JUNOS™ For Dummies®

Cheat Sheet

JUNOS for IOS Users

While the JUNOS software command line interface (CLI) has many built-in tools to guide you, if you already know the command language for Cisco's IOS, you can anticipate many of the JUNOS software commands. Note the fundamental differences between JUNOS and IOS:

- JUNOS software organizes commands in a structured hierarchy as opposed to a flat file, showing the configuration and commands of each level within its own set of curly braces {}.
- JUNOS software stores changes into a candidate configuration instea[illegible] impactin[illegible] ou do[illegible] ou *co*[illegible]

Because [illegible] e command[illegible] you already know wor[illegible] the keyword. For example, `show ip` [illegible]`ute` becomes `show route`.

Table 1 — Basic CLI and Systems Management Commands

JUNOS Command	*IOS Command*
`set date`	`clock set`
`ping`	`ping`
`request system reboot`	`reload`
`request message`	`send`
`show system uptime`	`show clock`
`show chassis environment`	`show environment-`
`show cli history`	`show history`
`show system statistics`	`show ip traffic`
`show logshow log file name`	`show logging-`
`show system processes`	`show processes`
`show configuration`	`show running config`
`request support information`	`show tech-support`
`show system users`	`show users`
`show version`	`show version`
`traceroute`	`trace`

Table 2 — Switching Commands

JUNOS Command	*IOS Command*
`show ethernet-switching interfaces`	No equivalent command
`show spanning-tree bridge`	`show spanning-tree`
`show ethernet-switching table`	`show mac address-table`
`show log messages`	`show logging`

JUNOS™ For Dummies®

Table 3 Interface Commands

JUNOS Command	*IOS Command*
`clear interfaces statistics`	`clear counters`

`show interfaces`
`show interfaces detail`
`show interfaces extensive`
	`show interfaces`

`show interfaces`
`show interfaces detail`
`show interfaces extensive`
	`show ip interface`

`show interfaces terse`	`show ip interface brief`

Table 4 Routing Protocol Commands

JUNOS Command	*IOS Command*
`clear arp`	`clear arp-cache`
`show arp`	`show arp`
`show route`	`show ip route`
`show route summary`	`show ip route summary`
`show policy` `show policy policy-name`	`show route-map`
`show system connections`	`show tcp`
`show ospf database`	`show ip ospf database`
`show ospf interface`	`show ip ospf interface`
`show ospf neighbor`	`show ip ospf neighbor`
`clear bgp neighbor`	`clear ip bgp`
`clear bgp damping`	`clear ip bgp dampening`
`show route protocol bgp`	`show ip bgp`
`show route community`	`show ip bgp community`
`show route damping decayed`	`show ip bgp dampened paths`
`show bgp neighbor`	`show ip bgp neighbors`
`show route advertising-protocolbgp` *address*	`show ip bgp neighbors` *address* `advertised-routes`
`show route receive-protocolbgp` *address*	`show ip bgp neighbors` *address* `received-routes`
`show bgp group`	`show ip bgp peer-group`
`show route aspath-regex`	`show ip bgp regexp`
`show bgp summary`	`show ip bgp summary`

For Dummies: Bestselling Book Series for Beginners

JUNOS®
FOR
DUMMIES®

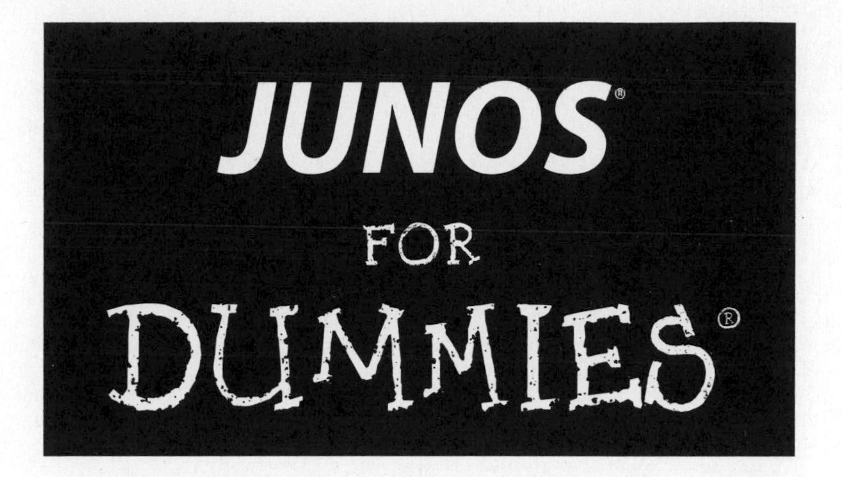

by Michael Bushong, Cathy Gadecki, Aviva Garrett

Wiley Publishing, Inc.

JUNOS® For Dummies®

Published by
Wiley Publishing, Inc.
111 River Street
Hoboken, NJ 07030-5774

www.wiley.com

Published by Wiley Publishing, Inc., Indianapolis, Indiana

Published simultaneously in Canada

For general information on our other products and services, please contact our Customer Care Department within the U.S. at 800-762-2974, outside the U.S. at 317-572-3993, or fax 317-572-4002.

For technical support, please visit www.wiley.com/techsupport.

Wiley also publishes its books in a variety of electronic formats. Some content that appears in print may not be available in electronic books.

Library of Congress Control Number: 2008934805

ISBN: 978-0-470-27796-6

Manufactured in the United States of America

10 9 8 7 6 5 4 3 2

About the Authors

Michael Bushong: A Senior Product Manager at Juniper Networks, Michael is tasked with managing JUNOS software. Michael has spent the past seven years working at Juniper Networks in several capacities. Originally hired to train JUNOS engineers on architectural, design, and application principles, Michael developed detailed materials covering everything from software architecture to broader applications deployed using JUNOS software. Michael has since transitioned to product management, where he has focused on the constant evolution of the operating system, spearheading major infrastructure efforts designed to scale the operating system to meet tomorrow's needs. Having majored in mechanical engineering with a specialized focus on advanced fluid mechanics and heat transfer, Michael began his professional career working on research in aerodynamics. He has since spent time with databases at Sybase and, more recently, in ASIC design tools at both Synopsis and Magma Design Automation.

Cathy Gadecki: A Senior Product Marketing Manager at Juniper Networks, Cathy is responsible for marketing JUNOS software. Since joining Juniper Networks four years ago, she has held multiple product and solution marketing positions addressing the needs of enterprise customers. Cathy has more than 20 years in marketing and product management positions with a focus on creating new markets for network equipment and services, for both startup and established firms. Cathy is the co-author of *ATM For Dummies* (Wiley), which has been reprinted seven times and published in multiple languages. Among other publications, Cathy authored *Roll Out*, a column discussing new product and service introduction, which appeared regularly in Tele.com. She earned her master's degree in electrical engineering from the Georgia Institute of Technology with a focus on data communications.

Aviva Garrett: Aviva Garrett has documented Juniper Networks technologies since joining the company as its first writer in 1997. She wrote the first JUNOS manuals and then oversaw the documentation as the company grew from a startup to an established network equipment provider. She recently stepped down as the Juniper Networks Director of Technical Publications to pursue other writing and business assignments. She is the author of the *JUNOS Cookbook* (OReilly, 2006). Prior to Juniper Networks, Aviva worked at Cisco Systems for six years. She also worked for Excelan/Novell, Gavilan, and other technology companies and startups.

Dedication

Michael Bushong: To Stacy Prager, now Stacy Bushong, but not when I began writing the book. Thank you, Patrick Ames. And to Chloe and, of course, to Steve and Linda Bushong.

Cathy Gadecki: To Steve and our five children.

Aviva Garrett: To David and Sage.

Authors' Acknowledgments

The authors wish to thank the many people who helped bring about this book. Our in-house editors, Jonathan Looney and Patrick Ames, were critical to the completion of this book. Our lead technical editor, Mario Puras, tested and confirmed our configurations and output. A large group of Juniper field engineers reviewed the manuscript and made invaluable suggestions for improvement: Pedro Cutillas, Christian Graf, Joe Green, Imran Khan, Stefan Lager, and Michael Pergament, On security matters, Monear Jalal reviewed and helped us along. On matters of switching, Lenny Bonsall, Bobby Guhasarkar, Joseph Li, David Nguyen, and Michael Peachy offered their expertise. Other key subject matter experts checked our work and took our phone calls: Daniel Backman, David Boland, Atif Khan, Kannan Kothandaram, Mike Marshall. Ananth Nagarajan, Brian Pavane, Naren Prabhu, Doug Radcliff, Alan Sardella, and Don Wheeler.

Publisher's Acknowledgments

We're proud of this book; please send us your comments through our online registration form located at www.dummies.com/register/.

Some of the people who helped bring this book to market include the following:

Acquisitions and Editorial

Project Editor: Kelly Ewing

Senior Acquisitions Editor: Katie Feltman

Editorial Manager: Jodi Jensen

Editorial Assistant: Amanda Foxworth

Sr. Editorial Assistant: Cherie Case

Cartoons: Rich Tennant (www.the5thwave.com)

Composition Services

Project Coordinator: Kristie Rees

Layout and Graphics: Nikki Gately, Melissa K. Jester, Laura Pence, Christin Swinford, Christine Williams

Proofreaders: Christopher M. Jones

Indexer: Broccoli Information Mgt.

Publishing and Editorial for Technology Dummies

Richard Swadley, Vice President and Executive Group Publisher

Andy Cummings, Vice President and Publisher

Mary Bednarek, Executive Acquisitions Director

Mary C. Corder, Editorial Director

Publishing for Consumer Dummies

Diane Graves Steele, Vice President and Publisher

Composition Services

Gerry Fahey, Vice President of Production Services

Debbie Stailey, Director of Composition Services

Contents at a Glance

Table of Contents

Introduction

Welcome to *JUNOS For Dummies*. This book provides you with a handy reference for configuring and running JUNOS software on Juniper Networks products and includes relevant background on the related networking concepts. (You can discover more about Juniper Networks and the evolution of JUNOS software at `www.juniper.net/company`.)

JUNOS software is deployed extensively throughout the world running Juniper Networks platforms designed for switching, routing, and security. You can find it in both the largest and smallest service provider networks and in the networks at tens of thousands of offices, campuses, and data centers of enterprise organizations, as well as in the public sector and education.

See whether you can identify with any of the follow scenarios:

- **In your data centers:** You may be looking for ways to reduce the power usage of your data center, collapse networking tiers and infrastructure, converge your data centers into fewer sites, scale existing ones, or build out a new data center.
- **In your branch offices:** You may be updating your branch gateway with an integrated platform, deploying access control or Voice over IP (VoIP), supporting new users, introducing application acceleration, or upgrading older switching and routing infrastructure.
- **In your headquarters or regional office campuses:** You may be adding access control to protect your network, deploying Voice over IP (VoIP), supporting a new location, adding new users or deploying new web or other servers, or upgrading older switching and routing infrastructure.
- **In your metropolitan or wide area networks:** You may be transitioning to new optical, Ethernet, or MPLS carrier services; building a new core for your metro, wide area, or data center backbone network; rolling out MPLS; or upgrading older switching and routing infrastructure.

This book helps you with all these scenarios and a whole lot more. We made this book a fast and easy way to understand, deploy, and use JUNOS software in your network today.

About This Book

We wrote this book thinking that you're probably a lot like us: too many projects, with too little uninterrupted time. So we created this book to help you do the following:

- Understand what JUNOS software can do for you and how you can use it in your own network.
- Quickly use the CLI so that you can configure and change your network with JUNOS software.
- Run, operate, and maintain JUNOS software with high uptime, performance, and security.
- Give you a set of references for quick look-up and review into the world of JUNOS software and its many features and uses.

Conventions Used in This Book

Device output and configuration samples are printed in a monospace font. When you see a bold monospace font within an output snippet, that is something you, the user, keys into the command line interface (CLI) to launch the command and receive the subsequent output. We don't bold configuration samples, however, as the entire configuration would be a bolded monospace font.

By the way, at this book's writing, JUNOS 9.2 version release was used. More software versions are coming, on a predictable JUNOS release train (see Chapter 1) that incorporates new networking and security features. It's important for you to know that subsequent release versions don't negate what you find out in this book, but simply extend the functionality of what you have learned.

What You're Not to Read

We place text you don't need to read in self-contained sidebars and clearly mark them as Technical Stuff. You can skip these items if you're in a hurry or don't want to lose your train of thought. Return to them later or browse through the book some day during lunch and read them in one lump. They're good preparation for a cocktail party with networking engineers.

Foolish Assumptions

When we wrote this book, we made a few assumptions about you:

- We assume that you're a network professional, although you don't have to be one. Because our objective is to get you up and running, we include a few basics on how various protocols work, but don't discuss the operations of the protocols in detail.
- You may design or operate networks with devices running JUNOS software — or are about to, are considering it, or are just curious about what JUNOS software is all about. If you know another network operating system, such as Cisco IOS, this book is a good introduction to JUNOS software and the day to day administration of the Juniper devices that run it.
- You may be an IT manager. Or you may procure networks or otherwise work with people who plan and manage networks running on JUNOS software.
- You may be a student entering the networking profession.

How This Book Is Organized

This book is divided into five parts.

Part I: Exploring JUNOS Software

This part introduces JUNOS software for switching, routing, MPLS, and security.

Part II: Working with JUNOS

This part helps you set up the basics of your network. You find out how to work with the command-line interface and discover the basic commands for routing, switching, and securing your device.

Part III: Deploying JUNOS

In this part, we help you set up additional functionality, including remote management, interfaces, peering, policy, class-of-service, MPLS, and VPNs.

Part IV: Managing JUNOS Software

This part helps you run your network. We offer guidance on monitoring, troubleshooting, and automating your network.

Part V: The Part of Tens

This part offers a quick reference of the top-ten most helpful commands, the key differences in the user interface from IOS, and other places you can go for more information.

Icons Used in the Book

We use icons throughout this book to key you into time-saving tips, things you really need to know, and the occasional warning or interesting backgrounder. Look for them throughout these pages.

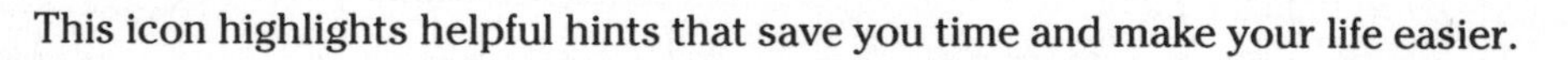

This icon highlights helpful hints that save you time and make your life easier.

Be careful when you see this icon. It marks information that can keep you out of trouble.

Whenever you see this icon, you know that it highlights key information you'll use often.

If you're in a hurry or aren't interested in the details, you can skip the text marked by this icon. But careful; sometimes it's really pertinent.

Where to Go from Here

You can go anywhere with your network if you use this book and JUNOS software. That's the whole point. As authors, we teach and train hundreds of network administrators and engineers about JUNOS software each year, and every day we work with someone just like you who is improving their network response time, traffic handling, or expanding services. Browse through the Table of Contents and consider a starting point and then just dip in. Ramble around a little. You can't get lost with JUNOS. You can only get better.

Part I

Exploring JUNOS Software

"It's all here, Warden. Routers, hubs, switches, all pieced together from scraps found in the machine shop. I guess the prospect of unregulated telecommunications was just too sweet to pass up."

In this part . . .

In this part, we introduce you to JUNOS software for running your high-performance network infrastructure, including its functionality for routing, switching, and security.

We also strive to answer the key questions that you're likely to have. How is JUNOS different? How does it work? How can it help you? Where can it help you? Why is it better? Why does it matter?

Chapter 1

Getting Familiar with JUNOS Software

In This Chapter

- Understanding the purpose of a network operating system
- Discovering how JUNOS software is different
- Looking inside JUNOS software
- Realizing why the JUNOS development process matters

Have you ever considered what it takes for the operating system (OS) on your computer to keep everything running smoothly? How it must allocate system resources and manage tasks so that you can keep typing, even while you're printing or an application is performing an autosave? If you type for most of the day, you probably notice it a lot.

Now, consider everything that a network operating system (NOS) must do to keep your network running smoothly. Not only does it need to process a gazillion details, such as figuring out how to direct traffic from each point A to each point Z, but it also has the weighty task of delivering the bazillions of packets cruising your network to their destinations. And, don't forget the NOS has to track and apply all those special services and security rules that you've requested.

The engineers of a network operating system have their work cut out for them, not only because of all the different design and development options, but because everyone wants their network to be always ready, and fast, without pauses, such as a momentary freezing of the cursor. Just as the OS that you use on your desktop affects the way that you do certain tasks and the efficiency of your computer, the operating system that runs your networking platforms impacts their speed and ease of management, not to mention your network's reliability and security. In this chapter, we explore JUNOS software.

Exploring the Functions of Network Operating Systems

Network operating system (NOS) describes a broad category of software —from basic systems that support only the functions of local connections, such as printer sharing and file system, to sophisticated systems running on platforms specifically designed as networking infrastructure. Our focus is on the latter—the software systems that support not only local, but also metro and wide area networking infrastructure, including the networking platforms of the world-wide Internet.

It's all about control

In building your network, you use various types of specialized devices that pass along traffic from one to another. We speak of *internetworks* when we interconnect these individual networks. Before a network can safely deliver traffic, each device node must first know where to send each bundle of traffic, or *packet,* that enters through its interfaces.

This essential map for connectivity and other orchestrating processes are the functions of the network operating system's *control plane.*

In simplest terms, the *control plane* is the brain of the networking device with the *forwarding plane* providing the brawn to quickly move packets through the system.

The processes and information of the control plane must provide answers to two essential questions:

- How does the network direct the delivery of packets from one place to another? In other words, what are the routes or paths to establish, how do they change, and how does each device know which to use for each packet?
- What does the network do with each of the packets along its journey? In other words, what are the handling rules, or *policies,* established for traffic delivery?

While the questions can be simply stated, the possible responses are virtually limitless. You can define dozens and dozens of protocols to answer these questions for different types of network maps and all the different types of traffic, not to mention how the control plane monitors and manages it all. The many processes to control the network delivery of packets fills the industry with all those three- and four-letter acronyms that you've somehow managed to file into your memory (or if you're like us, you've just filed away the place to look them up when you need them).

Moving on: Packet forwarding

Along with assembling the intelligence to properly deliver the traffic from one place to another, the network operating system (and its hardware) must actually deliver packets to the correct destination using this intelligence. Moving packets through a networking device is the function of the network operating system's *forwarding plane*, also sometimes known as the *data plane*.

Packet forwarding takes care of the needed handling to move each packet quickly from its inbound device interface to the proper outbound interface(s). For large networking devices that carry terabits of traffic, this handling must occur at an ultra-über fast rate to maintain the high packet throughput of the machines.

The sophisticated service demands of today's users and applications have further added to these responsibilities. While forwarding the packets, the networking devices must also typically apply a range of filters, policies, and services for protecting the network (and its clients and applications) and assigning priorities for the use of its resources. Visualize watching a YouTube video. Now visualize all your users watching the video all at the same time because some clown in your office passed along an e-mail with the link to everyone. And now think about all the traffic hitting your network all at once, just as your president is on a critical call with your biggest customer. Oofta! It's just one example of where you may want to define a few of those extra rules that your network can follow in making its packet deliveries. (We provide Chapter 15 to help you out.)

Taking Advantage of One Network OS

Network operating systems have a lot do and can have a big impact on the performance, ease of operations, reliability, and security of your network. JUNOS software is different, in that it's one operating system enhanced along one software release train built in one modular architecture. But, why does having one operating system matter?

One operating system means the Juniper engineers build upon the same, single source code base and then share this code, as appropriate, across all the platforms running JUNOS software. For example, enterprise platforms use the same hardened implementation of the routing protocol Open Shortest Path First (OSPF) that has been running in large service provider networks for many years. It's not a different code set, but the same one. (To set up OSPF, see Chapter 8.)

So, if your responsibilities include administrating the network, you find that many features are configured and managed in the same way on the different platforms. One operating system therefore saves you time, potentially lots of

20/20 through the rear view

Most of the engineers writing the early releases of JUNOS software came from other companies where they had previously built network software. They had first-hand knowledge of what worked well, and what could be improved because they'd experienced the issues that occur when they didn't have good control over the code development. The software became difficult to manage, and changes could result in unpredictable problems that often became visible only in the operational networks of customers.

So, in engineering the principles of development and architecture for JUNOS software, these engineers found new ways to solve the limitations that they'd experienced in building the older operating systems (the ones that still exist today in many networks, surviving through lots of different versions, patches, and administrator workarounds). These innovations in JUNOS software are rooted in its earliest design stages. They can't be retrofitted or reverse-engineered into existing systems. The founding engineering team built them into the origins of JUNOS software, and they have passionately preserved them over the years.

it, in everything from training to setup to ongoing operations. And, if you plan changes in the network, one operating system can save you time there, too. With far less variation to evaluate, test, and deploy, it's less effort for feature roll out, software upgrades, and other network modifications.

Taking a Peek Inside JUNOS Software

Another area impacting the reliability, performance, security, and many aspects of your devices (and therefore your network) is the way that the engineers architect the network operating system — in other words, how they organize its many processes and how these processes work together.

Fundamental to the architecture design of JUNOS software are its modularity and Juniper's innovation to separate the functions of control from packet forwarding. (For more on packet forwarding, see the section "Moving On: Packet forwarding," earlier in this chapter.)

Going their separate ways: Functions

In JUNOS software, the functions of control and forwarding are cleanly divided. The explicit division of responsibility allows the software to run on two different engines of processing, memory, and other resources. Separation of the control and forwarding planes is a key reason why JUNOS software can support so many different types of hardware platforms from a single code base.

Figure 1-1 provides a high-level view of the JUNOS software architecture with its two functional processing planes. Shown above the dashed line is the control plane that runs on what is known as the *Routing Engine* (RE) of the Juniper device. Below the dashed line is the packet forwarding plane, which usually runs on a separate *Packet Forwarding Engine* (PFE) of the device, along with switching boards and services cards in larger Juniper platforms.

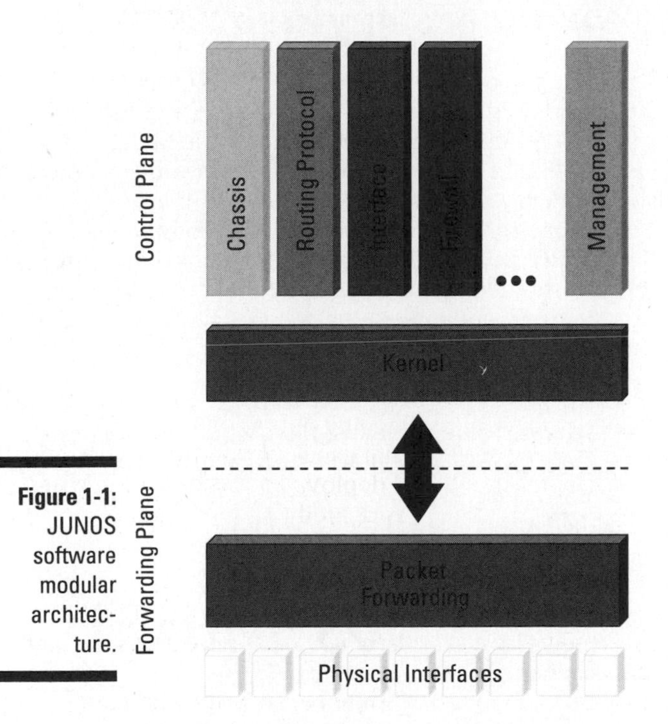

Figure 1-1: JUNOS software modular architecture.

The fundamental architecture decision to separate control from forwarding provides important design benefits in scalability and reliability.

Do you want faster platforms in your network? That's like asking if you'd like to have today off (with pay, of course). Yes, it would be good to have the network go a little faster. Faster, faster, faster is a constant drum beat for networks. And, in its ten years of product delivery, Juniper has scaled the throughput of its fastest devices from 40GB per second to multiple terabits per second. The use of separate processors for the RE and the PFE has been the essential architecture element to each performance breakthrough. In particular, separation lets the PFE throughput scale with the increasing speeds of the custom *application-specific integrated circuits* (ASICs) on which it runs.

Separating the engines also reduces interdependencies between them. Not only does this separation help preserve the operation of each when the other is experiencing problems, it also gives the Juniper engineers more ways to provide system redundancy and failover. For example, you find dual REs in some platforms, while the EX 4200 Ethernet switches offer a capability called Virtual Chassis to provide redundancy, among other benefits. (See Chapter 3 for the details of this switching feature).

Plain smart: The planes of JUNOS software

All the necessary functions of the control plane run on the Routing Engine (whether you have a router, switch, or security platform running JUNOS software). Figure 1-1, shown earlier in this chapter, shows the high-level design of the control plane — a set of modules, with clean interfaces between them, and an underlying kernel that controls the modules and manages all the needed communication back and forth between all the components. The kernel also handles the RE communications with the Packet Forwarding Engine. Each of the different modules provides a different control process, such as control for the chassis components, Ethernet switching, routing protocols, interfaces, management, and so on.

The basis of the JUNOS kernel comes from the FreeBSD UNIX operating system, an open source software system. This mature, general-purpose system provides many of the essential basic functions of an operating system, such as the scheduling of resources. To transform it into a network operating system, the Juniper engineers extensively modified and hardened the code for the specialized requirements of networking.

You may be wondering if you have a way in JUNOS software to protect the control plane itself from a security attack. Yes, you can configure filters and rate limit the traffic that reaches your RE. (For more on this topic, go to Chapter 9).

The Packet Forwarding Engine is the central processing element of the forwarding plane, systematically moving the packets in and out of the device. In JUNOS software, the PFE has a locally stored *forwarding table*. The forwarding table is a synchronized copy of all the information from the RE that the forwarding plane needs to handle each packet, including outgoing interfaces, addresses, and so on. Storing a local copy of this information allows the PFE to get its job done without going to the control plane every time that it needs to process a packet.

Another benefit to having a local copy? The PFE can continue forwarding packets, even when a disruption occurs to the control plane, such as when a routing or other process issue happens. (Find out more about this capability and what other features are important to preserving high uptime in the operating system in Chapter 5.)

That's not a problem: The many benefits of modular architecture

Have you ever had a router continually reboot, and when you look on the console, you see that an error occurred in a single nonessential process?

With JUNOS software, you don't see that problem. The modular architecture of JUNOS software allows individual control plane processes to run in their own module (also sometimes called a daemon). Each module has specified processing resources and runs in its own protected memory space, avoiding the processing conflicts that can occur.

What about a minor hiccup in SNMP bringing down your whole system? That's another misfortune that you won't miss with JUNOS software, because its clean separation between control processes helps to isolate small problems so that they can't create worse havoc. If a malfunction in a module causes an issue, the rest of the system can continue to function. For example, one module can't disrupt another by scribbling on its memory.

In our many discussions with users, we hear over and over again that the stability of JUNOS software is the biggest difference that they see after deploying Juniper platforms in their network. They tell us about their boxes running for months and months, even years without interruption. How they popped it in the rack, set up the configurations, and never looked back. It just keeps going and going and going.

Want to know another benefit of the modular architecture? It eases fault isolation. With each process functioning within its own module, when the occasional problem does occur, pinpointing the exact reason is far less complicated for both you and the Juniper support team. With quick identification and a good understanding of the root cause, you can apply a fix that works, from the first time.

We have one more benefit to highlight — flexible innovation. The organized structure of the JUNOS software architecture enables deep integration of new capabilities with highly functional interaction with existing processes. What does it mean for you? Native support of new services and features delivers a richness of capability with the high performance that you expect. For example, among recent integrations to JUNOS software are the security services being derived from Juniper's ScreenOS operating system.

Developing JUNOS Software

Software development probably isn't a topic that you expected to find in a networking book. After all, you don't need to build JUNOS software. Juniper's engineers already do that for you.

However, we include this topic because we think it's important. Software development is an essential reason why JUNOS software is different and why organizations see such a difference in the stability of their networking devices when they put JUNOS software into their infrastructure. When a development process produces code that is consistently more stable and predictable, all aspects of operations just get a lot easier.

You may be wondering how Juniper engineers can use only a single base of the source code, given all the different features and platforms supported by JUNOS software. (We discuss the single source code base in this chapter in the section "Taking Advantage of One Network OS.")

It does take a well-defined process with lots of discipline to stick to the principles. The answer begins by following a single software release train for development. The Juniper engineers extend the one source code base of JUNOS software in highly scheduled, incremental steps, where everyone adds their code (and any needed fixes) to that same repository. The expanding repository forms the main line of code, released in a series of numbered versions, as shown in Figure 1-2.

With all those versions, you may be wondering about the answers to a few questions:

- **How can you find out whether a feature that you're using is also available in a new version that you want to deploy?** Well, you don't have to worry about that. If it's in your current JUNOS software release, it's generally in the new version. By following a main line, the Juniper engineers deliver supersets of features with each release.
- **How will you choose which release to use?** With other systems, you may be used to having to make decisions about tradeoffs. One software train has all the features you need, but doesn't support the latest hardware; this other train has all the features you want, but has a critical bug in one critical feature you need; and yet another train has all the critical features, but lacks two less important features you have used.

  With JUNOS software you don't have these trade-offs. For each new version, the Juniper engineers compile the full set of release binaries so that each version is available to run all the Juniper platforms run by JUNOS software. Each binary brings together the features from the repository that are relevant (and tested) for the particular platform that it runs.

- **What about when you report a bug?** How will you know whether it's fixed on every platform? Because all platforms share much of the core code, most bug fixes automatically get integrated into all the devices where you find that feature. So if it's fixed in one platform, it's fixed in all (unless it's minor and missed the test window for that platform, but even then, it won't be too far behind).

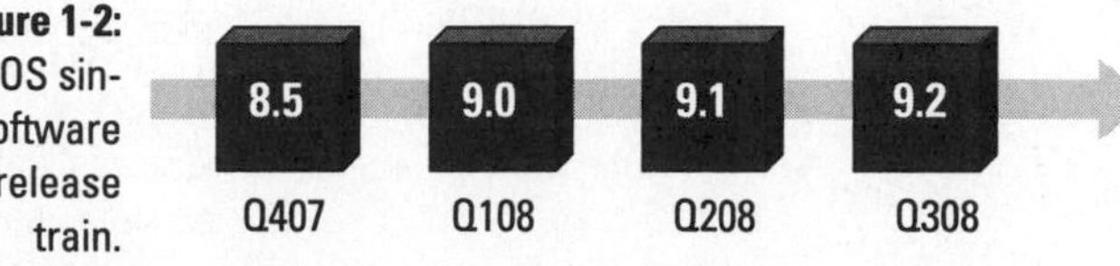

Figure 1-2: JUNOS single software release train.

Reaping the benefits of a single release train

A single software release train is extremely rare, not only for networking equipment, but for any software development. The more common approach, particularly when rapid changes are needed, is to branch code — in other words, to create a new release train by taking a copy or a subset of the existing code. Then two main lines exist in which the developers work and add new features. And sometimes, for any given feature, two different developers might create the code for the same feature. And when the pressure mounts for rapid changes, the code might be copied again, starting up yet another

Testing, testing

Juniper's testing processes are extensive and highly automated. With only the one code base to worry about, they can really put it through the ringer. Ask someone from Juniper about it sometime. All these development disciplines are there to deliver highly stable code to you.

Automated regression testing takes days to run in Juniper's high-speed test beds. The regressions tests check that previously released features still work as expected, while new test scripts check the new features of the release. Here the single release train discipline aids Juniper's engineers because they can focus on just one set of code and not have to worry about many, many different trains, or branches, or patches of code. It's one of the secrets of how they keep on track, delivering new versions four times a year.

Asking the right questions

Consider reviewing the software development processes of vendors as a part of your evaluation process for new network and security equipment, because it can save you time and money down the road. Here are some questions that you can ask your vendors about their software development process:

- How many different software versions exist for the products you are buying? How do you know when to use one version versus another?
- What steps do development engineers follow when adding new feature code? How do they support different software versions or release trains? How do they decide which features to add to which version?
- What are the steps for adding fixes to the code? What procedures ensure that a new fix is a part of all releases, including those in the future?
- How are newly developed features (and fixes) tested? What guidelines determine when a release is ready for customers? Can a new release affect previously working features?

train. Over time, these tactical decisions can end up in hundreds and even thousands of different strains of the software. And that's within what is supposedly the same operating system. We haven't even discussed the situation where a vendor might create a whole new operating system for each new platform.

So what does it all mean to you? The bottom line is that you get lots of new features in a series of stable releases.

When deploying JUNOS software for the first time in their networks, administrators tell us that they immediately notice its stability and reliability. We hear about big drops (20, 40, 50 percent, sometimes even higher) in the total number and the duration of their unplanned system events. More stable code just makes their jobs a lot easier because it reduces their risk of business disruption and the frequency of their unplanned maintenance, as well as streamlining upgrade procedures when they do want to make changes to the version running their machines.

Hup 1, 2, 3, 4: JUNOS software release numbering

Essential to the success of the single software release train of JUNOS is the frequent release of new versions. Otherwise, you and other users may become impatient waiting for new functionality. Each new major release of JUNOS software is called a new version. Juniper numbers its new versions to the first decimal point, as in the 9.2 JUNOS software release. You sometimes see jumps in the release numbering to the next whole number. It used to mean the delivery of extensive new functionality, but now frankly, it's a more arbitrary decision.

Juniper also issues maintenance and service releases to fix issues found in a version after its first release. *Maintenance releases* are standard releases provided to all customers. Juniper delivers *service releases* between maintenance releases when it needs to address a specific issue for a specific customer.

The easiest way to understand the release name is to look at an example:

```
jinstall-9.2R2.10-domestic-signed.tgz
```

- The descriptor `jinstall` indicates the binary of the release; in this case, the image is for the routing platforms.
- Next, is the release version: 9.2.
- Following, is a letter that indicates the type of release. As a customer, you generally see R for released software (another type is B for Beta releases).
- Next appears the maintenance release number (2 in our example).
- The last number is the spin of that maintenance release, in this case 10. The Juniper engineers create different spins for different testing versions of the software and also to create the service releases.
- Finally, this name indicates that the software is for domestic use (in the United States and Canada). The other type is worldwide. The difference is primarily their inclusion of encryption capabilities.

Chapter 2

Operating Your Network with JUNOS Software

In This Chapter

- Discovering the error-resistant configuration tools of the CLI
- Exploring available automation tools
- Working with what you already have
- Taking advantage of software support and new versions

When is the last time on the job that you had an hour of uninterrupted time to focus on one task? Can't remember? How about when you had an uninterrupted 30 minutes, or even 15? If you run a network, constant interruptions and multitasking are far more common than quiet spans for engrossed accomplishment.

This chapter looks at the operations features that can help you proactively run your network. You won't find some of these tools in many other network operating systems, so they may be new to you. If you want to know how JUNOS software can help you in easing the time, effort, and stress of running your network, this chapter is for you.

Introducing the Command-Line Interface

The command-line interface (CLI) is the starting point to many operational tasks. The CLI of JUNOS software is an intuitive, text-based command shell. If you've used a UNIX-based host system, you'll see many similarities.

Most users find the JUNOS software CLI fairly straightforward to pick up. Within a few minutes of looking around the interface, they begin to find some of the advanced tools that the Juniper engineers have provided for making configuration, monitoring, and management easier. Among the many features of the CLI is a structured command hierarchy, extensive fail-safe mechanisms that help to catch any configuration mistakes and errors, automation tools for speeding (and delivering accuracy to) your daily operations tasks, and comprehensive online help.

The CLI provides two different modes:

- An operational mode for monitoring and managing your Juniper device
- A configuration mode for configuring your device

Part II shows you how to set up and run your devices and network using the CLI.

Handy command-line tools

The commands of the CLI are organized into a structured hierarchy. This structure is quite handy as it allows you to quickly jump around the interface, speeding you to wherever you need to go.

You find lots of help tools intuitively integrated into the interface. For example, you can enter a **?** at any prompt, or even within commands, to find out the possible valid command entries or command completions at that particular point. And, with a press of the Tab key, the CLI automatically completes your partially typed commands, filenames, and user names so that you don't have to recall the exact syntax or names every time you use them.

Examples of other handy tools include

- **Syntax checking:** Checks for small errors as you're typing. The CLI immediately lets you know if an entered line doesn't conform to valid syntax and offers tips for you to correct it.
- **Annotations:** Use `annotate` followed by your notes when you want to leave comments for other team members.
- **Rescue configuration:** Lets you `rollback rescue` quickly to a known working configuration.
- **Access permissions:** Set authorization privileges for different users. You can use predefined user classes as well as customize who can access what command hierarchy, or even specific individual commands.
- **Predefined changes and installs:** Use `deactivate` when you want to input configuration changes and leave them inactive until needed or schedule the specific time with the `commit at` command. As an example, you can set everything up ahead of time for a technician installing a new card at a remote site.
- **Filtering of the command output:** Pipe (`|`) lets you display just the information that you need.

Commit, confirm, and rollback functions

In the JUNOS CLI, you're not making changes to the actual configuration on the device, but rather to a *candidate configuration* that you can later check and commit to. Figure 2-1 outlines the configuration process of the JUNOS CLI, something the Juniper engineers put a lot of thought into as a process with a lot of help from customers. It can save you from much hassle and headache.

Perhaps you're among the unfortunate with a story to tell about your worst configuration nightmare, how during a bleary-eyed 3 a.m. trouble call, you made matters worse with some fat-thumb move. Or, maybe it's about the time you mixed up the exact order of your line-by-line command entries and found yourself with more to clean up. (Ever remember adding security to a remote box from a tradeshow, only to find that the new firewall locked you out of the very interface that you were using to get into the box?)

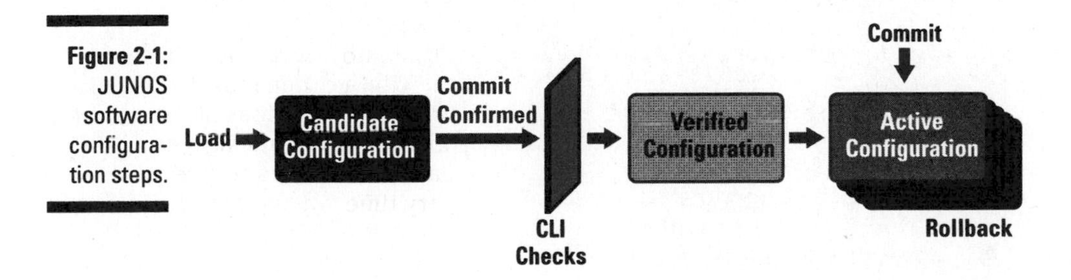

Figure 2-1: JUNOS software configuration steps.

Whatever your story, you're not alone. Many different studies show that more than 60 percent of network downtime can be attributed to human factors (a.k.a. absent-minded errors).

So how can the JUNOS CLI help you to avoid being 3 a.m. stupid, any time of the day? Here's a short list of command-line features (the instructions on how to use them appear in Chapter 6):

- **Candidate configuration:** You always enter your configuration or its changes as a candidate file. The rich set of text editing tools save you lots of typing.
- **Show | Compare:** See exactly what changes you made and look for any last-minute typos or omissions with `show | compare`, such as when you copy a configuration to a new interface.
- **Commit Check:** When your changes are ready (or any time while you're entering changes), use `commit check` to see whether the CLI agrees with you. The system verifies the logic and completeness of your new candidate configuration entries without activating any changes. If the CLI finds a problem, it lets you know.

- **Commit Confirmed:** When you're ready to activate your candidate as the active configuration. You have two options: `commit` or `commit confirmed`. `commit confirmed` is the better choice because it saves you in case your changes accidently isolate your device. You see, if you don't confirm your changes (by then entering `commit` or `commit check`) within ten minutes of activation (or other interval that you can set), the device reverts back to the prior configuration.
- **Rollback:** The JUNOS CLI gives you one other piece of safety equipment that not only helps to protect you, but also makes changes easier. `roll-back` lets you restore the rescue or any of the prior 50 configurations. A quick rollback is much easier than undoing one command at a time.

The `confirmed` function is there to help you. We've heard stories of folks who didn't bother using it and then later regretted it when they were stuck trying to figure out how to fix what they had just done that isolated a remote site. Get in the habit and take the little extra step to `commit confirmed`.

Boosting Productivity with Automated Tools

Along with the extensive hands-on tools for your day-to-day tasks, JUNOS software provides many automation tools that can boost your productivity, giving you more time for other things that you need to get done. Together, the many tools outlined in the following sections provide you with a helpful edge in configuration, monitoring, diagnostics, restoration, maintenance, and other operations tasks.

Automation scripts

Automation scripts give you the power to automate the commands of the command-line, both configuration and operational, as well as to set event policies. Chapter 20 provides a longer introduction to the JUNOScripting capabilities described here.

First, *commit scripts* allow you to customize the commit verifications that run before a candidate configuration becomes active — for example, when you enter a `commit` or `commit confirmed` command. With commit scripts, you can do things like make sure that all your outbound interfaces are configured with a proper set of security measures, such as firewalls. As another example, you can make sure that the *Maximum Transfer Unit* (MTU) (the maximum size allowed for a packet) is set correctly for each interface.

Included in the commit script tool set is a macro capability that can condense repeated complex configuration tasks, such as setting up a Stateful firewall, to an entry that is just a few configuration lines with its set of variables. Over time, you can develop a library of commit scripts, maintained by the most experienced engineers on your team, to ensure that your configurations are not only error-free, but also compliant to your business and network policies.

One of the characteristics of complex systems is the cascade effect of errors. Small problems can rapidly escalate into major ones. Instead of waiting for an outage that is significant enough to trip alarms and notify administrators, operation (op) scripts and event policies allow you to automate steps in the operational command mode of the command-line.

These tools provide immediate, on-box problem detection and resolution. The scripts are always running, alert to potential early warning issues and ready to take action. *Op scripts* can receive command output, inspect it, and determine the next appropriate action, repeating the process until finding the source of the problem, and then report it to the CLI. For specifically defined events, *event policies* can correlate the events and perform a set of actions, including calling upon an op script to help diagnose an issue or take corrective steps.

By capturing your operational procedures in automated scripts, you can help everyone to follow best practices. Scripting also gives you a continuous improvement capability. As you diagnose each network outage, add the solution as one of the automated scripting tools, and you can administer the proactive avoidance steps to prevent the outage from occurring again.

On-board monitoring, logging and support

Complementing the scripting features is an extensive set of on-board instrumentation tools for monitoring and managing your network and devices. Handling these functions on-board a network device itself speeds problem-solving. (Chapter 18 provides the how to for monitoring, and Chapters 7, 11, and 19 examine the how to of the management logging functions.)

Be prepared: Monitoring and logging

On-board instrumentation enables you to proactively gather information from the JUNOS software itself, giving you advance notification of issues before they create service-impacting havoc. Self-monitoring allows continuous feedback from the devices and lets you capture network-wide down to highly granular perspectives on the operations of your network. It can save you a lot of time from manually gathering data for analysis.

Available tools for automating network monitoring include

- **Real-time performance monitoring (RPM):** Measures the performance of traffic as it travels between network devices so that you can continuously monitor traffic as it moves along those paths. The RPM probes can collect round-trip time minimums, averages, maximums, jitter, and other data on both a per-destination and application basis.
- **Flow accounting:** Provides a method for collecting traffic flow statistics, enabling operations teams to track link utilization for capacity planning, security analysis, fault isolation, internal billing, and more. You can gather statistics on an individual physical device, logical device, interface, or subinterface.
- **Health monitor:** Notifies your network management system (NMS) when something requires attention. Health monitor extends the Remote Network Monitoring (RMON) alarm infrastructure of JUNOS software with minimum user configuration requirements, by providing predefined monitoring of the operating system processes and device hardware, for example: file system usage, CPU usage, and memory usage.

The logging and tracing operations of JUNOS software allow you to find out about events that occur in your device — normal operations, as well as error conditions. You can use the following tools to trace and analyze the sequence of events leading to network or device issues for really fast resolution. (See Chapter 7 on how to set them up.)

- **System logging:** Generates system log messages (syslog messages) for recording events that occur on the device, including hardware and within the processes of the operating system. A few examples, among the thousands that we can cite: An interface starting up, login failure, or hardware failure conditions.
- **Trace logging (tracing options):** Provides a wide range of variables for observing network and system events of protocol operations. (Examples include BGP state changes, graceful restart events, and even tracking SNMP operations and statistics). They're a valuable tool when you need to find out what's going on in your device running JUNOS.

For the most efficient debugging, it's good practice to set the appropriate `traceoptions` parameters ahead of time in the configuration and leave them disabled. Then, when you need them, they're ready, and you can quickly get started finding out what's going on.

Advanced Insight Solutions

Advanced Insight Solutions (AIS) is another set of tools and services of JUNOS software that you're likely to find helpful to your daily tasks. AIS uses operation scripts and event policies defined by engineers in the Juniper Networks Technical Assistance Center (JTAC), the Juniper group that provides customer support. These scripts are specially designed to automatically perform the steps that a JTAC engineer would use to help you resolve issues in your network. They're available to organizations with a support contract and can speed detection, diagnosis, and remediation of issues requiring JTAC assistance.

Beyond the AIS scripts, you can subscribe to Juniper technical services that extend AIS functionality. These services dynamically automate the steps in your Juniper gear to detect system events, analyze them, notify you, and contact JTAC for assistance. You can optionally choose for your systems to securely send collected data directly to JTAC, saving you significant time and effort, especially when every minute counts during a problem event. Another aspect of the offering provides proactive expert analysis of your device deployment, and is particularly useful when you have a very large number of devices to maintain.

You can find out more about Advanced Insight Solutions by visiting the Web site at `http://juniper.net/products_and_services/technical.html`.

Integrating with Other Vendors' Systems

Do you have only one vendor in your network? We didn't think so. Just as you likely have multiple vendors for your computers, servers, storage, and other IT systems, it's good practice (as you're most likely to get a better solution for less cost) to use multiple networking vendors and carefully evaluate the right choice for each of your purchases.

So, how easily you can manage new devices running JUNOS software and how well it works with your existing equipment and systems is probably a key consideration for you. The flexibility of JUNOS software to coexist with your existing network can be divided into four arenas: interoperability, management, integration, and open development.

Interoperability

Juniper is a strong advocate of open standards. It takes leadership roles in industry efforts to specify open standards in organizations such as the Internet Engineering Task Force (IETF), the group providing the standards describing the Internet protocol suites. JUNOS software supports hundreds of networking protocols — standards such as spanning tree, OSPF, BGP, IPv6, and MPLS, to name just a few.

Nonetheless, the practicalities of interoperability require that Juniper goes beyond simply implementing the standards and conduct its own interoperability tests. It's no secret that the specifications of standards often leave openings for interpretation or that misinterpretations can occur, which can lead to interoperability gaps in actual implementation.

Juniper fills these gaps, where necessary, with new development projects. This practical approach is necessary to support the tens of thousands of customers of JUNOS software. Interoperability between Juniper and other large networking vendors has been proven several times over, in the best possible way, with live network implementations over the past decade.

Management

Beyond the CLI, Juniper provides several tools for managing JUNOS software, including a web GUI and element management tools. Additionally, JUNOS software provides a broad complement of SNMP MIBs for managing the software, hardware and protocols of the system.

Simple Network Management Protocol (SNMP) is an Internet standard protocol for network management. It is used for collecting and setting various types of management information using basic commands and defined Management Information Bases (MIBs). JUNOS software supports SNMP Versions 1, 2c, and 3. (Find out more about its support in Chapter 7.)

The J-Web tool is a web-based graphical user interface embedded in many of the devices running JUNOS software. It lets you do some of the same things that you can do at the command-line interface, providing simple-to-use tools to monitor, configure, troubleshoot, and manage your device. (For more on the command-line interface, see the section "Introducing the Command-Line Interface," earlier in this chapter.) Among the friendly configuration and diagnostic tools and wizards of J-Web is a tool for comparing different configurations that lists files side by side and can highlight their differences for you.

Juniper is expanding its NSM management system to support devices running JUNOS software, providing a common management system across most of its portfolio. NSM provides system-level fault, configuration, and performance monitoring. Additionally, the JUNOScope IP Service Manager provides monitoring, configuration, inventory, and software management applications for the routing product lines. Service-level management is available through Juniper's portfolio of Session Resource Control (SRC) products for policy-driven control of network resources

Integration

Operations teams use tens, sometimes hundreds, of different tools to manage their networks. You probably have a few of them in your own network environment to help you with various operations activities, such as inventory, configuration, provisioning, monitoring, and managing faults. You may have developed some of these tools yourself, or you may have purchased them from one of the many independent software vendors who develop network management products. Juniper works in close partnership with these vendors to integrate management of JUNOS software into their solutions.

Juniper streamlines integration of partner and customer systems by providing a number of open, standard interfaces in JUNOS software. In addition to the CLI, standardized system logging messages, SNMP interfaces, and on-board instrumentation systems, JUNOS software also provides an XML (eXtensible Markup Language) interface. All these open options let network management tools interact with JUNOS software in a reliable and predictable way.

XML is a widely adopted specification from the W3C (World Wide Web Consortium) for creating custom markup languages for exchanging data in structured formats. It provides a way to define a set of markers, called *tags,* applied to a data set or document. These tags describe the function of individual data elements and codify hierarchical relationships among them.

The XML interface provides a consistent, well-defined way to exchange device configuration and state information with other systems. Recently, Juniper has led the IETF standardization effort to create the Network Configuration (NETCONF) protocol, defining an XML-based data encoding for configuration data as well as the protocol messages. The NETCONF API of JUNOS software enables other systems to request and change configuration information in a standard way.

The NETCONF API is described in RFC 4741, NETCONF Configuration Protocol, available at `www.ietf.org/rfc/rfc4741.txt`.

Open development

Juniper also provides tools that enable customers and partners to build applications to run on JUNOS software. The Partner Solution Development Platform (PSDP) provides a set of secure tools and resources, including a software development kit (SDK), to build applications that can run on the control plane and services card.

Building with the platform does require networking and software engineering experience, and developers must become licensed partners of Juniper to get access to certain information. You can build the applications on your own or work with system integrators to build customized solutions that fit your network and its needs.

Upgrading to New Releases

Another topic that is essential to operating your network is software upgrades. The single release train and strict development processes of

JUNOS software make upgrading to new releases easier than with other networking systems. (For more on these topics, see Chapter 1.) The algorithm for selecting which new version to use is straightforward: Choose a higher numbered release, and you get all your existing capabilities along with the new functionality.

Unlike most other network operating systems, you don't have to worry about different software trains (see Chapter 1). Nor do you have to worry about choosing the right package for the features you want, on the platforms you need, or losing functionality when you upgrade.

Any organization with a valid support contract can download new releases of JUNOS software from the Juniper support site. Having the images of each new quarterly release available at the same time for all platforms, with consistency in the code and setup of many new features, streamlines upgrade planning and deployment. Depending upon the complexity of your network, it can literally save days, or sometimes even weeks, of your time.

JUNOS software support

The current policy of Juniper is to support each new version of JUNOS software until Juniper has delivered some specified number of releases. Assuming that Juniper continues its midquarter release cycle, Table 2-1 shows the expected length of support. JUNOS software support consists of a period of active engineering support followed by a period of only JTAC support:

Table 2-1 JUNOS Software Support — Typical Duration

Juniper Support	*Standard Support*	*EEOL Support*
Engineering/JTAC support	9 months	36 months
JTAC (only) support	EOE + 6 months	EOE + 6 months

- During *engineering support* of a release, the engineering teams create updated releases (maintenance, service, and patch) to address any coding issues.
- During the time of only *JTAC support,* the JTAC engineers help to resolve issues with solutions and workarounds that don't require changes in the release code.

Juniper describes the end of engineering support as End of Engineering (EOE) and the end of JTAC support as the End of Life (EOL) of the JUNOS software release. Juniper provides six months' notice of the EOL for each of the version releases. When the release reaches EOL, Juniper removes the software images from its site, and JTAC provides support on a commercially reasonable effort basis.

The last release of the year is known as an Extended End of Life (EEOL) release and provides active engineering support for three years, followed by six months of JTAC support. The first release providing EEOL support was the JUNOS 8.1 release in 2006.

Downloading new releases

You can find the latest supported releases of JUNOS software on Juniper's download site. Navigate to `www.juniper.net/customers/csc/software`.

Find the image for the particular platform that you're upgrading. Choose between the domestic image, for use in the United States and Canada (domestic), and a worldwide image (export). The technical documentation for each platform is freely available in multiple formats.

While they don't necessarily need to, many users upgrade the release of JUNOS software running on their devices at least once a year. Regular upgrades ensure that they have ready access to the latest features. If their network requires a new feature, it's already a part of the software on their devices, and they simply activate it in their deployed release whenever they're ready.

Chapter 3
Switching to JUNOS

In This Chapter

- Switching in the network
- Enhancing your network using switches
- Comparing the Juniper switches

Switches provide cost-effective network access for endpoints, such as PCs, phones, printers, servers, storage, and virtually any other IP-enabled device, and connect to each other to expand your network. Switches typically support the aggregation points of more local links, while routers support larger intersections of links, usually where traffic comes together from distant points or even from other networks.

In this chapter, we introduce the basics of how switches work (for the less technical members of our audience) and discuss recent developments in switching. We also compare the Juniper switches so that you know what to use where. (If you're looking for basic switch setup and configuration details, turn to Chapter 10.)

It's All about Perspective: Switching and Your Network

What's outside your office? You may have answered, "A bunch of cubicles." But if you happened to jump on Google Earth when I asked the question, your answer may be very different. The switches in your network most often move traffic around based on a small, local field of view, like just standing up and looking around from your office; but they can also turn to a wider view of the network if needed, such as using Google Earth to figure out where to head to get most anywhere.

Specifically, the switches running JUNOS software are Ethernet switches. The Ethernet protocol defines how the switch's interfaces, (also known as *ports),* send frames of traffic over physical media links. You can send and receive Ethernet frames over different types of copper, coaxial and fiber media, and at various bit-rate speeds, including the most common, 10/100/1000BASE-T Ethernet interfaces for twisted pair.

Layers of switching

In a common network configuration, your endpoint devices directly connect to one of the ports of their local Ethernet switch in what is known as the *access layer* of the network (see Figure 3-1). For larger sites with scores of devices, these access Ethernet switches then connect to each other, often through another layer of larger switches, known as the aggregation layer, and in the largest networks there may be another layer to connect these aggregation switches, known as the *core layer* of the network.

Together, the access, aggregation, and core layers provide a hierarchical structure for physically connecting many switches and endpoints.

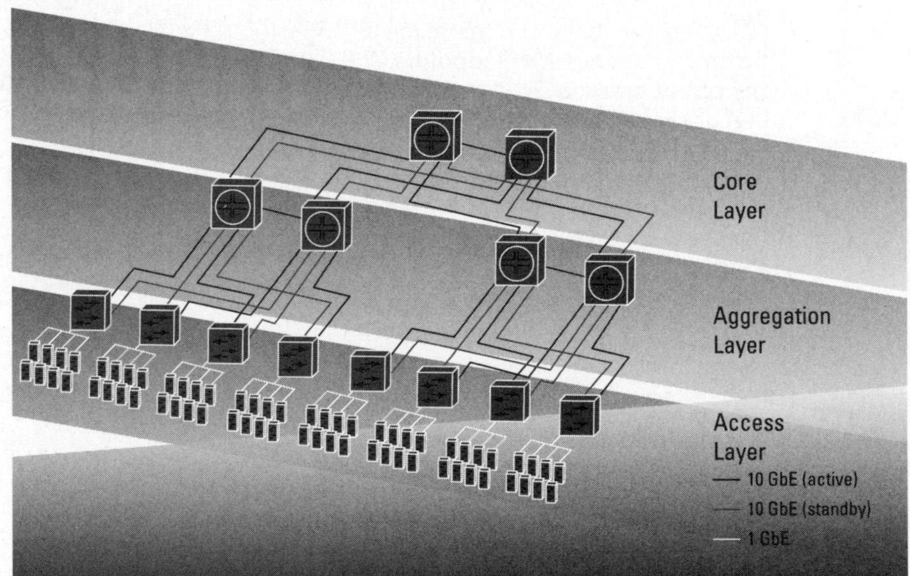

Figure 3-1: Switching layers of the network.

Switching away to the destination

The switches need a way to determine how to send each Ethernet frame (or *packet*) across the maze of links that make up your Ethernet network so that the packets safely arrive at their intended destination(s).

When sending packets through the network, Ethernet initially relies on broadcast communication, whereby the network delivers all traffic to all points, one (or more) of which is the right next destination. We speak of groups of Ethernet endpoints that are all reachable by a broadcasted message as being in the same broadcast domain. Ethernet identifies each of the endpoints on the network by its Media Access Control (MAC) address. A switching network that sends traffic between endpoints (in this case) using their MAC addresses is known as a Layer 2 (L2) network. (It's one step above the view seen by the actual physical media, or Layer 1.)

Over time, an Ethernet switch learns which MAC addresses lie on which downstream links and only forwards packets where they're needed, using a methodology known as *transparent bridging.* The switch stores the discovered addresses in its switching tables. The ability of an Ethernet switch to learn how to reach endpoints on its own is a huge advantage in automating network setup.

Even though each switch gradually gets smarter about which traffic to forward to which link, the large volume of broadcast traffic, even for small networks with only a handful of chatty endpoints, would quickly overwhelm the network links. That's why administrators typically split a local area network (LAN) into segments so that each segment only includes and carries traffic for a set number of endpoints. (The terms LAN, MAN, and WAN indicate the physical reach of the network. A *LAN* is a network within a floor, building, or a group of nearby buildings. It compares to a *metropolitan area network (MAN)* that reaches across a city and a *wide area network (WAN)* that extends between cities.)

For greater flexibility, *virtual local area networks (VLANs)* offer administrators a way to segment a network without regard to the physical locations of the endpoints — that is, a VLAN is a broadcast domain where the endpoints can be virtually anywhere in the corporate network.

In setting up a VLAN, administrators group devices that communicate with each other most frequently. This approach minimizes the amount of traffic that the network must carry — think of it as having the flexibility to pick whoever you want to talk to over the walls of your cubicle. By configuring VLANs in software instead of physically relocating devices on the LAN, administrators have the flexibility to change the network whenever they need.

Links that form loops in the network may be beneficial for redundancy, but they can cause many problems for switches trying to discover the best way to reach the endpoints of each VLAN. *Spanning Tree Protocol* (STP) clears up the confusion by specifying a single path through the network for a switch to reach each endpoint. Several different standardized STP algorithms now exist to meet different requirements, such as support for multiple VLANs and for more rapid convergence. (Configure VLANs and spanning tree in JUNOS software following the how-to steps in Chapter 10.)

What about the L3 view?

If the final destination of a packet lies somewhere outside the L2 view of the switching network (discussed in the prior section), then at some point the network needs to refer to the IP address of the packet to figure out where to send it. IP addresses offer a much wider view of the network for reaching many more endpoints. (For more on IP addresses, see Chapter 4.)

Devices that use IP addresses to make traffic forwarding decisions are said to operate at Layer 3 (L3) of the network. Routers were traditionally the only devices that had an L3 view of the network, but today many switches can also use IP addresses to determine where to send a packet. These devices are commonly known as a Layer 3 switch. Any time a packet needs to leave its VLAN, one of the switches (or a router) must refer to an L3 view of its network to point the packet in the right direction. (We talk about the L3 protocols used to set up the L3 view of the network — the routing tables — in Chapter 4.)

When a switched network carries traffic for many different types of devices and applications, another handy protocol to know about is the *Link Layer Discovery Protocol* (LLDP). LLDP is a standard protocol for discovering the topology and devices of the physical LAN, regardless of whether they're available at Layer 2 or Layer 3 of the network. You can use LLDP when you want to help your endpoints find their neighbors, no matter what protocol they're running. (Chapter 10 shows how to configure LLDP in JUNOS software.)

A Switch of All Trades: Doing More than Just Switching

The functionality of Ethernet switches has moved well beyond their initial role of just delivering packets through local area networks. Nowadays, you design your switching network to also consider the performance, reliability, and security of the packet delivery method — not just for the client-server traffic that dominated networks a few years ago, but also for the diverse and growing mix of unified communications, Web, video, and other application traffic pulsing along your network.

What do the changing demands of your users, business, school or organization mean for your switched Ethernet network?

Delivering unified communications

Is your organization introducing unified communications or voice over IP (VoIP)? Today's Ethernet switches can deliver power, predictable performance, and high availability to meet the needs of these newer applications.

Unified communications integrates the delivery of calls, voicemail, e-mail, instant messaging, web conferencing, and other modern communication tools into a single integrated system so that users can more quickly find and respond to each other. *VoIP* technology allows you to move voice traffic onto your packet-based IP network, easing voice/data convergence within applications while eliminating the need to manage a separate voice network.

Power over Ethernet

Do you have local power outlets for your phones? Ethernet switches can deliver power alongside Ethernet packets over twisted–pair copper cabling using *Power over Ethernet* (PoE) interfaces. So you don't need local outlets to transition your voice network to a converged IP infrastructure.

PoE interfaces can power security cameras, badge readers, environmental controls and other small electronic devices. Retire other types of proprietary networks in your buildings by also migrating these devices to your access switches.

Class of Service

If you run unified communications or VoIP applications on your network, consider what can happen if one user decides to download a large video file at the same time that others are talking on the phone. If the video file consumes most of the bandwidth and switching resources, the sound quality of the calls may suffer from delays and clipping (also known as *jitter effect*) that make it difficult to have a conversation.

Class of Service (CoS), also interchangeably called Quality of Service (QoS), lets you define service mechanisms in your switches (and routers) to prioritize, rate limit and in general manage traffic congestion and bandwidth consumption. When using class of service, the devices follow the configured rules to *mark* the new packets entering the network with one or more CoS designators so that all downstream devices know how to handle the packets. (Chapter 15 discusses how to set up basic Class of Service in devices running JUNOS software.)

CoS tools are most effective when interfaces can support different queues as it provides more flexibility in choosing how to handle the traffic — for example, temporarily buffering big video packets while prioritizing small voice packets so that they can quickly get by.

High availability

High availability is another critical aspect of delivering unified communications and related VoIP traffic.

Many different types of events and errors can cause disruption in network availability. Whether it's your switches, routers, or the links in between that fail, the result is the same — your users are without their network. (In Chapter 5, we discuss the challenges to high availability and consider the key role of both preventive and fail-safe mechanisms in delivering high network uptime.)

Controlling network access

In the past, a generally shared assumption of network managers was that they could trust whatever or whoever used the network from inside any of their buildings. However, for many organizations, this assumption is increasingly invalid, introducing a whole new set of responsibilities for switches.

Do you have users who use their laptops at home or on the road and then come back into your offices and connect to your LAN? How about contractors or other visitors who use their own laptops on your network? In these cases (and many others), the possibility that someone could introduce a virus into or otherwise harm your network from the inside becomes very real. A related issue is controlling access through your internal network to restricted applications, confidential information, and other resources.

Network Access Control (NAC) is a security solution that enables your switch to check users and devices as they enter your internal network but before they attach to the system. Additionally, a NAC solution allows you to monitor these endpoints with mechanisms designed to mitigate and quarantine any problems that may arise after network admission. Essentially, NAC provides a protective layer of security wherever devices can access your internal network, broadly complementing the many other defenses at work in your infrastructure.

The switch can be a NAC enforcer. It's up to the switch to stop traffic if the NAC solution determines the new user or device isn't in compliance with network policies. For example, if a laptop isn't running the latest version of virus definitions, you can prohibit access to your network *before* any damage occurs. And if your organization manages the device, your network can redirect users to appropriate remediation tools. NAC solutions can perform many different types of checks, such as user and device identity, device health, and device security state. You can also use NAC to control where each user can go within your network and what applications they can access.

IEEE 802.1X standardizes the mechanisms for port-based network access control. All Juniper Networks EX-series switches support 802.1X . The complete solution includes a separate policy device, such as the Juniper Networks

Unified Access Control (UAC) platform, to set up and manage network policies, as shown in Figure 3-2. (Find out how to set up admission control in Chapter 10.)

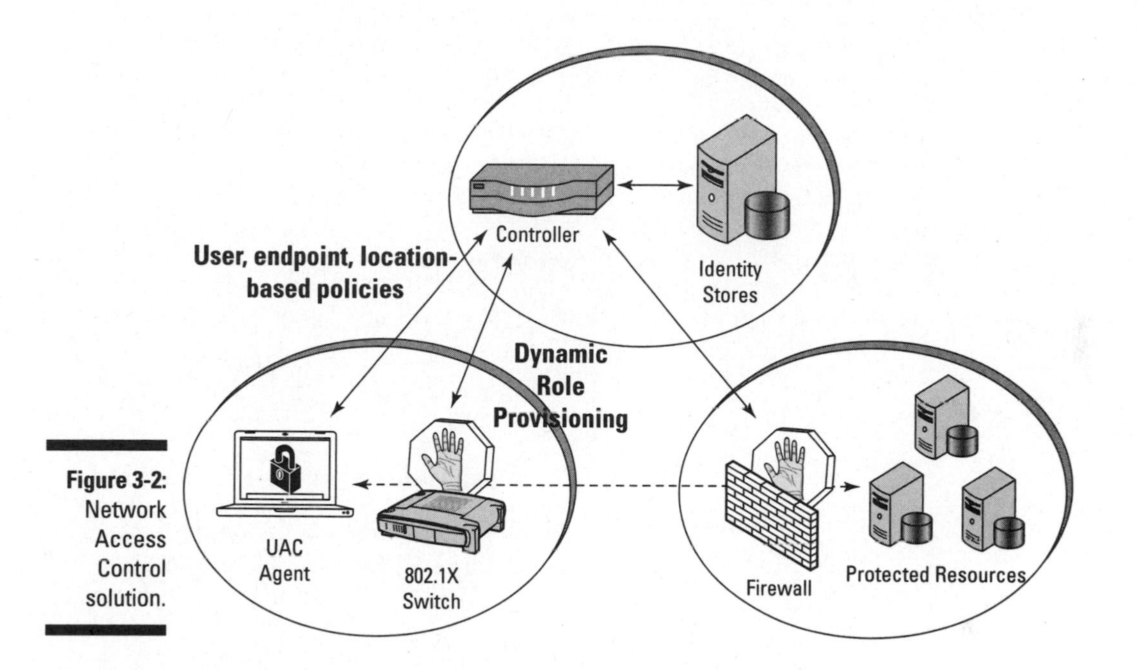

Figure 3-2: Network Access Control solution.

You don't need to deploy a comprehensive NAC solution everywhere in your network to start realizing its benefits. Introduce the capabilities in phases where you address the most immediate needs and then add more functionality and benefits over time. For example, you may begin by only checking devices and traffic that traverse to another segment of your network through a Layer 3 device. Or, perhaps it makes most sense to start by protecting the traffic coming in from your wireless access points (perhaps a visitor or contractor segment). Or, you may have a particular group of users or applications where you want to initially focus your rollout.

Scaling the data center

Is your organization consolidating or redesigning data centers, or perhaps even building a new one? If so, you may be thinking about new ways to optimize the switching infrastructure. Certainly, high availability, performance, operational simplicity, and cost remain key considerations. However, scalability and power consumption may be top of mind as the challenges you most want to solve.

Mountains of gear

In the data center, the access layer provides network access to servers, storage, security, and other IP devices. In a typical configuration, aggregation switches interconnect these access switches, while a core layer provides connectivity between the aggregation layer and the gateway routers that link to the Internet and/or the WAN that interconnects all your sites.

While this three-layer breakout is useful for adding new devices and switches without requiring a major overhaul to the existing network, in many data centers, more than 50 percent of available switching ports are thereby used to connect to other switches. The compounding complexity of scaling across three layers not only adds wiring but also can increase the risk of failure and the effort to manage the infrastructure. And, the power and space needed to run all those switches can further strain energy and financial budgets.

For many organizations, the challenges are only growing. Forecasts predict not just more traffic, but an aggressive acceleration, especially in video and graphics (consider the rocket rise of YouTube). Other causes of traffic growth include migration to:

- **Service-Oriented Architecture (SOA):** SOA approaches large structure applications as a collection of smaller independent modules called services. SOA helps to unify business processes by enabling different applications to use the same code for the same task. As such, SOA approaches are being broadly adopted across many different business applications. In a major business application supporting millions of tasks and transactions, these services can generate millions of messages multiplying bandwidth needs across your network.
- **Software as a Service (SaaS):** SaaS is an application delivery model where the software runs on a central host that users can access from anywhere. The benefits are many, not the least of which are the savings from not having to purchase and manage the application on each and every user machine. However, with the typical Web-based service requiring ten times the bandwidth of comparable client-server applications, the adoption of SaaS application delivery is another potentially significant driver of bandwidth on your network.

As the number of endpoints and traffic in your data center(s) rise, consider how the physical dimensions of your switches affect the efficiency of the network architecture as it scales, particularly:

- **Port density** determines how many interfaces you can physically connect into each switch and how much rack space each switch requires.
- **Interface speed** rates how fast the switch interfaces run, previously limited to 1 Gigabit per second (Gbps) — that is, Gigabit per second Ethernet (GbE or GigE). 10 Gbps interface options are now coming to market, with 40 Gbps and 100 Gbps on the horizon.

- **Port expansion** incrementally adds new ports to existing switches as opposed to investing in and managing more new switches.

With forecasts predicting more traffic growth and with current architectures devouring more and more ports just for interconnecting the infrastructure, you may be looking at design alternatives for your data center networks. New switching solutions with higher port densities, faster interface speeds, and more flexible ways to expand ports offer new options for optimizing your data center network for growth.

Scaling the access switching layer

How are the access switches in your data center organized? Perhaps your preference is to locate them at the top of the rack (TOR) because it simplifies wiring, keeping more cables within the rack. Yet, many of the small, fixed-configuration switches used in these TOR designs have limited features and functionality. Additionally, administrators must manage each switch individually, increasing operational demands.

Perhaps the access switches in your data center are at the end of the row (EOR) where you can justify larger chassis switches with greater functionality. However, cables must run from all the boxes on the network to the end of the row. And, if each row doesn't require all the ports of the large chassis switch, port utilization is low. Also, even a partially configured chassis can have significant space, power, and cooling requirements. Ideally, you want an architecture that delivers the benefits of each design option, without their drawbacks. If you had a platform that distributed the ports of a chassis solution across the row or, alternatively, allowed you to incrementally grow at the end of the row as needed, these alternatives may be attractive to your existing design.

Juniper's Virtual Chassis technology, available on all EX 4200 series Ethernet switches, enables both of these alternative designs, as shown in Figure 3-3.

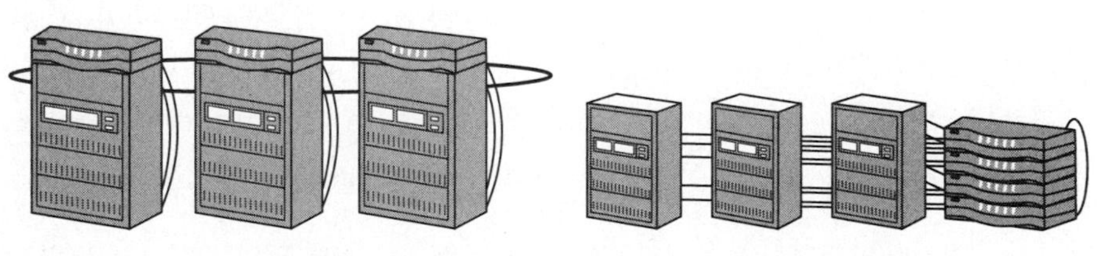

Figure 3-3: Top of the rack and end of the row designs with virtual chassis technology.

The technology currently enables up to ten Juniper EX 4200 series switches to interconnect over a 128 Gbps backplane and act as a single logical device, sharing a common operating system and configuration file. It's also possible to connect switches located on different floors or in different buildings, using the front-panel 10 Gigabit Ethernet fiber uplink ports. (Chapter 10 helps you in setting up the solution). When arranged in a Virtual Chassis configuration, interconnected EX 4200 switches can work together as a single system, offering some unique advantages:

- **Pay-as-you–grow scalability:** Expand port densities only as you need, so you can begin economically with a single switch (1 RU) and avoid the up-front investment of chassis-based solutions.
- **Reduced power, cooling and space needs:** Each switch uses far less power and generates far less heat than chassis-based systems, and because you can incrementally add new platforms as you need, you don't have to pay to power and cool capacity that you aren't using, or take up valuable rack space with a largely empty chassis.
- **High availability:** Interconnect the switches to automatically leverage the multiple Routing Engines present to deliver Graceful Routing Engine Switchover (GRES) and nonstop forwarding (see Chapter 5) in the rare event of a master switch failure.
- **Location independence:** Distribute switches beyond one rack to wiring closets, other floors, and even different buildings, giving you more configuration flexibility. The only distance limitation becomes that of the physical media.
- **Ease of management:** Manage and operate up to ten switches as though they were a single physical chassis, simplifying configuration, maintenance, upgrading, and troubleshooting.

Collapsing the aggregation and core layers

Another design option that you may be considering to optimize your data center network is reducing the number of switch layers. The availability of larger, higher-density chassis switches with many more high-speed 10 Gigabit Ethernet interfaces allow you to consider collapsing the aggregation and core layers of your network(s). In this design, the access switches directly connect to the core over wire-speed 10 Gigabit Ethernet links.

By reducing the number of switches, the design can save not only capital cost but also reduce power, cooling, and space requirements. Additionally, collapsing layers removes potential points of failure and simplifies network operations — including OS upgrades; moves, adds, changes; and troubleshooting. Consider the throughput and the number of 10 Gigabit Ethernet interfaces on your selected chassis platform as well as your expected pace of future growth when determining if this is a good option for your data center.

Choosing the Right Hardware

The primary consideration in choosing the right Juniper Networks products for your switching infrastructure needs is the hardware, particularly its performance, interface capacity, richness of packet handling, and High Availability design. In this section, we discuss the EX-series switches; the MX-series, described in Chapter 4, may be an option when you need to combine high-density switching with deep carrier-class routing functionality. For the latest on the Juniper products running JUNOS software visit `http://juniper.net/products_and_services`.The EX-series Ethernet switches offer Layer 2 and Layer 3 capabilities in a range of high port density platforms offering wire-speed connectivity as detailed in Table 3-1.

Table 3-1 Juniper Networks EX-Series Ethernet Switches

EX-Series	*General Usage Tips*	*Form Factors*
EX 3200 series Ethernet switches	A simple, cost-effective access switch solution for low-density branch and regional offices, as well as campus wiring closets.	Models include 24 and 48 10/100/1000BASE-T Ethernet ports, with options for a full or partial set of Power over Ethernet (PoE) interfaces. Also include support for optional four-port Gigabit Ethernet and two-port 10 Gigabit Ethernet uplink modules with pluggable optics.
EX 4200 series Ethernet switches with Virtual Chassis technology	A solution for access and aggregation switching in your branch and campus, as well as for access in your data center. The EX 4200 series combine the compact, pay-as-you-grow economics of stackable switches with the performance, availability and high port densities of chassis-based platforms.	Models include configurations described for the EX 3200 series and a 24-port 100BASE-FX/1000BASE-X SFP-based platform for Gigabit aggregation deployments requiring the long distance links enabled by fiber. Individual units can group together into a Virtual Chassis configuration, delivering up to 480 10/100/1000BASE-T ports and up to 40 Gigabit Ethernet or 20 10 Gigabit Ethernet uplinks. The EX 4200 series also provides an internal redundant power supply option.

(continued)

Table 3-1 *(continued)*

EX-Series	*General Usage Tips*	*Form Factors*
EX 8200 series Terabit-chassis Ethernet switches	High-speed, high-density platforms for aggregation and core deployments in the campus and data center. The series includes integrated security features for protecting against intrusion and other external threats, such as Distributed Denial of Service (DDoS) attacks. Taking advantage of behavioral threat detection algorithms, the switches are also capable of identifying and closing half-open sessions — important for defending against zero-day threats for which no signatures exist.	Models include the EX 8208, an eight-slot 1.6TB chassis supporting up to 64 10 Gigabit Ethernet ports, and the EX 8216, a 16-slot 3.2TB chassis supporting up to 128 10 Gigabit Ethernet ports. Two of the EX 8216 switches can fit in a single 42-unit rack, delivering 256 10 Gigabit Ethernet ports per rack. Both the EX 8208 and EX 8216 switches deliver 200 Gbps of switching capacity per slot, enabling the future addition of 100 GbE ports.

Chapter 4

Ramping Up to Routing

In This Chapter

- Discovering the ins and outs of routing
- Checking out MPLS
- Matching up Juniper routers with your projects

Routing is the process of selecting paths through the network. Routers (and Layer 3 switches — see Chapter 3) then use this routing information to pass IP addressed packets through a network of nodes from their source to their destination. Here, we introduce the basics of routing. (Chapter 8 helps you to get routing up and running).

This chapter also takes a peek at MPLS, which can be useful in very large private backbone networks — not to mention the networks of your service providers.

The View, Routing Style

The role of *routing* is to select paths, one step at a time, in a network or across a network of networks. Each device knows the next step (the *next hop,* in IP networking lingo) to send each packet on its journey. Any switch or router that performs routing is a *Layer 3 device* because it can forward traffic along these end-to-end paths. Each Layer 3 device knows where to forward each incoming packet for all reachable destinations, a process known as *hop-by-hop routing* (see Figure 4-1).

Switches are a good, cost-effective solution for routing within a building or a nearby group of buildings. Juniper's switches require no additional licensing to use the most common Layer 3 features. This approach offers you more flexibility in choosing where to use Layer 3 networking within your switching infrastructure.

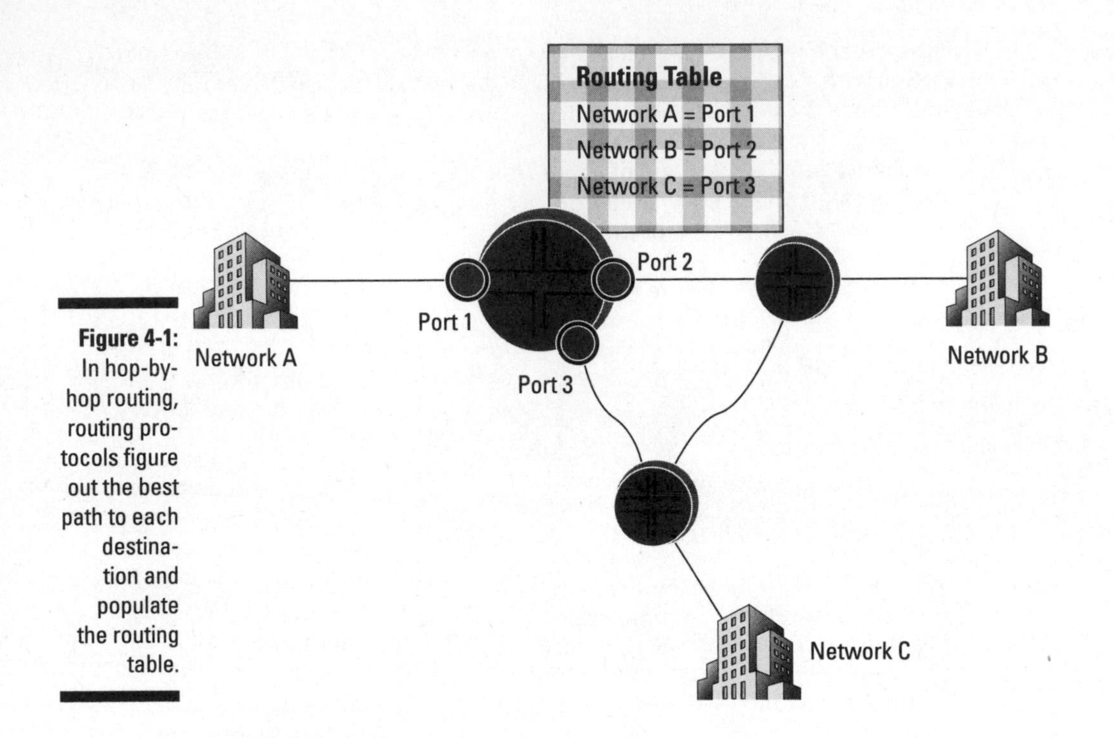

Figure 4-1: In hop-by-hop routing, routing protocols figure out the best path to each destination and populate the routing table.

Addressing the packet

Routers excel at connecting to the outside world. They offer a broad range of interface types to different provider services, the internal design to manage the large routing tables of the Internet, and the fast packet handling power to provide diverse security, policy, accounting, and other services to traffic.

Routing generally uses IP addresses to set up the network paths, and Layer 3 devices use the IP address of incoming packets to forward each along these paths to their intended destination(s). The most fundamental values of IP addressing are its scalability and adoption by networks all around the world. Many IP addresses are public IP addresses, which are globally unique throughout the Internet. A *public IP address* is similar to your phone number. No one else has the same phone number, so anyone calling that phone number will reach you. With a public IP address on the Internet, you can reach any other publicly reachable *host* (the name for an endpoint of an IP network).

Private IP addresses are another type. They are unique only within an individual network, such as a business, school, or other organization. A private IP address is similar to phone extensions in a hotel. While many different hotels may have an extension to get to room 201 or room 7201, this private extension isn't a problem, because within each hotel, only one room has a given extension.

The typical IP address (technically known as an *IPv4 address*) is a 32-bit number, written with a decimal separating each of its octets as in: 207.17.137.229. Each *octet* (that's the numbers between the dots) has the possible range of 0–255.

IETF has defined a new type of IP address known as *IPv6,* which uses a 128-bit address. IPv6 provides greater address scaling and other benefits, but we don't cover it here. Many of the basic concepts are similar in IPv4 and IPv6.

Most organizations receive their public IP addresses for use on the Internet from their service provider. An *address block* is a set of addresses that are contiguous. If you need a lot of addresses, you may get more than one address block from your provider. It's common, but not necessary, to break an address block into smaller portions known as *subnetworks*, or subnets, also typically made up of a set of contiguous addresses.

If you look at all the addresses in any given block or subnet as written in binary form, you see that they share a same set of leading bits — in other words, the same sequence of 1s and 0s makes up the first part of their address. This identical sequence is because the addresses are contiguous. The total count of the common address bits is known as a *mask.* (Find out how to assign IP addresses to your device interface in Chapter 7.)

To identify an address block or a subnet, you need both an address and a mask. You see them written together with the IP address followed by a slash and then the mask as in 207.16.0.0/14.This example identifies a group of addresses ranging from 207.16.0.0 through 207.19.255.255. If you write the addresses within this range in binary form, you see that they all share the same sequence of 1s and 0s in the first 14 bits — for example, 11001111000100.

All the devices (both hosts and routing nodes) communicating on the network know how to interpret the IP addresses and their masks and use this information to determine which IP addresses are on each network. So anytime you use an IP address in a network, you must also indicate its related mask.

The subnet mask can also be written in the same form as an IP address. The subnet mask of 14 means 14 1s followed by 18 0s, which in IP address form is 255.252.0.0. When you write the mask as an IP address, a bit position with a 1 means an exact match must be found in a related address, whereas 0 means that either a 1 or 0 is a match. Here's an example for a host with an address 207.17.137.229 and a mask of 255.252.0.0. The vertical bar denotes the end of the network ID and the start of the host ID.

```
Address:   11001111.000100 |01.01001001.11100101
Mask:      11111111.111111 |00.00000000.00000000
```

Within your private network, you can make your own IP address assignments, following the guidelines of IETF RFC 1918. Each host within your network must have its own unique IP address, and it must know its IP address. You can assign the IP addresses on your network manually, but that would be a lot of work to not only set up but also maintain (and likely an inefficient use of addresses), so most administrators rely on a Dynamic Host Configuration Protocol (DHCP) server to automate assignment of a unique IP address to each host.

In a private network, the addresses that you assign to your endpoints aren't generally visible on the Internet. A gateway device securing your Internet connection shields the private addresses from others through a process called Network Address Translation (NAT). NAT can translate private addresses to public addresses, so only public addresses are known (and seen) on the Internet. (For more on this topic, see Chapter 5.)

When hosts send IP packets headed to destinations outside their local network, they send them to their assigned default gateway on the Layer 3 network. The *default gateway* is a router (or Layer 3 switch) that starts the packet on its way, providing the entrance to the network leading to its final destination IP address.

Your Layer 3 networking devices use the IP addresses to move packets across the network from source to destination. How they do it can be broken into two broad sets of activities:

- Determining each next hop
- Forwarding the incoming packets to the next hop

Each L3 device stores the information it needs to send the packets along their journey in *routing tables,* also sometimes called Routing Information Bases (RIBs). For each destination entry, the stored routes include the next hop along with other key information about the route. Figure 4-1, earlier in this chapter, shows a simplified routing table of destinations and next hops for each of the network nodes. When a packet comes into the L3 device, the device determines what to do with it by looking for the *longest match* to the destination address in its routing table or, more specifically, for JUNOS software in its forwarding table, which is a copy of the information in the routing table. (*Longest match* refers to the most specific match. The *long* refers to the length of the network mask, in units of bits. Think about the mask as a string of 1s followed by 0s, the longer the string of 1s, the longer the match. An exact match would be a host, typically on a subnet directly connected to the router.)

With the method of longest match, the router can use one entry (the *prefix*) in the routing table to represent a contiguous set of addresses reached in the same way, while also allowing entries for specific addresses in that range that you want to somehow route in a different manner. Using prefixes that group addresses together significantly reduces the number of unique entries that the routing table must maintain, speeding both setup and lookup of the routing table.

In a Juniper device, the route lookup references the locally stored forwarding table of the PFE. (For more on this topic, see Chapter 1.) The JUNOS software routing process maintains a number of different routing tables to support different types of traffic, such as *unicast* (traffic sent to only one specific place), multicast (traffic going to a group of destinations), and MPLS. For each destination entry, the routing process determines an *active route* and copies all active routes to the Forwarding Information Base (FIB). The PFE forwarding table is a synchronized copy of the FIB.

Setting up the table with routing protocols

You can manually configure the routing table for each of your L3 devices, which is known as *static routing*, or you can automate the process (*dynamic routing*) using a routing protocol. Unless your network is small without many changes, you're going to want to use a routing protocol to set up most of the routes in your routing table. Your routing table may also likely include a few statics routes that you set up, such as default and null routes. (Chapter 8 describes these routes and shows you how to set them up.)

Routing protocols let your L3 devices exchange information about what they know about their networks and determine the best next hops to destinations. As each L3 device receives routing information from others, it must sort through the new data to revise its routing table(s). When network topology changes, such as new or failed devices and links, update messages enable the L3 devices to determine new best routes to affected destinations.

To assess whether one way is better than another, the protocols use *routing metrics*. How do you determine how to get to someplace? What is best for you — a wide highway with a high speed limit or small back roads with low speed limits? Normally, you might choose the shortest route. However, many people would choose to drive a few extra miles to go on the highway. Why? They're using something called metrics. In early routing protocols, the only metric was the count of the number of hops to get to a destination. Newer, more sophisticated protocols now make routing decisions using a combination of metrics that may also include bandwidth, reliability, delay, load, and economic cost among others.

In defining the next hops for each L3 device, the routing protocols must converge quickly while avoiding loops. *Convergence* is a measure of how long it takes for the updates of network changes to be reflected in the routing tables of each L3 device in the network so that each has accurate routing information about the best routes in its routing tables.

Problems that can arise from rapid changes with long convergence times include

- **Black holing:** Sends traffic to a nonexistent next hop — in other words, the packet is dropped and never reaches its destination. It's as if you followed a sign toward your destination and suddenly ended up at a dead-end.
- **Route flapping:** Occurs when a link or device repeatedly and rapidly fails and then returns. It's as if a road is repeatedly closed due to a common problem. Keeping up with the latest status is more hassle than it's worth, so you may want to temporarily ignore it until it's permanently repaired. If your routers try to keep up with the latest status of a flapping element, it causes a quick succession of routing updates that can slow convergence and otherwise create instabilities in the network.

Each protocol has a different method and set of messages for exchanging routing information and calculating the next hop for the routing tables. Two classes of routing protocols are Interior Gateway Protocols (IGPs) and Exterior Gateway Protocols (EGPs). Conveniently, these names are very descriptive. *IGPs* enable the Layer 3 devices to exchange information within a network to determine routes. *EGPs* define the mechanisms to exchange routing information between independent networks — for example, among the networks that make up the Internet.

Two broad categories of methods for routing used by IGPs are the following:

- **Distance-vector algorithms** send the routing table of each device only to adjacent neighbors and use accumulated cost metrics, such as hop count, for assessing best routes.
- **Link-state algorithms** independently determine the next hops in each device by creating a map of the network using topology information received from every other L3 device in the network. Each routing device advertises *local changes* — that is, recognized changes in the state of its directly connected links/devices — by flooding the network with a message about the changes.

Hierarchical routing is a way to speed up routing and route convergence in networks by breaking the network up into regions. Each routing device then needs to know only how to get to the other destinations within its own region and how to get to other regions. Hierarchical routing is formally used only by protocols based on link-state algorithms.

For the devices to exchange information, they must be running the same routing protocol. A single device can run multiple routing protocols at a time. In JUNOS software, the routing process uses a predefined preference to choose which of the discovered routes becomes the active route to the destination.

JUNOS software's predefined preference is similar to the concept of administrative distance in Cisco's routers, which selects the best path when two or more different routes exist to the same destination from two different routing protocols.

Here we provide a brief description of the most common routing protocols:

- **Routing Information Protocol (RIP)** is a distance-vector protocol that uses only hop count to assess the best paths through the network
- **Intermediate System – Intermediate System (IS-IS)** uses link-state and enables you to set up network hierarchy within your IP network. IS-IS is most often found in service provider networks.
- **Open Shortest Path First (OSPF)** uses link-state and enables you to set up network hierarchy within your IP network. OSPF is found in both service provider and enterprise networks.

These long-standing, widely deployed standard protocols for routing let you use equipment from different vendors, yet still run a stable, highly functional network. The standards specify all the details so that different L3 devices can affectively exchange the messages and execute the decisions of the defined routing protocols. (Chapter 8 discusses further the common, standard IGP routing protocols that you can use inside your network for *unicast* traffic.)

If you still run Enhanced Interior Gateway Routing Protocol (EIGRP), a proprietary IGP, migrating to OSPF gives you additional capabilities and improved scaling, along with a standard protocol that lets you deploy different vendors in your network. With proper planning, the transition may not be as challenging as you might think, as you can simultaneously run EIGRP and OSPF in your routers to enable the transition. A good place to start is your backbone. Juniper provides documents about this migration on its Web site: `www.juniper.net/junos`.

Chapter 13 discusses the routing protocol used within the Internet, known as Border Gateway Protocol (BGP). BGP provides a mechanism to exchange routes among *autonomous systems* (AS). An AS is a collection of networks under the control of one administrative entity, such as an ISP.

If you use only one access point to one service provider to connect to the Internet, you can use static routes. However, if you want to route across the link (for example, to know when it is up or down), or if you use more than one service provider or multiple access points from the same provider and want traffic destined to some or all of the addresses at that site to be able to use either access point — you want to *multihome* your site — you need to provision BGP on the routers connecting the site to the Internet. If you're a large organization, you may also use BGP within your own network to connect a number of large OSPF networks.

Remembering policy

As part of your routing protocol decisions, you can factor in the perspective of policies that you set through configuration. Routing policy applies to routing protocols, affecting the selection of routes, how they're stored in the routing tables, provided to the forwarding table, and advertised to peers.

An example of how you might use routing policy is to direct voice packets to specific low-latency paths of your network. In this case, your Level 3 device can use the packet's classification for CoS (see Chapter 3) in its determination of the best next hop to use.

Routing policy gives you powerful control over how the routing protocols behave in your network, and you can use it anytime the default policy of a routing protocol doesn't meet your requirements. (Chapter 14 discusses routing policy in detail.)

The View, MPLS Style

Multiprotocol Label Switching (MPLS) is another way to send packets through an IP network. Instead of using hop-by-hop routing to forward traffic, the protocol forwards the packets along preset end-to-end paths through your network. The IETF has developed an extensive set of standards for MPLS.

MPLS thereby combines the strengths of end-to-end circuit design with packet-driven flexibility so as to support a converged infrastructure that offers any-to-any connectivity with high levels of control and resiliency. This section introduces the why and how of MPLS, while Chapter 16 discusses its setup in JUNOS software.

MPLS services

You may already subscribe to MPLS services or a service that a provider supports internally with MPLS but gives it another name, such as IP VPN services. Regardless of the name, MPLS services deliver a private VPN that combines the flexibility of any-to-any connectivity with high-performance.

To use these services, you don't need to run MPLS in your network. Your handoff can be a standard IP connection over which you send IP addressed packets. Your provider then uses MPLS within its network, leveraging the flexibility of the protocol so that your packets can go around failures and congestion, engineering the network for delivery of predictable performance.

If you build your WAN with services from providers, you can benefit from MPLS by migrating to MPLS services offerings, shown in Figure 4-2. If you run your own private WAN backbone, you're a candidate to run a private MPLS network, using MPLS services to connect smaller sites to your backbone.

MPLS can run over Generic Routing Encapsulation (GRE) tunnels so that you can use your provider's IP network for some of your private MPLS links.

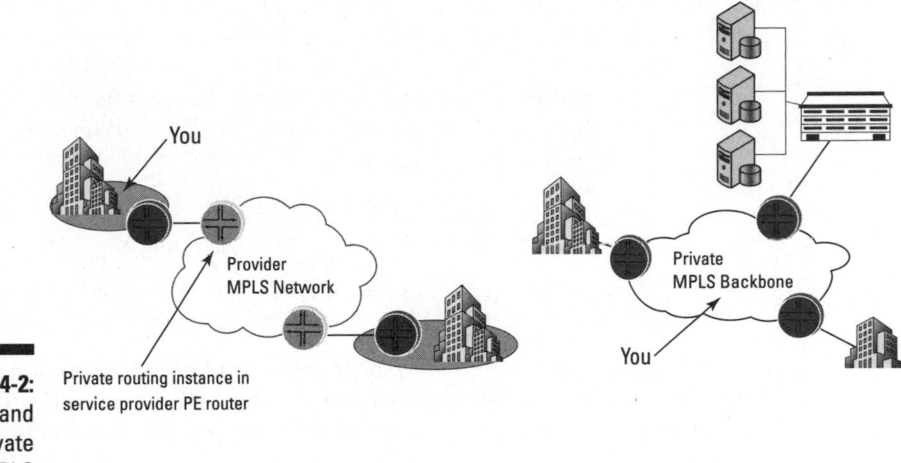

Figure 4-2: Public and private MPLS services.

Reasons to use MPLS

While often perceived as complex, MPLS can actually help you simplify your converged backbone with many points of control.

MPLS adds functionality in three new areas not generally available in hop-by-hop routing (see Figure 4-1). If you have advanced requirements in any of these areas, you should consider using MPLS in your own private network:

- **Traffic engineering** enables the selection of specific end-to-end paths to send given types of traffic through your network. The engineering of defined paths provides greater control in your network design to:
    - Assure predictable performance for traffic by engineering paths for different levels of service. For example, you can designate highly available, low-latency paths to carry your voice traffic.
    - Balance traffic across redundant paths and intelligently route around congested links for efficient utilization of the network.
    - Lower WAN costs by preventing unnecessary use of costly links.

- **Fast failover** rapidly moves traffic from one engineered path to another for failover that is generally much faster than route reconvergence. MPLS *Fast-Reroute (FRR)* occurs in under 50 ms (often much more quickly) to preserve time-sensitive applications, such as voice calls.
- **Virtualization** enables the creation of fully separated and independent virtual networks within one physical network. MPLS Virtual Private Networks (VPNs) offers the flexibility for:
    - Different organizations to secure and fully administer as well as control their own virtual network, independent to and without impact on other organizations sharing the same backbone. This approach allows the members of a large organization to share the same backbone, while enabling autonomy for different business groups, operations, and processes.
    - Quick provisioning of new services over the backbone without involvement or coordination with your service provider.
    - Fast integration (or divesture) of new networks resulting from acquisitions, mergers, and other business organization changes.
    - Different applications to run with differentiated qualities of service in their own virtual network, over a converged infrastructure, yet segregated from the traffic and demands of other applications.
    - Inherent security zones between the virtualized networks, which can greatly reduce the number of Access Control Lists (ACLs) you need to configure in your devices. (Chapter 5 describes ACLs.)
    - Ease of carrying legacy traffic, including proprietary, non-IP protocols, through encapsulation mechanisms to deliver almost any traffic, including point-to-point links, over one shared backbone.

The workings of MPLS

MPLS is among the most acronym-rich protocols, which can get a little confusing and certainly challenges the memory, but its basic principles are fairly straightforward. As in any IP network, each MPLS device has to know what to do with incoming packets. Here's the super-short description of how it works:

1. **The mechanisms of MPLS attach a label (the label in the MPLS name) to each packet.**
2. **The MPLS devices then use this label (instead of the destination IP address) to look up where to forward the packet.**

   The labels must be unique only to a specific physical link, so to perform a lookup, the device uses both the port and label information.

3. **Through this forwarding process, the packets move from one device to the next, traversing a path that has been set up in the network.**

The use of labels facilitates convergence of many different types of networks (the multiprotocol in the MPLS name). The IETF has also established standards for attaching MPLS labels to non-IP traffic types, including ATM, frame relay, Ethernet, point-to-point circuits, and many others. For these other types of traffic, MPLS uses an existing header field or adds a short shim to the transported data that contains the label information, enabling stacking, so you can design hierarchy within your network.

To set up the forwarding tables, the MPLS network uses various protocols, described in Chapter 16.

Common terms used in describing MPLS networks include

- **Label Switched Path (LSP):** The end-to-end, unidirectional path established through the MPLS network.
- **Label Switching Router (LSR):** A networking device that can run the MPLS protocols.
- **Forward Equivalency Class (FEC):** The set of IP packets assigned to a particular path and identified by its label.
- **Label Distribution Protocol (LDP):** The MPLS-specific protocol that LSRs can use to exchange information about the labels for each FEC so that they can assign the correct labels to each of their forwarding paths.

An MPLS network tasks the ingress router with sorting the IP packets and assigning them to their FEC (and so also their path) as they enter the MPLS network. The downstream routers need to make only forwarding decisions — that is, they need to select the outgoing link based on the label. As such, the ingress routers do most of the heavy lifting for the control needs of the network, which is a factor contributing to the high scalability of MPLS.

Following are two common methods for MPLS transport of non-IP traffic:

- **Virtual Private LAN Services (VPLS)** transports multipoint Ethernet LAN traffic across the MPLS network. The existence of the MPLS network is transparent to the LANs, appearing as just another Layer 2 switch of the network. VPLS is well suited for the distributed enterprise or data center or service provider network.
- **Pseudo wire emulation** transports other protocols using a small shim attached to a packaged stream of the traffic, effectively enabling you to replace any physical link with your converged MPLS backbone (and without having to first encapsulate the traffic in IP). The shim provides the label header used by the MPLS network in its forwarding decisions.

Choosing the Right Hardware

Routers are the most common hardware choice for the Layer 3 networking requirements of your large campus, metro, and wide area network backbones, as well as at the gateway points connecting your branch and regional offices, data centers, and other sites to your wide area network and the Internet. Some routers also provide a full suite of Layer 2 capabilities should you need that, too, so check the specs of the model you're interested in. The decision of what routers to use depends upon where you're deploying them, and thereby, the required throughput and feature set needed. Table 4-1 summarizes the array of choices you have from Juniper Networks.

If you're looking for a routing backbone for the switching infrastructure inside your buildings, you may also consider the EX-series Ethernet switches (see Chapter 3). For the latest on the Juniper products running JUNOS software, visit `http://juniper.net/products_and_services`.

Scaling from small branch offices to the largest TeraPop sites in the world, JUNOS routing platforms include IPv4 and IPv6 addressing, all standard routing protocols, routing policy, *multicast* (traffic from one point that must go to many points) and MPLS VPNs. Additionally, the platforms offer stateful firewall, many types of tunneling and other security features, classification and accounting of traffic, and other services that require rich packet processing for your L3 packets along with many High Availability features.

Table 4-1 Juniper Networks Routing Platform Series

Routing Series	*General Usage Tips*	*Form Factor*
J-series services routers	Family of routing platforms providing a broad set of integrated functionality that includes routing, security, IP telephony and WAN acceleration with rich functionality and high performance. The series meets branch office needs and can also be a fit for small regional offices and small data centers. Security capabilities derived from Juniper's ScreenOS operating system include stateful firewalls with security zones, simplified set up of VPNs, and clustering of platforms for High Availability.	The models offer four fixed 10/100/1000 LAN ports with the option to add more ports with interface cards supporting up to 16 10/100/1000 BASE-T Ethernet. Other interfaces available include serial, T1/E1, DS3/E3, ISDN, ADSL2/2+ and G.SHDSL. The optional Avaya IG550 Media Gateway is a set of plug-in modules that offers media gateway capabilities and a variety of traditional telephony interfaces for analog, digital and ISDN trunks, as well as analog and IP stations.

Routing Series	*General Usage Tips*	*Form Factor*
M-series multiservice edge routers	High capacity routing platforms for network gateway points in large head office, campus and data center sites as well as for large backbones of your network infrastructure. Service providers use M-series at the edge and core of their network.	The series spans from 5 Gbps up to 320 Gbps of throughput in several different models that offer a diverse set of Ethernet and wide area interfaces.
MX-series Ethernet services routers	High capacity routing platform for environments requiring both L2 switching and routing along with support for large Internet routing tables or extensive packet handling. Service providers use MX-series at the edge and core of their network.	Models offer 240G to 960G of performance with high density 10/100/1000 Ethernet, Gigabit Ethernet and 10 Gigabit Ethernet interfaces.
T-series core platforms	Core routing platform for large service provider networks, but may also be used in the backbones of businesses, schools and governments requiring very high throughput rates.	Models deliver terabit capacities with multi-chassis scalability along with a wide range of interfaces that include various optical options.

Chapter 5

Locking-in on JUNOS Software Security and High Availability

In This Chapter

- Adding security to your network
- Understanding firewall filters, firewalls, NAT, and VPNs
- Avoiding network downtime

In this chapter, we provide short descriptions of various security functions for those new to the topic and also introduce a few of the ways that JUNOS software can help you secure your network, as well as provide high network availability to users. (Chapter 3 discusses switch security solutions for Network Access Control).

Security is one of those feature areas where product families running on JUNOS software can vary most in what each provides and how they work. For example, you probably look for a broad spectrum of integrated security functionality in your smaller routing devices, but less in your larger platforms, where most organizations continue to use specialized devices for performance and other reasons. So if you're implementing security in JUNOS software, you want to look at documentation written specifically for that product.

Securing Your Network

The protocols for switching and routing assume a single-purpose mission: Take any packet entering the network and pass it on as quickly as possible for fast delivery to whatever destination the packet requests.

Of course, in reality, just like your mailbox at home, you don't always want all the traffic sent to your network. Moreover, unlike your mailbox, unwanted

For more on security

Juniper is expanding the set of security features within JUNOS software, some of which we cover, and some of which will have to wait for the next edition of this book. The Juniper engineers are deriving many of these features from Juniper's ScreenOS operating system widely used by organizations to secure their infrastructure. So, if you're interested in all the security capabilities and functionality that you can get in products running on JUNOS software (and perhaps even a few new products), you can complement what we provide with a visit to the Web site `www.juniper.net/products_and_services/security.html`, even if you're reading this book only a few months after publication.

traffic is not only a minor annoyance, but it can be a major threat to your organization as well, with long term impact to customer relationships and its financial health. Security helps you restrict the rote forwarding of switches and routers by making informed decisions about where, when, and how much to deliver certain types of traffic in your network. Actions to secure your network occur throughout your infrastructure. You likely have specialized devices, particularly at your large central sites. For example, a basic *firewall* controls what traffic can come in and out of, or move across, your network based on specified data fields of the packet header (contains the addresses and other handling instructions). As another example, devices providing *intrusion detection and prevention* read into the application data of the packet (also known as the payload), for greater granularity and insight into the traffic coming and going on the network.

The security features of JUNOS software running on Juniper's switching and routing platforms can complement your existing security infrastructure. In addition, an expanding set of security features derived from the ScreenOS operating system gives you more options for different needs in your network. One example is Juniper's platforms designed for the branch that integrate routing, security, application acceleration, and other functions into one device, offering cost and management benefits for your smaller sites.

Firewall filters — what you let in and out

So, how do you let some traffic into your network, yet filter out the unwanted traffic or *rate limit* (in other words, restrict the flow of) less important traffic that is trying to get in? A first step is to define firewall filters to control the traffic passing in and out of an interface. You can use this first step on routing, switching, and security platforms running on JUNOS software. You may already be familiar with them by another name: *access control lists* (ACLs). The firewall filters are *stateless* — in other words, they can't statefully inspect the traffic. (Chapter 9 tells you how to set up the filters.)

Unsure what the term *stateful* firewall refers to? Above Layer 3 of the network is another: Layer 4 (L4) enables a host to distinguish among the many different flows of application data that they're exchanging with another host. For many types of applications, the hosts identify their back and forth exchange of information as a single *transport session*. The session stays in place as long as the communicating applications require it to complete a particular task or a set of activities. If an intermediate device sitting between the hosts is monitoring their back and forth packets and tracking the progress of the sessions, it's aware of the changing *state* of each session. The L4 header includes information about the particular session of the transported application, such as its *transport protocol, port numbers,* and so on.

Firewall filters can take actions based on one or a combination of different L2, L3, and L4 packet header parameters, so they're extremely useful in monitoring and controlling the traffic on your network. For example, you can block unexpected (and potentially harmful) traffic such as *Telnet* (a protocol to access devices remotely) or apply needed filters to rate limit traffic by type or inbound/outbound address to thwart Distributed Denial of Service attacks.

To set up a firewall filter, you first define the filter and its associated terms of condition and then apply the filter to specific interfaces. Breaking this process into two provides a convenient way for you to use the same filters over and over in your device. Then, when you need to update the conditions or consequences of a filter, you have to make the change only in one place.

The filter terms include both the criteria for a match and the requested actions to take for matched packets. After you activate the firewall filters, the interfaces then inspect all incoming and outgoing packet headers looking for the matches to the defined conditions. Upon finding a match, the interface can accept, discard, log, count, or rate limit the incoming/outgoing packet.

Juniper platforms hold multiple advantages over competing solutions in setting up and processing firewall filters by

- Easing configuration by using the flexible editing tools of the JUNOS CLI.
- Activating all firewall filters of an interface in one step: the commit of the complete candidate configuration. (In many other systems, activation is line-by-line through the CLI with the potential of unexpected consequences of partially entered configurations). (Chapter 2 describes the configuration process.)
- Supporting very large numbers of firewall filter terms with high performance throughput.
- Enabling the use of multiple match criteria to establish conditional actions by nesting and chaining of filters.

Stateful firewall — what's going on

Beyond the static verification checks on the IP packet headers made by firewall filters, gateway routers and security devices can track the state of each traffic flow or stream looking for problematic anomalies. This capability, known as *stateful firewall*, protects hosts from being fooled into communicating with compromised or faulty users and applications.

For example, instead of letting in any traffic masquerading as part of one of potentially many, many established web sessions, the stateful firewall checks that the packets truly belong to an existing session. By constricting the openings into your network to only the small, specific holes necessary to support the expected communications, stateful firewalls protect against many different types of security risks.

Stateful firewalls work by maintaining a table of the active, permitted sessions. For each session, the stateful firewall records key parameters that allow it to detect unanticipated changes, such as the source and destination IP addresses, port numbers, and the current sequence number of the session packets.

For most applications, the conventions that a stateful firewall uses to determine valid packets of a session are straightforward. However, more complex applications require Application Layer Gateways (ALGs) to provide the stateful firewall with details on how the application works. Examples of applications requiring ALGs include File Transfer Protocol (FTP) and many protocols used in transporting Voice over IP (VoIP).

Further discussion of specific implementations of stateful firewall and ALGs for different platforms is beyond the scope of this book, but you can turn to the technical documentation of each platform for details.

Address translation — secret identities

Many private networks translate IP addresses in packets as they enter (and leave) the network. This translation function is straightforwardly enough called *Network Address Translation* (NAT).

Organizations use NAT in their network for two primary reasons:

- They want to enhance security by disguising host addresses and shielding other details of the network from the outside world.
- They want to let multiple hosts access the Internet with a single public IP address.

The latter also aids address conservation. Prevalent use of NAT has lessened concerns that the world is running out of public IP addresses.

For hosts with direct connections to the Internet, the translation function can simply convert between the public and the private address on a static one-to-one basis. Alternatively, all traffic can appear to originate from the nctwork gateway where translation is dynamic, supporting the conversion of many-to-one. In this configuration, the gateway must track destination addresses, port numbers, and other information as the packets leave your network. Then, when the responding packets of a given exchange return, your gateway uses this information to translate them back to the private addresses and port numbers expected by your hosts. (Chapter 17 discusses the setup of a basic NAT configuration.)

Secure VPNs tunnels — armored traffic

Secure *Virtual Private Network* (VPN) tunnels enable the safe exchange of traffic over public IP services. Our focus in this book is site-to-site VPNS to secure communications between gateway points of your network. For example, you can send all the traffic from a small remote office to a central regional site for forwarding to the next hop in its destination. The VPN tunnel protects the traffic from tampering or interception by others as it traverses across the public IP network. The IPSec (IP security) protocols are a commonly used form of tunnels for site-to-site VPNs.

IPSec is a suite of protocols for securing IP packets that define mechanisms to *authenticate* (verify the identity of the tunnel endpoints) and/or encrypt each packet in a data stream, including how the endpoints will exchange cryptographic keys. Encryption provides mathematical manipulation of the traffic using a *cryptographic key* (a string of information) so that only the intended tunnel endpoint can read the data by undoing the manipulation.

In setting up the VPN tunnel, the gateways on both sides must determine how they will secure the traffic, as IPSec offers several options. (Chapter 17 helps you set up IPSec tunnels with JUNOS software to create a VPN for interconnecting the sites of your network.)

Delivering without Down Time

Along with ensuring that your network protects your users and applications (and itself), you want it to be always available for its primary purpose of carrying traffic among them. Many different types of events and errors can cause disruption to network availability. Whether it's your switches, routers, or links in between that fail, the result is the same: Your users are without critical services.

The following sections explore the different causes of network downtime and the mechanisms and features of JUNOS software for delivering high availability.

Planned events

How much downtime do planned events cause in your network? Maintenance time for software upgrades and needed fixes can quickly add up, sabotaging efforts to deliver high uptime. Reducing the number of these events, as well as their duration, can get you much closer to your targeted nines of reliability.

The single release train of JUNOS software (see Chapter 1) can help you reduce the downtime caused by planned events. For example:

- Have you ever had to upgrade in order to change over to a different software package because what you were running didn't have a feature that you needed? As JUNOS software provides new releases with existing features, there's a good chance that when you need to turn on a new feature, it's already available in the software running on your platforms.
- How often do you need to update software with fixes and patches from your vendor? How many times do these work the first time? You're likely to find that with JUNOS software, you just don't need to deploy new fixes and patches as much as you do with other operating systems.

Additionally, JUNOS software offers in-service software upgrades (requires dual REs and platform support) that can further reduce downtime by enabling the transition to new software versions with minimal disruption in service delivery to users.

Unplanned events

Unplanned events occur due to failures in your devices, links, and network services. The inherent stability of the modular design and single release train of JUNOS software contributes to its high uptime in the field (see Chapter 1).

JUNOS software also offers High Availability features to minimize downtime due to unplanned events. These features include automated mechanisms for rapid detection and response to events, fast failover to redundant systems, and self-healing of networks, among other means. These automated mechanisms help avert downtime and the stressful chain of events that it can trigger.

Advanced High Availability capabilities of JUNOS software include

- **Graceful Routing Engine Switchover (GRES)** provides stateful replication between a master and backup Routing Engine, with both engines maintaining a copy of all important entities. If the PFE detects failure in the master RE, it switches to use the backup. In groups of Ethernet switches with Virtual Chassis technology (see Chapter 3), if the master RE should happen to fail, GRES enables the control of the overall chassis to pass from that system to another.

- **Graceful Restart Protocol Extensions** enable adjoining routing peers (or switches) to recognize an RE failover from the master to the backup as a transitional event so that they don't begin the process of reconverging network paths (or spanning trees) to route (or bridge) around the transitioning node. The solution requires that the peers run the standardized protocol extensions.
- **Nonstop Active Routing (NSR)** and nonstop bridging provide mechanisms for transparent switchover of the routing engine, without restart of supported routing and bridging protocols. Both REs are fully active in processing protocol sessions and so can take over for the other. The solution is self-contained, and the switchover is transparent to neighbors.
- **Bidirectional Forwarding Detection (BFD)** provides rapid detection of failures between certain pairs of connected systems. The lightweight protocol works by having the endpoints exchange high-speed HELLOs (a form of ping) that verify connectivity between the pairs.
- **Event policies and operation scripts** enable automation of early warning systems and response in the software to not only detect emerging problems but also to take immediate steps to avert further issues. By automating your troubleshooting and response practices, these scripts enable fast diagnosis and action when events do occur (see Chapter 20).

Furthermore, JUNOS software supports many other methods for high availability, including failover of the default gateway and rapid recovery and self-healing of the network topology, as defined by various networking standards and protocols.

Human factors

Various studies investigating the causes of network downtime have estimated human factors as the primary cause in a majority of the cases. Given all the details to track in running a modern network, it's no surprise that a few errors occur now and again, but unfortunately, an absentminded error at the wrong place or a misunderstanding of the result of an action can cause millions of dollars in damages in lost transactions and customers that may never return.

While human factors may most often cause downtime, they're also often the least understood and examined malfunctions. However, a systematic approach to proactively identifying, correcting, and preventing errors can result in significant gains to network uptime. The focus is on what happened, what aspects of the system made the error possible in the first place, and how to prevent the same error from occurring in the future. Changes to reduce human error must recognize that despite best efforts, mistakes can always happen, and so fail-safe mechanisms are a key part of any effective solution.

The engineers building JUNOS software anticipate that mistakes will happen and so provide fail-safe mechanisms and ways to learn from errors so that they do not happen again. (Chapter 2 outlines many of the operations tools available in JUNOS software for preventing human error.)

By defining and changing configurations in a candidate, checking for proper syntax and context, enabling fast rollback, and restoring working configurations on systems that become isolated, the JUNOS CLI helps you catch mistakes before they become a problem. Commit scripts provide further capabilities by allowing you to customize the checks performed on your configuration. The most experienced engineers on your team can define commit scripts that enforce the setup and policies of your network and check that past errors aren't repeated. A macro capability of commit scripts lets you condense commonly used, lengthy configurations to a few lines of variable input. (See Chapter 20 to learn more about commit and other types of scripts.)

Part II
Working with JUNOS

"If it works, it works. I've just never seen network cabling connected with Chinese handcuffs before."

In this part . . .

There's no better way to master JUNOS software than by doing JUNOS software. Part of its built-in sophistication is its ease of use. We can tell you about this feature and that trick, but it is so much easier to just *do* it yourself.

In this part, we take you on a hands-on tour of the JUNOS software. We show you the basics of how to set up your network by working with the command-line interface (CLI), and then running the base commands for routing, switching, and securing your device.

Chapter 6

Getting to Know Command-Line Interface Essentials

In This Chapter

- Understanding the difference between operational mode and configuration mode
- Helping control and configure the router with hierarchies
- Knowing the difference between commands and JUNOS statements
- Initially starting and configuring a Juniper Networks router

When you first get your router (or switch), you'll want to turn it on and start playing with it right away. So this chapter lays out the basics of how to log in and gives a guided tour of what you will find using the router's command-line interface (CLI). It also tells you how to configure the router the first time.

Logging in to Your Router for the First Time

Most Juniper routers are part of a large network used by your business, organization, or school in many locations. More than likely, a separate team has installed and connected the router to the network. (If you're installing the router yourself, see the sidebar "DIY: Installing the router.")

When the router is already connected to your network, you need to find out from the installer or your network team what they've named the router. This *hostname,* or name, is your entry key. From your PC or laptop, use a terminal program, such as Telnet, to open a connection to the router.

The router is like any other secured device on the network. You need to have a username and a password to log in. The first time you log in to a router that has never been configured, it will be as `root`, and the router will not require a password. This user is a super-administrator who can perform any operation,

> ### DIY: Installing the router
>
> If you're installing the router, or if you have a smaller router, such as a J-series, and are sitting next to it, you can connect to the router with your laptop by attaching an RS-232 cable from your computer into the router's console port. The location of this port varies from router to router, but is generally on the front of the router. You connect to the router's console port with a terminal program (such as HyperTerminal on Windows). Configure the terminal program to communicate at 9600 baud (or bps), 8 data bits, no parity, and 1 stop bit (sometimes referred to as "9600 8-N-1").

from benign checks such as looking at the status of the router to disruptive operations such as changing the configuration and rebooting the router.

One of the first things you should do is create login accounts for regular users to limit the scope of what normal users can do on the router. (We talk about that topic in the next chapter.)

To take a quick look around on a router, first log in:

```
fred-laptop> telnet junos-router
junos-router (ttyp0)

login: fred
Password: *******

--- JUNOS 9.0R1 built 2007-07-26 20:06:09 UTC
fred@junos-router>
```

After you log in, you see a command-line prompt, which shows the name you used to log in, followed by an @ sign and the name of the router. When you are using the CLI, you type all commands after a prompt. If you log in with the `root` username, you see a shell, similar to a UNIX shell. You type `cli` to enter the JUNOS CLI.

Taking a Look at Two Command Modes

Juniper routers support many different types of interface connections to the network and several dozen different protocols for communicating with other devices on the network (see Part I). JUNOS software provides many hundreds of commands to control the router, all the interface types, and network communications. The commands are grouped into two distinct groups, called *modes:*

- **Operational mode** is where you are each time you log in to the router (except when you log in as `root`). Here, you monitor the router hardware and software and perform maintenance tasks, such as upgrading software or managing the files on the router. Operational mode commands show you how the router hardware and software are functioning.
- **Configuration mode** is where you configure the router to work in your network. You enter this mode using the configure command in operational mode, such as

```
fred@junos-router> configure
Entering configuration mode
 [edit]
fred@junos-router#
```

To figure out which mode you're in, just look at the prompt. In operational command mode, a > appears after the username and router name, such as the first line in the preceding output example. In configuration mode, you see a hash mark (#), such as in the last line of the output example. You can spot one more clue for configuration mode, which is the line before the prompt. This line shows your current location in the configuration hierarchy. When you enter configuration mode, you're at the top of the hierarchy, represented by `[edit]`.

Bringing Order to Chaos: Hierarchy of Commands

Even when all JUNOS commands are split between operational and configuration mode (see preceding section), each mode can still have hundreds of possible commands. If the CLI showed them all in a single list, it would fill many screens and be difficult to use. So JUNOS software arranges them into a hierarchy that groups together related commands.

The hierarchy is like the directory structure on your PC or Mac. On the PC's desktop, you see primary directories, such as Documents, Applications, Pictures, and Music. At the top of the JUNOS command hierarchy, you see a few top-level commands. If you look in each of your PC's folders, you see more folders or files, and in the JUNOS hierarchy, you see a group of commands related to the top-level command. And just like a PC's folder can have many levels of subfolders, the JUNOS hierarchy can have many levels of related subcommands.

Figure 6-1 shows a sample of hierarchies under the `clear` and `show` commands. Notice that under the top-level command, both have `bgp`, `interfaces`, and `system` commands. Then the next level down has different options in the hierarchies. From these hierarchies, some of the commands available are `clear bgp neighbor` *`neighbor-name`*, `show bgp neighbor` *`neighbor-name`*, and `show interfaces`.

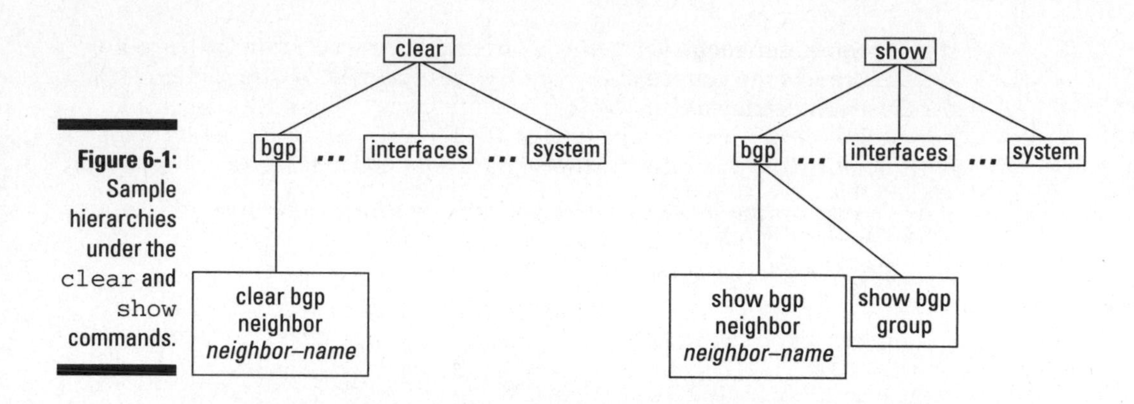

Figure 6-1: Sample hierarchies under the `clear` and `show` commands.

A commanding hierarchy: Operational mode

When you log in to the router and are in operational mode, simply type a `?` to list the commands at the top level of the command hierarchy, as shown in Listing 6-1.

Listing 6-1: A Sampling of the Operational Mode Command Hierarchy

```
fred@junos-router> ?
Possible completions:
  clear                  Clear information in the system
  configure              Manipulate software configuration information
  file                   Perform file operations
  help                   Provide help information
  monitor                Show real-time debugging information
  ping                   Ping remote target
  quit                   Exit the management session
  request                Make system-level requests
  restart                Restart software process
  set                    Set CLI properties, date/time, craft interface message
  show                   Show system information
  ssh                    Start secure shell on another host
  telnet                 Telnet to another host
  traceroute             Trace route to remote host
```

Listing 6-1 shows an abbreviated version of the JUNOS operational commands. The command name is on the left and a description is to the right. We use the `?` throughout this chapter to explore the JUNOS software, and we talk more about these commands in the upcoming section "Keeping One Eye Open at All Times: Operational Mode Commands."

If you peek under each command, you see the next level in the hierarchy. Because one of the commands you use most often in JUNOS is `show`, Listing 6-2 illustrates a truncated list of the different varieties of `show` command.

Listing 6-2: A Truncated List of the `show` Command

```
fred@junos-router> show ?
Possible completions:
  accounting           Show accounting profiles and records
  aps                  Show Automatic Protection Switching information
  arp                  Show system Address Resolution Protocol table entries
  as-path              Show table of known autonomous system paths
  bfd                  Show Bidirectional Forwarding Detection information
  bgp                  Show Border Gateway Protocol information
  chassis              Show chassis information
  class-of-service     Show class-of-service (CoS) information
  cli                  Show command-line interface settings
  configuration        Show current configuration
```

Using `?` allows you to see the subordinate commands in the next level of the hierarchy. Drill down one more level of the hierarchy, into the `show chassis` hierarchy, and you see

```
fred@junos-router> show chassis ?
Possible completions:
  alarms               Show alarm status
  environment          Show component status, temperature, cooling system speeds
  firmware             Show firmware and operating system version for components
  fpc                  Show Flexible PIC Concentrator status
  hardware             Show installed hardware components
  location             Show physical location of chassis
  mac-addresses        Show media access control addresses
  pic                  Show Physical Interface Card state, type, and uptime
  routing-engine       Show Routing Engine status
```

Where does the hierarchy for a command end? When you see `Enter` as one of the possible command completions, such as

```
fred@junose-router> show chassis hardware ?
Possible completions:
  <[Enter]>            Execute this command
  detail               Include RAM and disk information in output
  extensive            Display ID EEPROM information
  models               Display serial number and model number for orderable FRUs
  |                    Pipe through a command
```

So when you finally reach the end of the hierarchy, press Enter to see output data, as shown in Listing 6-3.

Listing 6-3: The Output Data at the End of the Hierarchy

```
fred@junos-router> show chassis hardware
Hardware inventory:
Item               Version  Part number  Serial number     Description
Chassis                                  25708             M20
Backplane          REV 03   710-002334   BB9738            M20 Backplane
Power Supply A     REV 06   740-001465   005234            AC Power Supply
Display            REV 04   710-001519   BA4681            M20 FPM Board
Routing Engine 0   REV 06   740-003239   1000224893        RE-2.0
Routing Engine 1   REV 06   740-003239   9000022146        RE-2.0
SSB 0              REV 02   710-001951   AZ8112            Internet Processor IIv1
SSB 1              N/A      N/A          N/A               Backup
FPC 0              REV 03   710-003308   BD8455            E-FPC
  PIC 0            REV 08   750-002303   AZ5310            4x F/E, 100 BASE-TX
  PIC 1            REV 07   750-004745   BC9368            2x CT3-NxDS0
  PIC 2            REV 03   750-002965   HC9279            4x CT3
Fan Tray 0                                                 Front Upper Fan Tray
Fan Tray 1                                                 Front Middle Fan Tray
Fan Tray 2                                                 Front Bottom Fan Tray
Fan Tray 3                                                 Rear Fan Tray
```

You can filter the output of an operational (or a configuration) mode command by adding the | (pipe) symbol as part of the command. This handy JUNOS software tool lets you quickly display exactly what you need in one command step.

Making a statement: Configuration mode

Configuration mode has a hierarchy of JUNOS configuration keywords, called *statements*, that explicitly spell out the configuration of the router. They're the programming language that the router interprets and translates into real operation.

To begin, enter configuration mode by using the `configure` command from operational mode:

```
fred@junos-router> configure
Entering configuration mode

[edit]
fred@junos-router#
```

Now enter `set ?` after the configuration mode prompt # to see the hierarchy of configuration statements that organize all JUNOS statements into related groups, as shown in Listing 6-4. (If you type just a `?` at the prompt, you see the configuration mode commands. We use the `set` command to display the hierarchy of configuration statements.)

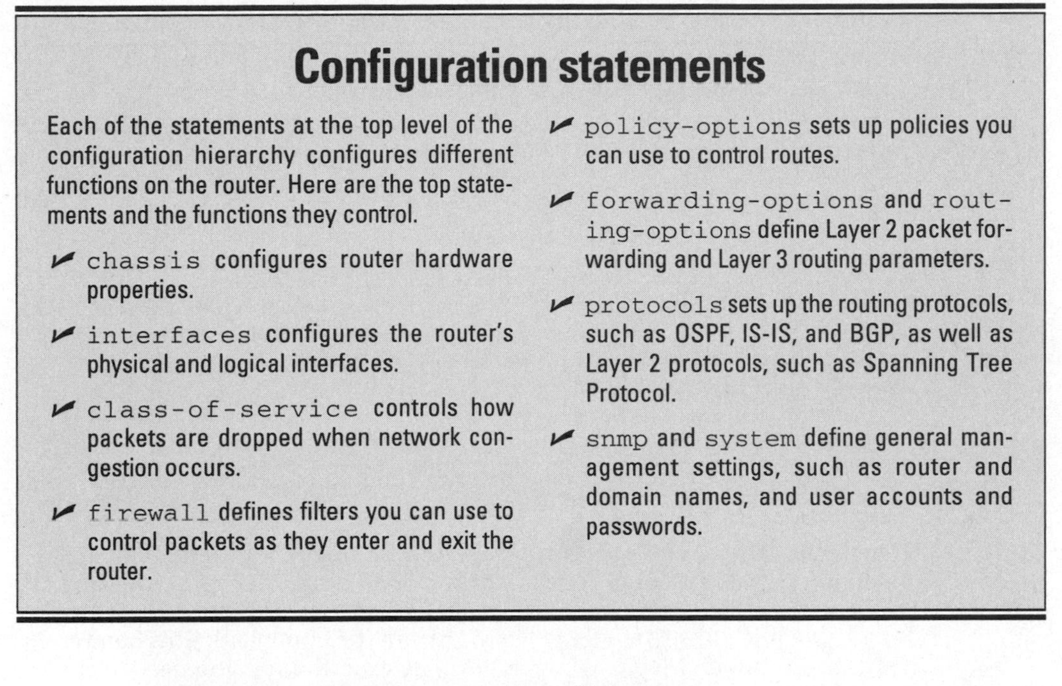

Configuration statements

Each of the statements at the top level of the configuration hierarchy configures different functions on the router. Here are the top statements and the functions they control.

- `chassis` configures router hardware properties.
- `interfaces` configures the router's physical and logical interfaces.
- `class-of-service` controls how packets are dropped when network congestion occurs.
- `firewall` defines filters you can use to control packets as they enter and exit the router.
- `policy-options` sets up policies you can use to control routes.
- `forwarding-options` and `routing-options` define Layer 2 packet forwarding and Layer 3 routing parameters.
- `protocols` sets up the routing protocols, such as OSPF, IS-IS, and BGP, as well as Layer 2 protocols, such as Spanning Tree Protocol.
- `snmp` and `system` define general management settings, such as router and domain names, and user accounts and passwords.

Listing 6-4: Using `set ?` to View Statements

```
[edit]
fred@junos-router# set ?
Possible completions:
> chassis              Chassis configuration
> class-of-service     Class-of-service configuration
> firewall             Define a firewall configuration
> forwarding-options   Configure options to control packet forwarding
> interfaces           Interface configuration
> policy-options       Routing policy option configuration
> protocols            Routing protocol configuration
> routing-instances    Routing instance configuration
> routing-options      Protocol-independent routing option configuration
> snmp                 Simple Network Management Protocol configuration
> system               System parameters
```

Just like in operational mode, you can look down into the hierarchy. (See the preceding section for more on operational mode.) For example, drilling down into one of the configuration statements, `system`, shows the next level of the hierarchy, as shown in Listing 6-5.

Listing 6-5: Using `system` to Examine a Single Configuration Statement

```
[edit]
fred@junos-router# set system ?
Possible completions:

+ authentication-order Order in which authentication methods are invoked
> backup-router        IPv4 router to use while booting
  domain-name          Domain name for this router
  host-name            Hostname for this router
> location             Location of the system, in various forms
> login                Names, login classes, and passwords for users
> name-server          DNS name servers
> ntp                  Network Time Protocol services
> radius-options       RADIUS options
> radius-server        RADIUS server configuration
> root-authentication  Authentication information for the root login
> syslog               System logging facility
> time-zone            Time zone name or POSIX-compliant time zone string
```

Identifying the end of a configuration statement hierarchy is a bit different than for operational commands. When the first column is blank, you have reached the bottom of the hierarchy. In Listing 6-5, the `domain-name`, `host-name`, and `time-zone` statements are at the bottom of the hierarchy. For these statements, you just type a value and press Enter. For example:

```
[edit]
fred@junos-router# set system time-zone UTC
```

The statement you type becomes part of the router's configuration:

```
[edit]
fred@junos-router# show system
time-zone UTC;
```

When the first column contains a >, the arrow points to a further hierarchy level.

Keeping One Eye Open at All Times: Operational Mode Commands

Operational mode commands run the router and keep an eye on what the router software and hardware are doing. Listing 6-6 lists some common operational mode commands.

Listing 6-6: Operational Mode Commands

```
fred@junos-router> ?
Possible completions:
  clear                 Clear information in the system
  configure             Manipulate software configuration information
  file                  Perform file operations
  help                  Provide help information
  …
  ping                  Ping remote target
  quit                  Exit the management session
  request               Make system-level requests
  restart               Restart software process
  set                   Set CLI properties, date/time, craft interface message
  show                  Show system information
  ssh                   Start secure shell on another host
  telnet                Telnet to another host
  …
  traceroute            Trace route to remote host
```

You use the `show` command to display status and statistics for just about everything on the router, from the network interfaces (`show interfaces`) to the hardware (`show chassis hardware`) to the routing protocols (`show ospf, show bgp`, and so on). You use the `clear` command to clear, or zero, statistics collected by the router.

Some commands, such as the following, provide router management capabilities:

- `file` allows you to manage files on the router. The `file list` command is similar to the UNIX `ls` command and shows the files in the router's directories. For creating and archiving configuration files, the `file copy` command moves files to and from file servers on your network.
- `request` is the command you use to install new versions of JUNOS software, or to reboot or shut down the router.
- `restart` allows you to restart specific processes on the router.

You may recognize a few commands in the JUNOS list from UNIX and other operating systems, too:

- `ping` is the standard IP command to test whether other routers, interface cards, or nodes are reachable on the network.
- `ssh` is the standard UNIX secure shell program for opening a user shell on another router or host on the network.
- `telnet` opens a terminal connection to another router or host on the network.
- `traceroute` reports the path taken by packets from your router to a destination on an IP network.

Changing the Router's Look: Configuration Mode Commands

You use configuration mode commands for creating, modifying, and activating the router configuration, as shown in Listing 6-7.

Listing 6-7: Configuration Mode Commands

```
[edit]
fred@junos-router# ?
Possible completions:
  <[Enter]>            Execute this command
  activate             Remove the inactive tag from a statement
  annotate             Annotate the statement with a comment
  commit               Commit current set of changes
  copy                 Copy a statement
  deactivate           Add the inactive tag to a statement
  delete               Delete a data element
  edit                 Edit a sub-element
  exit                 Exit from this level
  help                 Provide help information
  insert               Insert a new ordered data element
  load                 Load configuration from ASCII file
  quit                 Quit from this level
  rename               Rename a statement
  replace              Replace character string in configuration
  rollback             Roll back to previous committed configuration
  run                  Run an operational-mode command
  save                 Save configuration to ASCII file
  set                  Set a parameter
  show                 Show a parameter
  status               Show users currently editing configuration
  top                  Exit to top level of configuration
  up                   Exit one level of configuration
  wildcard             Wildcard operations
```

The main commands for creating and modifying a configuration are `edit` and `set`. The `edit` command moves you to desired level in the statement hierarchy. The `set` command inserts a statement into the router's configuration. If you want to configure a BGP peer, you first use the `edit` command to move into the BGP portion of the statement hierarchy:

```
[edit]
fred@junos-router# edit protocols bgp

[edit protocols bgp]
fred@junos-router#
```

Configuration commands at a glance

The commands in configuration mode manipulate the configuration file itself. Here's how they work:

- **Moving around the configuration hierarchy:** `edit` moves down to a statement hierarchy level, `up` moves up one level in the hierarchy, and `top` moves to the top level.
- **Adding and removing statements:** `set` inserts a statement into the configuration, and `delete` removes a statement from the configuration. `deactivate` keeps a statement from operating, but doesn't remove it from the configuration.
- **Manipulating existing statements:** `copy` duplicates a statement, and `rename` and `replace` rename user-defined variables in configuration statements. `insert` rearranges statements whose operation depends on the order in which they appear in the configuration. (For most statements, order doesn't matter, and they're listed alphabetically.)
- **Displaying the configuration:** The `show` command lists the statements in the configuration. Use this command to show changes you haven't yet activated. The operational-mode command `show configuration` always shows the current active configuration.
- **Returning to a previous configuration:** Use the `rollback` command. (We talk about this command in "A Blast from the Past: Working with Archived Configurations.")
- **Activating a configuration:** The `commit` command activates the statements in the candidate configuration. (We talk about this topic in the section "Confirm before you commit.")
- **Leaving configuration mode:** Use the `quit` or `exit` commands to return to operational command mode.

Notice that the configuration prompt changed from `[edit]` to `[edit protocols bgp]`, showing that you've moved into the "protocol" hierarchy and then into the "bgp" hierarchy. To configure a BGP peer, use the `set` command:

```
[edit protocols bgp]
fred@junos-router# set group bgp-group-name neighbor 192.168.1.2
```

After you issue the `set` command, you see the BGP configuration:

```
[edit protocols bgp]
fred@junos-router# show
group bgp-group-name {
  neighbor 192.168.1.2;
}
```

If you move to the top of the configuration hierarchy, you see a different view of the configuration:

```
[edit protocols bgp]
fred@junos-router# top

[edit]
 fred@junos-router# show
protocols {
  bgp {
    group bgp-group-name {
      neighbor 192.168.1.2;
    }
  }
}
```

Lending a Helping Hand: The Help Command

Everyone who works on a Juniper router, from beginners to experts, uses the question-mark help (?) all the time to get a list of available CLI options. Because almost all the information about the router is built into the CLI itself, you don't have to constantly refer to the product documentation.

Each time you type `?`, the JUNOS software will display a two-column output. The left column lists commands and statements you can use, and the right column provides a short description of what the command or statement does. It always provides a clue or reminder so that you can decide what you want to do.

You may have also noticed the `help` command in both operational and configuration modes. Under this command, you can use the `help topic` and `help reference` commands to provide usage guidelines and command syntax descriptions for configuration statements.

A Need for Speed: Command Completion and Keyboard Sequences

Most JUNOS administrators like the CLI because it's generally quicker to configure and monitor with a CLI than with a GUI. The downside of using a CLI is that sometimes you have to type long commands or statements. JUNOS software provides two types of shortcuts to minimize the amount of typing you have to do: command completion and keyboard sequences.

Command completion

Command completion is just what the name implies: You type the first few characters of a command or statement, press the spacebar or the Tab key, and the JUNOS software completes the word.

You can use either the spacebar or Tab key to complete most command arguments, but only the Tab key will complete user-defined variables (such as a firewall filter name).

For example, you can use the `show interfaces` command, which displays the status of the router's interfaces, when checking or troubleshooting the router's operation. With command completion, you can simply type

```
fred@junos-router> show int<press spacebar>
```

JUNOS software completes the command, and you see the entire command in the CLI:

```
fred@junos-router> show interface
```

Now press the Enter key to see the interface information in the CLI.

If the portion of the command string you're entering is ambiguous, the JUNOS software will list the options so that you can choose the one you intended:

```
fred@junos-router> show r<spacebar>
Possible completions:
  rip                Show Routing Information Protocol information
  route              Show routing table information
  rsvp               Show Resource Reservation Protocol information
```

So, type an **o** and press the Enter key to complete:

```
fred@junos-router> show ro<spacebar>
fred@junos-router> show route
```

Keyboard sequences

Keyboard sequences are when you press a letter or an arrow key while simultaneously pressing the Ctrl or Esc key. Use keyboard sequences to modify the text on the current command line or to modify a command that you recently issued. JUNOS software maintains a history of the commands you've typed, and the arrow keys allow you to scroll through the history to reuse commands, either as you typed them or after modifying them first. When you have the command you want, press Enter to execute it.

Keyboard sequences (see Table 6-1) are particularly useful when you're configuring similar items on the router, such as a large number of the same type of interface. They're also useful when you're debugging a problem on the network and need to re-use the same commands over and over.

Table 6-1 Keyboard Sequences Shortcuts

Keyboard Sequence	*Action*
Up arrow (or Ctrl+p) and down arrow (or Ctrl+n)	Move backward and forward through the most recently executed commands.
Left arrow (or Ctrl+b) and right arrow (or Ctrl+f)	Move the cursor, character by character, through the text on the command line.
Esc+b	Move back one word.
Esc+f	Move forward one word.
Ctrl+a	Move to beginning of command line.
Ctrl+e	Move to end of command line.
Ctrl+k	Delete all text from cursor to end of command line.
Esc+d	Delete the word after the cursor.
Esc+Backspace	Delete the word before the cursor.
Ctrl+y	Paste the deleted text at the cursor.

Committing a Configuration

The configuration contains the statements that actually operate the router. (For more information, see the section "Changing the Router's Look: Configuration Mode Commands," earlier in this chapter.) The version of the configuration currently operating the router is called the active configuration. The configuration itself is stored in a file. When you go into configuration mode to modify the configuration, you're modifying the candidate configuration, which is a copy of the active configuration. You can change the candidate configuration all you want without any effect on router operation until you activate the configuration, which changes the candidate configuration into the active configuration.

The commit process

A JUNOS configuration is simply text — just a set of statements in a file on the router. You can create and modify this file in configuration mode on the router, or you can create the file on a network file server and then load it onto the router.

The configuration file is a candidate configuration and has no special powers until you activate it using the `commit` configuration mode command, which transforms the configuration into the active configuration:

```
[edit]
fred@junos-router# commit
commit complete
```

As part of the commit process, the JUNOS software verifies that all the statements in the configuration are formatted correctly. When the activation is done, you see the `commit complete` message, which indicates that all the statements in your configuration have started operating.

An important point to note is that the JUNOS activation is a batch process: All the router configuration statements start operating at the same time. Activating the router configuration in a single operation is especially important for interdependent statements to start running at the same time instead of with a delay between them.

Confirm before you commit

Having a JUNOS candidate configuration activate all at once can be a scary process. What happens if the configuration starts going haywire, and network performance starts deteriorating? Worse, what happens if the configuration you committed locks you out of the router so that you can no longer log in?

JUNOS software provides a path for the timid and the cautious user alike. You can try out a candidate configuration; if you don't like it once it becomes the active configuration, JUNOS software will return to the previous version of the configuration automatically. This approach is an easy way to get out of a jam. To try out a candidate configuration, instead of using the `commit` command, you use the `commit confirmed`:

```
[edit]
fred@junos-router# commit confirmed
commit confirmed will be automatically rolled back in 10 minutes unless
                confirmed
commit complete
```

The default wait is 10 minutes, and you have to explicitly accept the commitment, either by typing the `commit` command again or by typing the `commit check` command. Then you see the `commit complete` message.

If 10 minutes is too long to wait in your functional network, use a shorter delay, such as 1 minute, to tell whether the configuration is working:

```
[edit]
fred@junos-router# commit confirmed 1
commit confirmed will be automatically rolled back in 1 minutes unless confirmed
commit complete
```

If you see that the router operation isn't correct, when the confirm time expires, the JUNOS software automatically returns to the previous configuration, which you know was a working configuration:

```
Broadcast Message from root@junos-router
        (no tty) at 16:36 PDT…
Commit was not confirmed; automatic rollback complete.
```

Even the most experienced JUNOS engineers and administrators use the `commit confirmed` command as an insurance policy on their own work. It can sometimes save days of digging out from under what might go wrong.

Working with Archived Configurations

JUNOS software automatically keeps an archive of the previous active configuration when you activate a new configuration. This automatic backup mechanism lets you return quickly to a previous configuration. In addition, you can also copy the currently active or a previous configuration from the router to a file server on the network, and if you need to return to a backed-up version, you can reload the configuration file onto the router.

To return to a configuration that JUNOS software has automatically archived, use the `rollback` command in configuration mode:

```
[edit]
fred@junos-router# rollback 1
load complete
```

This `rollback` command loads the previous configuration but stops short of activating it. If you need to change what's in the configuration, you can modify it. To see what statements are in the configuration, use the configuration mode `show` command:

```
[edit]
fred@junos-router# show
```

The `show` command displays all the statements in a configuration one screen at a time. To see the next screen, press the Enter or the spacebar.

When you're ready to activate the configuration, use the `commit` command:

```
[edit]
fred@junos-router# commit
commit complete
```

In addition to archiving the last version of the configuration, JUNOS software stores the last 50 active configurations. These files are on the router's flash and hard disks, so you can restore the configuration saved in a particular file.

Use help with the `rollback` command to list the full archive:

```
[edit]
fred@junos-router# rollback ?
Possible completions:
<[Enter]>                Execute this command
0                        2007-10-31 12:34:56 PST by fred via cli
1                        2007-10-31 12:30:03 PST by fred via cli
2                        2007-10-30 14:23:44 PST by fred via cli
…
48                       2007-09-03 08:00:03 PST by root via cli
49                       2007-09-03 07:45:21 PST by root via cli
  |                      Pipe through a command
```

Pick the configuration by date and time and specify the number in the `rollback` command to load that configuration:

```
[edit]
fred@junos-router# rollback 2
load complete
```

Verify it's what you want by using the `show` command, and then activate it with the `commit` command:

```
[edit]
fred@junos-router# show
...

[edit]
fred@junos-router# commit
commit complete
```

Archiving manually from a server

You can manually archive configuration files by copying them to a file server on your network. To begin, use the JUNOS `file copy` operational mode command to copy the active configuration, the file `juniper.conf.gz`, in the router's `/config` directory:

```
fred@junos-router> file copy /config/juniper.conf.gz server1:/homes/fred/tmp
fred@server1's password:
juniper.conf.gz                                    100% 2127      2.1KB/s   00:00
```

Once the file is on the server, you want to rename it so the next time you copy the active configuration, you don't overwrite the previous one. For example:

```
fred@server1> mv juniper.conf.gz juniper.conf.gz-20071031
```

If you need to return to that active configuration, copy it back to the router by using the `file copy` command again to put it back in your home directory on the router:

```
fred@junos-router> file copy server1:/homes/fred/tmp/juniper.conf.gz-20071031
fred@server1's password:
juniper.conf.gz-20071031                     100% 2127      2.1KB/s   00:00
```

After the copy operation completes, look at the files in your home directory to make sure the file has arrived safely:

```
fred@junos-router> file list
juniper.conf.gz-20071031
```

Next, change from operational mode to configuration mode by using the `configure` command, load the configuration file with the `load` command, and review it with the `show` command. Finally, activate it using the `commit` command:

```
fred@junos-router> configure
Entering configuration mode

[edit]
fred@junos-router# load juniper.conf.gz-20071031
load complete

[edit]
fred@junos-router# show
...

[edit]
fred@junos-router# commit
commit complete
```

Creating and saving configurations

When you add new equipment or customers to your network, change the design of the network and its services, or install new network cards or hardware in the router, you need to modify the router's configuration to define and activate the new features. You can modify the configuration when you're rolling out the new equipment or services, or you can modify it beforehand, in anticipation of the hardware arrival or the service start date, and then flip the activation switch at the appropriate time.

As you become more familiar with JUNOS software, creating configurations in advance — when you're not under deadline pressure — can be a very useful technique for managing time and reducing stress.

For network cards, which provide the physical interfaces to the network, you can add the configuration statements whenever you want, even before the card arrives. When you activate a router configuration, JUNOS software compares the interfaces you have in the configuration to the network cards it detects in the router. If the correct card is present in the correct slot, the software applies the configuration to it, and the card starts operating. If the card isn't present in that slot, the software simply ignores that part of the configuration.

For example, if you've ordered a new Gigabit Ethernet card and you're planning to put it in position 1 of slot 1, you can add it to the configuration beforehand:

```
[edit]
fred@junos-router# edit interfaces ge-1/1/0

[edit interfaces ge-1/1/0]
fred@junos-router# set description New GigE network card

[edit interfaces ge-1/1/0]
fred@junos-router# set unit 0 family inet address 172.168.1.2/24

[edit interfaces ge-1/1/0]
fred@junos-router# commit
commit complete
```

Because no hardware is present yet, when you look at the interface status, nothing is reported about this interface:

```
fred@junos-router> show interfaces terse
Interface               Admin Link Proto    Local                 Remote
fe-0/0/0                up    up
fe-0/0/0.0              up    up
fe-0/0/1                up    up
fe-0/0/2                up    up
ge-1/0/0                up    up
ge-1/0/1                up    up
```

The output shows Fast Ethernet interfaces in slot 0 and Gigabit Ethernet interfaces in slot 1, position 0 only. You can also look at the hardware inventory to confirm that no network hardware is in the slot yet:

```
fred@junos-router> show chassis hardware
Hardware inventory:
Item            Version   Part number  Serial number    Description
Chassis                                25708            M20
…
FPC 0           REV 03    710-003308   BD8455           E-FPC
  PIC 0         REV 08    750-002303   AZ5310           4x F/E, 100 BASE-TX
  PIC 1         REV 07    750-004745   BC9368           2x CT3-NxDS0
  PIC 2         REV 03    750-002965   HC9279           4x CT3
FPC 1           REV 03    710-003308   BB9032           E-FPC
  PIC 0         REV 03    750-002914   BC0131           2x OC-3 ATM, MM
…
```

On M-series routers, the slots are called FPCs (Flexible PIC Concentrators), and the positions hold PICs (Physical Interface Cards). Slots and positions are numbered starting at 0, so FPC 1 is in the second slot, and PIC 1 is in the second position on the FPC.

Getting the Router Up on the Network

After you know how to get around the CLI, you're ready to configure the router. Initially, you need to configure it just enough so that the router is accessible on the network and other users can log in to it.

In new Juniper devices that you buy, JUNOS software is already installed. When you first turn on the device, the software automatically starts. Log in as the user root. You won't need a password yet. Once logged in, you can set a few basic properties of the router.

First, start the CLI and enter configuration mode:

```
root@%  cli
root> configure
Entering configuration mode

[edit]
root#
```

Set the name of the router and the router's domain name:

```
[edit]
root# set system host-name junos-router

[edit]
root# set system domain-name mynetwork.com
```

Next, set the IP address of the router's Ethernet management interface, if your router has one. (The J-series routers don't have a dedicated Ethernet management interface, but you can configure a normal Ethernet interface instead.) On M-series routers, the dedicated Ethernet management interface is named `fxp0`. This interface provides a separate out-of-band management connection to the router, which you use to get information about the router without interfering with actual traffic being transmitted on the router. Use an IP address in the same address space as your network's management network. For this example, we use the address prefix 192.168.0.1/24:

```
[edit]
root# set interfaces fxp0 unit 0 family inet address 192.168.0.1/24
```

On your management network, identify a backup router and a DNS name server. Your router uses the backup router, which should be directly connected to your router, only when booting and only if the JUNOS routing software doesn't start. When your router is booting, it creates a static route to the backup router and removes the route when it successfully starts up. Your router also needs to know the address of a DNS name server so that it can translate host names into IP addresses:

```
[edit]
root# set system backup-router 192.168.0.23

[edit]
root# set system name-server 192.168.0.32
```

When you initially start the router, the root account has no password. Now is a good time to assign one for the account:

```
[cdit]
root# set system root-authentication plain-text-password
New password:
Retype password:
```

JUNOS software prompts you to type and retype the password. The password must be a mixture of uppercase and lowercase letters and must contain at least one digit.

Before activating the initial configuration, review the contents to make sure they're correct, as shown in Listing 6-8.

Listing 6-8: Reviewing Your Configuration

```
[edit]
root# show
system {
  host-name junos-router;
  domain-name mynetwork.com;
  backup-router 192.168.0.23;
  root-authentication {
    encrypted-password $1$ZulES4dp$OuwWo1g7cLof/aMWpHucn/; ## SECRET-DATA
  }
  name-server {
    192.168.0.32
  }
}
interfaces {
  fxpo {
    unit 0 {
      family inet {
        192.168.0.1/24;
      }
    }
  }
}
```

Each statement ends with a semicolon. Each group of statements is enclosed in braces.

Check that everything is what you want. Here, the only odd statement is `system root-authentication`, because you didn't type the encrypted-password shown. When you set the password, the JUNOS software immediately encrypts it after you enter it so that no one can read it.

Finally, activate the configuration with the `commit` command and exit from configuration mode:

```
[edit]
root# commit
commit complete

[edit]
root@junos-router# exit
Exiting configuration mode

root@junos-router>
```

Chapter 7

Setting Up the Routers

In This Chapter

- Displaying a banner
- Logging out of the router
- Setting up user accounts
- Tracking (and collecting) router events
- Setting the time and time zone for the router
- Configuring interfaces and assigning IP addresses to them

In this chapter, we cover basic setup tasks to get the router working on your network. (If you haven't configured your router, see Chapter 6.) We show you how to provide access for the different people who will need to log in to the router, set the proper time on the router, and enable the router to track events that occur on it. We also explore configuring the network cards that are installed in the router.

Creating a Banner at Login

When you log in to the router, you're immediately placed into the CLI and can start working. The prompt shows the username you used to log in and the name of the router:

```
fred@junos-router>
```

Because the router is a shared device on the network, you may want to send a message to all the router users who log in. One way is to display a message on the screen each time someone logs in. The banner containing the message is displayed before or after the login prompt, depending on which command you use.

After entering configuration mode, the banner command `set system login message` places your message before the login prompt. The `\n` puts one blank line (a new line) after the text and before the login prompt:

```
[edit]
fred@junos-router# set system login message "JUNOS router
            managed by Corporate Network team\n"
```

The following banner appears each time someone logs in to the router:

```
fred@server# ssh junos-router
JUNOS router managed by Corporate Network team

junos-router (ttyp0)
login:
```

If your company has legal requirements in place to limit access to key network devices, such as routers, you can use the login banner to warn that only certain people are allowed to work on the router. Be sure to use the specific language the legal department provides for the banner.

Any text that you do include in a banner should never welcome or otherwise encourage people to use the router. Here's an example of a warning login message:

```
[edit]
fred@junos-router# set system login message "----------------------------
            -----\nWARNING: Unauthorized access prohibited.\n-----------
            ------------------------"
```

And here's what the login message looks like:

```
fred@server# ssh junos-router
-----------------------------------------
WARNING: Unauthorized access prohibited.
-----------------------------------------

junos-router (ttyp0)
login:
```

You can also use banners to make announcements for such things as network or router down time, or a scheduled network maintenance window, by using the `set system announcement` command:

```
[edit]
fred@junos-router# set system announcement "Network
            maintenance will occur Saturday night from 2000
            to 2300; log out before then"
```

Announcement command banners show up *after* the user logs in so that you don't broadcast sensitive things, such as maintenance schedules:

```
junos-router (ttyp0)

login: fred
password: ********

--- JUNOS 9.0R1.8 built 2008-02-12 19:51:10 UTC
Network maintenance will occur Saturday night from 2000 to
           2300; log out before then
fred@junos-router>
```

Logging Out

Whenever you finish your work on the router, don't just walk away from your terminal session. Log out! This action prevents anyone from randomly walking up to your terminal or PC and accessing the router. If you're working in operational command mode, you can log out with a simple `exit` command:

```
fred@junos-router> exit
logout
Connection closed by foreign host.
fred@server#
```

Because you can log out only from operational command mode, when you're working in configuration mode, you'll need to finish your configuration session and return to operational mode:

```
[edit system]
fred@junos-router# exit configuration-mode
Exiting configuration mode

fred@junos-router> exit
logout
Connection closed by foreign host.
fred@server>
```

Setting Up Router User Accounts

Routers are shared network devices, and you must have an account to log in to the router. JUNOS software has several ways to set up user accounts. You can set up individual accounts locally on the router, and you can also set them up on remote centralized authentication servers, running RADIUS or TACACS+, which are authentication protocols. You can also set up group accounts.

If you manage a small group of routers, setting up individual accounts is a straightforward way to provide access for your network administrators. Although you'll need to manually configure the account information on each router, if the number of routers is small and you don't have to modify the information very often, this method is the best way. For larger networks, however, using a centralized authentication server is much easier because you can store all account information in one place, and you update it only once when changes occur.

When you create an account on the router for an individual user, you assign a login name, password, and privileges, and you provide information about the user. Here's an example that sets up an account for the user Mike:

```
[edit system login]
fred@junos-router# set user mike class super-user

[edit system login]
fred@junos-router# set user mike full-name "Mike Bushong"

[edit system login]
fred@junos-router# set user mike authentication plain-
        text-password
New password:
Retype new password:
```

The first command defines an account for the user Mike and gives him super-user privileges, which allow him to perform all operations on the router (see Table 7-1). The second command defines his full name. And the third command creates a password for Mike. Even though the command says it's a plain-text (ASCII) command, JUNOS software encrypts the password, as you can see when you display the configuration:

```
[edit system login]
fred@junos-router# show
user mike {
  uid 2001;
  class super-user;
  authentication {
    encrypted-password "$1$BmFLXWlx$sYKMY7XrTRHv40AD3/
          Z7U1"; ## SECRET-DATA
  }
}
```

Table 7-1 Four Standard Login Privilege Classes

Name	*Description*	*Usage Recommendation*
Super-user	A super-user can perform any and all operations on the router.	Reserve this privilege level for the key people who monitor and maintain all aspects of your routers.
Operator	An operator is allowed to work in operational mode to check the status of the router and the routing protocols, clear statistics, and perform reset operations, including restarting routing processes and rebooting the router.	This class can look at the router configuration, but can't modify it. This privilege level is for the network operations team that is responsible for monitoring your routers.
Read-only	Someone with read-only can only monitor the status of the router and routing protocols.	Give to low-level watchers of the network who must get an engineer or administrator when they see something.
Unauthorized	Unauthorized is a class with no privileges at all on the router.	When users in this class log in, the JUNOS software immediately logs them out.

JUNOS software encrypts all passwords that you type in the configuration and marks them as `## SECRET-DATA`. It allows you to hide the fact that a password is even present in the configuration, because you can filter out the line completely by using

```
[edit system login]
fred@junos-router# show | except SECRET-DATA
user mike {
  uid 2001;
  class super-user;
  authentication {
  }
}
```

Larger organizations generally centralize the authentication process, setting up RADIUS (or TACACS+) servers on the network. (Here, we talk about RADIUS, which is the Remote Authentication Dial-In User Service.) All account information — username, password, and privilege class — is stored on the server. When a user attempts to log in to the router, the router queries the RADIUS server to validate the user.

Here's how you set up centralized authentication:

1. **Enter configuration mode and configure the IP address and password (which RADIUS calls a "secret") of the RADIUS server:**

```
[edit system]
fred@junos-router# set radius-server 192.168.10.1
        secret 123456

[edit system]
fred@junos-router# show
radius-server {
  192.168.10.1 secret "$9$ZQUk.fTz6Ct5TcyevLX"; ##
        SECRET-DATA
}
```

   Again, when you display the RADIUS server configuration, the password is encrypted.

2. **Make RADIUS the primary authentication method:**

```
[edit system]
fred@junos-router# set authentication-order [ radius
        password ]
```

With this configuration, when users try to log in to the router, the JUNOS software first attempts to authenticate them against the RADIUS database. If this step succeeds and the user's credentials match those on the server, the user is allowed to log in. If it fails, or if the RADIUS server is down, the software checks for accounts configured locally on the router. If the user has a local account and the credentials match, they can log in. Otherwise, access to the router is denied.

Using a RADIUS server for authentication also lets you set up a single account for a group of users. Instead of setting up lots of individual accounts for people who have the same job responsibilities, you can create a shared account for the entire group. On the router, create the group account

```
[edit system login]
fred@junos-router# set user architects class super-user

[edit system login]
fred@junos-router# set user architects full-name "Network
        design team"
```

The next step is to map the users on the RADIUS server to the group account name you just gave them on the router. How you do this step depends on which RADIUS software you're using on the server.

Tracking Events with SNMP and Logging

Keeping records of what happens on your routers allows you to know how the routers operate under normal conditions and alerts you when things start going haywire. SNMP and logging are two commons ways to track router operation.

Tracking with SNMP

SNMP (Simple Network Management Protocol) is an Internet standard protocol for managing all devices on an IP network. SNMP has centralized systems called *clients* (which SNMP calls *managers*) that actively monitor servers (which SNMP calls *agents*) by querying them and collecting status information and statistics from them. The managers generally run on dedicated computers called *Network Management Systems* (NMSs), and routers are one type of agent.

SNMP acronyms/definitions

SNMP uses a set of acronyms all its own:

- **SMI**: Structure of Management Information defines the way data is stored in a Management Information Base (MIB).
- **MIB**: Management Information Bases (not Men In Black!) are hierarchical databases, like a directory structure on a PC or Mac, in which SNMP agents (such as a router) store their status information and statistics. The information in each MIB is arranged as a hierarchical tree structure, with branches that move down from the root node. Each branch eventually ends at a leaf. Branches are just like directories on a computer, and leaves are just like the files in directories. One difference between MIBs and computer directories is that each branch and leaf in the MIB is identified not only by a name, but also by a number. SNMP defines standard MIBs, and individual network equipment vendors can also define proprietary MIBs. The standard MIB for use in TCP/IP networks is called MIB-II because it is the second version of this MIB. For your SNMP client to be able to retrieve information stored in these MIBs, it must know the structure of the MIB. You can download all Juniper router MIBs, both the standard and proprietary ones, from the Juniper Web site (`www.juniper.net/techpubs/software/junos/mibs.html`).
- **OID**: Object Identifier is the number that uniquely identifies a branch or leaf in the MIB. The OID is actually a string of numbers, with one number for each branch in the hierarchy and one number for the final leaf in the hierarchy. The OID generally begins with a period to indicate the top of the tree (the root node), and each subsequent number is separated by a period. An example of an OID from the standard MIB-II MIB is .1.3.6.1.2.1.1.1, which points to the device's description (sysDescr).

When you want the NMS systems on your network to be able to monitor the router, you need to configure the router to be an SNMP agent:

```
[edit]
fred@junos-router# set snmp community public authorization
          read-only
```

To transform the router into an agent, you place the router into an SNMP community using `set snmp community public authorization read-only`. This command uses one of the common SNMP communities, `public`. The second part of the command defines how the agent (your router) will respond to requests from the NMS system. An authorization of `read-only` means that the router will send its information to the NMS, but the NMS will not be able to modify any settings on the router (which it could do if you specified an authorization of `read-write`). You can configure the router to respond to multiple communities, each with its own authorization level.

You can configure basic information about the router for the NMS to collect when it queries the router, such as the router's location and description and whom to contact about the router. This information corresponds to leaves in the `system` group in the standard MIB-II, and NMS systems on the network can collect it when querying the router:

```
[edit snmp]
fred@junos-router# set description "Juniper Router"

[edit snmp]
fred@junos-router# set location "Sunnyvale, California
          machine room"

[edit snmp]
fred@junos-router# set contact "page-fred@juniper.net,
          cell phone +1-408-555-2000"
```

In normal SNMP operation, the NMS periodically queries the router. If any unexpected events occur on the router, the NMS will find out only after sending a query. The router can be configured to send notifications to the NMS when unexpected events occur. This notification means that the NMS, and the people monitoring the NMS, can find out about router problems more quickly. These notifications are called *traps,* and you can configure the types of events that trigger the router to send traps. (Table 7-2 lists a variety of trap categories used in the JUNOS software.)

The following command configures the router to send traps when an NMS system uses the wrong community when trying to access the router:

```
[edit snmp]
fred@junos-router# set trap-group authentication-traps
          targets 192.168.10.30
fred@junos-router# set trap-group authentication-traps
          categories authentication
```

Table 7-2 SNMP Trap Categories

Configuration Option	*MIB*	*Description*
`authentication`	Standard MIB-II	Authentication failures on the agent (router)
`chassis`	Juniper proprietary	Chassis and router environment notifications
`configuration`	Juniper proprietary	Configuration mode notifications
`link`	Juniper proprietary	Interface transitions, such as transitioning from up to down
`rmon-alarm`	Juniper proprietary	SNMP remote monitoring (RMON) events
`routing`	Juniper proprietary	Routing protocol notifications
`startup`	Standard MIB-II	Router reboots (soft/warm and full reboots)

Using logs to track the router's events

Another way to track the events that occur on the router is to use the router's logging facility. You can watch events as they happen in real time (though it may slow down the router's operation), and you can save event history to files on the router.

JUNOS software has two types of logging facilities:

- *System logging* (also called *syslog*), which records router-wide events
- *Trace logging* (also called *tracing*), which records events related to specific operations (such as routing protocols)

Collecting syslog messages is straightforward: You configure the file in which to store them, the type of events you want to track, and the event severity.

Here's an example that stores logs of all router events that have a severity level of "warning" (or more severe) in a file named "messages":

```
[edit system]
fred@junos-router# set syslog file messages any warning
```

In this configuration, `any warning` indicates the event (`any`) and severity level (`warning`). Tables 7-3 and 7-4 provide different types of logging events and severity levels you can use in collecting syslog messages, such as `authorization error` or `change-log notice` to chart activity on the router that might be suspicious and damaging to the current router setup. To look at the syslog messages in the file on the router, use the `show log` command followed by the name of the log file:

```
fred@junos-router> show log messages
```

Table 7-3 Types of Logging Events

Configuration Option	*Type of Event*
`any`	Any router event
`authorization`	Authentication and authorization attempts
`change-log`	Changes to the router's configuration
`conflict-log`	Changes to the router's configuration that are inappropriate for the router hardware
`daemon`	JUNOS software processes
`firewall`	Packet filtering performed by firewall filters
`ftp`	File transfers done with FTP
`interactive-commands`	Commands typed at the command-line interface or by a JUNOScript client application
`kernel`	JUNOS kernel
`Pfe`	Packet forwarding software
`user`	User processes

Table 7-4 Logging Severity Levels

Name	*Number*	*Description*
any	---	All severity levels (in other words, include all events)
none	---	No severity levels (in other words, discard all events)

Name	Number	Description
debug	7	Debugging information
info	6	General router operation
notice	5	General router operational events of more interest than "info"
warning	4	General warnings
error	3	General errors
critical	2	Critical errors that might affect router operation
alert	1	Errors requiring immediate attention
emergency	0	Errors that cause the router to stop operating

In addition to the syslog feature, you can use the `traceoptions` feature to get more detailed information about a particular operation on the router. (This process provides information similar to that produced by the `debug` feature on some other companies' devices.) For example, you may want to keep an eye on routing protocol operation. When you do, you can turn tracing on for all routing protocols or for an individual routing protocol.

To get an idea of the general routing protocol operation on the router, configure a file in which to store the operational events and a list of flags that define the types of events you want to record. The following configuration collects information about all events (flags) in the file trace-events:

```
[edit]
fred@junos-router# set routing-options traceoptions file
          trace-events world-readable

[edit]
fred@junos-router# set routing-options traceoptions flag
          all
```

Logging is an excellent way to monitor and keep track of your router, and the permutations are open enough to adapt to the size, complexity, and security of your network. For more on logging, SNMP traps, and generally managing your router from a remote station, see Chapter 11.

Setting the Router's Time and Time Zone

To accurately know what (and when) events happened on a single router, the router needs to have the correct time and time zone. And on a whole network of routers, all the routers must have the same time, especially when you're trying to track events and problems. Otherwise, you'll have difficulty tracking sequences of events and determining what went wrong exactly when.

JUNOS software lets you set the router time simply, just like you're setting a watch. This task is reasonably easy to do in a small network. Simply set the time from operational mode:

```
fred@junos-router> set date 200802121646
Tue Feb 12 16:45:00 UTC 2008
```

The time the router displays is not the local time (unless you're in the United Kingdom in winter), but rather it's UTC (Universal Coordinated Time, once called Greenwich Mean Time, or GMT). If you want to use the local time zone instead, set it in configuration mode. For Western Europe, set the local time zone with this configuration:

```
[edit system]
fred@junos-router# set time-zone GMT+1
```

If you operate a larger network or have networks with routers in different time zones, use UTC across the entire network. These networks generally also have a centralized time server of some kind, and you use the Network Time Protocol (NTP) on the router to have the router automatically synchronize itself to the time server. The router can synchronize its time whenever it boots if it knows the IP address of the NTP server:

```
[edit system]
fred@junos-router# set ntp boot-server 192.168.10.20
```

In a stable network, you don't reboot routers very often, but the time on the router can slowly drift. You can have the router periodically synchronize its time with the NTP server:

```
[edit system]
fred@junos-router# set ntp server 192.168.10.20
```

Configuring Interfaces

The interfaces on the router connect the router to the network so that traffic can be sent to and from the router.

You can install different types of interface cards in the router, depending on the type of network your router is attached to. Juniper Network cards for the M-series routers are called PICs. Common examples of PICs are Fast Ethernet and Gigabit Ethernet for Ethernet networks, T1 and ISDN PICs, and, for large carriers, SONET and SDH PICs.

Juniper routers also have another type of PIC — service PICs — that can be installed into the router and can manipulate traffic before sending it. Service PICs are used for such things as monitoring traffic entering and exiting from the router and performing Network Address Translation (NAT). Tunnel PICs allow the router to encapsulate traffic in tunnels and de-encapsulate traffic received from tunnels.

Finally, special interfaces within the router don't correspond to any hardware card. These interfaces are used for communication within the router itself, for router management interfaces, and for the router's loopback address.

If you simply install the router interface cards into the router and start the router, the cards won't work. You need to configure them, at a minimum assigning an IP address to the interface.

To configure an interface, you need to know the type of PIC it is and which slot in the router the card is installed in, because you configure the interface based on its type and location in the router. Each interface name has two parts:

- A text string that identifies the interface type, as listed in Table 7-5
- Numbers that correspond to the interface's location in the router

Table 7-5 Common Interface Types and Their Identifiers

Interface Type	*Interface Text Identifier*
ATM over SONET/SDH	`at`
Encryption Services	`es`
Fast Ethernet	`fe`
Gigabit Ethernet	`ge`
Loopback	`lo0`
Router internal interface for out-of-band management	`fxp0`
Router interface for internal management	`fxp1`
Serial	`se`
Services for specialized services PICs	`sp`
SONET/SDH	`so`
T1	`t1`

The location portion of the name varies from router model to router model, depending on how many slots it has for network cards. Slots hold a larger board, generally called a Flexible PIC Concentrator (FPC).

To illustrate interface naming, suppose that you're configuring a Juniper router with eight FPC slots. The FPCs in the router are numbered from 0 through 7, with FPC 0 being in the first slot and FPC 7 being in the eighth one. The first FPC slot in all routers is slot 0. (You generally insert network cards in the front of the router, and the slot numbers are usually well labeled.)

Each FPC has fixed positions on it for PICs, generally for four PICs. The PIC positions on an FPC are numbered starting again at 0, from 0 through 3. (Be sure to check your specific router model for PIC slot orientation.)

To illustrate how interfaces are named, suppose a Gigabit Ethernet PIC is installed in the third PIC position in an FPC installed in the router's second slot. You'd use the following name in the configuration for one of the interfaces on that PIC:

```
ge-1/2/0
```

The `ge` indicates a Gigabit Ethernet PIC; the `1` identifies the second FPC slot; and the `2` indicates the third position on the FPC. The last number, `0`, corresponds to a port number on the PIC. Ports are numbered sequentially, beginning with 0. Therefore, a 0 here indicates the first port on the PIC.

Assigning an IP Address to an Interface

Each interface on the router has an IP address so that network traffic can be sent to and from that interface. You set the address when you configure the interface. For a Gigabit Ethernet interface named ge-1/2/0, here's how to assign it an IP address:

```
[edit]
fred@junos-router# set interfaces ge-1/2/0 unit 0 family
          inet address 192.168.10.40/24
```

It's worth seeing how the address is displayed in the configuration file because it visually shows the different sections of the interface configuration by the layers of indentation:

```
[edit]
fred@junos-router# show
interfaces {
  ge-1/2/0 {
    unit 0 {
```

```
        family inet {
          address 192.168.10.40/24
        }
      }
    }
  }
```

The output shows four levels of indention under the interfaces statement:

- The first level, `ge-1/2/0`, is the container for the Gigabit Ethernet physical interface. Any statements configured directly under this level apply to the entire physical interface.
- The second level has the statement `unit 0`. A *unit* is a smaller portion of the physical interface that is called a logical interface. A physical interface must have at least one logical interface, and the first one is numbered 0 (not 1).
- The third level is the family portion, which identifies a protocol that will be processed on this logical interface. You almost always want to configure at least one family on each logical interface. Here the protocol is `inet`, which is the JUNOS software way of saying IPv4.

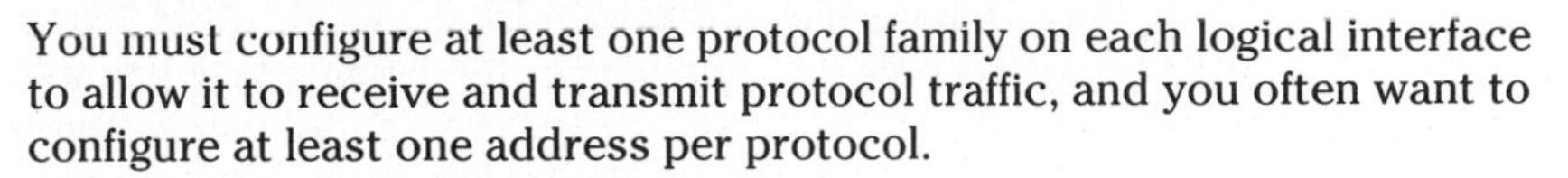

You must configure at least one protocol family on each logical interface to allow it to receive and transmit protocol traffic, and you often want to configure at least one address per protocol.

- At the final level, most families have an address portion to associate an address with the interface.

Protocols on interfaces

Some of the more common protocols you can configure on interfaces are

- `inet`: For IPv4. Specify a 32-bit IPv4 prefix, followed by a slash and the prefix length (as shown in this section).
- `inet6`: For IPv6. Specify a 64-bit IPv6 prefix, followed by a slash and the prefix length.
- `iso`: For interfaces that need to support CLNS, which is the ISO network layer service protocol that is used by IS-IS. You also need to configure one or more addresses on the router's loopback (lo0) interface, which IS-IS uses for its interface addresses.
- `mpls`: For interfaces that need to send and receive Multiprotocol Label Switching traffic. You don't need to configure an address.

A loopback interface

Once each interface has an address, it can send and receive traffic. However, if the interface goes down or if you need to remove it from the router for some reason, the router may no longer be reachable on the network by applications such as SNMP that monitor the router. To prevent this issue, you assign an address to the router itself by configuring the router's loopback interface:

```
[edit interfaces]
fred@junos-router# set lo0 unit 0 family inet address
          192.168.10.1/32
```

The loopback address is a special internal interface within the router and is not associated with any physical hardware, so you don't need to specify an FPC or a PIC slot or a port number. Note its identifier name, lo0 (refer to Table 7-5, earlier in this chapter).

The management interface

Another interface you should set up on the router is the router's management interface, which is called `fxp0` on M-series routers. You use this interface for out-of-band access to the router. Unlike normal interfaces on the router, which receive and transmit traffic flowing between different network interfaces on the router (*transit traffic*), the out-of-band management interface accepts traffic only to and from the router itself.

Using a separate, dedicated interface for managing the router is good for two reasons:

- It doesn't interfere with network traffic.
- The interface is available even if other network interfaces go down.

The `fxp0` interface is an Ethernet interface running IPv4, so you configure it like so:

```
[edit interfaces]
fred@junos-router# set fxp0 unit 0 family inet address
          192.168.50.2/24
```

Tracking interfaces

Because each interface in the router has one or more addresses, you often need to find out which addresses are associated with the router, especially when you're debugging a network problem or working on the router's configuration. The `show interfaces terse` command shows the addresses along with the basic operational status of each of the router's interfaces:

```
fred@junos-router# show interfaces terse
Interface               Admin Link Proto Local              Remote
fe-0/0/0                up    up
fe-0/0/0.0              up    up   inet  192.168.10.2/24
fe-1/1/0                up    up
fe-1/1/0.0              up    up   inet  192.168.10.41/24
ge-1/2/0                up    up
ge-1/2/0.0              up    up   inet  10.0.0.1/24
ge-1/3/0                up    up
ge-1/3/0.0              up    up   inet6 3001::2/64
                                   iso
lo0                     up    up
lo0.0                   up    up   inet  192.168.10.1/32
```

The `Local` column in the output lists the interface addresses.

Putting the Interfaces to Work

Juniper routers come in many models, and each supports different types of interface cards. Because we don't know your exact router and network needs, in this section, we show you how to perform a basic configuration on a few of the more common interfaces. Careful examination of the various output will help you understand how to configure your specific router model and interface.

The basic configuration for Ethernet interfaces — both Fast and Gigabit Ethernet PICs — is straightforward: Simply configure network addresses, and you're up and running. Here's the configuration for setting up an IPv4 address on a Fast Ethernet interface:

```
[edit interfaces]
fred@junos-router# set fe-1/1/0 unit 0 family inet address
        192.168.10.41/24
```

And here are sample configuration commands for setting up a Gigabit Ethernet interface on an IPv6 network, also allowing it to send and receive CLNS traffic for IS-IS:

```
[edit interfaces]
fred@junos-router# set ge-1/3/0 unit 0 family inet6
        address 3001::2/64

[edit interfaces]
fred@junos-router# set ge-1/3/0 unit 0 family iso
```

With these configuration commands, the interfaces are up and running. When you activate the configuration with the `commit` command (see Chapter 6), the JUNOS software checks whether hardware is actually present on the second FPC (FPC 1) in positions 2 and 4 (which the JUNOS software numbers 1 and 3, respectively). If the hardware matches the media type (Fast Ethernet and Gigabit Ethernet, respectively), the hardware starts operating with the new configuration. If no PICs are present or if they're of a different media type, the JUNOS software simply ignores that part of the configuration.

You can configure router interfaces whether or not the PICs are installed in the router — for example, after you've ordered them but before they have arrived. In fact, whenever you have a maintenance window to work on the router's configuration, you can add the configuration for the PIC. The JUNOS software will ignore it until you physically install the PIC in the router.

If you're managing a service provider router that has high-speed SONET interfaces, the basic interface configuration is just as straightforward. You simply configure an address on the interface. After you activate the configuration, it will start working:

```
[edit interfaces]
fred@junos-router# set so-3/0/0 unit 0 family inet address
        192.168.20.41/24
```

Matching your network needs

For each interface and PIC type, you can configure a wide range of parameters to meet the needs of your network. While there are far too many options to discuss in this book, we do illustrate a few.

Parameters that apply to the physical interface itself are often grouped under an -options hierarchy immediately under the name of the interface. The name of this -options hierarchy varies with the physical media type. For example:

- **Fast Ethernet:** `[edit interfaces fe-x/y/z fastether-options]`
- **Gigabit Ethernet:** `[edit interfaces ge-x/y/z gigether-options]`
- **SONET and SDH:** `[edit interfaces so-x/y/z sonet-options]`
- **T1:** `[edit interface t1-x/y/z t1-options]`
- **ATM:** `[edit interfaces at-x/y/z atm-options]`
- **Ethernet on EX-series switches:** `[edit interfaces ge-x/y/z ether-options]`

Parameters for logical interfaces are set under the unit statement. Some interface encapsulations (for example, Ethernet interfaces with 802.1q VLAN tags or Frame Relay) allow you to have multiple logical connections on a single physical interface. In these cases, you can associate the logical connections with individual logical interfaces, and you configure each logical interface under a separate `unit` statement.

Information about a specific protocol, including the protocol addresses for the interface, is set under the `family` statement. You can set any details about a specific address under the address itself.

Chapter 8
Setting Up the Network

In This Chapter

- Routing on a network
- Reading and using router tables
- Touching on RIP on your network
- Exploring OSPF and IS-IS

All Juniper routers have a common job to do: Move messages and traffic across the network from the person (or application) sending the message to a specific destination. The movement of messages and traffic is called routing.

This chapter explains the basic principles of routing and how routers route traffic. It also talks about the common routing protocols used to move traffic across the network and how to set them up on your network.

Understanding Network Routing

The most basic *routing* concept is that of a route. Routes on a network, whether the global Internet or the network within your company, are the path that messages take to reach their destination.

The way routes are determined is similar to how you might choose to drive from your home to work. Most people know several different ways to get to work and each day choose the one that will be best because it's less congested or avoids a construction project or whatever. Network routes work the same way. The router's job is to keep track of available routes and to send network traffic along the route that it decides is best at that moment.

Most of the time, however, we tend to take the same route to work everyday. This route is unchanging, or static. On a network, you (as the administrator) may want packets from a specific router to always follow the same path to reach another router. The administrator explicitly configures these *static routes* on the router.

Static routes are the simplest way to direct traffic along a path in the network and to always know what that path will be. A static route provides straightforward directions to the router. When the router sees a packet destined for a particular address in the network, the static route instructs the router to send the message to a specific IP address or out a specific interface. The IP address that the message goes to isn't necessarily the destination network, but it's generally just the next router in the right direction. This next router then has to determine how it will continue forwarding the message toward its destination.

Unlike your drive to work, where you decide the route to take, each router along the path decides the route in IP networks. So even if a static route on Router A always moves packets to Router B, Router A has no control over the path that Router B will choose to move that packet along.

Most of the time, you want to let a router determine the best path for a packet to take as it travels through the network. But sometimes a router should always use the same path — for example, when an enterprise router connects directly to your upstream service provider. In this case, you need to hard-code a static route on the router such as a static route from your router to the SP's router.

If you want to be able to reach a system on the network that doesn't or can't run a dynamic routing protocol for some reason, use a static route.

Here's how to create a static route:

```
[edit routing-options]
fred@junos-router# set static route 192.168.1.1 next-hop
          10.1.0.1
```

This command says that any packets that are destined for the system at 192.168.1.1 should be sent through the router at 10.1.0.1.

Dynamic routing protocols

When you drive to work along your normal route, you might listen to the radio for traffic reports on traffic conditions ahead. If you hear about an accident, you can use your knowledge of the city (and perhaps the advice from the traffic report) to decide on a different route. Routers use dynamic routing protocols to do essentially the same thing. *Dynamic* routing protocols dynamically keep track of which routers are present in the network and which paths are being used to send traffic. Dynamic routing protocols use this network traffic information to decide which path is the best one to reach a certain destination and to dynamically decide on alternate routes.

Why use routes that are subject to change?

Why would you want the router to use routes that are subject to change if the router already knows how to reach a destination? Well, just as traffic conditions tend to be stable when you drive to work (apologies to those with a killer commute), the routes through the network tend to be, but are not always, stable. So if a neighboring router goes down, or a physical cable connecting two cities on the Internet is severed, dynamic routing protocols become aware of these network topology changes and automatically perform calculations to choose different routes. Best of all, the protocols perform the route calculations by themselves, without any intervention from a network administrator!

Dynamic IP routing protocols choose the best route toward a destination, the best route being the shortest one. The protocols define what *short* means in two basic ways:

- Some protocols count how many routers it takes to get to the destination. Each router is a *hop* along the way, and the next router in the path is called the *next-hop router*. Each destination has a hop count associated with it, which is the number of hops, or routers, to reach that destination. This routing algorithm is called a *distance-vector algorithm*. On JUNOS routers, the only protocol that uses this algorithm is RIP (Routing Information Protocol), which is one of the original Internet routing protocols.
- *Link-state protocols* use a different mechanism to determine the best route. Two of the newer routing protocols, Open Shortest Path First (OSPF) and Intermediate system to intermediate system (IS-IS), use this mechanism. These protocols send out special packets — OSPF calls them link-state advertisements (LSAs) and IS-IS calls them link-state protocol data units, or link-state PDUs (LSPs) — to find out who their neighboring routers are and what speed the connections are between routers. From this information, the routing protocols create a database that defines the network topology. They then run the Dijkstra shortest-path first (SPF) algorithm on the information in the database to determine the shortest path to each destination in the network.

Routing tables

When you select your route to work, you may consult a map or ask your coworkers or friends for suggestions. You probably store all this information in your head and then use it to make choices depending on the commute conditions each day.

Routers have a mechanism that is similar to a map, called a *routing table,* that they use to store information about destinations on the network that they know how to reach. A routing table entry contains two basic types of information: a network destination and the address of a next-hop router, which can accept traffic for that destination. The destination is a network address or prefix that has been learned from static and dynamic routing protocols or directly from the router's network interfaces.

The destination may be reached through an interface on another router somewhere on the network, or it may be right on the router itself. When the network is reached through another router, the next-hop router is one of the router's directly connected neighbors. When the router receives a packet destined to a network address, the router determines which destination in the routing table best matches the destination address in the IP packet. The router then forwards the packets to the next-hop router (or neighbor) associated with that destination in the routing table. This process moves the packet one step closer to its destination.

Routers actually maintain several routing tables to separate the information they learn from different types of routing protocols, for example IPv4, IPv6, ISO, and multicast routes (see Table 8-1).

Table 8-1 JUNOS Routing Tables

Routing Table Name	*Description*
inet.0	Default table for IPv4 unicast routes, including configured static routes. RIP, OSPF, IS-IS, and BGP stored their routes in this table.
inet.1	Multicast forwarding cache, used by DVMRP and PIM.
inet.3	Stores paths and label information for traffic engineering (MPLS).
inet6.0	Default table for IPv6 unicast routes.
iso.0	ISO routes for IS-IS.
mpls.0	Next hops for MPLS label-switched paths (LSPs).

What do the entries in the routing table look like? The `show route` command lists all the entries in the routing table, as detailed in Listing 8-1.

Listing 8-1: Show Route to List a Router's Routing Table

```
fred@junos-router> show route

inet.0: 6 destinations, 6 routes (6 active, 0 holddown, 0 hidden)
+ = Active Route, - = Last Active, * = Both

2.0.0.0/24         *[Direct/0] 06:01:36
                    > via fe-0/0/2.0
2.0.0.120/32       *[Local/0] 06:01:36
                      Local via fe-0/0/2.0
10.5.0.0/16        *[Static/5] 5d 00:25:00
                    > to 10.93.15.254 via fxp0.0
10.10.0.0/16       *[Static/5] 5d 00:25:00
                    > to 10.93.15.254 via fxp0.0
10.93.4.52/32      *[Direct/0] 5d 00:25:00
                    > via lo0.0
10.93.8.0/21       *[Direct/0] 5d 00:25:00
                    > via fxp0.0
                    [Static/5] 5d 00:25:00

__juniper_private1__.inet.0: 14 destinations, 14 routes (8 active, 0 holddown,
              6 hidden)
+ = Active Route, - = Last Active, * = Both

10.0.0.0/8         *[Direct/0] 5d 00:25:00
                    > via fxp1.0
10.0.0.1/32        *[Local/0] 5d 00:23:09
                      Local

__juniper_private1__.inet6.0: 2 destinations, 2 routes (2 active, 0 holddown,
              0 hidden)
+ = Active Route, - = Last Active, * = Both

fe80::/64          *[Direct/0] 5d 00:25:00
                    > via fxp1.0
fe80::200:ff:fe00:4/128
                   *[Local/0] 5d 00:25:00
                      Local via fxp1.0
```

The command lists the contents of all the routing tables that the JUNOS routing process (RPD) is using. Scan the output of the `show route` command in Listing 8-1 and notice that the routing table has both IPv4 and IPv6 routes. Notice, too, the first part of the output shows the contents of the `inet.0` routing table, which is the default IPv4 routing table. The prefixes starting with `2.0.0.0` and ending with `10.93.8.0` are IPv4 unicast routes that are used to route traffic. The prefixes listed under `__juniper_private1__.inet.0` and `__juniper_private1__.inet.6` are the routes in internal routing tables that only JUNOS software uses.

If you closely examine the entries in the routing table in Listing 8-1 (look just at the IPv4 routes because the detail is the same for both IPv4 and IPv6 routes), the first line summarizes the contents of the `inet.0` routing table. The router has learned six destinations and has six routes, all of which are active. No routes are in hold-down state, which occurs just before a route is removed from the routing table, and no routes are hidden as a result of a policy that you've configured on the router or a problem with the route.

The second line of output in Listing 8-1 is just a key to symbols used in the output. An active route is one that the router is currently using as the best route to reach a destination. All the routes shown in the output are active, so they're marked with an asterisk (*) in the right column.

The first column in the routing table lists all the prefixes that the router knows how to reach.

The text in the brackets lists how the router learned about the route. This router has learned routes directly, from local interfaces, and from configured static routes. If any routing protocols, such as OSPF or BGP, were running on the router, the routing table would also show the routes learned from these protocols. The final text on the first line of each routing table entry shows how long the route has been in the routing table.

Inside the brackets, the number after the slash is a value the router uses to choose between multiple routes to the same destination. This value is called the route's preference, and we talk about it more in the next section.

The second line of each routing table entry shows which interface the router will use to forward traffic towards the prefix and, in some cases, the IP address of the next-hop router. Some of the prefixes in this routing table are reached through the Fast Ethernet interface `fe-0/0/2`.

You can practice this kind of close examination on your own routing tables, which are chock full of network and routing information.

Choosing the Best Route

The router chooses the best routes from all the routes it learns about (see the preceding section). It makes the decision about which route is the best by looking at a route's *preference.* The route preference is a number from 0 through 4,294,967,295 ($2^{32} - 1$) that is assigned based on the protocol from which the route was learned (see Table 8-2). If the router learns several routes to the same destination, it chooses the one with the lowest preference value, marks it as the active route, and uses that route to forward packets.

The other routes remain in the routing table, but are inactive and not marked with an asterisk.

Table 8-2 Default Route Preferences in JUNOS Software

How Route Is Learned	*Default Route Preference*
Directly connected router or network	0
Configured static routes	5
MPLS	7
LDP	9
OSPF internal routes	10
IS-IS Level 1 internal routes	15
IS-IS Level 2 internal routes	18
SNMP	50
RIP	100
PIM	105
DVMRP	110
Aggregate	130
OSPF external routes	150
IS-IS Level 1 external routes	160
IS-IS Level 2 external routes	165
BGP	170
MSDP	175

Sometimes two routes will have the same preference, and the router still has to pick one of them to be the active route. The JUNOS software goes through a fairly complex decision tree for choosing the best route. Because you generally don't need to know how this decision-making process works unless you're analyzing the overall flow of traffic through your network, we're punting to the Juniper product documentation, which has dozens and dozens of pages devoted to the actual decision tree.

Running RIP on Your Network

RIP is a distance-vector protocol and uses the distance, measured in hops, to determine the best route to a destination. Each hop corresponds to a single router, and the number of hops to a destination is the sum of the number of routers a packet has to pass through, starting at its origin.

Let 'er RIP!

The Routing Information Protocol (RIP) is one of the first routing protocols, developed as part of the ARPANET project in 1969. It was included in the UNIX BSD operating system in the early 1980s, before specialized devices called routers had even been developed, and as a result, became the de facto routing protocol and was widely used. RIP is an IGP, meaning that it routes traffic within a single administrative domain, such as a company or a university. RIP was standardized by the IETF in 1988 and became known as RIP version 1. The protocol was updated to version 2 in 1994 to add support for Classless Interdomain Routing (CIDR) and MD5 authentication.

RIP is generally used in smaller or less complex networks, partly because it's something of a simple protocol, and partly because of a design limitation. The maximum hop count that a route can have is 15. If a destination is more than 15 routers away, RIP can't forward packets to that destination and simply discards (drops) the packets. The two other IGPs discussed later in this chapter, OSPF and IS-IS, don't have this limitation. For this reason, and also because OSPF and IS-IS provide more features than RIP, they're used more often for a network's IGP (which is why this discussion of RIP is fairly short!).

You'd want to use RIP on the Juniper router when you're connecting the router to a network that is already running RIPv2. The router configuration is very straightforward. You turn on RIP on each interface that is directly connected to a neighboring router that is running RIP. In the following configuration, the JUNOS router connects to the neighbor using the Fast Ethernet interface fe-0/0/1's unit 0 logical interface:

```
[edit protocols]
fred@junos-router# set rip group fred-group neighbor
          fe-0/0/1.0
```

The JUNOS configuration requires that all RIP neighbors be part of a group, which you define with the group keyword. Here, the group has a name of `fred-group`, but you can name it anything you like. For a simple network, you can configure all the RIP interfaces and routers to be in a single group. If you want to enable RIP packet authentication and want routers to have different passwords, you need to configure the routers to be in different groups.

The RIP configuration on the neighboring router is similar. You can use the same group name and the appropriate interface. Use the `show rip neighbor` command to check that the interface is configured:

```
fred@junos-router> show rip neighbor
                       Source       Destination    Send   Receive   In
Neighbor        State  Address      Address        Mode   Mode      Met
--------        -----  -------      -----------    ----   -------   ---
fe-0/0/1.0         Up  10.0.29.2    224.0.0.9      mcast  both        1
```

The first column of the output shows that you're running RIP on the configured interface, `fe-0/0/1.0`, and the State column shows that the connection is Up. The two address columns show the address of the local interface and the interface to which the router is sending updates. (In this case, a well-known multicast address used by RIP routers.) The last column reports the inbound metric, which is how many hops will be added to received routes. Here, the metric is the expected value of 1.

Running OSPF on Your Network

OSPF is a more advanced interior gateway routing protocol. Unlike RIP, which is a distance-vector protocol, OSPF is a link-state protocol. Instead of determining the best route by looking at the distance (number of hops), link-state protocols run a shortest-path first (SPF) algorithm to create a database of the network's topology and, from that database, to determine the best (that is, shortest) path to a destination.

As an IGP, OSPF operates within a single network administrative boundary or domain, which is sometimes called an autonomous system (AS).

Each router running OSPF goes through the following process to discover the network topology and determine the best path to each destination:

1. **OSPF creates link-state advertisements (LSAs), which describe the network topology that the router has in its link-state database.**
2. **The router floods the LSAs to all routers in the domain.**
3. **When the router receives LSAs from other routers, it adds the information to its link-state database.**
4. **The router runs the Dijkstra SPF calculation to determine the shortest path to each destination in the domain.**

   The result of the calculation is a pair of values for each destination, consisting of the destination address and the next hop toward that destination. OSPF places this information in its OSPF routing database. While each router performs the SPF calculation independently, all routers end up with identical link-state databases (though the routers may have different next hops for the destinations).

All OSPF routers within a domain must have the same link-state databases for OSPF to work.

5. **When changes occur in the administrative domain, this information is transmitted in LSAs, and all the OSPF routers rerun the SPF calculation and update their link-state databases.**

Dividing an OSPF network into areas

As an OSPF network gets larger, one of the challenges is keeping all the link-state statements on all the routers in sync. One way to control the size of the OSPF network is to divide it into smaller pieces, which OSPF calls *areas*. Each area has the same properties: All the routers within the area exchange their network topology information in LSAs, and this smaller group of routers run the SPF calculation to keep their link-state databases identical.

Routers that connect only to other routers within an area are called *internal routers*.

Some of the routers within an OSPF area sit on the boundary of two areas. These *area border routers* (ABRs) connect the areas within the larger OSPF network. They run two SPF calculations, one for each area to which they're connected, and they maintain two link-state databases, one for each area. The ABRs pass route information between the two areas, but condense (summarize) it before sending it into the neighboring area. The summarization improves the overall stability of the OSPF network.

Areas and area border routers sit in a single OSPF administrative domain. Another type of router sits at the boundary between one OSPF administrative domain and another administrative domain or routing protocol. This router is the AS boundary router (ASBR). These routers are responsible to advertise externally learned routes into the OSPF administrative domains.

Areas come in several different flavors. The main one is the backbone area because it forms the backbone of the OSPF network. The backbone area has the area ID 0, which is normally written as the 32-bit value 0.0.0.0. All areas in the OSPF network connect to the backbone, and as a result, all area border routers are part of the backbone area. Also, any networks that have an area ID of 0.0.0.0 must also connect to the backbone area.

All routers in the OSPF backbone must be physically connected to each other. If any routers aren't physically contiguous, they must be connected by an OSPF virtual link so that they appear to be contiguous.

In a simple (if you can conceive of that right now) OSPF network, all nonbackbone areas connect directly to the backbone area. By default, these nonbackbone areas are referred to as *regular areas.* To minimize the amount of LSA traffic on segments of the OSPF network, OSPF has two other types of areas that don't advertise route information into other areas. *Stub areas* receive only summarized routing information about other areas within the OSPF domain, and they don't receive any information about external OSPF routes. As a result, stub areas can't connect to external networks. Not-so-stubby areas (NSSAs) are a slight variant of a stub network. These areas can connect to external networks.

Configuring and monitoring OSPF

While OSPF in theory may seem overly complicated, configuring OSPF on a JUNOS router is straightforward and easy. First, you must define the OSPF areas to which the router will connect, and then you must enable OSPF on the interfaces on which you want OSPF to run. You configure these two properties with a single command:

```
[edit protocols]
fred@junos-router# set ospf area 0.0.0.0 interface
          interface-name
```

Once OSPF is configured, you can use the commands listed in Table 8-3 to monitor OSPF routing on your network.

Table 8-3 Commands to Monitor OSPF

Command	*Purpose*
`show ospf database`	Displays entries in the OSPF link-state database.
`show ospf interface`	Displays the interfaces on which OSPF is configured.
`show ospf neighbor`	Displays the router's OSPF neighbors.
`show ospf route`	Displays the contents of the OSPF routing table.
`show route protocol ospf`	Displays the routes learned by OSPF.

Running IS-IS on Your Network

Like OSPF, IS-IS is another link-state interior gateway routing protocol. Like OSPF, IS-IS also runs the Dijkstra shortest-path first (SPF) algorithm to create a database of the network's topology and, from that database, to determine the best (that is, shortest) path to a destination.

Unlike OSPF, which was developed and standardized by the Internet Engineering Task Force (IETF), IS-IS is an ANSI ISO protocol and was originally based on the Digital Equipment Corporation DECNET Phase V Network Technology.

IS-IS uses a slightly different terminology than OSPF for naming its protocol packets. When IS-IS routers send packets to each other describing the network topology, these packets are called *link-state protocol data units* (link-state PDUs, or LSPs). In addition to describing the network topology that the router knows about, the link-state PDUs include IP routes, checksums, and other information.

Similar to OSPF, all IS-IS routers place the information in the received link-stated PDUs into their link-state database, and all routers have the same view of the network's topology. IS-IS runs the SPF algorithm on the information in the link-state database to determine the shortest path to each destination on the network, placing the destination/next-hop pairs that result from the SPF calculation into the IS-IS routing database.

Using IS-IS addresses only when needed

Unlike other IP routing protocols, which typically run on TCP, UDP, or IP, which are OSI Layer 3 or Layer 4 protocols, IS-IS runs directly on the data link layer (Layer 2). As a result, each interface that runs IS-IS doesn't need an IP address to exchange IS-IS information, and you don't need to configure an inet family on any interfaces running IS-IS. Rather, only the router itself needs an IP address, which makes the router configuration simpler.

Because it was developed as part of the OSI network protocols and not part of TCP/IP, IS-IS doesn't use IP addresses. IS-IS addresses are called NETs, or network entity titles. While IP addresses are 32 bits long and are normally written in dotted quad notation (such as 192.168.1.2), NETs can be 8 to 20 bytes long, but are generally 10 bytes long and are written as shown in this example:

```
49.0001.1921.6800.1002.00
```

The IS-IS address consists of three parts:

- **Area identifier:** The first three bytes are the area ID. IS-IS areas are similar to OSPF areas (see the preceding section), but for this example, the area ID is 49.0001. The first byte of this — 49 — is the address family identifier (AFI) of the authority, which is equivalent to the IP address space that is assigned to an autonomous system. The AFI value 49 is what IS-IS uses for private addressing, which is the equivalent of RFC 1918 address space for IP protocols. The second two bytes of the area ID — 0001 — represent the IS-IS area number. In this example, the area number is 1.
- **System identifier:** The next six bytes identify the node (that is, the router) on the network. The system identifier is equivalent to the host or address portion on an IP address. While you can choose any value for the system identifier, a commonly used method is to use binary-coded decimal (BCD) which involves taking the router's IP address (the address you assigned to the `lo0loopback` interface), filling in all leading zeros, and then repositioning the decimal points to form three two-byte numbers. In our example, if you pad the IP address 192.168.1.2 with zeros, the result is 192.168.001.002. Re-arranging the decimal points gives you 1921.6800.1002.

  Another common way to assign the system identifier is to start with the router's media access control (MAC) address, which is a six-byte address and re-arrange the decimal points to create three two-byte numbers. So, for example, for a router MAC address of 00:1B:63:31:86:BE, the IS-IS system identifier is 001b.6331.86be.
- **NET selector:** The final two bytes are the NET selector (NSEL). For IS-IS they must always be 00, to indicate "this system."

Minding your IS-IS areas

To control the amount of IS-IS protocol traffic sent within the local network, IS-IS networks are divided into areas, just as OSPF networks have areas. Each IS-IS area consists of a set of networks and routers that are administratively grouped together. All the routers within an area exchange their network topology information in IS-IS LSPs, and this smaller group of routers run the SPF calculation to keep their link-state databases identical. Routers within an area share the information in their link-state databases with each other by exchanging LSPs. This process ensures that all the link-state databases in the area are identical, and hence that all routers within an area have the same view of the area's network topology. Routers within an area can send summaries of their routes to other areas in the IS-IS network.

IS-IS areas contain two types of routers:

- **Level 1 systems:** These routers route traffic within an IS-IS area. When they receive traffic destined for somewhere outside the area, they send the packet towards a Level 2 system.
- **Level 2 systems:** Route traffic between two IS-IS areas. They also route traffic to other ASs.

A single IS-IS router can be both a Level 1 and a Level 2 system, which is similar to the OSPF area border router (ABR). These routers maintain two link-state databases, one for the Level 1 area and a second one for the Level 2 area.

Configuring and monitoring IS-IS

To configure IS-IS on a JUNOS router, you must enable family `iso` processing on the interfaces on which you want IS-IS, and then you must tell the router to form IS-IS adjacencies over that interface. Here's how you do it for the `ge-1/2/0.0` interface:

```
[edit]
fred@junos-router# set interfaces ge-1/2/0 unit 0 family
           iso

[edit]
fred@junos-router# set protocols isis interface ge-1/2/0.0
```

Once configured, you can use the commands listed in Table 8-4 to monitor IS-IS routing on your network.

Table 8-4 Commands to Monitor IS-IS

Command	*Purpose*
`show isis adjacency`	Displays the router's IS-IS neighbors.
`show isis database`	Displays entries in the IS-IS link-state database.
`show isis interface`	Displays the interfaces on which IS-IS is configured.
`show isis route`	Displays the contents of the IS-IS routing table.
`show route protocol isis`	Displays the routes learned by IS-IS.

Chapter 9

Adding Security

In This Chapter

- Deploying basic physical security
- Understanding the default JUNOS security settings
- Designing custom security principles
- Deploying authentication

On the Internet, routers are the primary devices responsible for distributing traffic, whether that traffic is e-mail messages, documents, videos, or unwanted spam. Traffic transmission rates were initially limited by the speed of the network routers. However, in the past ten years, Juniper has introduced routers with interfaces that run at line speed (that is, at the maximum speed supported by the link connecting to the router interface). Over this decade, interface speeds have increased dramatically, with both faster SONET/SDH and Ethernet interfaces.

These advances mean that you can now move traffic, both wanted and unwanted, very quickly across the Internet. A hacker who can take control of an unsecured or an improperly secured router can wreak havoc on your network and can use the router as a launching pad for denial-of-service and other types of attacks. And all of it can happen faster than you can make a sandwich and eat it.

Fortunately, in this chapter, we cover several security features and practices you can take advantage of.

Stop! Physical Security

A basic way to secure your router is to limit physical access to it. This precaution prevents someone from accidentally or deliberately turning off the router or removing or replacing cables and power cords connected to the router.

Also, anyone who has physical access to a router can connect to the router's console port. If someone manages to log in as the root user, he can take control of the router, issuing any and all commands and modifying the router configuration.

To physically isolate routers, keep them in an area with restricted access, such as a locked room or a room that requires badge access. Then, limit the number of people who have access to that area.

This advice may seem like basic stuff, but you'd be surprised at the number of routers operating in the corner of some administrator's open cube.

Go! JUNOS Default Security Features

JUNOS software has a number of default behaviors that contribute to router security. These behaviors immediately take effect after you perform the initial router configuration (see Chapter 6).

- **Router access:** By default, the only way to access the router is by physically connecting to the router's console port. To configure the router initially, you must connect a laptop or other terminal directly to the console port. All other remote management access and management access protocols, such as Telnet, FTP, and SSH (secure shell), are disabled. (On the J-series routers, the Web interface is enabled by default to aid in initial system configuration.) Once the initial configuration is complete, you need to enable a way to remotely log in to the router so you don't have to physically be there, connected to the router's console port. SSH provides the best security, and you configure it as follows:

```
[edit]
fred@router# set system services ssh
```

- **Configuring the router with SNMP Set commands:** JUNOS software does not support the SNMP Set capability for editing configuration data, which allows an NMS to modify the configurations on managed network devices. JUNOS software does, by default, allow SNMP to query the status of the router, although no known security risks are associated with this.
- **Directed broadcast messages:** JUNOS software doesn't forward these messages, which are datagrams with a destination address of an IP subnetwork broadcast address. Directed broadcasts are easy to spoof, which is a method used in denial-of-service (DoS) attacks.
- **Martian addresses:** JUNOS software ignores routes for several reserved addresses (but not including the private addresses defined in RFC 1918). Martian addresses should never be seen on the Internet, but routes for

these addresses are sometimes advertised by misconfigured routers. You can modify the list of martian addresses, if you so desire.

- **Password encryption:** When configuring the router, you should enter passwords for various features. All these passwords are secured — either by *encryption* (a one-to-one mapping, which is possible to decrypt) or *hashing* (a many-to-many mapping, which is impossible to unhash) algorithms — to keep them from being discovered. Even in cases where the JUNOS software prompts you for a plain-text password, the software encrypts it immediately after you type it. When you display the password in the configuration file, you see only the encrypted version, marked as SECRET-DATA. For example, if you configure a plain-text password for a user login account, you see that the JUNOS CLI encrypts it right away using SHA1:

```
[edit system]
fred@router# set login user mike authentication plain-
        text-password
New password:
Retype new password:

[edit system]
fred@router# show
user mike {
  authentication {
    encrypted-password "$1$bRzNS9Tm$yG6vt2U0aXHBR5f9U1
        twy/"; ## SECRET-DATA
  }
}
```

- **Partial enforcement of strong passwords:** JUNOS software enforces the use of strong passwords to a certain extent, requiring that all passwords you configure be at least six characters long and have a change of cases and contain either digits or punctuation. The software rejects passwords that don't meet these criteria:

```
[edit system]
fred@router# set login user mike authentication plain-
        text-password
New password:
error: require change of case, digits or punctuation
```

You can enhance the enforcement of strong passwords by configuring a longer minimum password length and by increasing the minimum number of case, digit, and punctuation changes:

```
[edit system]
fred@router# set login password minimum-length number

[edit system]
fred@router# set login password minimum-changes number
```

Choosing passwords

Password selection is one of the most important ways to protect a router from hackers and other types of unwanted attacks. The root and user accounts you create on the router should all have passwords and the passwords should be strong:

- Choose a password that is a combination of uppercase and lowercase letters, digits, and punctuation characters.
- Choose a password that is a phrase or a shortened version of a phrase that you can easily remember without writing down.
- Don't choose the router vendor name (such as juniper), the string "admin," or the string "password."
- Don't choose an easily guessable password, such as your birthday or spouse's name.
- Don't use a word that's in a dictionary in any language. Brute-force, automated programs can rapidly try all words in all online dictionaries when attempting to break into a router.

Encryption and hashing algorithms

If security is your issue, it may be important for you to know that JUNOS software uses the following encryption and hashing algorithms to protect data and packets:

- **DES:** An encryption algorithm that uses a 56-bit key.
- **MD5:** A message-hashing algorithm that produces a 128-bit hash function. Because of the longer hash, it's more secure than DES.
- **SHA1:** Produces a 160-bit message digest. It has the longest length and hence is the most secure of the algorithms.
- **SSH:** A security protocol that creates keys for authentication. You configure the public key on the router and only users with the corresponding private key will be able to authenticate against that key. It is generally considered to be impossible to determine a private key from a public key.

Tighten the root login account

During the initial configuration of a new router, you set the root password as a plain-text password. Because the root user is able to perform any and all operations on the router, tightening access to the root login account is a good idea. One way is to configure the root password using SSH key authentication, which is more secure that the plain-text password (provided you protect the private key appropriately):

```
[edit system]
fred@router# set root-authentication ssh-dsa "ssh-dss
             AAAAB3NzaC1kc3MAAACBAMQrfP2bZyBXJ6PC7XXZ+MzEr
             I8Jl6jah5L4/O8BsfP2hC7EvRfNoX7MqbrtCX/9gUH9g
             ChVuBCB+ERULMdgRvM5uGhC/gs4UX+4dBbfBgKYYwgm
             isM8EoT25m7qI8ybpl2YZvHNznvO8h7kr4kpYuQEpKvg
             sTdH/Jle4Uqnjv7DAAAAFQDZaqA6QAgbW3O/zveaLCID
             j6p0dwAAAIB1iL+kWrXiD8NPpY+w4dWXEqaV3bnobzPC4
             eyxQKBUCOr80Q5YBlWXVBHx9elwBWZwj0SF4hLKHznEx
             nLerVsMuTMA846RbQmSz62vM6kGM13HFonWeQvWia0
             TDr78+rOEgWF2KHBSIxL51lmIDW8Gql9hJfD/Dr/NKP
             97w3L0wAAAIEAr3FkWU8XbYytQYEKxsIN9P1UQ1ERXB
             3G40YwqFO484SlyKyYCfaz+yNsaAJu2C8UebDIR3Giey
             NcOAKf3inCG8jQwjLvZskuZwrvlsz/xtcxSoAh9axJc
             dUfSJYMW/g+mD26JK1Cliw5rwp2nH9kUrJxeI7IRe
             Dp4egNkM4i15o= root@router"
```

As you can see, that is a lot to type! If you don't feel like entering that, you can also load an SSH key file from a network server:

```
[edit system]
fred@router# set root-authentication load-key-file server-
             name:/dir/filename
```

When SSH is enabled, anyone with the root password or SSH private key can log in as the root user from anywhere on the network. This ability is useful in large networks or when you can't get physical access to the router.

Generally, however, no one on the network should have any reason to log in to the router using the root account, so you can ratchet up the router security one level more by forcing anyone logging in as root to log in directly from the router's console port. To do so, you disable root login through SSH:

```
[edit system]
fred@router# set services ssh root-login deny
```

What happens if you ever lose network access to the router? While it's unlikely, you may find that you can't connect to a router over the network as you would usually do. If this issue occurs, the only way to access the router is to connect a laptop or terminal to the router's console port. This port is enabled by default on all JUNOS routers. While you can disable console access to the router, we really don't recommend it. Also, the only way you can remain logged in to a router while its rebooting is by connecting to the console port. You may want to do so when trying to troubleshoot and debug problems with the router or the JUNOS software.

Checking Who's on the Router

More than one person can log in to a Juniper router at any given time, logging in either with an individual user account name or with a group name that is shared by many users. (An example of a group account is root.) Each person who is on the router can perform whatever operations they're allowed depending on their privileges (see Chapter 7), and it's possible that another person's work may interfere with what you're doing.

Knowing who's logged in

When you log in to the router, the CLI doesn't tell you whether anyone else is already logged in. You need to check manually:

```
fred@router> show system users
```

If you discover that an unwanted user is logged in to the router or if you need to perform an operation, such as rebooting the router or installing new software, that would be easier if no one else were logged in to the router, you can forcibly log people out. The `show system users` command shows you the names of who is logged in. Use the name to forcibly log the person out, herewith logging out Mike:

```
fred@router> request system logout mike
```

Mike sees the following on his terminal window:

```
mike@router> Connection closed by foreign host.
[server.mycompany.com] mike@server%
```

You can also ask people to log out. You can ask an individual with a command like this one, with any message you want:

```
fred@router> request message user mike message "End router
             session now!"
```

You can also have the message go to everyone currently logged in to the router:

```
fred@router> request message all message "End router
             session now!"
```

Figuring out who's configuring

JUNOS software also allows multiple people to be in configuration mode at the same time. When you enter configuration mode, the CLI displays a message letting you know whether anyone else is also editing the configuration. However, if someone enters configuration mode after you, you won't receive any kind of message. You can check periodically using the `status` configuration mode command:

```
[edit]
fred@router# status
Users currently editing the configuration:
  fred terminal p0 (pid 13329) on since 2008-03-23
          15:15:12 UTC
       [edit]
```

If more than one person is changing the configuration, when one of them issues a `commit` command to activate the configuration, all changes made by all users are activated. To check the changes before committing the configuration, move to the top of the configuration hierarchy and use the following version of the `show` configuration mode command to look at the differences:

```
[edit]
fred@router# show | compare
[edit protocols]
+   mstp;
[edit interfaces]
-  ge-0/0/1 {
-    unit 0 {
-      family inet {
-        address 192.168.1.4;
-      }
-    }
- }
```

The plus sign (+) indicates lines that have been added to the configuration since it was last activated, and the minus sign (-) shows what has been deleted. In the preceding example, the MSTP protocol has been enabled, and one of the Gigabit Ethernet interfaces has been removed from the configuration.

If you need to ensure that no one else can modify the router configuration while you're editing, lock it when you enter configuration mode with this command:

```
fred@router> configure exclusive
```

If someone else has an exclusive lock on the configuration, the CLI displays a message when you enter configuration mode:

```
fred@router> configure
Users currently editing the configuration:
  mike terminal p0 (pid 13329) on since 2008-03-23
          15:15:12 UTC
  exclusive [edit]
```

Logging Out

Most people remember to log out when they're no longer working on the router to monitor it or modify the configuration, but even when you walk away from your desk or office, you should log out to prevent unauthorized people from walking up to your keyboard and accessing the router.

Log out with this simple operational mode command:

```
fred@router> exit
```

If you're in configuration mode, use the `exit` or `quit` command to return to operational mode first. If you're not at the top level of the configuration, use one of the following command sequences to get there:

```
[edit protocols bgp group isp-group]
fred@router# top

[edit]
fred@router# exit
Exiting configuration mode

fred@router>
```

or

```
[edit protocols bgp group isp-group]
fred@router# exit configuration-mode
Exiting configuration mode

fred@router>
```

Controlling SSH and Telnet Access to the Router

SSH and Telnet are the two common ways for users to access the router. Both require password authentication, either through an account configured on the router or an account set on a centralized authentication server, such as a RADIUS server. Even with a password, Telnet sessions are inherently insecure, and SSH can be attacked by brute-force attempts to guess passwords.

One way to limit the number of people who can log in to the router is to restrict which network systems people can use to connect to the router.

You restrict SSH and Telnet access by creating a firewall filter, which regulates the traffic on a specific interface, deciding what to allow and what to discard. (Firewall filters are discussed in more detail in Chapter 14.) Creating a filter is a two-part process:

1. **You define the filtering details.**
2. **You apply the filter to a router interface.**

Now, when you want to control access to the router, you'd normally need to apply those restrictions to every interface as the router can be contacted through any interface. However, to make things easier, JUNOS software allows you to apply firewall filters to the lo0 interface. Firewall filters applied to the lo0 interface affect all traffic destined to the router's control plane, regardless of the interface on which the packet arrived. So to limit SSH and Telnet access to the router, you apply the filter to the lo0 interface.

To create a filter, you name it and define the filtering conditions. A firewall filter looks at the contents of packets on an interface and compares them to conditions you define. It the packet matches all conditions, the filter takes the actions you configure.

The filter below is called `limit-ssh-telnet`, and it has two parts, or terms. The JUNOS software evaluates the two terms sequentially. Traffic that matches the first term is processed immediately, and traffic that fails is evaluated by the second term. Here's how the process works:

1. **The first term, `limit-ssh-telnet`, looks for SSH and Telnet access attempts only from devices on the 192.168.0.1/24 subnetwork.**

   Packets will match this term only if the IP header includes a source address from the 192.168.0.1/24 prefix, the IP header shows the packet is a TCP packet, and only if the TCP packet header shows that traffic is headed for the SSH or Telnet destination ports.

If all these criteria are met, the filter's action is to accept the access attempt and traffic:

```
[edit firewall]
fred@router# set filter limit-ssh-telnet term access-
        term from source-address 192.168.0.1/24

[edit firewall]
fred@router# set filter limit-ssh-telnet term access-
        term from protocol tcp

[edit firewall]
fred@router# set filter limit-ssh-telnet term access-
        term from destination-port [ssh telnet]

[edit firewall]
fred@router# set filter limit-ssh-telnet term access-
        term then accept
```

2. **The second term, called `block-all-else`, blocks all traffic that does not meet the criteria in Step 1.**

   You can do this step with a basic `reject` command. This term contains no criteria to match, so, by default, it's applied to all traffic that fails the first term:

```
[edit firewall]
fred@router# set filter limit-ssh-telnet term block-
        all-else term reject
```

From a vigilance point of view, you should track failed attempts to access the router so that you can determine whether a concerted attack might be underway. The `block-all-else` term counts the number of failed access attempts (the first command in the next example keeps track of these attempts in a counter named `bad-access`), logging the packet, and sending information to the syslog process about the packet. (These actions are taken in addition to the `reject` command you already configured):

```
[edit firewall]
fred@router# set filter limit-ssh-telnet term block-all-
          else term count bad-access

[edit firewall]
fred@router# set filter limit-ssh-telnet term block-all-
          else term count log

[edit firewall]
fred@router# set filter limit-ssh-telnet term block-all-
          else term count syslog
```

Creating a filter is half the process. The second half is to apply it to a router interface, in this case to the router's loopback interface, lo0:

```
[edit interfaces]
fred@router# set lo0 unit 0 family inet filter input
        limit-ssh-telnet
```

You apply the filter as an input filter, which means that the JUNOS software applies it to all incoming traffic destined to the control plane.

Firewall filters have two basic characteristics that you need to consider to design them properly:

- On most devices, you can apply multiple firewall filters in an ordered chain. If you apply the `limit-ssh-telnet` filter to the router's loopback interface, this interface accepts SSH and Telnet traffic but nothing else. So if you've configured other protocols, such as SNMP, BGP, OSPF, and IS-IS, to use the loopback address as the router address, packets from those protocols are blocked and don't reach the router.

  However, you can write a number of smaller firewall filters and apply them in a chain, which allows you to reuse smaller pieces of firewall filters multiple times instead of writing custom firewall filters for each interface. When you configure a chain of firewall filters, the JUNOS software acts as if you had just created one large firewall filter, composed of the terms of each filter in order. (That means if you put this `limit-ssh-telnet` filter first in a chain, all other traffic would be rejected regardless of the remaining firewall filters, because the second term of the chain would reject all traffic.)

- JUNOS software evaluates the terms in a firewall filter (or chain of firewall filters) in order, starting with the first one. The router processes each packet through the terms in a firewall filter in order until it finds a match. When it finds a match, it takes the actions indicated by that term's `then` clause, which means that you must ensure traffic will be accepted or rejected at the right place, but not sooner. So, for example, if you want to allow all Telnet traffic, but deny all other TCP traffic, you need to put the term allowing Telnet traffic before the term denying TCP traffic. If you put them in the reverse order, the router will deny the Telnet traffic (because Telnet uses TCP) and never reach the term to allow Telnet traffic. You do not, however, need to worry about optimizing your firewall filters, as the JUNOS software takes care of that for you. Having the software take care of your filtering makes your job easy: You just worry about making sure that the filter logic is in the correct order, and the router will take care of optimizing it for you.

Limiting Traffic on Router Interfaces

Some DoS attacks on routers work by inundating the router with traffic, sending so much traffic to router interfaces so quickly that the interfaces are overwhelmed and can't handle the regular traffic that should be passing through the interface. One method to combat this attack is to use JUNOS policers, which you can specify when you define the action a firewall filter should take. *Policers* allow you to place limits on the amount of traffic (or even just a type of traffic) an interface can receive, which can limit the impact of DoS attacks. Policers control the maximum allowed bandwidth (the average number of bits per second) and the maximum allowed size of a single burst of traffic when the bandwidth limit is exceeded. Any traffic received beyond the set limits is dropped.

Policers are used in the action (`then`) portion of a firewall filter. To use them in a firewall filter, you first define the policer. The following example creates a policer called `police-ssh-telnet` that sets a maximum traffic rate (bandwidth) of 1 Mbps and the maximum size of a traffic burst exceeding this limit (burst size) of 25 KB. Traffic exceeding these limits is discarded.

```
[edit firewall]
fred@router# set policer police-ssh-telnet if-exceeding bandwidth-limit 1m

[edit firewall]
fred@router# set policer police-ssh-telnet if-exceeding burst-size-limit 25k

[edit firewall]
fred@router# set policer police-ssh-telnet then discard
```

Then include the policer in a firewall filter action. As an example, we add it to the SSH-Telnet firewall filter from the previous section that we applied to the router's loopback interface:

```
[edit firewall]
fred@router# set filter limit-ssh-telnet term access-term then policer police-
             ssh-telnet

[edit firewall]
fred@router# set filter limit-ssh-telnet term access-term then accept
```

Traffic that conforms to the limits in the policer will take the action you specify in the firewall term (in this case, it will be accepted), while traffic that exceeds the limits in the policer will take the action specified there (in this case, it will be discarded). (In case you were paying close attention, we didn't need to re-specify the `accept` action that we had already configured earlier, but we did it for clarity in case you skipped over that part.)

Rate-limiting traffic flow to the Routing Engine by defining policers is a good security practice to prevent the Routing Engine from being overwhelmed by unwanted traffic or by possible attacks on the router. All the routing protocol processes run on the Routing Engine, which are critical to the core operation of the router itself. When these processes can't run normally, the result can be a destabilization of the network.

Protecting the Routing Engine: A More Complete Strategy

While all interfaces are important, the loopback (lo0) interface is perhaps the most important because it is the link to the Routing Engine, which runs and monitors all the control protocols.

This section shows the skeleton of a firewall filter that protects the Routing Engine by allowing only desired traffic and rejecting all other traffic. You can use this example as a blueprint to design the appropriate filter for your router. The filter is applied to the router's lo0 interface.

This filter is for a router configured for a common IPv4 setup:

- IPv4
- BGP and IS-IS routing protocols
- RADIUS, SSH, and Telnet access
- SNMP NMS access
- NTP

Because firewall filters are evaluated in order, place the most time-critical items — the routing protocols — first. Accept traffic from your known BGP peers and from the known IS-IS neighbors with the AS using the following `set` commands:

```
[edit firewall filter routing-engine]
set term bgp-filter from source-address peer-address1
set term bgp-filter from source-address peer-address2
set term bgp-filter from protocol tcp
set term bgp-filter from port bgp
set term bgp-filter then accept
```

Then accept DNS traffic (for hostname resolution):

```
[edit firewall-filter routing-engine]
set term dns-filter from source-address network-address
set term dns-filter from protocol [ tcp udp ]
set term dns-filter from port domain
set term dns-filter then accept
```

Next, accept RADIUS, SSH, Telnet, and SNMP NMS traffic:

```
[edit firewall-filter routing-engine]
set term radius-filter from source-address radius-server-address1
set term radius-filter from source-address radius-server-address2
set term radius-filter from source-port radius
set term radius-filter then accept
set term ssh-telnet-filter from source-address network-address1
set term ssh-telnet-filter from source-address network-address2
set term ssh-telnet-filter from protocol tcp
set term ssh-telnet-filter from destination-port [ ssh telnet ]
set term ssh-telnet-filter then accept
set term snmp-filter from source-address network-address1
set term snmp-filter from source-address network-address2
set term snmp-filter from protocol udp
set term snmp-filter from destination-port snmp
set term snmp-filter then accept
```

The last traffic to accept is from the NTP time servers and the ICMP protocol (which sends IPv4 error messages):

```
[edit firewall-filter routing-engine]
set term ntp-filter from source-address server-address1
set term ntp-filter from source-address server-address2
set term ntp-filter from source-address 127.0.0.1
set term ntp-filter from protocol udp
set term ntp-filter from port ntp
set term ntp-filter then accept
set term icmp-filter from protocol icmp
set term icmp-filter from icmp-type [ echo-request echo-reply unreachable time-
            exceeded source-quench ]
set term icmp-filter then accept
```

The final part of the filter explicitly discards all other traffic:

```
[edit firewall-filter routing-engine]
set term discard-the-rest then count counter-filename
set term discard-the-rest then log
set term discard-the-rest then syslog
set term discard-the-rest then reject
```

You need to create the file in which to place the syslog messages:

```
[edit system]
fred@router# set syslog file filename firewall any
```

And lastly, apply the firewall filter to the router's loopback interface:

```
[edit interfaces]
fred@router# set lo0 unit 0 family inet filter input routing-engine
```

Securing Routing Protocols

Another way to protect the routing protocols is to enable authentication so that the protocols accept traffic only from routers known to you. This approach ensures that only trusted routers contribute routes to the routing table and hence participate in determining how traffic is routed through your network.

You enable authentication for each routing protocol separately.

Securing RIP

The most secure authentication RIP supports is MD5:

```
[edit protocols]
fred@router# set rip authentication-type md5

[edit protocols]
fred@router# set rip authentication-key key-string
```

MD5 creates an encoded checksum, which is verified by the receiving router before it accepts packets. You must configure the same password on all RIP routers on the network and the same authentication type. (RIP also lets you use a simple, unencrypted password for authentication.)

Securing IS-IS and OSPF

IS-IS supports MD5 and a simple password authentication, which uses a clear-text, unencrypted password. When authentication is enabled, IS-IS validates that all LSPs are received from trusted routers.

Each IS-IS area can have its own encryption method and password. The following commands set encryption in the IS-IS Level 2 area:

```
[edit protocols]
fred@router# set isis level 2 authentication-type md5

[edit protocols]
fred@router# set isis level 2 authentication-key key-string
```

All routers within the same area must have the same authentication key.

Securing OSPF

OSPF also supports MD5 and a simple password authentication. When authentication is enabled, OSPF validates its Hello and LSA protocol packets.

The following command sets the OSPF encryption for an interface in an area, here the backbone area. For OSPF, you must set the encryption on each interface separately:

```
[edit protocols]
fred@router# set ospf area 0.0.0.0 interface interface-name authentication md5 1
            key key-string
```

Routers will be able to form adjacencies only over interfaces with other routers that are configured to use the same authentication key for that network.

Authenticating BGP peers

BGP sessions are often the subject of external attacks on the network because the sessions are visible on the Internet. Enabling the authentication of the BGP packets exchanged by EBGP peers prevents the router from accepting unauthorized packets. For BGP, you also use MD5. Each BGP group can have its own authentication password:

```
[edit protocols]
fred@router# set bgp group group-name authentication-key key-string
```

You can also set individual authentication passwords between each BGP peer in an EBGP session:

```
[edit protocols]
fred@router# set bgp group group-name neighbor address authentication-key key-
            string
```

The neighbor in an EBGP session is often in another AS, so you need to coordinate authentication methods and keys with the administrator of the external AS.

You can also enable authentication between IBGP peer routers. Even if the IBGP peers are all within your administrative domain and you know them to be trusted routers, it may be worth enabling authentication in order to prevent attempts to maliciously spoof these sessions.

Enabling authentication on MPLS signaling protocols

You use a signaling protocol with MPLS — either LDP or RSVP — to allocate and distribute labels throughout an MPLS network. Enabling authentication for these two protocols ensure the security of the MPLS LSPs in the network.

Enabling authentication for LDP protects the TCP connection used for the LDP session against spoofing. JUNOS software uses an MD5 signature for LDP authentication. You configure the same key (password) on both sides of the LDP session:

```
[edit protocols]
fred@router# set ldp session address authentication-key key-string
```

RSVP authentication ensures that RSVP traffic accepted by the router comes from trusted sources. RSVP uses MD5 authentication, and all peers on a common network segment must use the same authentication key (password) in order to communicate with each other:

```
[edit protocols]
fred@router# set rsvp interface interface authentication-key key-string
```

Chapter 10

Setting Up the Switches

In This Chapter

- Getting started with your Juniper EX-series switches
- Racking and connecting switches together
- Configuring VLANs
- Connecting switches to create Virtual Chassis systems
- Using the switch as a router

You may think that routers and switches are the same because you use them to connect to the Internet or to a network in your office or campus. But from a technology point of view, they're different.

Routers, routing protocols, and the Internet Protocol (IP) operate at Layer 3, the network layer, of the OSI protocol stack. They use IP addresses to route traffic, and — for Ethernet networks — to map these addresses to each network device's media access control (MAC) address, which is the Layer 2 hardware address of the device. Switches operate at Layer 2, the data-link layer, of the OSI protocol stack, so they use only the MAC address to forward traffic through the network.

In this chapter, we set up the switch.

Setting Up the Switch

Juniper switches ship in individual shipping crates. The EX 3200 and EX 4200 devices come in cardboard boxes, and the EX 8200 device comes on a wooden pallet.

The EX 3200 and EX 4200 are 1U boxes (about 1.75 inches high), weighing about 22 pounds (10 kilograms) each, so unlike some of the larger Juniper routers, you can unpack and install these switches without forklifts or other mechanical aids.

The EX 8200 models are much larger — the smaller one is about 24 inches high and about 250 pounds, and the larger model is about 38 inches high and about 400 pounds — so to install these switches, you'll need mechanical moving and lifting equipment and a team of three people.

Racking the switch

You can install EX 3200 and 4200 switches in a rack or cabinet, or even on a desk or table. If you're mounting the switches in a rack or cabinet, screw the mounting brackets onto the sides of the switch and then install the switch in the rack or cabinet. If you plan to set the switch on a desk or table, insert the rubber feet into the holes in the bottom of the switch to keep the chassis from sliding on the desk and aid airflow around the device.

You can install the larger EX 8200 only in a rack or cabinet. Attach the mounting brackets and use a mechanical lift to move the switch into the proper position.

The smaller EX 3200 and EX 4200 switches don't have on/off switches. When you plug them in, they start booting. If you need to power down the switch, you have to halt the software and then unplug it. The larger EX 8200 switch has an on/off switch.

Configuring the switch initially

One easy way to initially configure the switch is to use the J-Web GUI interface. After the switch powers up, press the Menu button next to the LCD panel on the front of the box and navigate to the Maintenance Menu. Press Enter and then press the Menu button again until you see Enter EZ Setup. At this point, use an Ethernet cable to connect a PC to port 0 (which is called ge-0/0/0, the first Gigabit Ethernet interface) on the front panel of the switch. Then follow these steps to complete the initial configuration:

1. **From the laptop browser, go to the address 192.168.1.1.**
2. **Log in as the user `root` with no password.**
3. **On the Basic Settings page, set the name of the switch (the hostname), the root password, and the date and time.**
4. **On the Management Options page, use either the default VLAN (called `default`) or create a new VLAN.**

   We talk about VLANs in the section "Segmenting a LAN," later in this chapter.

5. **On the Manage Access page, you can enable Telnet, SSH, and SNMP services on the switch.**
6. **Click Finish to activate the initial configuration on the switch.**

Plugging devices into the switch

The ports for plugging network devices into the switch are on the front of the switch. On the models with copper ports, all the ports are 10/100/1000BASE-T ports, so you use the appropriate Ethernet cables to connect laptops, VoIP phones, wireless access points (WAPs), security cameras, and other network devices to the switch.

If you decided to use the `default` VLAN when you initially configured the switch, all the devices you connect to the switch are placed into this VLAN and can begin transmitting traffic on the network without further configuration of the switch. If you configure a different VLAN, you'll have to configure the switch to add the appropriate ports to that VLAN. We cover this topic in the section "Configuring more VLANs" later in this chapter.

Connecting switches together

When you want to create a Virtual Chassis unit from two or more (up to ten) EX 4200 switches, you normally interconnect them using the dedicated 64-Gbps Virtual Chassis ports (VCPs) on the back of the switch chassis, which are designed exclusively for interconnecting switches (and which require no extra configuration on the switch). You can also interconnect them using the 10-Gbps ports on the uplink module, but then you must configure these ports to be Virtual Chassis Extender Ports (VCEPs).

In the shipping box of each EX 4200, you will find one Virtual Chassis cable for the dedicated 64-Gbps VCPs.

The Virtual Chassis unit you create can be in a single rack or wiring closet, or it can be spread out across different racks or different wiring closets. The only restriction on where you can place the switches is the maximum length of the VCP cable, which is about 10 feet (3 meters).

If you need a longer distance, you must connect the switches by configuring ports on the 10-Gbps uplink module to be VCEPs. You can use both VCPs and VCEPs in a single Virtual Chassis unit, if necessary.

Design the connections between the individual chassis to form a ring topology that ensures that the distance between any two switches in the Virtual Chassis unit is as short as possible. A ring topology configuration provides up to 128 Gbps of bandwidth between member switches, which they use to pass data packets and out-of-band traffic. Figure 10-1 shows a simple ring topology for a Virtual Chassis unit in a single location.

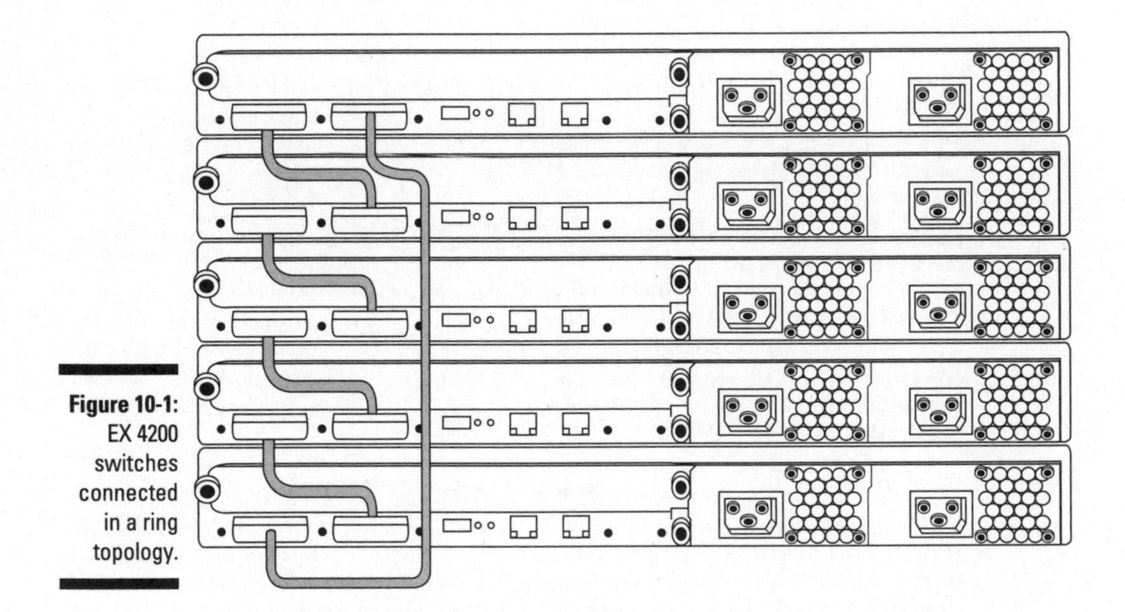

Figure 10-1: EX 4200 switches connected in a ring topology.

When you're connecting member switches that are in adjacent racks or that are in wiring closets scattered across a floor in your building or between floors, a *chain* topology that joins each member switch to the previous and next switch in a line is often easier than trying to loop back to form a ring topology. The maximum bandwidth between member switches in a chain is slower than that in a ring, only 64 Gbps. Additionally, this topology provides no redundancy in case of a switch or link failure in the middle of the chain. For that reason, you should try to form a loop wherever possible. Figure 10-2 illustrates the sample cabling for a chain topology.

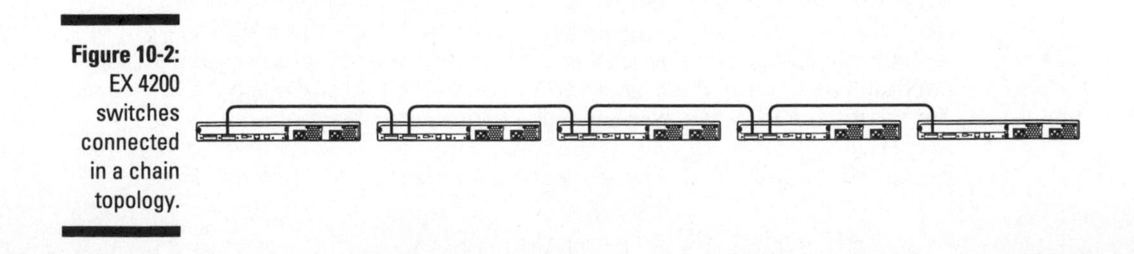

Figure 10-2: EX 4200 switches connected in a chain topology.

Segmenting a LAN

Switches connect devices on Ethernet local-area networks (LANs). Ethernet LANs were originally designed in the 1980s for small, simple networks that primarily carried data traffic. Ethernet design allows devices on the network to transmit traffic at any time. However, the physical cabling between the nodes originally could carry only one stream at a time. All stations on the LAN were connected together and received all traffic that was sent from all endstations. All the receiving devices examined the traffic to see whether it was destined for them. To account for packet collisions that occur with broadcasting, Ethernet uses the carrier-sense multiple access with collection detection (CSMA/CD) protocol to detect frame collisions and to signal each device on the network to retransmit frames that aren't successfully sent the first time because of collisions.

Over the years, Ethernet has become the most commonly used standard for enterprise networks, and these networks are carrying voice, graphics, and video traffic over interfaces that run considerably faster that the original Ethernet. The result is the potential for more and more packet collisions. The IEEE addressed this issue by defining transparent bridging, which is generally just called bridging, in the IEEE 802.1D-2004 standard.

Bridges reduce the chances for collisions by separating the network. Unlike the original Ethernet, where all stations on the Ethernet network received all traffic, bridges (the EX-series switches are a kind of bridge) receive traffic on a port, examine the traffic to determine the appropriate destination, and send the traffic on appropriate ports when able to do so. Bridging means that the *collision domain*, or the number of hosts that can be transmitting at the same time on an Ethernet segment and cause a collision, is reduced to just the single switch port and the devices attached to it. In fact, when just a single host is attached to a single switch port, you no longer need to worry about collisions. In these cases, you can enable *full-duplex* operation, where both sides can transmit simultaneously and ignore collisions.

However, LANs have another concern besides collisions. In some cases, switches can't determine the appropriate ports on which to transmit packets. In these cases, they *flood* packets, sending them on every switch port, to make sure that the traffic reaches its destination. Also, in the case of *broadcast* traffic (traffic intended to reach every host on the network), the switches must send the traffic on every port to ensure that it reaches every host. In this case, the entire LAN is a single broadcast domain. On a normally functioning network, hosts send broadcast traffic for many reasons. Because this broadcast traffic must reach every host in the network, it can produce increasingly large amounts of traffic when the broadcast domain grows. One way to reduce the size of a broadcast domain is to split LANs into smaller

LANs, but this approach normally requires separate equipment for each LAN. Thankfully, there is a better way: VLANs.

Instead of thinking of each network as a single LAN, a bridge can divide a LAN into subsets called virtual LANs, or VLANs. Bridges treat VLANs as if each VLAN was a separate LAN. So, when a switch receives broadcast traffic from a device within a VLAN, it sends the traffic only to those devices in the same VLAN. And, when it needs to flood traffic, it sends it only to other ports in the same VLAN on which the traffic was received. In this way, VLANs significantly reduce the amount of broadcast or flooded traffic that devices on the VLAN see, thus decreasing the amount of bandwidth used for this traffic.

Now, this separation may make you think that devices on different VLANs can't communicate with each other. And, in a sense, that is true, because the devices aren't on the same Layer 2 network, and they can't communicate with each other directly at Layer 2. But, do not fear! Traffic destined for a device outside one VLAN can be forwarded to a different VLAN by a router attached to both VLANs, or by the inter-VLAN routing feature of an EX-series switch. (See the section "Trunking together VLANs," later in this chapter.)

Configuring the default VLAN

On an EX 3200 (or an individual EX 4200 that isn't part of a Virtual Chassis unit), when you power it on, bridging is enabled on all the interfaces (ports) on the switch, and all the ports are part of a preconfigured VLAN named `default`. So for a small office or research lab, all you need to do to get the Juniper switch up and running is to power on the device, perform the initial configuration to give the switch a name and time, set the root password, and then connect your laptops, PCs, WAPs, printers, file servers, and any other devices to the ports on the front of the switch.

The great thing about this setup is that you don't need to open the switch's configuration file to set up anything. The JUNOS software handles everything automatically. You can at some point look in the configuration file to see the results of the automatic configuration. The automatic switching portion of the configuration will look like

```
[edit]
fred@switch# show
[...]
interfaces {
  ge-0/0/0 {
    unit 0 {
      family ethernet-switching;
    }
```

```
  }
  ge-0/0/1 {
    unit 0 {
      family ethernet-switching;
    }
  }
  [...]
}
protocols {
  lldp {
    interface all;
  }
  rstp;
}
poe {
  interface all;
}
```

Look at the configuration to see that the `ge-0/0/1` interface supports bridging. First, the interface is configured with the `ethernet-switching` keyword, which enables the JUNOS Ethernet switch protocol family. Second, the protocols section of the configuration shows that two bridging protocols are enabled, RSTP and LLDP. The switch uses the Link Layer Discovery Protocol (LLDP) to learn which network devices are attached to each port on the switch.

A switch may find multiple paths to another device, or the path that it finds might go in circles, creating a loop. The second protocol, RSTP, is a rapid version of the original Spanning Tree Protocol (STP) that prevents loops in a bridged LAN or within a VLAN. Spanning-tree protocols also determine new paths to devices on the VLAN after the topology in the VLAN changes — for example, when you add or move a laptop or a printer. The convergence times for RSTP are faster than those for STP.

The last protocol in the configuration is Power over Ethernet (PoE), which is enabled on all switch interfaces. This protocol ensures that PoE is enabled on all the ports that support PoE.

Another way to check that the `default` VLAN is configured on the switch is to use the `show vlans` command to list all the VLANs. We have configured only one interface, so the output of this command is short:

```
fred@switch> show vlans
Name           Tag     Interfaces
default
                       ge-0/0/0.0, ge-0/0/1.0, [...]
mgmt
                       me0.0
```

The output shows two VLANs: `default`, which contains the `ge-0/0/1` interface that you have plugged the laptop into, and `mgmt`, which is a switch management interface. The default VLAN has no VLAN ID, or tag, to identify which VLAN packets originated from, so no tag name is listed in the Tag column. (The VLAN IDs, or tags, are used for VLAN trunking using the 802.1q specification, which we discuss in the next section, "Configuring more VLANs.") All packets sent on this VLAN are untagged, which is fine because the network has only one VLAN.

Configuring more VLANs

The basic VLAN configuration that switches set up automatically creates a single VLAN. This setup is fine for a small network, but for anything larger than that, you will want to subdivide your LAN into a number of VLANs.

And when you have more than one VLAN, the switch needs a way to distinguish which packets originate where. To do so, each VLAN must have a unique name and a numeric tag, called a VLAN ID. Also, because each VLAN is a separate broadcast domain, any given IP subnet should usually not span VLANs.

As a simple example, look at two printers connected to the same switch, one in the physics department and the other in chemistry. First, you need to configure the ports that the printers are plugged in to, namely `ge-0/0/1` and `ge-0/0/2` (the second and third ports on the front of the switch) and associate the interfaces with the VLANs you're about to create:

```
[edit interfaces]
fred@switch# set ge-0/0/1 unit 0 family ethernet-switching vlan members physics

[edit interfaces]
fred@switch# set ge-0/0/2 unit 0 family ethernet-switching vlan members
             chemistry
```

Some people prefer an interface-centric approach to VLAN configuration, where you configure all the VLAN membership information in the interface configuration. Others prefer a VLAN-centric approach to VLAN configuration, where you configure all the VLAN membership information in the VLAN configuration. Fortunately, JUNOS offers a CLI syntax that supports both approaches.

Two strategies for architecting VLANs

The following are two common ways to design VLANs:

- **Group devices by type.** In this architecture, each VLAN contains only one type of network device, meaning you have one (or more) VLAN for printers, another one for office PCs and laptops, a third one for WAPs, a fourth one for VoIP telephones, another for IP security cameras, and so on. The advantage of this design is that the VLAN carries the same type of traffic, so less contention for bandwidth occurs between applications that use a lot of bandwidth, such as security cameras and computers simply sending e-mail to each.
- **Group devices by organizational structure.** This architecture segments network devices according to the organizational boundaries of your company or enterprise. For example, at a university, you can create separate VLANs for the physics, chemistry, and computer science departments when each department is responsible for procuring and maintaining their own network equipment.

The preceding example illustrates the interface-centric approach, which is the approach we will continue to demonstrate. If you instead want to use the VLAN-centric approach, you need to configure the `ge-0/0/1.0` and `ge-0/0/2.0` interfaces for `family ethernet-switching` (which is included in the factory-default configuration):

```
[edit interfaces]
fred@switch# set ge-0/0/1 unit 0 family ethernet-switching

[edit interfaces]
fred@switch# set ge-0/0/2 unit 0 family ethernet-switching
```

Then, you configure the VLAN membership under the VLAN configuration:

```
[edit vlans]
fred@switch# set physics interface ge-0/0/1.0

[edit vlans]
fred@switch# set chemistry interface ge-0/0/2.
```

Now, say that you want the EX-series switch to route traffic between these two VLANs. To do so, you must configure two VLAN Layer 3 interfaces and assign IP addresses for each VLAN interface:

```
[edit interfaces vlan]
fred@switch# set unit 100 family inet address 192.0.2.1/25

[edit interfaces vlan]
fred@switch# set unit 200 family inet address 192.0.2.129/25
```

Now define the VLAN ID so that all packets transmitted from the physics department are marked with the VLAN ID (or tag) 100 when the switch is performing VLAN trunking, while the chemistry packets are tagged with VLAN ID 200:

```
[edit vlans]
fred@switch# set physics vlan-id 100

[edit vlans]
fred@switch# set chemistry vlan-id 200
```

The final step is to associate the Layer 3 interface that you created with the two VLANs:

```
[edit vlans]
fred@switch# set physics l3-interface vlan.100

[edit vlans]
fred@switch# set chemistry l3-interface vlan.200
```

In these two statements, the last keyword (`vlan.100` and `vlan.200`) establishes the connection between Layer 3 routing and a VLAN, which performs Layer 2 switching. In assigning the IP addresses, we use two different logical units, or logical interfaces, for the VLAN. For physics, we use the command `set unit 100...` to create vlan.100, so unit 100 is the logical interface we specify as the physics department Layer 3 interface. For chemistry, we use `set unit 200...` to create vlan.200, so we specify vlan.200 as the logical interface. In this case, we have chosen to use the same numbers for the units and the VLAN IDs; however, you aren't required to do so.

In the JUNOS software, you can use `<interface>.<unit>` to refer to a particular unit on a physical interface. So, `ge-0/0/1 unit 0` is `ge-0/0/1.0`, and `vlan unit 10` is `vlan.10`. When you reference an interface elsewhere in the configuration, you almost always need to specify unit numbers. If you forget, the CLI usually will assume that you meant to specify unit 0, which can save you time — if it's the right choice!

Trunking together VLANs

Access ports are simply ports that connect to network devices. By default, all switch ports are in access mode, so you don't need to specify this mode in the configuration. When you connect one switch to another, or to a router, they are usually connected with trunk ports. On trunk ports, the devices add a short header to each Ethernet frame, which includes the VLAN ID. The receiving device reads the VLAN ID and puts the traffic into the correct

VLAN. This information in the header lets the two devices exchange traffic for multiple VLANs, while keeping all the data straight.

You convert a port into a trunk port simply by configuring it to be a trunk port. Although you can make any port a trunk port, you generally connect switches together using the uplink ports, which are numbered starting at `ge-0/1/0` or `xe-0/1/0`. (Depending on the uplink module, it will have either two or four ports.)

Suppose that the physics and chemistry departments have two separate switches and that you have connected them by plugging in a cable to `ge-0/1/0` on the physics side and to `ge-0/1/1` on the chemistry side. Here's how you configure the trunk port on the physics switch:

```
[edit interfaces]
fred@physics# set ge-0/1/0 unit 0 family ethernet-switching port-mode trunk

[edit interfaces]
fred@physics# set ge-0/1/0 unit 0 family ethernet-switching vlan members
              [ physics chemistry ]
```

The configuration on the chemistry switch is similar:

```
[edit interfaces]
fred@chemistry# set ge-0/1/1 unit 0 family ethernet-switching port-mode trunk
fred@chemistry# set ge-0/1/1 unit 0 family ethernet-switching vlan members
              [ physics chemistry ]
```

The remaining switch configuration is similar to what we describe in the previous section.

Controlling access to VLANs

The VLAN configuration described in the preceding sections of this chapter set up the network so that anyone who can plug their computer into the switch or who can get on the wireless network through your WAPs can use your network. To limit network use only to valid users, whether employees, department or group members, or anyone else, you need to set up network admission control (NAC) policies on the switches. Admission control allows you to strictly control who can access the network, preventing unauthorized users from logging in and enforcing policies for network access (such as ensuring authorized users have the latest antivirus software and operating system patches installed on their PCs and laptops).

JUNOS software on EX-series switches can use the IEEE 802.1X protocol (often just called dot-one-ex) to provide authentication of all devices when they initially connect to your LAN. The actual authentication is done by separate software or a separate server, generally a RADIUS authentication server that is connected to one of the switches on your LAN. When you have configured the EX-series switch to use 802.1X and a network device of any type attempts to connect to the LAN, it kicks off the following authentication process on the switch:

1. **When the switch detects that a device has connected to the LAN, the switch puts on its authenticator hat and blocks all traffic to and from the network device, which at this point is an unauthenticated device.**
2. **When the client indicates it would like to start 802.1X authentication, the switch asks for the client's identity and then sends an access request message to the RADIUS server, asking the server to verify whether the network device is allowed to access the LAN.**
3. **If the RADIUS server sends an access challenge to the switch, the switch sends an access challenge to the network device, asking for a password to connect to the network.**
4. **When the network device responds, the switch forwards this password to the RADIUS server.**
5. **If the RADIUS server accepts the response, it sends a message to the switch telling it to allow the user and, optionally, assigning certain parameters (such as VLAN assignment or firewall filters) that the switch should use for this client.**

   The device is then allowed to send and receive traffic on the LAN.

   If the RADIUS server rejects the access request or the user enters an invalid password, the network device remains unauthenticated and is denied access to the LAN.
6. **When the network device disconnects from the LAN, the switch moves the port into an unauthorized state in which all traffic to and from that port is again blocked.**

To set up admission control on the switch:

1. **Configure the address of the RADIUS servers, along with a password that the RADIUS server uses to validate requests from the switch.**

   This example uses the address 192.168.1.2:

   ```
   [edit access]
   fred@switch# set radius-server 192.168.1.2 secret my-password
   ```

   The `secret` keyword in this command configures the password that the switch uses to access the RADIUS server.

In case the switch has several interfaces that can reach the RADIUS server, you can assign an IP address that the switch can use for all its communication with the RADIUS server. In this example, you choose the address 192.168.0.1:

```
[edit access]
fred@switch# set radius-server 192.168.1.2 source-address 192.168.0.1
```

2. **Set up an authentication profile to be used by 802.1X:**

```
[edit access]
fred@switch# set profile my-profile authentication-order radius

[edit access]
fred@switch# set profile my-profile radius authentication-server
        192.168.1.2
```

The first command requires the switch to contact a RADIUS server when sending authentication messages. (The other available options are LDAP servers or local password authentication.) The second command shows the address of the authentication server (which you just configured in the previous step).

3. **Configure the 802.1X protocol itself, specifying the access permissions on the switch interfaces.**

You can do this interface by interface, as in

```
[edit protocols]
fred@switch# set dot1x authenticator authentication-profile-name my-profile
        interface ge-0/0/1.0

[edit protocols]
fred@switch# set dot1x authenticator authentication-profile-name my-profile
        interface ge-0/0/2.0 supplicant single-secure
```

The `authentication-profile-name` statement associates the authentication profile established in the previous step with this interface.

Note that you specify the logical interface name (ge-0/0/1.0), not the physical interface name (ge-0/0/1).

In Step 3, the keyword `supplicant` (which is the 802.1X term for a network device seeking authentication on a network port — in other words, the 802.1X client) defines the administrative mode for authentication on the LAN:

- **Single mode:** Authenticates only the first device that connects to the switch port and allows access to any devices that later connect to the same port without further authentication. When the first authenticated device logs out, all other devices are locked out of the LAN. This mode is the default, so you don't need to include it in the configuration.

- **Single-secure mode:** Authenticates only one network device per port. In this mode, additional devices that later connect to the same port are not allowed to send or receive traffic, nor are they allowed to authenticate.
- **Multiple:** Authenticates each device that connects to the switch port individually. In this mode, additional devices that later connect to the same port are allowed to authenticate and, if successful, to send and receive traffic.

When using single mode, only the first device is authenticated, and this configuration can be considered to be a security hole. If you foresee problems, use the single-secure or multiple mode.

If the authentication mode is the same on all switch ports, you can configure 802.1X parameters to apply to all interfaces by using the keyword `all` instead of an interface name:

```
[edit protocols]
fred@switch# set dot1x authenticator interface all
```

Interconnecting Switches

When you create a Virtual Chassis unit with interconnected EX 4200 switches, it creates a single unit that you can manage as if it were a single chassis. One switch member in the virtual chassis is the primary or master switch, and a second member is a backup that provides redundancy if the master member fails for some reason. The forwarding (and routing) tables remain synchronized with those of the master member. If a failover to the backup occurs, this member switch can immediately step in to continue the forwarding of traffic on the LAN.

Going virtual

As a basic example to illustrate interconnecting switches, consider a Virtual Chassis configuration where two EX 4200 switches are interconnected.

If you use the default configuration, you connect the two switches with the dedicated 64-Gbps Virtual Chassis ports (VCPs) on the rear panel of the switch and power on the switches, and the virtual chassis is operational. Connect each of the two VCPs on the chassis member to a VCP on the other member. You don't have to configure these ports.

After you power on the two switches in the Virtual Chassis unit, the JUNOS software picks one of them to be the master (the other becomes the backup) and assigns member IDs to each one. You can see this information on the switch's LCD display, which is on the front panel. The master will show `Member ID: 0, Role: Master`, and the backup will show `Member ID:1, Role Backup`.

If you want a particular switch to be the master, power it on first.

Another way to check the master-backup assignment is to view the status of the Virtual Chassis unit:

```
fred@switch> show virtual-chassis status

Virtual Chassis ID: 0019.e250.47a0
                                              Mastership            Neighbor List
Member ID  Status  Serial No    Model         priority    Role      ID  Interface
0 (FPC 0)  Prsnt   AK0207360276 ex4200-48p         128    Master*    1  vcp-0
                                                                     1  vcp-1
1 (FPC 1)  Prsnt   AK0207360281 ex4200-24t         128    Backup     0  vcp-0
                                                                     0  vcp-1

Member ID for next new member: 4 (FPC 4)
```

The `Mastership priority` column shows that both members have an equal chance of being elected as the master. In this case, member 0 is the master because it was powered on first. Also check that the dedicated VCPs are up and running:

```
fred@switch> show virtual-chassis vc-port all-members
fpc0:
--------------------------------------------------------------------------
Interface          Type              Status
or
PIC / Port
vcp-0              Dedicated         Up
vcp-1              Dedicated         Up

fpc1:
--------------------------------------------------------------------------
Interface          Type              Status
or
PIC / Port
vcp-0              Dedicated         Up
vcp-1              Dedicated         Up
```

The JUNOS software treats each switch in a Virtual Chassis unit as if it were a FPC in the slot of an M-series router chassis. So, the software calls the first member switch fpc0, and it calls the second switch fpc1.

As your network expands, you add another member to the Virtual Chassis unit. Start by cabling the VCPs on the rear of the third chassis, as shown in Figure 10-3. But do not power on this switch yet.

To ensure that the first switch remains the master when you add the new member so as not to disrupt the flow of traffic through the Virtual Chassis unit and to have the second switch to remain the backup, you need to configure the mastership priority. You configure the mastership priorities on the existing Virtual Chassis unit. To configure the first switch to be the master, the command is

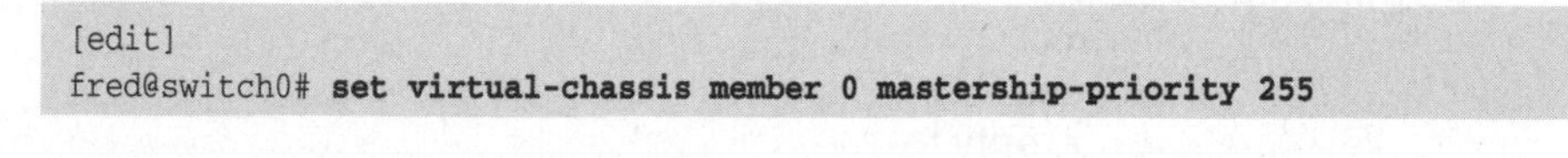

```
[edit]
fred@switch0# set virtual-chassis member 0 mastership-priority 255
```

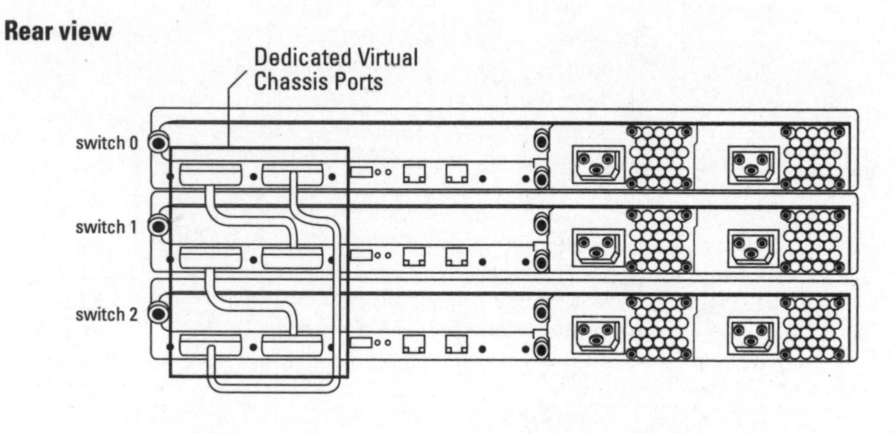

Front view

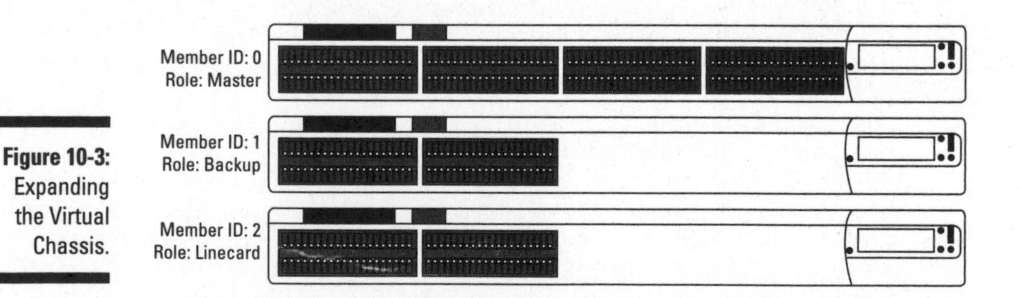

Figure 10-3: Expanding the Virtual Chassis.

You use the highest possible value for mastership priority to ensure that this switch continues to function as the master. Configure the second switch with the same priority so that it remains first in line to become the master:

```
[edit]
fred@switch0# set virtual-chassis member 1 mastership-priority 255
```

Note that this configuration will produce nondeterministic results on boot-up. It is possible that the second switch will become master if it boots first when the Virtual Chassis unit reboots. If you want switch 0 to always be master when it is available, you can set switch 0 to have a slightly higher priority than switch 1, but for both to have a higher priority than the default (128). In this case, switch 0 will assume the master role anytime it's available, even if switch 1 is already functioning as master and hasn't failed. (This behavior is commonly called *preemption.*) The one downside to this behavior is in a failure scenario: If switch 0 is continually rebooting, it will continue to become master, only to reboot a minute later. That's not so good! We recommend that you use the same mastership priority for master and backup.

When you commit any configuration changes to the Virtual Chassis unit (whether interface configuration, protocol configuration, or even Virtual Chassis configuration), use the `commit synchronize` command rather than the plain `commit` command. This command ensures that configuration changes are saved on both the master and backup switches.

Now you can power on the new third switch. You don't need to perform any configuration on this switch, and the expanded Virtual Chassis unit is ready to use.

Virtual chassis, real redundancy

Because each switch member in an EX 4200 Virtual Chassis unit has its own Routing Engine (RE), the Virtual Chassis unit has inherent redundancy. The configuration discussed throughout this chapter provides redundant failover. In addition, you can configure Graceful Routing Engine Switchover (GRES). Before explaining the difference between these two types of redundancy, we need to look at how the switch's REs work.

In a Virtual Chassis unit, the master member acts as the master RE, running the routing protocols, providing the forwarding table that the PFEs on all the member switches of the Virtual Chassis unit use to forward traffic on the LAN, and running management and control processes for the entire Virtual Chassis unit. When you issue a `commit synchronize` command, the master RE sends the new configuration to the backup RE to ensure the configuration is synchronized; however, the backup RE does not actively run routing protocols or keep state with the master RE.

With redundant failover, when the master member fails, the backup RE assumes mastership and begins acting like the master RE (running routing protocols, building forwarding tables, and so on). Because the two REs haven't been exchanging data, this change is rather traumatic for the PFEs.

Imagine being in the middle of intensely reviewing a spreadsheet and suddenly having all the numbers change on you! For this reason, the PFEs on all the member switches in the virtual chassis re-initialize their state to the boot-up state before connecting to the new RE. After they reboot, everything is better, and they begin talking to the new RE.

Graceful Routing Engine Switchover (GRES) allows the transition to the new master RE to occur with minimal interruption in network traffic. When you configure GRES, the master and backup REs synchronize certain control information. This synchronization allows the PFEs to seamlessly switch from one RE to another. The PFEs never re-initialize their state to the boot-up state, preventing a forwarding outage.

Configuring GRES requires a single command:

```
[edit]
fred@switch# set chassis redundancy graceful-switchover
```

Even though the switchover may be fairly seamless for the PFEs, the new master RE still needs to restart the sessions with all its routing protocol peers. By default, the switchover will cause a forwarding outage while the old sessions are torn down and the new sessions are established. For this reason, on switches that perform Layer 3 routing, you'll likely want to combine GRES with graceful restart, which allows Layer 3 forwarding to continue with the existing routing information while the new master RE starts sessions with routing protocol peers and builds routing and forwarding tables. Once the new master RE has completed building new routing and forwarding tables, it sends updates to the PFEs. These updates prevent an outage while the new master RE gets up to speed. You configure graceful restart with this command:

```
[edit]
fred@switch# set routing-options graceful-restart
```

For graceful restart to work correctly, the routing protocol peers of the switch must support graceful restart in *helper mode*. Just like it sounds, devices that support graceful restart in helper mode will help peers that have failed and want to perform a graceful switchover. These devices will maintain routes for a failed switch while the backup RE is taking over, resend all routing information to the new RE, and receive new routing information from the new RE. Once the restart is complete, the helper device will compare the routes it has received from the new RE with the routes it had received from the former master RE. If it finds differences, only then will it update its routing table. Helper mode allows the network to keep forwarding traffic with the routing and forwarding tables that existed at the time of the switchover until the new RE has had a chance to build all its routing protocol adjacencies and exchange routes with them.

Thankfully, by default, all routers running the JUNOS software support graceful restart helper mode for all protocols except BGP. So, if you use only Juniper Networks routers and don't run BGP, you don't need to do anything else. You can configure the JUNOS software to support graceful restart for BGP simply by configuring graceful restart on the device. If you use another vendor's routers, you will need to check their documentation to determine how to enable their devices to run graceful restart for particular protocols.

Using the Switch as a Router

EX series switches support many of the standard JUNOS routing protocols, including static routing, RIP, OSPF, IS-IS, and BGP, as well as additional features such as VRRP (see Chapters 7 and 8). To enable inter-VLAN communication, you configure a Layer 3 (routing) logical interface on the switch for each VLAN, as discussed in the section "Configuring more VLANs." The switch treats these just like any other interface, so you can route traffic to and from VLANs through these interfaces.

The switch maintains routing tables to compile information learned from the routing protocols and from other routing information sources. The switch creates the same routing tables (and forwarding tables) and uses them in the same way as JUNOS routers do (see Chapter 8).

Connecting to the Internet

In a small LAN that has a single connection to the Internet, an easy way to connect to your service provider's edge router is to configure a static route from the switch to the router. The static route configuration is straightforward, and the route remains in the switch's routing table until you remove it or until, for some reason, it becomes inactive.

You need just a few commands to configure the static route. First, set the IP address on the switch interface that connects to the service provider:

```
[edit interfaces]
fred@switch# set ge-0/0/10 unit 0 family inet address 192.168.0.2/30
```

As you can see in this example, you can configure any interface on an EX-series switch to be a Layer 3 routed interface instead of a switch interface. You configure the interface to be a Layer 3 interface by configuring a Layer 3 `family` statement on the interface. Of course, if you do so, you can't also configure the `family ethernet-switching` statement on the same interface.

That configuration would be very confusing — like telling your convertible car to have its top down and up at the same time — so the JUNOS software won't let you do that.

Then create a default route (a route with the address 0.0.0.0) to that switch interface:

```
[edit routing-options]
fred@switch# set static route 0.0.0.0/0 next-hop 192.168.0.1
```

Connecting to a router in your LAN

In larger networks, switches can perform different functions. Everything we describe in this chapter is for access switches, which are the switches that connect end user network devices, such as computers and printers, to the LAN. But large LANs can have dozens of switches that need to connect to the LAN core or to WAN edge layer switches. The switches at the LAN core or WAN edge are called *aggregation,* or *distribution, switches*. (In some cases, the network is large enough that the distribution switches need to be connected together at another layer of aggregation. In those cases, you might use *core switches* to aggregate the distribution switches together.)

You may need to configure a distribution switch if, for example, you move traffic between a number of different switches within your organization. The switches can be in the same building, or they may be geographically dispersed across a campus, city, country, or even around the world. The switches can communicate using the bridging, spanning tree, and other mechanisms.

Or you may need to move traffic between your network and the Internet. In this case, your distribution switches link to routers that in turn connect to the Internet. The switch interfaces that connect to the routers usually communicate either with a single Layer 3 interface or with a single Layer 2 interface with VLAN trunking enabled. If you choose to use a Layer 3 interface, you need to get routing information on the switches by either configuring static routes or using a dynamic routing protocol (such as OSPF or IS-IS). If you choose to configure routing protocols on the switch, you do so in the same way as you do on a JUNOS software router. (See Chapter 7 and Chapter 8, as well as those chapters in Part III that are applicable to your network.)

Part III

Deploying JUNOS

"It appears a server in Atlanta is about to go down, there's printer backup in Baltimore, and an accountant in Chicago is about to make level 3 of the game 'Tomb Pirate.'"

In this part . . .

In this part, you roll up your sleeves and get into the heart of the beast — JUNOS software in action. No matter the size of your responsibilities, the breadth of your domain, or the number of devices you operate, getting it all ticking like clockwork is just a matter of understanding how the whole network operates.

In this part, we show you how to set up the functionality your network requires, from remote management, interfaces, peering, policy, and class-of-service to MPLS and VPNs.

Chapter 11

Managing Remotely

In This Chapter

- Knowing the interfaces to manage the router
- Using the router
- Monitoring the router

Once you get your network up and running, you probably want to leave the lab and enjoy some time away from the wiring closets and fan noise. To safely leave your routers running, you have to be able to access and manage them remotely. This chapter describes how you access the routers, explaining everything from the physical interface that you use through the different monitoring tools that make it easy to monitor your router remotely.

Choosing an Interface

The most basic requirement of managing your router without having to physically be next to the router is having an interface through which you can communicate. So the question is, "Which interface do you want to use?"

Well, maybe the better question is, "Which interface *can* you use?" You have a couple of choices here depending on how you want to manage your network. And, of course, you have different options depending on your management requirements and the type of router you have. These choices boil down to two important questions:

- Do you want to use your network-facing interfaces or a specialized management interface?
- Do you need to access the router with root permissions?

The most basic decision you need to make when looking at how to remotely manage your router is whether you want that management to be out-of-band or in-band. So what's the difference?

- **Out-of-band management** identifies remote management through a network that is separate from the traffic-carrying network on which the router is deployed. Put simply, out-of-band management uses an interface that carries only management traffic, while the other interfaces on the router carry LAN/WAN traffic.
- **In-band management** is remote management where one of the LAN/WAN interfaces is used to manage the router. That is to say that you use the network to carry both network traffic and management traffic across the same links.

So which one is better? It depends. Generally speaking, most JUNOS administrators find it safer and more reliable to separate the traffic-bearing network from the management network, because when you have network issues, you want to guarantee access to your routers. Using the troubled network to resolve those issues makes you vulnerable. If you can't access the router during these times, your ability to remotely troubleshoot — and ultimately resolve — problems can be compromised.

The ports on a router are prime real estate. Using up one of those ports to handle management traffic reduces the ports available for network traffic. A router with only a few ports or one whose ports are all in use can become an issue.

The reason to use in-band management is a budget issue, because the benefits of an out-of-band management network don't come without a corresponding cost. It's expensive (sometimes prohibitively so) to have a separate network infrastructure to handle only management traffic. Such a management network requires the deployment of terminal servers and switches to pass management traffic, and those devices incur their own set of support costs both in terms of dollars and manpower.

The decision between out-of-band and in-band management is really one of cost: Do you have the resources to set up and maintain a separate management network? If you do, we recommend using the out-of-band approach to remote management. If you don't, in-band is the only other option.

Once you have made the decision about your remote management interface direction, you need to wire up your router and then configure the management interface.

Setting Up Out-of-Band Management

Out-of-band management is handled through special management interfaces on Juniper Networks routers. These interfaces are Fast Ethernet interfaces located on the front of all Juniper Networks routers. They're designed so that traffic that arrives on these interfaces does not get routed on other network interfaces on the router. This setup provides a separation of management traffic and network traffic.

To connect your out-of-band interface to your management network, follow these steps:

1. **Connect an Ethernet cable from your router's out-of-band interface to your management network (typically a switch in this case).**
2. **When your link lights are up, configure the IP address.**

   The out-of-band management interfaces on Juniper Networks routers are named fxp0 on M-, MX-, and T-series routers. On these product lines, the interface settings are configured under the interface name fxp0.

   On J-series routers, the management interfaces are named fe-0/0/0. Interface settings are configured under either fxp0 or fe-0/0/0. However, the router architecturally recognizes the J-series management interface as fe-0/0/0 and uses that name when reporting any interface information via operational commands. Therefore, using the fxp0 name when configuring J-series management interfaces is confusing; instead, use the fe-0/0/0 name.
3. **To configure the management interface, simply set the IP address on the interface:**

```
interfaces {
    fxp0 {
        unit 0 {
            family inet {
                address 192.168.71.246/21;
            }
        }
    }
}
```

Setting Up In-Band Management

For in-band management, you must first decide which interface you want as your management interface. Generally, management traffic is not excessive, so picking any of the slower interfaces on your router is likely to be enough. On most routers, a Fast Ethernet connection is more than sufficient to handle management traffic. On lower end routers, you might choose a serial interface or T1/E1 interface.

Connecting the interface is identical to connecting any other interface on the router.

1. **Connect the cable to the port and ensure that the remote connection is in place.**

   Once the link lights come up, you're ready to configure the interface.

   Some interfaces, such as serial interfaces, require some minimal configuration before the link is active. For such interfaces, you must configure the interface as you would with any other interface *before* the link lights will go on.

2. **After wiring up the management interface, configure the interface so that it has at least an IP address.**

   Typically, this configuration is enough to enable the interface:

```
interfaces {
    fe-0/1/0 {
        unit 0 {
            family inet {
                address 192.168.71.246/21;
            }
        }
    }
}
```

When you configure an in-band management interface, you need to be aware of how you have configured routing protocols and routing policies on your router.

Generally speaking, you don't want to enable protocols on the management interface because you want to prevent other routers from establishing adjacencies with your management interface. Ensure that any protocols configured on the router (especially those enabled using the `interface all` configuration statement) aren't active on the management interface. To disable a protocol on the management interface, use the `disable` statement:

```
[edit protocols]
user@Router# set ospf interface fe-0/1/0 disable

[edit protocols]
user@Router# show

ospf {
    interface all;
    interface fe-0/1/0.0 {
        disable;
    }
}
```

In this example, the OSPF protocol has been enabled on all interfaces on the router. The `disable` statement ensures that OSPF doesn't run on the management interface (`fe-0/1/0` in this case).

Similarly, route policies should not advertise management interface addresses to peering networks, which you can do by explicitly filtering management addresses using a route filter or by carefully constructing routing policies to ensure that routes are not leaked. For more information about routing policies and filtering routes, see Chapter 13.

Accessing Your Router

When attending a rock music concert, getting a backstage pass is the only way to be able to see or do anything really cool. You're with the band and not the traffic in the stands. Of course, you still have varying levels of access, depending on how good your pass is: You're with the band, you can only see the band from the backstage, you're tossed in with the groupies, and so on.

The following sections explore the kind of passes routers have and how close you can get to them.

Tel(net)

The most basic way of accessing a router is using Telnet. After you have configured an IP address on the management interface (whether that interface is out-of-band or in-band), you can access the router by opening up a telnet session to that address. For example, if you configure your router with a management interface address of 192.168.71.246, you should be able to access the router with the telnet session:

```
> telnet 192.168.71.246
Trying 192.168.71.246...
telnet: connect to address 192.168.71.246: Connection
          refused
telnet: Unable to connect to remote host
```

Oops, what went wrong? Access to the router must be explicitly configured on the router. And more specifically, particular modes of access must be explicitly enabled. In this case, you're trying to access the router using telnet, so you must tell the router to allow telnet connections. To configure the telnet service on the router:

```
 [edit]
system {
    services {
        telnet;
    }
}
```

Once telnet services are enabled on the router, the telnet request is successful:

```
> telnet 192.168.71.246
Trying 192.168.71.246...
Connected to router.domain.net.
Escape character is '^]'.

allspice (ttyp0)

login:
```

When your telnet session is established, access is then based on user authentication. The exact authentication mechanism is based on your configuration. (See Chapter 7 for information on setting up user names and authentication.)

Root access to the router is restricted to only those connections that are made via the console (indicating physical access to the router) or via an encrypted session (such as SSH or HTTPS). If you try to log in with the root user name, your login will fail regardless of the password you enter. If you must use telnet to access the router and you must have root access, try setting up a user ID with super-user privileges. (See Chapter 7 for details.)

SSH

While Telnet is the old-school original article and it may hold a fond place in your heart when it comes to accessing devices, it can be fairly insecure. Traffic exchanged via a telnet session isn't encrypted, and no safeguards ensure that traffic being sent across a telnet session is received by the end device and not intercepted somewhere between you and the machine you're accessing. Unfortunately, this setup makes it fairly simple to sniff the traffic and steal logins and passwords.

To be more protective with your login credentials, you want to use *Secure Shell* (SSH). SSH differs from telnet in that it enables the exchange of data between you and your router over a secure channel. Just as with telnet, you must explicitly enable the encrypted SSH service on the router:

```
[edit]
system {
    services {
        ssh;
        telnet;
    }
}
```

Once you have enabled SSH on the router, you can access the router through an encrypted session. And because this session is encrypted, you can now log in to the router remotely using the root login:

```
> ssh -l root router
root@router's password:

--- JUNOS 9.0I (JUNIPER) #3: 2007-11-30 02:18:17 UTC
root@router%
```

When you log into the router as `root`, you log in directly to the FreeBSD shell. To start the CLI, issue the cli command.

A fairly simple way to help strengthen your router against attack is to limit the number of access sessions that can be attempted per minute. If you imagine an automated script trying thousands, or even millions, of login/password combinations, you can see how a hacker might try to gain access to your box. Use the `rate-limit` statement to limit the number of tries to something reasonable:

```
[edit]
system {
    services {
        ssh {
            rate-limit 15;
        }
        telnet {
            rate-limit 15;
        }
    }
}
```

Monitoring a Router Using System Logging

Gaining access to the router box is essential for remote management, and it allows you to issue diagnostic commands to monitor the health and state of the router. However, monitoring even a single box in real-time using interactive commands is impossible. To monitor a router, and, by extension, your network, you have to be able to generate router messages that you can either act on, or use for historical data, without having to be actively on the router.

JUNOS software supports extensive system logging capabilities, as well as tracing functionality, to make watching over your network easier.

JUNOS software generates system messages (known as *syslog messages*) when system events occur. A *system event* can be anything from a user logging on the router, to a particular command being issued, or to a process on the router failing and restarting. These syslog messages are constantly being generated and are either saved or processed by the router, providing you with both the real-time and historical data you need to remotely monitor your network.

Delving into syslog messages

The most important aspect of logging is understanding what gets logged and when. Events across the entire system, covering both hardware and software conditions, have been included in the JUNOS software syslog repertoire:

- Every time the router is accessed, queried, or modified
- Every time a process starts, fails, or restarts
- Every physical threshold that is reached (temperature within the chassis, CPU utilization, fan speed, and so on)
- Various system conditions that affect or reflect the operation of the router

These events have been divided into different categories, called *syslog facilities.* Each of these facilities has been assigned a facility code, which ties a particular message to the syslog facility. Table 11-1 lists the JUNOS syslog facilities along with their corresponding facility code.

Table 11-1 JUNOS Syslog Facilities

Syslog Facility	*Facility Code*	*Event Source*
any	None	Any facility
authorization	AUTH, AUTHPRIV	Authentication and authorization attempts
change-log	CHANGE	Configuration changes on the router
conflict-log	CONFLICT	Configuration changes that are in conflict with the router's hardware
	CONSOLE	Kernel messages to the console
	CRON	Scheduled processes
daemon	DAEMON	Individual JUNOS software processes
firewall	FIREWALL	Packet filtering performed by fire-wall filters
ftp	FTP	FTP activities
interactive-commands	INTERACT	Commands executed from the CLI or through the XML API
kernel	KERNEL	JUNOS kernel
	NTP	Network Time Protocol process
pfe	PFE	Packet forwarding engine
	SYSLOG	System logging
user	USER	User processes

Each of these syslog facilities contains many different syslog events. To help differentiate between these events, in addition to the facility, each event is assigned a severity level. Table 11-2 lists the syslog severities. (We in the industry tend to list the worst severity last, because we never want to see them!)

Table 11-2 JUNOS Syslog Severities

Severity Name	*Severity Number*	*Severity Description*
any	None	All severity levels
none	None	No severity levels
debug	7	Information to be used for debugging

(continued)

Table 11-2 (continued)

Severity Name	*Severity Number*	*Severity Description*
info	6	Informational events about normal operations
notice	5	Conditions that aren't errors but are of more interest than normal operations
warning	4	General warnings for significant events
error	3	General errors
critical	2	Critical errors, including hardware failures
alert	1	Errors that require immediate intervention
emergency	0	Conditions that stop router function

All syslog messages contain both the facility and the severity. When searching through the hundreds, or even thousands, of log messages, you can match on these two values so that you can quickly identify the information you need when monitoring your network.

Here's what a syslog event, looks like:

```
Nov  2 19:02:49  router mgd[8039]: UI_LOAD_EVENT: User 'michael' is performing a
                 'rollback 2'
```

And here are the several key pieces of information of what this syslog event contains:

- **Timestamp:** The system time at which the event occurred. In this example, the event took place at 7:02pm on November 2.
- **Router name**: The configured name of the router. In this example, the router is creatively named `router`.
- **Process information:** The name of the process that generated the syslog event, including the process ID to uniquely identify the particular instance of the process. In this example, the MGD process created the event. Specifically, it was the MGD instance with process ID 8039.
- **Syslog message:** The syslog message, including the event name and relevant information to the event. In this example, the user `michael` has issued a `rollback 2` command on the router.

The timestamp associated with each syslog message does not indicate the time zone in which the router resides. If you have multiple routers across more than one time zone, you must remember the time zone each router is in. Imagine a situation where traffic between Los Angeles and Denver is interrupted at 1pm PST. For you to effectively sift through the syslog messages, you must know the system time on each router when the events would have been logged. And, in this case, the system times would be different, so you would have to know to look at 1 p.m. on the Los Angeles router and 2 p.m. on the Denver router. To simplify this kind of log perusal, configure the system time on each router using coordinated Universal Time Clock (UTC). If all the routers are configured within the same time zone, all the timestamps will show the same time, making your life much simpler when it comes to wading through log files. (See Chapter 7 to set your time and time zone.)

You can send syslog messages to a number of places. You can view them in real time by sending them to a console session. You can store them in files on the router so that you can look through them later. You can even store all the syslog messages from all your routers on a single syslog server so that you can go to a single place to monitor your network. How you configure your router determines which method you use.

Mood music: Turning on logging

To activate logging on the router, you must configure what you want logged and where you want to log it. You have to specify both the types of messages as well as where you want those messages to be sent.

The most common, and simplest, form of logging writes individual syslog messages to one or more log files stored locally on the router. Imagine that you want to log every interesting condition, regardless of the specific facility, as well as all user login activity on the box, and you want to store those messages in a file called `messages`. Turn on this logging by configuring system logs under the `[edit system]` configuration hierarchy:

```
[edit system]
syslog {
    file messages {
        any notice;
        authorization info;
    }
}
```

In this example, any message type of severity notice or higher, for all facilities, is to be logged. Also, all messages related to user authorizations (logins, authentications, and so on) of severity, info or higher, are to be logged.

When you specify a severity for logging, all events with that severity or higher are included in the logging.

Viewing syslog messages

Our previous syslog configuration is actually the default level of logging on the router — logs are saved to a file called `messages`, which resides in the default log file directory `/var/log/` (on M-,MX-, and T-series routers), or `/cf/var/log/` (on J-series routers).

To view the resulting log file from the configuration, you can start a shell process and view the file with the text viewer of your choice, or you can view the file from the router:

```
user@router> show log messages
Nov 7 15:24:36  router smartd[4239]: atastandbyarmset: ioctl: Inappropriate
               ioctl for device
Nov 7 15:24:36  router smartd[4239]: standby_request: Error:
               atastandbyarmset(TRUE): Inappropriate ioctl for device
Nov 7 15:31:01  router xntpd[4364]: kernel time sync enabled 2001
Nov 7 16:07:10  router mib2d[4365]: SNMP_TRAP_LINK_DOWN: ifIndex 195,
               ifAdminStatus up(1), ifOperStatus down(2), ifName at-1/0/0
```

In this kind of output, you can see a number of events, each timestamped and identified by its process and corresponding process ID. But the `show log messages` command basically concatenates the entire log file to the screen. If you're interested in only a subset of the entire log file or if you're searching for specific criteria, this kind of raw output is difficult to use — or, to be honest, bordering on completely useless. To filter the output from the command, specify filter criteria. For example:

```
user@router> show log messages | match mib2d
Nov 7 16:07:10  router mib2d[4365]: SNMP_TRAP_LINK_DOWN: ifIndex 195,
               ifAdminStatus up(1), ifOperStatus down(2), ifName at-1/0/0
```

By specifying the match condition, only the syslog event containing the string `mib2d` is returned.

Filtering syslog to different files

Dumping all syslog events to a single log file makes parsing out significant events difficult, especially those that may be of more critical importance than other events. For example, at a minimum, you may want to know who is accessing the box and when that happened so that you can determine whether your router has been a target of hacking attempts. You can configure logging so that these types of events are saved to a separate file called `security`:

```
[edit system]
syslog {
    file messages {
        any notice;
    }
    file security {
        authorization info;
    }
}
```

Here, you have a separate log file called `security` that has all the login attempts and authorization information. To view such a file:

```
user@router> show log security
Oct 28 12:41:44  router mgd[27893]: UI_AUTH_EVENT: Authenticated user 'michael'
            at permission level 'j-superuser'
Oct 28 12:41:44  router mgd[27893]: UI_LOGIN_EVENT: User 'michael' login, class
            'j-superuser' [27893]
Oct 28 12:41:45  router mgd[27893]: UI_CMDLINE_READ_LINE: User 'michael',
            command 'start shell sh '
```

This log file shows that the user `michael` was authenticated and then logged in. This user had super-user privileges and logged into the shell using the `start shell sh` command.

Refining your access to events

You often have two separate files with logging information in them: a `messages` file with all syslog events with a `severity` of notice or higher and a `security` file with all authorization events with a severity of `info` or higher.

Even with this separation, the syslog messages can still be cumbersome to sift through when viewing the files from the router. What if you want to view the `messages` file, but you only want to see events of severity warning or higher? The severity value doesn't appear in any of the syslog events.

To include both the syslog facility and the severity values in each message, configure the `explicit-priority` statement:

```
[edit system]
syslog {
    file messages {
        any notice;
        explicit-priority;
    }
    file security {
        authorization info;
    }
}
```

This syslog configuration includes the facility and severity values for all the syslog messages included in the `messages` file. Now you can view the log file and see only the messages of severity warning or above:

```
user@router> show log messages | match -4-
Nov 30 16:07:10  router mib2d[4365]: %DAEMON-4-SNMP_TRAP_LINK_DOWN: ifIndex 196,
            ifAdminStatus up(1), ifOperStatus down(2), ifName at-1/0/1
```

In this output, we filter the messages and retrieve only the message that has `-4-`. This returns the SNMP link down trap, which has a facility of `DAEMON` and a severity of `4`. Using the `explicit-priority` configuration statement, we can make our log files substantially easier to parse.

Managing your log files

If you've managed to create oodles of log files, ushering off different types of events to different types of files for ease of consumption, you need to manage those files.

By default, JUNOS software limits the size of the log files that are created to 128K. As events are logged, when the total size of the messages exceeds 128K, something has to give. You don't want to stop logging, but you also don't want to lose any historical information that may be useful or necessary.

When files reach the 128K limit, those files are compressed and archived on the router, using a file extension that identifies the file's relative age. Looking at the `/var/log/` directory shows this behavior:

```
% ls /var/log/messages*
messages              Size: 62145, Last changed: October 27 17:15:45
messages.0.gz         Size : 9213, Last changed: October 25 09:23:01
messages.1.gz         Size : 7814, Last changed: October 24 23:14:53
messages.10.gz        Size : 8467, Last changed: October 17 03:11:28
messages.2.gz         Size : 8863, Last changed: October 24 06:31:09
messages.3.gz         Size : 8749, Last changed: October 23 19:51:00
messages.4.gz         Size : 9003, Last changed: October 22 22:05:37
messages.5.gz         Size : 7191, Last changed: October 20 14:10:22
messages.6.gz         Size : 9059, Last changed: October 19 14:21:59
messages.7.gz         Size : 7834, Last changed: October 19 02:46:01
messages.8.gz         Size : 8559, Last changed: October 18 09:29:52
messages.9.gz         Size : 8272, Last changed: October 17 21:45:38
```

The JUNOS software rotates the log files. Each time the current file reaches the file size limit, that file is compressed and saved with the `.0` file extension. Each file's extension is then incremented, and the tenth file is deleted.

If you're using log files to actively troubleshoot a current problem, you may find it useful to clean up the log files so that you can reduce the number of old messages you have to sort through while debugging the issue. To clear the messages for a particular log, use the `clear log` command:

```
user@router> clear log messages
```

Upon issuing this command, the messages log file is emptied, which makes sorting through incoming syslog messages considerably easier.

Using Trace Logging to Monitor the Router

In addition to logging system events, JUNOS software allows you to monitor routing events through trace logging. Trace logging is configured and behaves in almost the exact same way as syslogging (see preceding section). That is, you specify what you want to trace and where you want the messages to be stored. The biggest difference in trace logging is where you configure it in the command-line hierarchy.

Because trace logging is used to monitor and troubleshoot routing protocols, tracing isn't enabled at the `[edit system syslog]` level in the configuration hierarchy. Instead, the tracing options (or `traceoptions`) are configured at the various routing protocol levels in the configuration hierarchy. For example, if you want to enable `traceoptions` to monitor OSPF activities, you configure `traceoptions` under the `[edit protocols ospf]` hierarchy in the configuration. For example:

```
[edit protocols]
ospf {
    area 0.0.0.0 {
        interface fe-0/0/0.0;
        interface fe-0/0/1.0;
    }
    traceoptions {
        file ospf-log {
            flag hello error general;
}
```

In this example, `traceoptions` are configured for OSPF. Whenever a hello, error, or general OSPF event occurs, the message is written to the file `ospf-log`. The trace log file is very similar to the syslog files:

```
user@router> show log ospf-log
Nov 30 16:07:10  OSPF rcvd Hello 10.0.16.2 -> 224.0.0.5 (fe-0/0/0.0, IFL 0x42)
Nov 30 16:07:10  OSPF Version 2, length 48, ID 192.168.19.1, area 0.0.0.1
Nov 30 16:07:10  checksum 0x0, authtype 0
Nov 30 16:07:10  mask 255.255.255.0, hello_ivl 10, opts 0x2, prio 128
Nov 30 16:07:10  dead_ivl 40, DR 10.0.16.1, BDR 10.0.16.2
```

The trace file has the timestamped OSPF events specified by the traceoptions. Using `traceoptions` can be quite useful when debugging routing issues within your network.

Chapter 12

Configuring Interfaces

In This Chapter

- Understanding what physical interfaces are used in networks
- Configuring T1, DS1, DS3, and serial interfaces
- Using digital subscriber line (DSL) interfaces
- Configuring Point-to-Point Protocol and CHAPS

Ethernet is certainly a popular choice these days, but you can send traffic through other physical media. This chapter is about those other guys, the physical interfaces that have taken a back seat to Ethernet but are still very much needed in your network. In this chapter, you find out what you need to know about T1, DS1, DS3, and serial interfaces. You also discover how to configure DSL interfaces. Our goal is to leverage your existing interface knowledge to round out your router and establish connectivity with your branch office.

Types of Physical Interfaces

Ethernet is by far the most popular interface, but it's anything but the only game in town. Several other types of physical interfaces are used in various networks. Because we focus on those interfaces that most commonly appear in enterprise branch offices, the larger interfaces (such as SONET interfaces) are beyond the scope of this particular chapter.

The primary interfaces that are applicable include

- T1 and DS1 interfaces
- Serial interfaces
- Digital subscriber line (DSL) interfaces

T1 interfaces

When people talk about T1 interfaces and DS1 interfaces, they're really talking about the same thing. *T1* is basically a digital data transmission medium that can handle traffic at speeds of 1.544 Mbps.

You may also hear people mention E1 interfaces. *E1 interfaces* are the European equivalents to T1 interfaces, which are more common in North America. E1 interfaces are actually a bit faster, clocking in at 2.048 Mbps. Aside from the difference in speed, their signal properties (clocking, framing, and so on) are the same. Which one you use will depend mostly on what you are connecting to, so don't get too caught up with the difference in bandwidth.

T1/E1 interfaces are digital data transmission media that operate on a basic principle: The interface receives voltage across a wire. The presence of a positive voltage indicates a positive value, or 1. The absence of voltage is a 0. So as these voltages fluctuate, the interface (and, by extension, the router) is reading in 0s and 1s. Those 0s and 1s make up the information that is being transmitted.

By the way, T1 interfaces have two separate wires that make up the connection. One of the wires is used to send signals to the device on the other end, and the other wire is used to receive signals from that same device. And within the signals that are exchanged, a clock signal tells the router when to sample the wires for voltage. Because the clock signal determines when the router will check the line, it's a good example of one of the physical characteristics of the line that must be configured identically on both sides of the connection.

Serial interfaces

Serial links are perhaps the simplest bidirectional links used in networks. Depending on the specific type, serial interfaces can transmit data at speeds anywhere between 200 Kbps to over 10 Mbps.

Serial cables connect two ends of a serial link. Typically, one of these ends is a modem, and the other is a router in the telephony network. This distinction is important, because the serial cables have different connectors depending on which device is which, and you have to be spot-on with your cabling or else traffic will not flow.

The modem is actually considered data communications equipment (DCE) and would require the DCE end of the serial cable. The device to which that modem is connected would be considered *data terminal equipment* (DTE). So just make sure that you have the cabling correct before configuring the devices, because improper cabling is one of the more common problems when setting up serial interfaces.

Once the interfaces are connected, the two endpoints exchange information using one of several serial line protocols. These protocols determine how information is passed back and forth. Essentially, they perform a handshake so that each endpoint knows the other is present. Once the connection is made, traffic can flow. Almost.

Before one device can send information to the other, the receiving device has to tell the sender that it is okay to transmit. The receiver sends a signal indicating that he's ready, and upon receiving that signal, the sender begins transmitting data. Because data can be transmitted only when the receiver is ready, flooding too much traffic across the link is impossible.

Common serial line protocols include EIA530, X.21, RS-232, and RS-422. The good news is that you don't have to decide which to use; the router will detect what the end device is using and just use that protocol. The bad news is that other portions of the configuration are dependent upon which protocol is in use, so you do actually need to be aware.

ADSL

One of the more common means to connect customer sites to service provider networks over the last mile of the network is via *asymmetric digital subscriber lines* (ADSL). ADSL is really just a particular type of the more commonly used DSL.

The asymmetric portion of ADSL stems from the fact that typical users want to download far more information than they want to upload. If you look at typical web browsing as an example, you send a request to some web server somewhere in the world. The server receives that request and then sends you a pile of information that is stored within that Web site. If you look at a more corporate example, most end-users who are using applications over the network are downloading information to be used locally on their computer.

Because of this basic usage scenario, ADSL provides more bandwidth downstream than upstream. A typical ADSL link supports 1.5 Mbps to 2.0 Mbps downstream and 16Kbps upstream.

ADSL is a clever beast. ADSL uses the same twisted-pair wires that your telephone uses. When you connect a couple of ADSL modems across one of these links, the two modems form a circuit over which they transmit data. The neat part is that the ADSL connection is dual-purpose; it can support both voice and data traffic.

A normal home has a single connection running from the home to your carrier. That connection has to support both types of traffic: voice and data. But usually different networks carry the different types of traffic. So both the telephone lines and the DSL lines are connected to a plain old telephone service (POTS) splitter, which basically filters the voice traffic and sends it to the voice network. The data traffic is then filtered and sent to the ADSL modem, which, in turn, connects to your carrier's data network.

Then if you imagine a neighborhood with many ADSL connections, those connections are all sent to a multiplexer, which processes and routes traffic from multiple POTS splitters. A typical setup resembles something akin to what's shown in Figure 12-1.

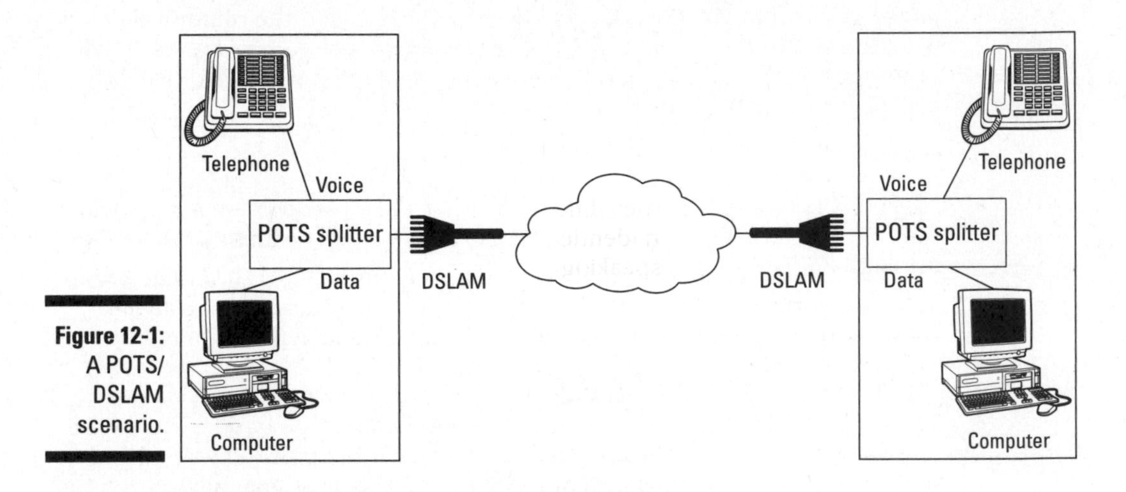

Figure 12-1: A POTS/ DSLAM scenario.

The Logical and Physical Properties of Interfaces

The first thing that probably pops into your mind when you think about interfaces is IP addresses. IP addresses are assigned to individual interfaces, and those addresses are used by protocols and other routing features to control traffic within the router and within the network to which that router is connected.

However, nothing about an interface says that it has to have a specific IP address assigned to it. In fact, you can assign the same address to a T1 interface and then delete it and assign the exact same address to a serial interface. The address is really a logical property of the link, not inherently associated with any of the physical characteristics of the line.

Logical properties

These types of properties (that is, those that are not intrinsically linked to the physical wire) are considered *logical properties.* Logical properties certainly govern how the interface and router behave, but they don't affect whether the underlying connection on that link can be made.

In addition to the IP address, other logical properties include the types of protocol families (MPLS, ISO, and so on) as well as the type of address (IPv4 or IPv6).

Physical properties

Physical characteristics of links dictate how signals are sent. These properties include *clocking* (how often signals are sampled), *encapsulation* (how traffic is framed), *encryption* (how traffic is scrambled), and so on.

Physical interface properties differ from logical properties in that they generally have to be configured identically on both ends of the link to ensure that the two end devices are speaking the same language.

Configuring Interfaces

The basics of interface configuration are the same for all interfaces, regardless of the type, which means that much of what we used to configure Ethernet interfaces in Chapter 7 applies when configuring these other types of the interfaces. We cover the basics, but focus more on the media-specific types of configuration.

Configuring T1 interfaces

T1 interfaces are really pretty simple to configure. To get a connection across a T1 link, all you really need to do is specify the interface name, protocol family, logical interface, and IP address on the interface:

```
[edit interfaces]
t1-0/0/1 {
    unit 0 {
        family inet {
            address 10.0.22.1/24;
        }
    }
}
```

The interface name is determined by the physical location of the interface card. If you use a name that doesn't match the slot into which the card is inserted, the configuration will not work.

The configuration for T1 interfaces is identical on both ends of the link, so you can use the same basic configuration (with different IP addresses, of course). The only requirement is that both IP addresses have the same subnet (which should probably go without saying, but consider it a quick test).

This configuration is simple because most of the properties on a T1 link don't need to be explicitly set. The default values are such that if you just configure an address, you should be able to establish a connection between your interface and the remote interface.

By default, your T1 connection will assume an MTU of 1504, it will use the router's system clock to sample the line, and it will use PPP to establish the connection.

So how do you know if the interfaces are configured correctly and the link between them is up? From the router, you should be able to ping both your own router's interface and the interface to which it is directly connected, such as

```
user@router1> ping 10.0.22.1
64 bytes from 10.0.22.1: icmp_seq=0 ttl=255 time=0.382 ms
64 bytes from 10.0.22.1: icmp_seq=1 ttl=255 time=0.337 ms
```

Configuring serial interfaces

Serial interfaces require a smidge more involvement than T1 interfaces (see preceding section). To get a serial link up and running, you have to correctly configure both sides of the connection. You have to identify which router is the DCE and which is the DTE.

For example, say that router 1 is the DCE, and router 2 is the DTE, which isn't the typical scenario. Normally, the DCE is a modem, and the DTE is the router, but it illustrates how the interface is configured as both a DCE and a DTE device. To complete the configuration, you must also know the serial line protocol used. In this example, assume that it's RS-232. Despite the serial-specific configuration, the following basic configuration is still required:

```
Router 1
[edit interfaces]
se-1/0/0 {
   unit 0 {
      family inet {
         address 10.0.22.1/24;
      }
```

```
    }
}

Router 2
[edit interfaces]
se-2/0/0 {
   description "Connected to DCE device router 1";
   unit 0 {
      family inet {
         address 10.0.22.2/24;
      }
   }
}
```

Troubleshooting an interface when you don't know what it's connected to can be a major headache. Always include a detailed interface description to ensure that, should something go wrong, you or your operations team can log on to the router and quickly determine where the interface is connected. This step can shave precious time off the total time it takes to diagnose and correct an issue.

If the serial interface being configured was a T1 interface, the configuration would be enough to establish connectivity between the devices. However, if you tried to ping the interfaces now, you would see that the link is not yet active. Another way to check this is to look at the output from `show interfaces detail` as shown in Listing 12-1.

Listing 12-1: Serial Interfaces Output Showing Unactive Link

```
user@router1> show interfaces detail
Physical interface: se-1/0/0, Enabled, Physical link is Down
  Interface index: 134, SNMP ifIndex: 27, Generation: 17
  Link-level type: Serial, MTU: 1514, Speed: 10mbps, Loopback: Disabled,
  Source filtering: Disabled, Flow control: Enabled
  Device flags   : Present Running
  Interface flags: SNMP-Traps 16384
  Link flags     : None
  CoS queues     : 4 supported
  Hold-times     : Up 0 ms, Down 0 ms
  Current address: 00:90:69:87:44:9d, Hardware address: 00:90:69:87:44:9d
  Last flapped   : 2004-08-25 15:42:30 PDT (4w5d 22:49 ago)
  Statistics last cleared: Never
  Traffic statistics:
   Input  bytes  :                0                    0 bps
   Output bytes  :                0                    0 bps
   Input  packets:                0                    0 pps
   Output packets:                0                    0 pps
  Queue counters:    Queued packets  Transmitted packets  Dropped packets
    0 best-effort                0                    0                0
```

(continued)

Listing 12-1 *(continued)*

```
    1 expedited-fo                0                    0                0
    2 assured-forw                0                    0                0
    3 network-cont                0                    0                0
  Active alarms  : None
  Active defects : None
```

In Listing 12-1, the first line indicates that the physical link is down, verifying that configuring the addresses on the two endpoints isn't sufficient for establishing connectivity between the interfaces. In Listing 12-1, router 1 is identified as the DCE. The DCE will provide the clock signal, so you have to configure router 1 to generate the clock and you must specify the clock frequency:

```
Router 1
[edit interfaces]
se-1/0/0 {
   clocking-mode internal;
   clock-rate 125;
   unit 0 {
      family inet {
         address 10.0.22.1/24;
      }
   }
}
```

This configuration ensures that router 1 generates a clock signal with a frequency of 125.0 KHz and transmits it to router 2. The configuration on router 2 must then reflect that it's a DTE device receiving a clock signal:

```
Router 2
[edit interfaces]
se-2/0/0 {
   clocking-mode dce;
   description "Connected to DCE device router 1";
   unit 0 {
      family inet {
         address 10.0.22.2/24;
      }
   }
}
```

After this configuration is complete, the interface connection should be established. A simple look at the `show interfaces detail` command reveals that the connection is established, as shown in Listing 12-2.

Listing 12-2: Serial Interfaces Output Showing Link Is Active (Up)

```
user@router1> show interfaces detail
Physical interface: se-1/0/0, Enabled, Physical link is Up
  Interface index: 134, SNMP ifIndex: 27, Generation: 17
  Link-level type: Serial, MTU: 1514, Speed: 10mbps, Loopback: Disabled,
  Source filtering: Disabled, Flow control: Enabled
  Device flags   : Present Running
  Interface flags: SNMP-Traps 16384
  Link flags     : None
  CoS queues     : 4 supported
  Hold-times     : Up 0 ms, Down 0 ms
  Current address: 00:90:69:87:44:9d, Hardware address: 00:90:69:87:44:9d
  Last flapped   : 2004-08-25 15:42:30 PDT (4w5d 22:49 ago)
  Statistics last cleared: Never
  Traffic statistics:
   Input  bytes  :                  0                    0 bps
   Output bytes  :                  0                    0 bps
   Input  packets:                  0                    0 pps
   Output packets:                  0                    0 pps
  Queue counters:     Queued packets  Transmitted packets    Dropped packets
    0 best-effort                  0                    0                  0
    1 expedited-fo                 0                    0                  0
    2 assured-forw                 0                    0                  0
    3 network-cont                 0                    0                  0
  Active alarms  : None
  Active defects : None
```

Note that the physical link is now listed as Up.

Configuring ADSL interfaces

JUNOS software supports ADSL over an Asynchronous Transfer Mode (ADSL)-over-ATM interface, meaning that the underlying interface configuration is actually done as if the interface were an ATM interface. Essentially, the transport is handled by ATM.

Because the underlying transport is ATM, you can use a lot of ATM configuration options. The assumption here is that if you're using an ADSL interface, you already understand at least some of the finer points of ATM. In other words, you should have a decent understanding of cell relays, packet-switched networks, virtual channels, and virtual paths. This section really focuses on how to configure this within JUNOS software.

As with the other interfaces, the base configuration for ADSL interfaces is very straightforward. The configuration does assume an underlying ATM interface, so the interface name looks like ATM:

```
[edit interfaces]
at-4/0/1 {
   description "Connected to DSLAM 314";
   unit 0 {
      family inet {
         address 10.0.22.2/24;
      }
   }
}
```

You now layer the various physical and logical properties onto the base configuration. First, as with all ATM connections, this link is associated with a virtual path. You must configure the virtual path identifier (VPI) that will relay the packet through the ATM network:

```
[edit interfaces]
at-4/0/1 {
   description "Connected to DSLAM 314";
   atm-options {
      vpi 25;
   }
unit 0 {
      family inet {
         address 10.0.22.2/24;
      }
   }
}
```

The VPI identifies the set of *endpoints* (your router and the remote destination) that makes up the virtual path. Different flows or channels are within that path. Typical practice is to set up an interface that you link to a virtual path from your router to some destination. Then you set up multiple logical interfaces within that physical interface, each of which represents a different virtual channel. The virtual channel is defined using the `vci` statement within the logical interface:

```
[edit interfaces]
at-4/0/1 {
   description "Connected to DSLAM 314";
   atm-options {
      vpi 25;
   }
   unit 37 {
      vci 37;
      family inet {
         address 10.0.22.2/24;
      }
   }
}
```

Notice that the logical interface number (specified with the unit statement) has changed from 0 to 37. The value 37 matches the virtual channel identifier. If you have many virtual channels configured on a single ATM interface, tracking them is easier if you use the VCI as the unit number. Using the VCI also makes it much easier to read the configuration and troubleshoot.

You must now configure the type of DSL operating mode for the interface. When an ADSL connection is established, the two interfaces negotiate properties before the connection is complete. Because there are various types of communications to perform this negotiation, you must configure how you want it to occur. The easiest and most reliable way is to configure the interface to *auto-negotiate* settings (so that your method matches whatever is configured on the DSLAM). To enable auto-negotiation, set the DSL options as follows:

```
[edit interfaces]
at-4/0/1 {
    description "Connected to DSLAM 314";
    atm-options {
      vpi 25;
   }
   dsl-options {
      operating-mode auto;
   }
   unit 37 {
      vci 37;
      family inet {
         address 10.0.22.2/24;
      }
   }
}
```

To verify this configuration, use the `show interfaces extensive` command, shown in Listing 12-3.

Listing 12-3: Sample Output to Verify auto-negotiate

```
user@host> show interfaces at-3/0/0 extensive
Physical interface: at-3/0/0, Enabled, Physical link is Up
  Interface index: 141, SNMP ifIndex: 23, Generation: 48
  Link-level type: ATM-PVC, MTU: 4482, Clocking: Internal, ADSL mode, Speed:
            ADSL,
  Loopback: None
  Device flags   : Present Running
  Link flags     : None
  CoS queues     : 8 supported
  Hold-times     : Up 0 ms, Down 0 ms
  Current address: 00:05:85:c7:44:3c
  Last flapped   : 2005-05-16 05:54:41 PDT (00:41:42 ago)
```

(continued)

Listing 12-3 *(continued)*

```
  Statistics last cleared: Never
  Traffic statistics:
   Input  bytes  :                4520                 0 bps
   Output bytes  :               39250                 0 bps
   Input  packets:                  71                 0 pps
   Output packets:                1309                 0 pps
  Input errors:
    Errors: 0, Drops: 0, Invalid VCs: 0, Framing errors: 0, Policed discards:
     0,L3 incompletes: 0, L2 channel errors: 1, L2 mismatch timeouts: 0,
Resource errors: 0
  Output errors:
    Carrier transitions: 3, Errors: 0, Drops: 0, Aged packets: 0, MTU errors:
    0, Resource errors: 0
  Queue counters:    Queued packets  Transmitted packets   Dropped packets
    0 best-effort                4                    4                 0
    1 expedited-fo               0                    0                 0
    2 assured-forw               0                    0                 0
    3 network-cont            2340                 2340                 0
  ADSL  alarms   : LOS, LOM, LOCDNI, FAR_LOF,  FAR_LOS, FAR_LOCDNI
  ADSL  defects  : LOF, LOS, LOCDNI, FAR_LOF,  FAR_LOS, FAR_LOCDNI
  ADSL media:            Seconds        Count  State
    LOF                  239206             2  OK
    LOS                  239208             1  OK
    LOM                       3             1  OK
    LOP                       0             0  OK
    LOCDI                     3             1  OK
    LOCDNI               239205             1  OK
  ADSL status:
    Modem status   : Showtime
    DSL mode       :      Auto    Annex A
    Last fail code: ATU-C not detected
  ADSL Statistics:                      ATU-R                  ATU-C
    Attenuation (dB)          :           0.5                    0.0
    Capacity used (%)         :            81                     72
    Noise margin (dB)         :           9.0                    9.5
Output power (dBm)         :           7.5                    8.5
                              Interleave       Fast  Interleave       Fast
    Bit rate (kbps)   :                0       8128           0        896
    CRC               :                0          3           0          0
    FEC               :                0          0           0          0
    HEC               :                0          3           0          0
    Received cells    :                0        287
    Transmitted cells :                0       4900
    Bit error rate    :                0          0
  ATM status:
    HCS state:     Hunt
    LOC     :        OK
  ATM Statistics:
```

Listing 12-3 *(continued)*

```
    Uncorrectable HCS errors: 0, Correctable HCS errors: 0, Tx cell FIFO
           overruns:
 0,
    Rx cell FIFO overruns: 0, Rx cell FIFO underruns: 0, Input cell count: 0,
    Output cell count: 0, Output idle cell count: 0, Output VC queue drops: 0,
    Input no buffers: 0, Input length errors: 0, Input timeouts: 0, Input
           invalid
 VCs: 0,
    Input bad CRCs: 0, Input OAM cell no buffers: 0
  Packet Forwarding Engine configuration:
    Destination slot: 3
    CoS transmit queue           Bandwidth          Buffer Priority
Limit
                          %            bps     %       bytes
    0 best-effort        95        7600000    95           0       low
none
    3 network-control     5         400000     5           0       low
none
  Logical interface at-3/0/0.0 (Index 66) (SNMP ifIndex 28) (Generation 23)
    Flags: Point-To-Point SNMP-Traps 16384 Encapsulation: ATM-PPP-LLC
    Traffic statistics:
     Input  bytes  :                   2432
     Output bytes  :                      0
     Input  packets:                    116
     Output packets:                      0
    Local statistics:
     Input  bytes  :                   1810
     Output bytes  :                      0
     Input  packets:                     78
     Output packets:                      0
    Transit statistics:
     Input  bytes  :                    622                  0 bps
     Output bytes  :                      0                  0 bps
     Input  packets:                     38                  0 pps
     Output packets:                      0                  0 pps
  Keepalive settings: Interval 10 seconds, Up-count 1, Down-count 3
  Keepalive statistics:
    Input : 33 (last seen 00:00:03 ago)
    Output: 34 (last sent 00:00:03 ago)
  LCP state: Opened
  NCP state: inet: Opened, inet6: Not-configured, iso: Not-configured, mpls:
Not-configured
  CHAP state: Success
    Protocol inet, MTU: 4470, Generation: 24, Route table: 0
      Flags: None
      Addresses, Flags: Is-Preferred Is-Primary
        Destination: 155.55.5.1, Local: 155.55.5.2, Broadcast: Unspecified,
Generation: 45
```

Listing 12-3 contains a ton of output that can be difficult to parse. However, the output's key elements are actually very simple:

- Ensure that the interface is Enabled in the first line of the output.
- Check that the physical link is Up in the first line of the output.
- See that no ADSL alarms or defects appear that can render the interface unable to pass packets. If you're unsure what the alarms are, you should consult the nearest ATM expert, be it man or book.

Configuring the point-to-point protocol

The point-to-point protocol (PPP) is one of the more common ways to establish a direct connection between two devices on, or across, a network. PPP is made up of three primary components:

- **Link control protocol (LCP):** Establishes working connections between two endpoints.
- **Authentication protocols:** Enable secure connections between two endpoints.
- **Network control protocols (NCPs):** Negotiate optional configuration parameters.

Why use PPP? Imagine that you have two devices that you want to make sure always have connectivity to each other, such as a computer in a branch office and the gateway router in your core. You can set up a PPP session, and if one side is unreachable from the other, the PPP session will terminate and generate an error. Additionally, PPP supports some authentication protocols that allow you to apply strict security to the connections to your router.

In this scenario, the remote host wants to set up a PPP session with the router. Because PPP is a layer 2 protocol, packets are encapsulated with the PPP header and then transported via some layer 3 protocol, allowing the PPP session to be established even when the two devices aren't connected via a direct link.

To configure PPP, you have to enable the encapsulation of PPP on the interface and specify a destination address for the PPP session:

```
[edit interfaces]
t1-1/0/0 {
    encapsulation ppp;
    unit 0 {
        family inet {
            address 10.0.22.1/24 {
```

```
                destination 10.0.45.2/24;
            }
        }
    }
}
```

In this configuration, a PPP session is configured from router 1 on interface t1-1/0/0 to the host's interface, which resides on a different subnet. If you want to make sure that connection is secure, you have to add a little security.

Of the interfaces we discuss in this book, PPP is supported on all except ADSL.

Using CHAP to authenticate PPP sessions

Using PPP gives you access to a great way to ensure that connections are secure by supporting the Challenge Handshake Authentication Protocol (CHAP).

Using PPP, you can establish a link between two devices. But imagine a situation where your users are dialing into your network and you want to grant them access, yet restrict outsiders from establishing connections with your network. You can use CHAP to authenticate those sessions, thereby granting access only to trusted hosts.

CHAP works by configuring a shared password (called a *secret*) on both the connecting device and the host. When the PPP session is established, the host challenges the connecting device by sending a random number (a *challenge value*) to the device. The device responds with a value that is calculated using the challenge value and a hash algorithm, based on the shared secret. If this value matches the value calculated by the host using the same information, the session is authenticated. If it doesn't match, the session is terminated. Because the challenge value is chosen randomly and changes with each challenge, CHAP provides a secure means of ensuring that the requesting device is trusted.

To configure CHAP, you have to first enable CHAP on your router and then you have to configure the secret. This step is most easily done using a default CHAP secret:

```
[edit interfaces]
t1-1/0/0 {
encapsulation ppp;
   ppp-options {
      chap {
         default-chap-secret "password";
      }
   unit 0 {
      family inet {
```

```
            address 10.0.22.1/24 {
               destination 10.0.45.2/24;
            }
         }
      }
   }
```

In this output, the default secret "password" is used for all PPP sessions established with this T1 interface. Whenever a session is established with this interface, this secret is used to calculate the challenge values and verify authenticity of the PPP session.

Because PPP is not supported with ADSL interfaces, you can't use CHAP to authenticate connections made through your ADSL interfaces.

Measuring the bit error rate

After you configure your interfaces, enable PPP on those interfaces (or at least on the ones not called ADSL), and establish an authentication scheme to make sure that only trusted people can establish connections, you'll want to ensure that those interfaces stay active and error-free.

In networking, the *bit error rate* (BER) is the percentage of bits that have errors compared to the total number of bits received. This percentage is usually reported as a 10 to a negative power. For example, a stream of data with a BER of 10-6 indicates that 1 bit error occurs in every 1,000,000 bits received.

The BER is a measure of how often packets have to be re-sent because of errors in the transmission. If the BER is high, many packets are being re-sent. A high BER typically indicates some type of problem on the network, such as noise on the line, which may be from a problem with the physical link or the interfaces on either end of that link. If the BER is low, then everything is working as it should, and your network is functioning correctly.

To test one of your interfaces, you need to configure a router in your network to be a *BERT tester*. You need to specify the test to be run, how long it should last, and the number of bit errors the router will intentionally include in the test. Although you can choose from several algorithms, sending all 1s is usually sufficient to test the link. The configuration is

```
[edit interfaces]
t1-1/0/0 {
   t1-options {
   bert algorithm all-ones-repeating;
   bert-error-rate 4;
   bert-period 120;
   }
}
```

The test then sends out all 1s, injecting 1 bit error for every 104 bits, and it runs for 120 seconds. Now you have to execute the test:

```
user@host> test interface t1-1/0/0 t1-bert-start
```

Listing 12-4 shows the output of this test, which is included in the `show interfaces extensive` command.

Listing 12-4: Output of a BERT Test

```
user@host> show interfaces detail
Physical interface: ge-1/0/0, Enabled, Physical link is Up
  Interface index: 134, SNMP ifIndex: 27, Generation: 17
  Link-level type: Ethernet, MTU: 1514, Speed: 100mbps, Loopback: Disabled,
  Source filtering: Disabled, Flow control: Enabled
  Device flags   : Present Running
  Interface flags: SNMP-Traps 16384
  Link flags     : None
  CoS queues     : 4 supported
  Hold-times     : Up 0 ms, Down 0 ms
  Current address: 00:90:69:87:44:9d, Hardware address: 00:90:69:87:44:9d
  Last flapped   : 2004-08-25 15:42:30 PDT (4w5d 22:49 ago)
  Statistics last cleared: Never
  Traffic statistics:
   Input  bytes  :                0                    0 bps
   Output bytes  :                0                    0 bps
   Input  packets:                0                    0 pps
   Output packets:                0                    0 pps
  Queue counters:   Queued packets  Transmitted packets    Dropped packets
    0 best-effort                0                    0                   0
    1 expedited-fo               0                    0                   0
    2 assured-forw               0                    0                   0
    3 network-cont               0                    0                   0
  Active alarms  : None
  Active defects : None
  T1 BERT configuration:
    BERT time period: 120 seconds, Elapsed: 120 seconds
    Induced Error rate: 10e-4, Algorithm: 2^15 - 1
```

If you look at the output, the last lines show the BERT test as it's configured.

Chapter 13

Working with Border Gateway Protocol (BGP)

In This Chapter

- Understanding and connecting Autonomous Systems
- Configuring the Border Gateway Protocol (BGP)
- Creating routing policies that advertise their routes
- Using route reflection on larger networks

While interconnecting the routers in your own network is certainly an accomplishment, having your own network without any conduit to the rest of the world is kind of like living on a deserted island. If you want any kind of contact with the rest of the networking world, you need to have some way to talk to people on the mainland. That connectivity between your network island and the mainland Internet is typically provided via the Border Gateway Protocol (BGP).

In this chapter, we introduce you to BGP, describe why and how it is used, and how you can configure and tailor it to suit your specific network's needs.

An Island of Their Own: Autonomous Systems

Interior Gateway Protocols like OSPF and IS-IS enable you to set up networks and exchange routing information within your network. These IGPs let you create your own network island, which you can interconnect so that they can exchange information.

Because these island networks are fully functioning networks, they are, as such, completely *autonomous.* Given their autonomy, such networks have been aptly labeled *Autonomous Systems* (AS). An AS is a set of routers and devices, or even a set of networks, that are all controlled by a single entity.

Because they're all operated by a single entity, these ASs can freely exchange information amongst all the routers within. They can allocate addresses with full knowledge of the rest of the network. Security is important, but less than usual because all the information and traffic is self-contained.

Making AS Connections

An isolated AS cut off from the rest of the Internet is only marginally useful. If you have any need to access the Internet, either to grab information or to use it as a transport to other networks, you have to be able to connect outside the AS. These connections are established using peering relationships, where one AS connects to another (a peer) using Border Gateway Protocol (BGP).

To connect ASs to each other and establish a peering relationship, you must configure BGP on both peering routers.

Where an IGP like OSPF was simple to configure and worked on its own once you enabled it, you must explicitly configure BGP. And BGP can be rather unwieldy at times primarily because when you're using BGP, you're connecting to a router outside of your own control. Therefore, you're likely to want stricter security in terms of what information you make available to your peers as well as what they send to you.

Imagine you have a simple network with two ASs, each of which has a gateway router, as shown in Figure 13-1.

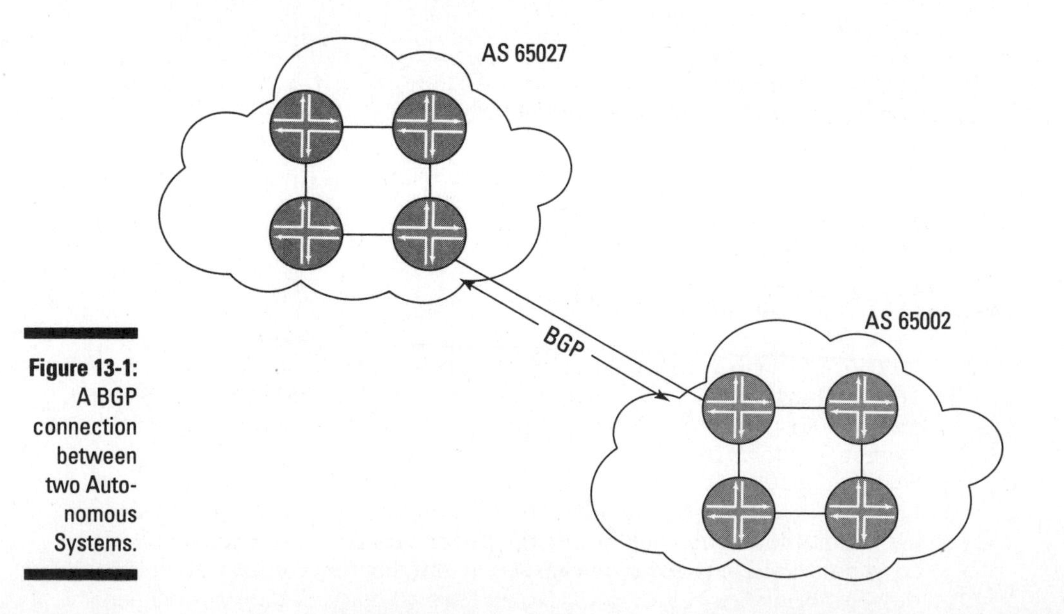

Figure 13-1: A BGP connection between two Autonomous Systems.

In Figure 13-1, you want to connect the two networks using BGP. To establish a connection, BGP requires a little bit of information:

- **You have to identify the AS to which each of the peering routers belongs.** Every AS in the world is uniquely identified by an AS number. These numbers are handed out by the Internet Assigned Numbers Authority (IANA) and are used to specify not only the peering router but also the peering AS for each BGP session.
- **You have to decide on a group for the peering session.** BGP groups everything so that you can have logical sets of connections that all behave more or less the same way.

  Imagine, for example, that you have multiple connections between your network and a neighbor network. You may have all the same configuration on these links except that they are between different routers (to provide a redundant link). To simplify the configuration, you group them and call them collectively "Those guys." All configuration for "Those guys" is employed on each individual session within the group.
- **You must know the specific IP address of the interface to which you're connecting.** This address is the neighbor address, as it's the neighboring interface with which you are peering.

The third bullet is the reason why BGP is an EGP and not an IGP. While you can use BGP to interconnect all of the routers within your network, the fact that you have to explicitly configure each connection can be a pain. It is far simpler to use a lighter-weight protocol like OSPF and save the heavy-duty protocols for the connections outside of your network. When we get to internal BGP (IBGP), you will see even more why BGP is not well-suited for easily managing connections within your network.

As a general rule and best practice, you want your IGP to carry local and interface routes. You want to leave the heavy lifting for BGP. BGP was built to handle large numbers of routes. IGPs, on the other hand, were designed to reconverge as fast as possible in the event of a failure (link, router, or other type of failure). For more on IGPs, see Chapter 8.

Keep in mind that the other guy has to know all the same information as well. For this session to work, both of you have to explicitly configure BGP to each other.

Configuring BGP

The configuration required for BGP to work can be broken into two parts:

- **A configuration that specifies who you are:** Who you are is really as simple as identifying your AS and specifying the address by which you want to be known. Configuring who you are is done by setting your AS under routing options:

```
[edit]
routing options {
   autonomous-system 65001;
}
```

A lot of protocols include an address for the router in their exchange of information with other routers. Explicitly configuring the address to be used for this type of communication is generally a good idea so that messages between routers are always clear, making it far easier to troubleshoot things down the road. You should always explicitly configure the router ID:

```
[edit]
routing-options {
   router-id 192.168.14.3
}
```

A common best practice is to have this router-id correspond to your loopback interface IP address.

- **A configuration that establishes a session with your neighbor:** After configuring your own information, you need to set up the BGP session to your external neighbor, as shown in Figure 13-2.

  Using Figure 13-2's topology, configure a BGP session from router 3 to router 5, and vice versa by working in the protocols section of the configuration hierarchy, such as:

```
[edit protocols]
bgp {
   group those-guys {
      type external;
      peer-as 65002;
      neighbor 10.0.26.2;
   }
}
```

  All you're doing here is explicitly defining the BGP session that will connect your AS to your peer AS. The neighbor address specified here is the interface address on the peer you're connecting to. The AS number you configure for this peer must match the AS number that peer has configured for itself. Also note that you have configured this neighbor as `type external`. This configuration means that the neighbor will be connected via the external flavor of BGP called *E*BGP.

If there is an external BGP, logic follows that there is also an internal version of BGP (IBGP). Where EBGP is configured between routers in different ASs, IBGP is configured between all routers within your internal network. Figure 13-3 shows the network topology.

The external BGP (EBGP) session you created established the connection between your AS and the peering AS. It did not, however, connect all your routers via BGP. You must configure IBGP between your routers. Configuring IBGP is very similar to configuring EBGP. To configure router 3:

```
  [edit protocols]
bgp {
group my-guys {
   type internal;
   neighbor 192.168.14.1;
   neighbor 192.168.14.2;
   neighbor 192.168.14.4;
   }
}
```

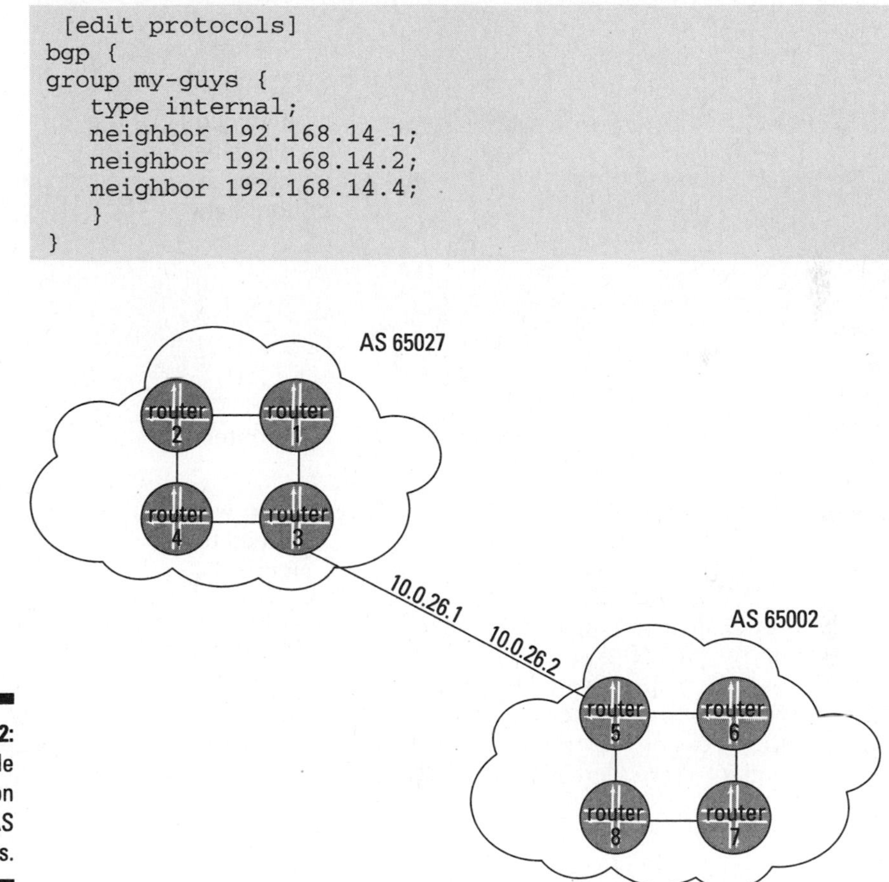

Figure 13-2: A sample BGP session between AS neighbors.

Notice the type of connection being configured here: type internal. Because these are internal neighbors, JUNOS is intelligent enough to know that the AS number is the same as the AS number configured under the routing-options. Also, notice that you have configured three neighbors, but the topology shows that you have only two immediate neighbors. Router 2 is only accessible via the other routers. Why is it included here?

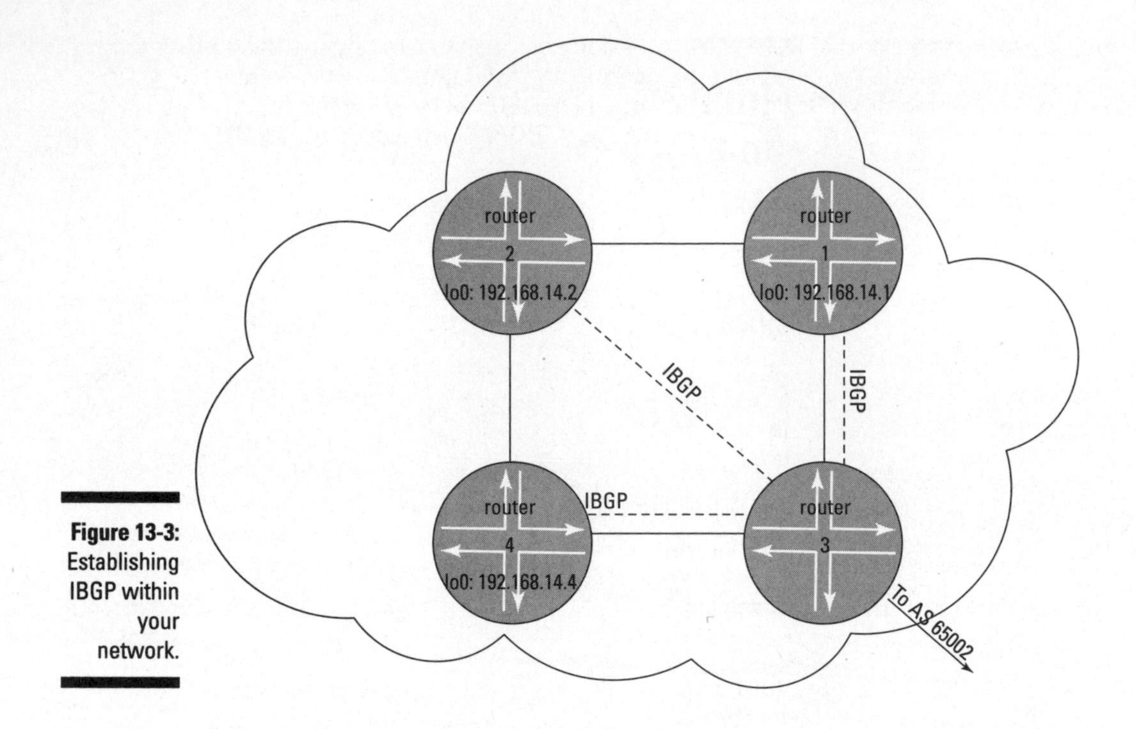

Figure 13-3: Establishing IBGP within your network.

That's because IBGP has some restrictions. By default, IBGP can't advertise routes learned via IBGP to other IBGP neighbors. So in Figure 13-2, earlier in this chapter, router 4 learns routes via EBGP from router 5. These routes have to be propagated to the rest of your network so that your router 2 can send traffic to router 7. Router 4 sends those routes to routers 1 and 3 via the IBGP session between them. Because IBGP cannot re-advertise those routes, it can't share them with router 2.

This kind of information is used to prevent routing loops, which has to do with IBGP and the AS-Path attribute (or lack thereof). The AS-Path attribute is carried inside BGP to advertise the AS numbers that the route has traversed to get to your router. Every time the prefix goes through a new AS, that AS is added to the AS-Path. The AS-Path attribute is only modified when the route traverses EBGP peers.

To get around this limitation, IBGP requires a *full mesh* configuration — that is, every router within your network must be configured as an internal peer to every other router in your network, regardless of whether they're physically connected via a link. This reason is why you see router 2 configured as a neighbor to router 3 when they're not physically linked.

BGP is now configured on your router.

Noting implementation differences between IOS and JUNOS software

Do you have extensive experience implementing BGP in another network operating system? If you're familiar with Cisco's IOS software, it's worth noting some differences in implementation. It's helpful to know that in BGP configurations, JUNOS software

- Enables the sending of communities to BGP peers. (Prevent the default by using an export policy to delete communities.)
- Uses route preference more so than local preference. JUNOS software has no concept of weight.
- Prefers all BGP-received routes over IGP internal routes. (Modify the default at the protocol, group, or neighbor level, or you can also use an import policy to modify the route preference on a per-route basis.)
- Enables deterministic MED. (Disable the default if you want the router to mimic the Cisco IOS nondeterministic MED behavior in order to provide compatibility with Cisco IOS routers.)
- Disables synchronization and auto-summarization as its default behavior.

Notice that the IBGP neighbor configuration differs slightly from the EBGP neighbor configuration (shown in Figure 13-3) in that the neighbor addresses for IBGP are *loopback addresses*. If a particular interface goes down within your network, the router may still be reachable via other routes provided by your IGP. You don't need to take down the IBGP session in this case. You peer with the loopback addresses because they're always up so long as the box is reachable. With EBGP, however, you generally peer with the interface you're directly connecting through. If that interface goes down, you have no other route to that host. So, in this case, you're better off taking the session down to prevent routing across that link.

Monitoring BGP

Perhaps you sometimes find it hard to tell whether BGP is really working. So how can you really tell if the session you configured is established? The `show bgp neighbor` command is the key, as shown in Listing 13-1.

Listing 13-1: Monitoring BPG with `show bgp neighbor` Command

```
mike@router1> show bgp neighbor
Peer: 10.245.245.1+179 AS 200  Local: 10.245.245.3+3770 AS 100
Type: External    State: Established    Flags: <ImportEval Sync>
Last State: OpenConfirm   Last Event: RecvKeepAlive
Last Error: None
Options: <Multihop Preference LocalAddress HoldTime AddressFamily PeerAS    Rib-
              group Refresh>
Address families configured: iso-vpn-unicast
Local Address: 10.245.245.3 Holdtime: 90 Preference: 170
Number of flaps: 0
Peer ID: 10.245.245.1     Local ID: 10.245.245.3     Active Holdtime: 90
Keepalive Interval: 30         Peer index: 0
NLRI advertised by peer: iso-vpn-unicast
NLRI for this session: iso-vpn-unicast
Peer supports Refresh capability (2)
Table bgp.isovpn.0 Bit: 10000
RIB State: BGP restart is complete
RIB State: VPN restart is complete
Send state: in sync
Active prefixes:             3
Received prefixes:           3
Suppressed due to damping:   0
Advertised prefixes:         3
Table aaaa.iso.0
RIB State: BGP restart is complete
RIB State: VPN restart is complete
Send state: not advertising
Active prefixes:             3
Received prefixes:           3
Suppressed due to damping:   0
Last traffic (seconds): Received 6    Sent 5  Checked 5
Input messages:  Total 1736   Updates 4     Refreshes 0    Octets 33385
Output messages: Total 1738   Updates 3     Refreshes 0    Octets 33305
Output Queue[0]: 0
Output Queue[1]: 0
```

The `show bgp neighbor` command shows a lot of information, most of which isn't terribly relevant most of the time. You should focus on a couple of key fields in the output, especially when determining whether a successful connection was established. Focus on only the first four lines of output:

```
mike@router1> show bgp neighbor
Peer: 10.245.245.1+179 AS 200  Local: 10.245.245.3+3770 AS 100
Type: External    State: Established    Flags: <ImportEval Sync>
Last State: OpenConfirm   Last Event: RecvKeepAlive
Last Error: None
```

The most basic part of determining whether a peering session is up is to identify the state of the session. In this case, the state is Established, which means the BGP configuration worked.

What might the state look like if it didn't work? And what would you do about it? Other possible states include

- **Idle:** This is the starting point for BGP sessions prior to any messages being exchanged. If you see an idle state, you probably just need to wait until BGP begins sending messages.
- **Connect:** Connect indicates that BGP messages are being exchanged and BGP is waiting for the underlying TCP connection to be established. This state means that things are either in progress, or they've stalled on the TCP side of things.
- **Active:** The most misleading of the state names, active does not mean that the BGP session is active; it means that BGP is *actively* looking for its peer. A common cause for these types of issues is misconfiguration, so check your AS numbers and make sure that they're configured correctly.
- **OpenSent** and **OpenConfirm:** These are transition states while BGP is negotiating. If you see these states, just enter the `show bgp neighbor` command a second time and see whether the states have transitioned to Established.

Depending on the state value, you can use the peering information at the top of the output in Listing 13-1 to determine whether the peering address and AS number are configured correctly. Remember that the BGP configuration on both sides of the peering session must be correct to establish the session correctly, so if you're having problems, the issue may not reside on your router but the peer it is trying to connect to.

Knowing why you can't ping

After you set up BGP between the two peering routers and among all your internal peers, similar to the topology shown in Figure 13-4, you'd think you should be able to ping router 7 from router 4, despite the two routers residing in different ASs.

You may be tempted to assume that you're finished configuring your network after the BGP session is up and running, but a simple ping command to any of the routers in the neighboring AS reveals that none of them are reachable. Why not?

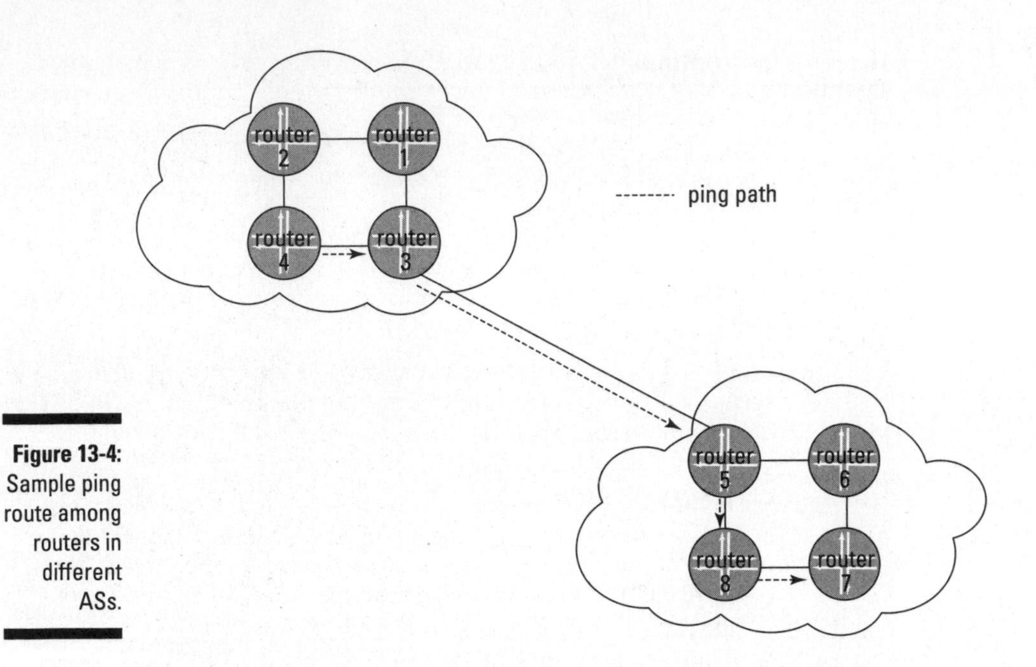

Figure 13-4: Sample ping route among routers in different ASs.

BGP differs from IGPs in that, by default, it doesn't share all the information about routes. OSPF's default behavior is to advertise all routes learned by OSPF to all OSPF neighbors and to import all routes learned by OSPF from those same neighbors. BGP, on the other hand, holds on to its routes and only exports them if they were learned through BGP. In this way, IGP routes are not sent to BGP peers.

For your ping between ASs, you must have a route to the destination AS. Look at the routing table in Listing 13-2 and see whether you have a route to that host.

Listing 13-2: Checking a Routing Table for a Ping Route

```
sally@router2> show route
inet.0: 16 destinations, 16 routes (15 active, 0 holddown, 1 hidden)
+ = Active Route, - = Last Active, * = Both

10.5.0.0/16        *[Static/5] 6w0d 00:18:22
to 192.168.71.254 via fxp0.0
10.10.0.0/16       *[Static/5] 6w0d 00:25:57
to 192.168.71.254 via fxp0.0
10.13.10.0/23      *[Static/5] 6w0d 00:18:22
to 192.168.71.254 via fxp0.0
10.84.0.0/16       *[Static/5] 6w0d 00:18:22
to 192.168.71.254 via fxp0.0
10.150.0.0/16      *[Static/5] 6w0d 00:18:22
to 192.168.71.254 via fxp0.0
```

Listing 13-2 (continued)

```
10.157.64.0/19     *[Static/5] 6w0d 00:18:22
to 192.168.71.254 via fxp0.0
10.209.0.0/16      *[Static/5] 6w0d 00:18:22
to 192.168.71.254 via fxp0.0
172.16.0.0/12      *[Static/5] 6w0d 00:25:57
to 192.168.71.254 via fxp0.0
192.168.0.0/16     *[Static/5] 6w0d 00:25:57
to 192.168.71.254 via fxp0.0
192.168.40.0/22    *[Static/5] 6w0d 00:18:22
to 192.168.71.254 via fxp0.0
192.168.64.0/21    *[Direct/0] 6w0d 00:25:57
via fxp0.0
192.168.71.246/32  *[Local/0] 6w0d 00:25:57
Local via fxp0.0
192.168.102.0/23   *[Static/5] 6w0d 00:25:57
to 192.168.71.254 via fxp0.0
207.17.136.0/24    *[Static/5] 6w0d 00:25:57
to 192.168.71.254 via fxp0.0
207.17.136.192/32  *[Static/5] 6w0d 00:18:22
to 192.168.71.254 via fxp0.0
```

In Listing 13-2, the interface address for router 5 is not in router 2's route table, meaning there is *no* route to that host, which verifies what you already know: You can't ping that interface.

Another way you can check on the route is to look at the BGP routes and see what route information BGP is sharing. A quick look at the `show route protocol bgp` output reveals that no BGP route exists:

```
user@router4> show route protocol bgp
```

```
inet.0: 16 destinations, 16 routes (15 active, 0 holddown, 1 hidden)
```

The question becomes how do you get BGP routes into the routing table?

Within your own network, the number of routes is relatively small or at least contained. If OSPF floods these routes to all other OSPF-enabled routers, it's probably not a big deal. And even OSPF has the ability to isolate routes through the use of areas to address the possibility of very large networks having tons of route advertisements.

So imagine BGP now. BGP connects networks to networks. If you took all the routes from your internal network and advertised those to your peering network, your peering network would have to track both its own internal routes and all of yours. And if a peer to your peer got all the routes from both you and your peer — well, you can see this situation would get very bad very fast.

Therefore, BGP requires you to explicitly state what you want to advertise and to whom. It brings sanity to what would otherwise be a chaotic world full of 220 thousand routes on every router.

Configuring routing policies that advertise their routes

Getting BGP routes into the routing table is a matter of advertising. The default behavior of BGP is to accept all nonlooped routes learned via BGP. You must configure routing policies to make sure that these routes get propagated through the network. Examine the topology in Figure 13-5.

Each link in the topology is a subnet to which the routers are connected. These subnets are included in the route table as static routes (direct routes, to be more precise). If you can advertise those subnets to your internal neighbors, you'll have BGP routes to all your internal peers.

Configuring routing policy requires the definition of the policy and the application of that policy on either the inbound (import) control traffic or the outbound (export) control traffic.

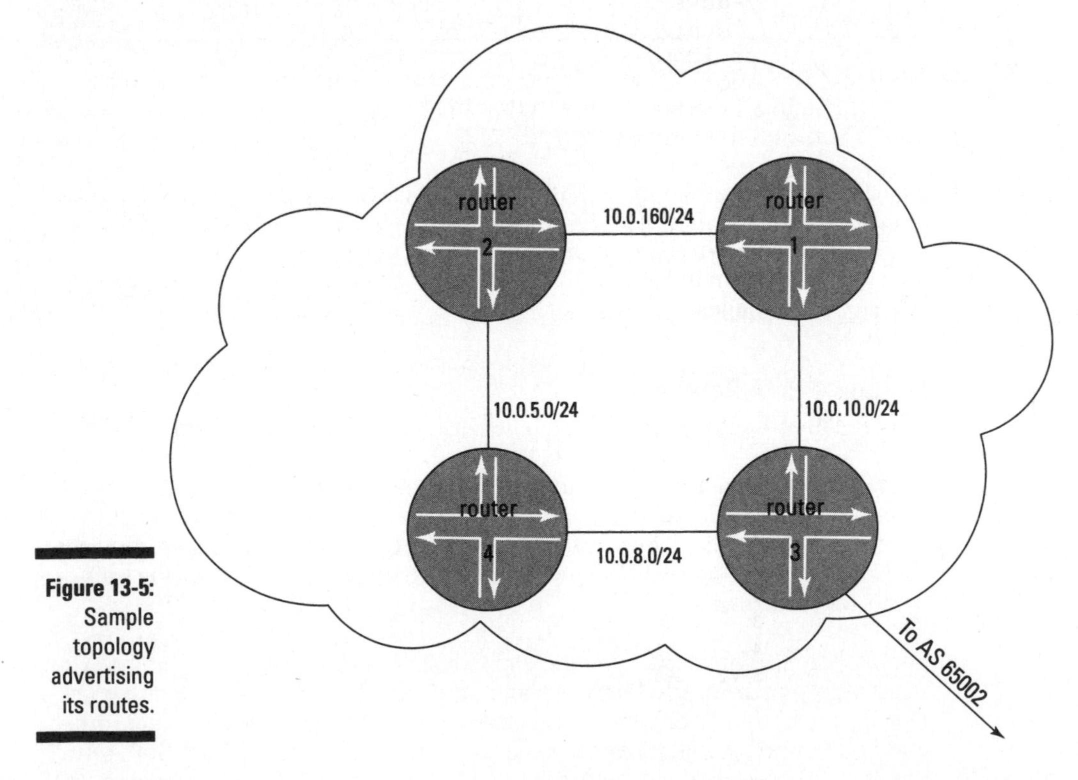

Figure 13-5: Sample topology advertising its routes.

In this case, you want to include static routes, so you want to use the `accept` action:

```
[edit policy-options]
policy-statement ibgp-export {
    term export-statics {
        from protocol static;
        then accept;
    }
}
```

In this routing policy, you accept all routes that are static. Whether you accept them as you receive control traffic or include them in your outbound control traffic depends on *where* you apply the policy. In this example, you want to include the routes in your outbound BGP advertisements, so you need to apply the policy as an export policy for your IBGP group:

```
[edit protocols]
bgp {
    group my-guys {
        type internal;
        export ibgp-export;
        neighbor 192.168.14.1;
        neighbor 192.168.14.2;
        neighbor 192.168.14.4;
    }
}
```

Issuing a `show route` command reveals that BGP routes are now in the routing table, as shown in Listing 13-3, which has been slightly truncated in order to fit on these pages:

Listing 13-3: A Routing Table Showing BGP Routes

```
mike@router2> show route

inet.0: 16 destinations, 16 routes (15 active, 0 holddown, 1 hidden)
+ = Active Route, - = Last Active, * = Both
192.168.14.1/24     *[BGP/100] 6w0d 01:56:10
to 192.168.14.3 via fe-0/0/0.0
192.168.14.2/24     *[BGP/100] 6w0d 01:56:10
to 192.168.14.3 via fe-0/0/0.0
192.168.14.4/24     *[BGP/100] 6w0d 01:56:10
to 192.168.14.3 via fe-0/0/0.0
192.168.64.0/21     *[Direct/0] 6w0d 02:03:45
via fxp0.0
192.168.71.246/32   *[Local/0] 6w0d 02:03:45
Local via fxp0.0
192.168.102.0/23    *[BGP/100] 6w0d 02:03:45
to 192.168.71.254 via fxp0.0
```

(continued)

Listing 13-3 (continued)

```
207.17.136.0/24    *[Static/5] 6w0d 02:03:45
to 192.168.71.254 via fxp0.0
207.17.136.192/32  *[Static/5] 6w0d 01:56:10
to 192.168.71.254 via fxp0.0
...
```

You can identify the BGP routes in Listing 13-3 by the content in brackets. It indicates how the route was learned and specifies the local preference.

The *local preference* is used to decide which route to use if there are two routes to the same destination. For example, if a static route has a local preference of 5, and BGP has a local preference of 100, the router will use the static route because of the higher preference value (lower number).

After configuring the routing policy for your IBGP routers, you must configure policy for your EBGP router. As it turns out, you can use a very similar policy and apply it on external group:

```
[edit policy-options]
policy-statement ebgp-export {
   term export-statics {
   from protocol static;
   then accept;
   }
}
```

Now apply it to your external group:

```
[edit protocols]
bgp {
   group those-guys {
      type external;
      export ebgp-export;
      peer-as 65002;
      neighbor 10.0.26.2;
   }
}
```

The application of these two routing policies ensures that routes are shared within your IBGP mesh and that those routes will not be leaked via the EBGP connection between ASs, which is important because you don't want to flood (or, by extension, be flooded by) internal routes into a neighboring network. Issuing a `show route` protocol bgp command on each of the routers should reveal that only the expected routes are included in the route tables.

Consider setting up an aggregate route to represent your entire set of addresses. As an example, if you have a lot of contiguous 192.168.x/24 addresses, you should configure an aggregate route and filter those routes. (For more details about route filtering, see Chapter 14.)

Using next-hop addresses

After the route table looks like it has all the necessary routes, you should be able to ping the routers in one AS from the other AS, right? Well, not quite. Understanding why pinging still doesn't work requires a little explanation of how BGP routes are exchanged and a look at Figure 13-6.

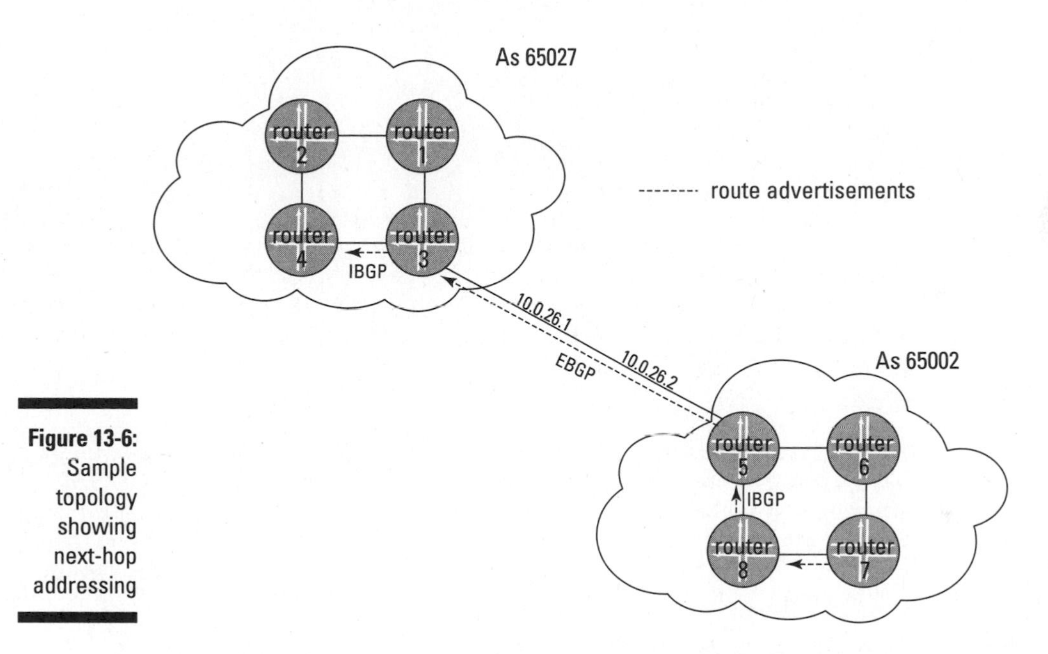

Figure 13-6: Sample topology showing next-hop addressing

When BGP shares a route via BGP messages, it includes next-hop information so that a router knows where to send traffic when forwarding to that particular destination. In Figure 13-5, earlier in this chapter, the peers that reside within AS 65502 send their routes through the gateway router 5. When that route gets passed to router 3 via EBGP, the advertisement includes the next-hop information tied to that EBGP link. Specifically, the interface address on router 5 (10.0.26.2) is marked as the next hop.

The problem is that when router 2 wants to send traffic to a peer within AS 65502, it must know where the 10.0.26.2/24 route is. But how does it get this information?

The simplest way of ensuring that a router has a route to the next-hop address is to set the next-hop address to something you know the router knows how to reach. In your AS, the routers all know each other's loopback addresses by virtue of OSPF. OSPF tells IBGP how to reach the loopback interface so that IBGP can establish its BGP session. So if router 3 can set the next-hop address to itself, overwriting the previous address, then all the routers in your AS will be able to send traffic.

To overwrite the previous next-hop address and use the router's own loopback as the next-hop address, use a routing policy to set next-hop self:

```
[edit policy-options]
policy-statement ibgp-export {
    term export-statics {
        from protocol static;
        then accept;
    }
    term next-hop-self {
        then {
            next-hop self;
        }
    }
}
```

The addition of a second term accomplishes this task. Routes are evaluated against the first term and accepted if they're static routes. Then those accepted BGP routes have the next-hop value set to the local router loopback address. When those routes are learned by other peers within your network, those peer routers will send traffic to the loopback address of your gateway router since they know how to reach the loopback address.

The alternative way to solve the problem of next-hop self is to ensure that you have a route to the peering subnet between your AS and the adjacent AS. If you run an IGP, the subnets are automatically advertised through that IGP to all your internal routers. If you run OSPF *passively* on that link (meaning that you don't want to establish an adjacency and flood routes there), your routers will learn the 10.0.26.0/24 subnet.

Given the simplicity of just setting next-hop self via a policy and the relatively more risky proposition of potentially flooding IGP routes across an unwanted link, you should generally use a routing policy to resolve this issue.

Pinging to the loopbacks

After you configure both EBGP and IBGP, the routing policies associated with each, and the next-hop information, it would be a shame if you couldn't ping a router in one AS from the other AS.

In Figure 13-7, notice that both router 2 and router 7 are in different ASs but aren't directly connected. If your BGP configuration is correct, you should be able to find a route to router 7 from router 2.

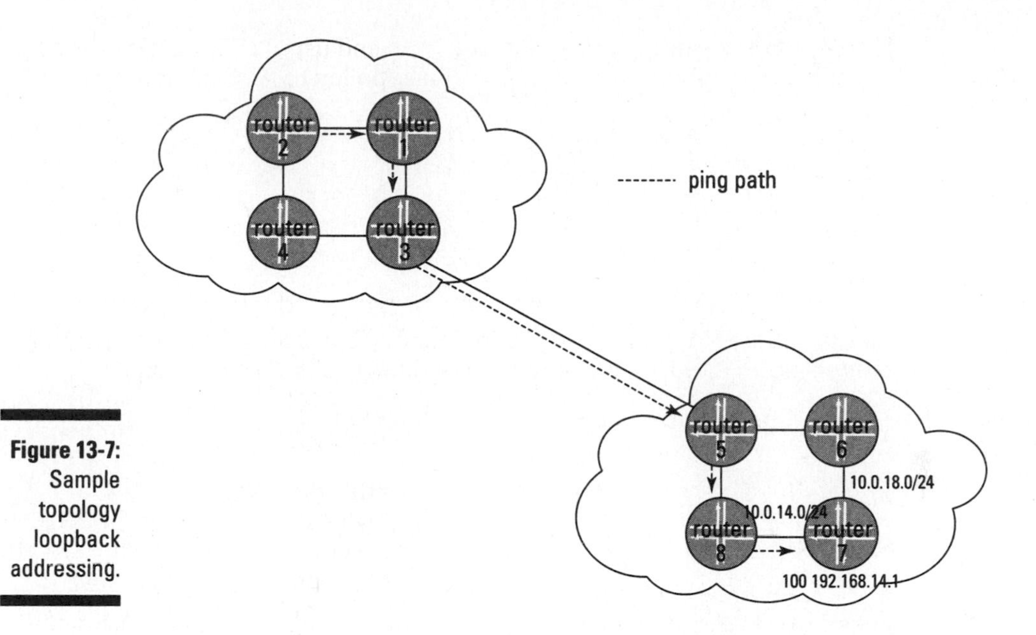

Figure 13-7: Sample topology loopback addressing.

To verify that the two are, in fact, reachable, issue a ping to the remote router, but look what happens when you issue the ping command:

```
mike@router2> ping 192.168.14.1
PING 192.168.14.1 (192.168.14.1): 56 data bytes
ping: sendto: No route to host
ping: sendto: No route to host
ping: sendto: No route to host
```

This ping command was supposed to work. What happened? Remember that your routing policies were advertising static routes, which were essentially all the directly connected routes. You weren't advertising all the loopback addresses of the individual routers. So the routing table on router 2 only contains routes to the subnets connecting all the routers, not routes to all the loopbacks.

If you examine the routing table in Listing 13-4, you should see a route to the subnets for router 7's outbound interfaces. (Note that the routing table has been truncated to fit on these pages.)

Listing 13-4: Routing Table Showing Routes to Loopbacks

```
mike@router2> show route

inet.0: 16 destinations, 16 routes (15 active, 0 holddown, 1 hidden)
+ = Active Route, - = Last Active, * = Both
```

(continued)

Listing 13-4 *(continued)*

```
10.5.0.0/16        *[Static/5] 6w0d 01:56:10
to 192.168.71.254 via fxp0.0
10.0.14.0/24       *[BGP/100] 6w0d 02:03:45
to 192.168.14.1 via fe-0/0/1.0
10.0.18.0/24   *[BGP/100] 6w0d 02:03:45
to 192.168.14.1 via fe-0/0/1.0
…
```

As expected, routes go to the 10.0.14/24 subnet and the 10.0.16/24 subnet. A ping to either of the interfaces on those subnets should yield results:

```
mike@router2> ping 10.0.14.1
PING 10.0.14.1 (10.0.14.1): 56 data bytes
64 bytes from 10.0.14.1: icmp_seq=0 ttl=63 time=0.917 ms
64 bytes from 10.0.14.1: icmp_seq=1 ttl=63 time=0.429 ms
64 bytes from 10.0.14.1: icmp_seq=2 ttl=63 time=0.452 ms
```

If you want to be able to ping to the loopback addresses of the routers in the neighboring AS, you need to configure a BGP routing policy to export those routes. In this case, you may want to advertise a single route aggregate for all the routes within the AS (see Chapter 14).

Configuring Route Reflection

Configuring BGP can be quite onerous, particularly with large numbers of peering sessions that must be configured manually. In fact, in a large network, the full-mesh requirement for IBGP can be a provisioning nightmare. If you have only 10 routers in your network, as shown in Figure 13-8, you have to configure an IBGP session between every pair of routers.

Looking at Figure 13-8, you realize that you have to configure a session on each router to each other router. Simple math reveals that you have 45 IBGP peering sessions that need configured — N*(N-1)/2, where N is the number of routers in your network.

If you've been wondering why BGP wasn't used everywhere instead of IGPs, it's because IBGP configuration is difficult to maintain. Adding a single router to your network requires that you touch the configuration of every other router that is already in the network. This task is challenging at best and downright unmanageable for large networks.

BGP's answer to the configuration nightmare that is the full mesh is called *route reflection.*

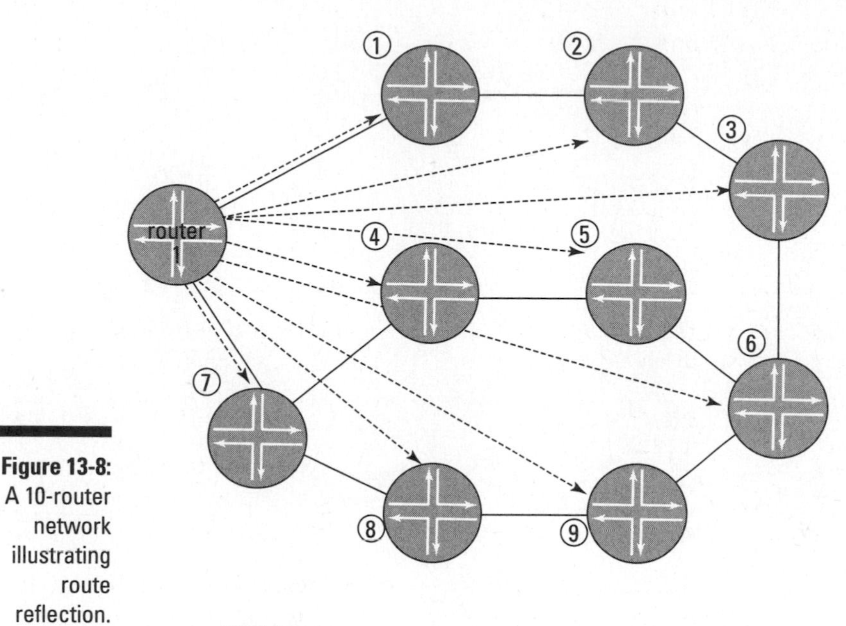

Figure 13-8: A 10-router network illustrating route reflection.

Route reflectors on large networks

IBGP comes with a significant restriction: IBGP peers should not re-advertise IBGP-learned routes to other IBGP speakers, which is why they all need to be fully meshed and have no loop prevention— the reason why you need route reflectors for large networks. If you can't re-advertise IBGP routes, then you must be directly connected to the originator of the route, hence the full mesh requirement.

The concept of *route reflection* allows you to designate one or more of your routers as route reflectors. BGP relaxes the re-advertising restriction on these route reflectors, allowing them to accept and propagate IBGP routes to their clients. Figure 13-9 shows a 16-router topology.

Because of the IBGP full-mesh requirement, this topology would require 15 IBGP peering sessions per router, or 120 distinct IBGP sessions within the network. However, if you designate router 4 as a route reflector, you can start to minimize this requirement. For example, look at what happens in Figure 13-10 with the routers directly connected to router 4.

In this part of the topology, router 4 has three directly connected routers. If just this part of the topology is running IBGP, you have to configure a full mesh between the 4 routers. However, if you designate router 4 as a route reflector, BGP only requires that every route reflector client have an IBGP connection to the route reflector (not to each other), as shown in Figure 13-11.

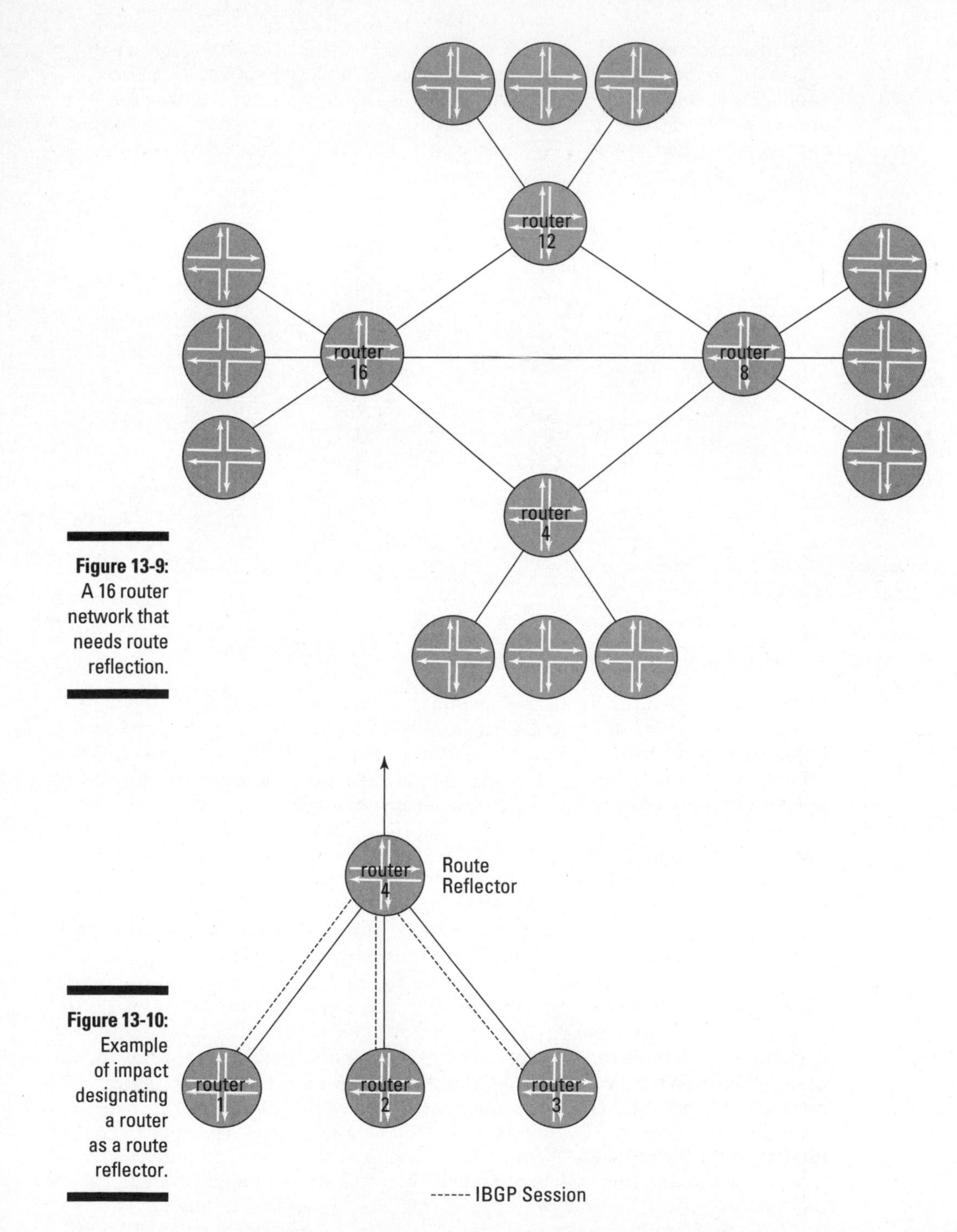

Figure 13-9: A 16 router network that needs route reflection.

Figure 13-10: Example of impact designating a router as a route reflector.

With this new configuration shown in Figure 13-11, the IBGP routes from routers 1, 2, and 3 are sent to the route reflector. Router 4, acting as the route reflector, re-advertises these routes to all of its clients. In this way, router 1 and router 2 are connected via IBGP, through their shared route reflector router 4. This group of routers is called a *cluster,* and each cluster is uniquely identified by its *cluster ID* (a 32-bit number similar to an IP address).

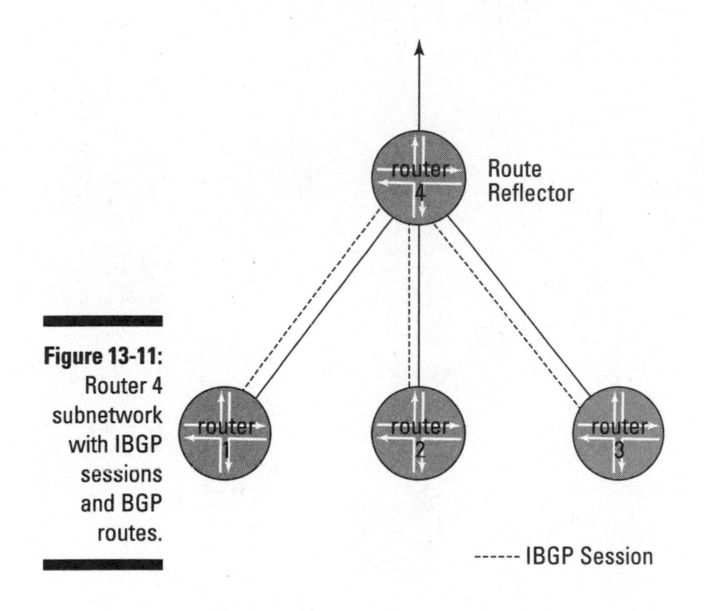

Figure 13-11: Router 4 subnetwork with IBGP sessions and BGP routes.

Looking back at the original 16-router network, if you make similar route reflectors with routers 8, 12, and 16, you can create four route reflectors and reduce the number of IBGP sessions, as shown in Figure 13-12.

However, all 16 routers are still in the same AS, which means that IBGP has to fully connect all 16 routers. How do you do this?

Ultimately, you must have connectivity somewhere. That connectivity occurs at the route reflector level. The route reflectors must be fully meshed, meaning that you must have IBGP peering sessions between each of the four route reflectors.

Essentially, you have drastically reduced the number of IBGP sessions in your network. Where you previously needed 120 sessions to fully mesh your network, you now need only three sessions from each route reflector to its clients and an additional six sessions to fully mesh the route reflectors (for a total of 18 IBGP sessions).

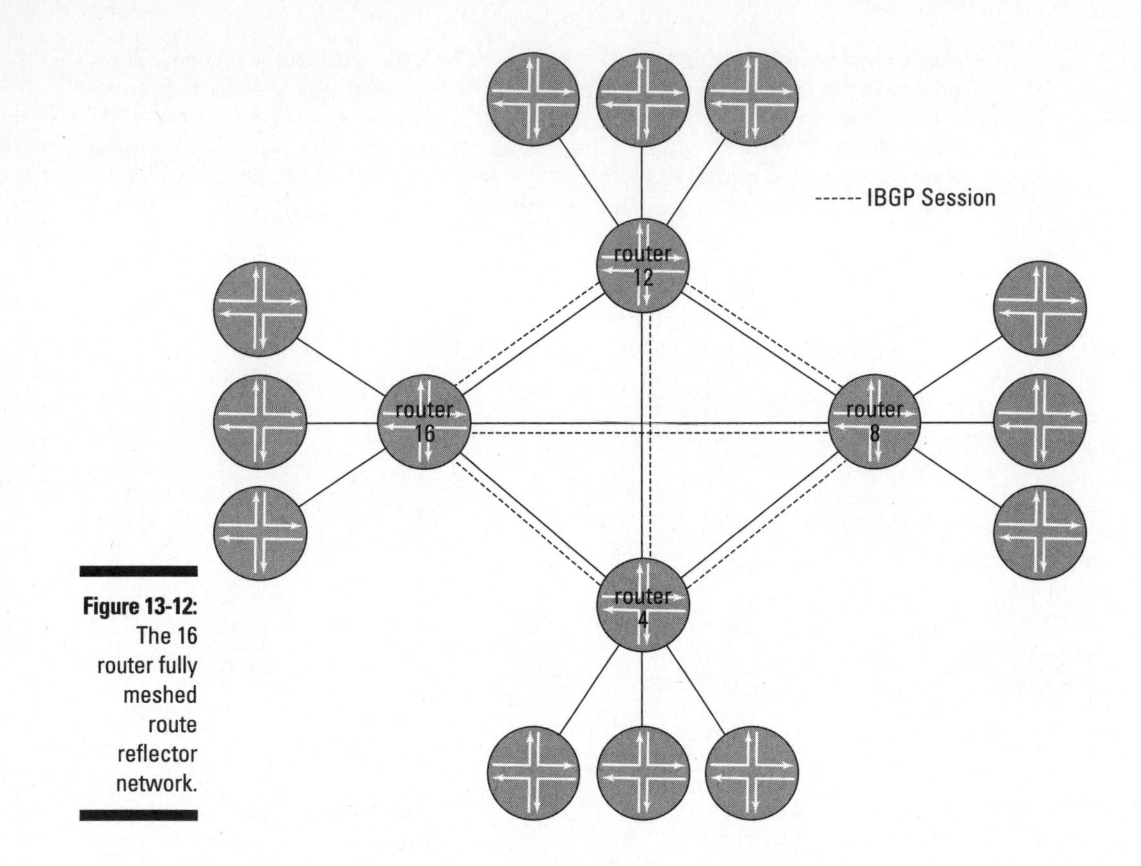

Figure 13-12: The 16 router fully meshed route reflector network.

Route reflector configuration

So how do you actually set up a router to act as a route reflector? The configuration of route reflectors has to happen on both the route reflector and on the client. Examine router 4's clients shown in Figure 13-13.

On the route reflector side, the configuration requires only that you identify routing cluster for which it is the reflector:

```
[edit protocols]
bgp {
   group reflector-peers {
      type internal;
      cluster 172.16.1.1;
      neighbor 172.16.2.2;
      neighbor 172.16.3.3;
      neighbor 172.16.4.4;
   }
}
```

The configuration is identical to a normal IBGP configuration except that a cluster ID has been specified.

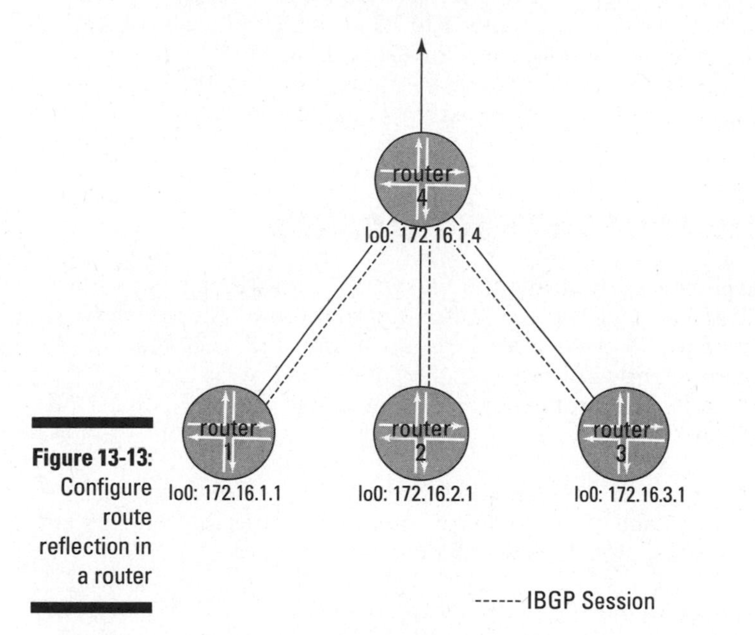

Figure 13-13: Configure route reflection in a router

Notice in this configuration that the cluster ID has been configured to be identical to the router ID. This configuration is generally a best practice because it makes it easier to track the originating cluster for routes that are advertised throughout your network.

On the client side, the configuration is identical to previous IBGP configurations except that you now have only a session configured between each client and the route reflector (not between each other):

```
[edit protocols]
bgp {
   group route-reflector {
      type internal;
      neighbor 172.16.1.1;
   }
}
```

Each client to the route reflector will have that route reflector configured as an internal peer.

You still have to configure the routing policy to ensure that routes are advertised as expected. The route reflector doesn't change that requirement. You, however, don't want to configure a next-hop-self policy on your route reflector because you don't want all your external-bound traffic to flow through the route reflectors. You want it to take the shortest path, which isn't generally through the route reflector. The exception to this rule is when the EBGP session from another AS is directly connected to your route reflector.

Dual route reflectors for backup

Basic route reflection is fairly straightforward but comes with a basic drawback: If you only had a single route reflector and that route reflector were to fail, your routers would be separated from your network, which means that you have inadvertently created a single point of failure for that part of your network. To solve this problem, you can choose to configure dual route reflectors (see Figure 13-14).

In this type of cluster, each client simply configures IBGP connections to both route reflectors. Each of the route reflectors configures its own cluster ID and forms peering relationships with its clients.

The two route reflectors themselves can interconnect in one of two ways: Either they can peer through a straight IBGP connection as per normal IBGP, or you can have each route reflector be a client to the other.

In the case where you have dual route reflectors, consider configuring each of them with the exact same cluster ID. This configuration reduces the total number of routes that have to be stored, and it tends to be far easier to understand when you depict the topology graphically (for example, the cluster has a single ID with two reflectors serving it).

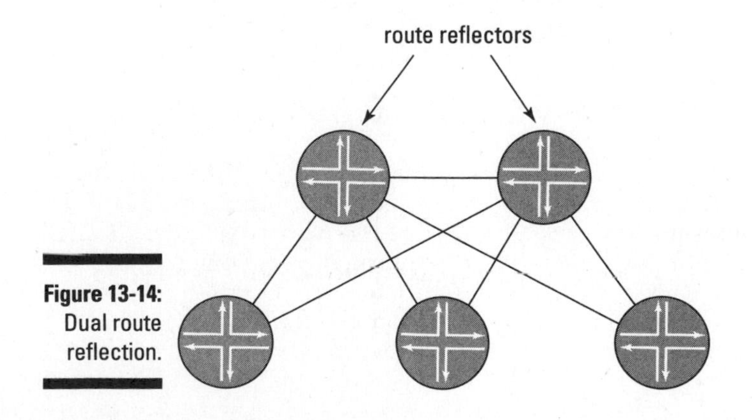

Figure 13-14: Dual route reflection.

Chapter 14

Working with Routing Policies

In This Chapter

- Applying routing policies
- Validating the routing policies
- Filtering your routes
- Understanding route aggregation

Your router (or other L3 device) gathers location information from routing protocols and stores it in its routing tables. These routing tables are then whittled down to include only the best information, and that information is stored in the forwarding table, which is ultimately responsible for where traffic is forwarded.

With all of that in place, what if the information being learned by the routing protocols are wrong? You're receiving information from your neighbors, and what if your neighbors are doing something you do not want them to do? You need a way of controlling how information is imported into your router. And on the flip side of the coin, you need a way to prevent your router from doing things that neighboring routers might not like. Routing policies are that way. Routing policies are your solution to monitoring, filtering, or even modifying what gets into and what comes out of your routing and forwarding tables.

Constructing Routing Policies

Routing protocols allow routers to exchange information and figure out where everyone is located. When a routing protocol like BGP shares information about the BGP routes it knows, these routes are received by your router and stored in the routing table. The *routing table* represents the collective knowledge of all the routing information that your router has. And from that repository of routing knowledge, your router selects only the best routes. These best routes form the *forwarding table,* which provides the final word on all forwarding decisions.

Routing policies are the constructs designed to control what goes into and what comes out of the routing table. That is, routing policies act as an inbound filter into the routing table and ultimately determine what information your router shares with other routers.

To understand how routing policies are configured, you must learn the basic building blocks and components that make up policies:

- Terms
- Match conditions
- Match actions
- Default actions
- Application of routing policies
- Evaluation of routing policies

The following sections describe these building blocks and components in detail.

Terms

The building blocks that make up routing policies are called *terms*. Each term contains match conditions that are checked. Based on the outcome of those checks, the router will lead to an evaluation against one or more actions, as illustrated in Figure 14-1. Terms are then strung together to form a routing policy.

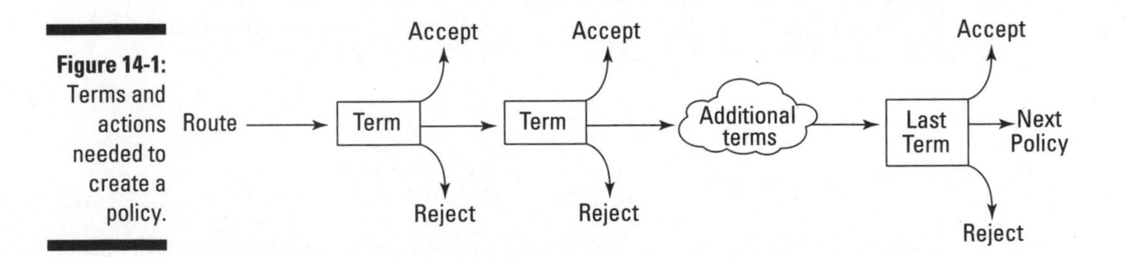

Figure 14-1: Terms and actions needed to create a policy.

Assume that a routing policy is applied to filter incoming routes. That routing policy is made up of several terms. As the route comes in, the policy is invoked. The first term in the policy is evaluated. If the route matches the conditions specified in the term, some action is taken. If it doesn't, the second term in the policy is evaluated. That second term's conditions are checked, and if they match, some action is taken. If they don't match, the third term in the policy is evaluated, and so on until all terms have been examined.

If none of the terms of the policy are a match for the route in question, then the next policy is evaluated, and so on until the default policy action is taken. (For more information, see the section "Default actions," later in this chapter.)

To configure a routing policy, you have to configure one or more terms within that policy. Configuration for policies is handled within the policy-options configuration hierarchy:

```
[edit policy-options]
policy-statement my-sample-policy {
    term my-first-term {
        from {
            match-conditions;
        }
        then {
            action;
        }
    term my-second-term {
        from {
            match-conditions;
        }
        then {
            action;
        }
}
```

In this configuration skeleton, you've configured a single routing policy called *my-sample-policy*. That policy is going to have two terms, each of which will have some match condition and a match action. If a route is evaluated against this policy and neither term matches, the default action will be executed. Once an action is taken, the policy is no longer evaluated. So if you have an action triggered in the first term, the second term will never even evaluate the second condition. You use this skeleton as you build up some basic routing policies throughout this chapter.

Terms within a policy are evaluated in a top-down manner. Put another way, the order of the terms within your configuration counts. The challenge here is that whenever you add a new term to an existing policy, by default, these terms are appended to the already configured terms. Newly added terms will always be evaluated after the terms initially configured. For example, examine the following configuration:

```
[edit policy-options]
policy-statement advertise-ospf-routes {
   term find-ospf {
      from {
         protocol ospf;
      }
      then {
         accept;
      }
   }
}
```

This policy simply accepts all OSPF routes. If you want to fine-tune this policy a little bit and accept all OSPF routes except those that originate from a particular area in your OSPF network, you need to add a term. Because terms are, by default, appended to existing terms, your configuration will be

```
[edit policy-options]
policy-statement advertise-ospf-routes {
   term find-ospf {
      from {
         protocol ospf;
      }
      then {
         accept;
      }
   }
   term reject-area-10 {
      from {
         protocol ospf;
         area 10;
      }
      then {
         reject;
      }
   }
}
```

What you want is for all OSPF routes to be accepted unless they come from area 10. However, when a route comes in, the first term is evaluated. If the route is an OSPF route, it's accepted, regardless of its area of origin. No routes from area 10 are ever rejected, because the first term accepts all OSPF routes.

If you want to add in the reject-area-10 term before the `find-ospf` term, you can use the `insert` command. Configure the two terms exactly as you did in the preceding code, but when you're done, insert the term where you want it:

```
user@host# insert policy-statement advertise-ospf-routes
           term reject-area-10 before term find-ospf
```

The `insert` command moves the configuration for the reject-area-10 term before the configuration to find all OSPF routes. The resulting configuration does what you want:

```
[edit policy-options]
policy-statement advertise-ospf-routes {
    term reject-area-10 {
        from {
            protocol ospf;
            area 10;
        }
        then {
            reject;
        }
    }
    term find-ospf {
        from {
            protocol ospf;
        }
        then {
            accept;
        }
    }
}
```

Match conditions

The whole point of routing policies is to take a particular route (and its corresponding attributes) and match it against some expected values. In this context, match conditions form the *if* part of an *if-then* construct. *If* a route matches the condition specified, *then* take some action. The match conditions, therefore, determine what your routing policies can detect. There are a number of match conditions, but only a subset of all the different conditions is typically used. Table 14-1 lists some of the more common match conditions.

Table 14-1 JUNOS Routing Policy Match Conditions

Summary	*Configuration Keyword*	*Description*
Route metric	metric	Corresponds to the metric value associated with the route
Route preference	preference	Matches on the route preference
Interface name	interface	Identifies the interface through which a route was received
Neighbor address	neighbor	Typically the peer from which a route was received

(continued)

Table 14-1 *(continued)*

Summary	*Configuration Keyword*	*Description*
Protocol	protocol	Typically the name of the protocol from which a route was learned
Area ID	area	For OSPF routes, identifies the area from which a route was learned
AS Path	as-path	For BGP routes, identifies the AS path associated with a particular route

You can't just know what the match conditions are — you must also know how they're oriented. Routes can be evaluated based on where they come from as well as where they are going. As an example, you can match on all routes that are learned through a particular neighbor or on all routes being exported to a particular neighbor.

That being said, you're probably best off just worrying about matching on where things are coming from. If you start to match on where things are going, you can overcomplicate things, which can have adverse effects on your network.

To configure a match condition (assuming that you're matching on where something is from), you use the `from` keyword:

```
[edit policy-options]
policy-statement my-sample-policy {
   term my-first-term {
      from {
         protocol static;
      }
      then {
         action;
      }
   term my-second-term {
      from {
         neighbor 10.22.32.1;
      }
      then {
         action;
      }
}
```

Applying a routing policy to all traffic

There are often times when you want a routing policy to apply to all traffic. In these cases, all you need to do is omit the `from` statement within the policy. If there is no `from` statement, JUNOS applies the match action to all traffic:

```
[edit policy-options]
policy-statement accept-all-
   routes {
   term accept-all {
      then accept;
   }
}
```

In this case, because there is nothing to match against, all traffic is subject to the specified action. In this case, all routes are accepted. Now whether that means they're imported or exported is a different story.

In the preceding configuration, a routing policy skeleton contains a pair of match conditions. If the first condition is met, then some action (yet to be specified) is taken. If it doesn't match, the second term is evaluated.

This last configuration is actually a little different than what you'll see on the router. Because you have only a single match condition, the router simplifies the configuration and collapses multiple lines into one:

```
[edit policy-options]
policy-statement my-sample-policy {
   term my-first-term {
      from protocol static;
      then {
         action;
      }
   term my-second-term {
      from neighbor 10.22.32.1;
      then {
         action;
      }
}
```

The configuration here is identical, but it's been streamlined a bit and matches what you'll see in the configuration file if you issue a `show configuration` command after creating the policy.

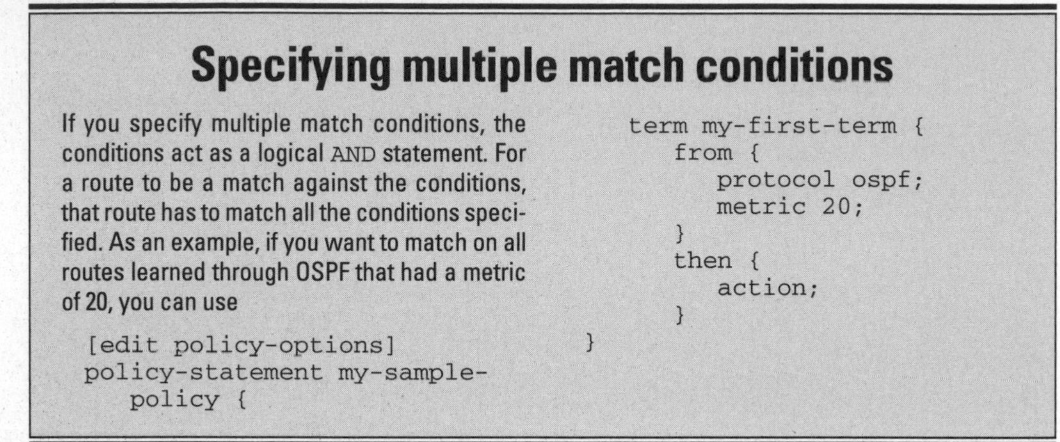

Specifying multiple match conditions

If you specify multiple match conditions, the conditions act as a logical AND statement. For a route to be a match against the conditions, that route has to match all the conditions specified. As an example, if you want to match on all routes learned through OSPF that had a metric of 20, you can use

```
[edit policy-options]
policy-statement my-sample-
   policy {
      term my-first-term {
         from {
            protocol ospf;
            metric 20;
         }
         then {
            action;
         }
      }
}
```

Match actions

While the match conditions are the IF, the match *actions* are the THEN. When a particular match condition is met, the action associated with that term is executed. Table 14-2 lists the actions you can choose from.

Table 14-2 JUNOS Routing Policy Match Actions

Action	*Description*
`Accept`	Accept the route and send it on.
`Reject`	Reject or suppress the route.
`Next-term`	Stop evaluating the current term in the policy and immediately move to the next term. In this case, any terminating action isn't executed, but all other actions are executed (meaning a route can be modified before passing to the next term).
`Next-policy`	Stop evaluating the current term in the policy and immediately move to the next policy. In this case, any terminating action is not executed, but all other actions are executed (exactly as the previous).
`Modify`	Several modifying actions manipulate values in the route, such as as-path, metric, preference, and so on. These actions are not terminating actions. The specified route attribute is modified as configured, and then any other match actions are executed (if more than one is configured for that particular term). If there are no terminating actions, the next term is evaluated (if one exists).
`Trace`	Log the match to a trace file. This is useful for debugging routing policy.

About 95 percent of the time (if not more), you'll be able to do what you want using only `accept` and `reject`. These actions are called *terminating actions,* because when they're executed, the routing policy evaluation stops and the decision is made. Your device needs to continue evaluating other terms in the policy or other policies in the chain.

The actions like `next-term` and `next-policy` provide some sophisticated flow control capabilities, but you'll probably not need them right away. Additionally, modifying route attributes is probably not something you want to deal with. Although you can do some interesting things by modifying route attributes, such constructs are more widely used in carrier networks.

If match actions form the THEN part of the IF-THEN statement, it probably makes sense to configure them using the `then` statement within a policy:

```
[edit policy-options]
policy-statement my-sample-policy {
   term my-first-term {
      from protocol static;
      then accept;
   term my-second-term {
      from neighbor 10.22.32.1;
      then reject;
   }
}
```

Notice that, just like with the match conditions, the configuration is collapsed when you have a single match action. In this example, the first term is evaluated. If the route is a static route, the route is accepted. If the route isn't a static route, the second term is evaluated. If the route is from the neighbor 10.22.31.1, the route is rejected.

Default actions

What if none of the terms in a match condition match? Examine this policy:

```
[edit policy-options]
policy-statement my-sample-policy {
   term my-first-term {
      from protocol bgp;
      then accept;
   }
}
```

Specifying more than one match action

Just like with match conditions, you can specify more than one match action. For example, you may want to modify a route metric so that it becomes the preferred route, and then you want to accept that route into the forwarding table. In this case, you need both a modifying action and the `accept` terminating action. You configuration would be

```
[edit policy-options]
policy-statement my-sample-
   policy {
      term my-first-term {
         from protocol ospf;
         then {
            metric 5;
            accept;
         }
      }
   }
```

In this example, you match on all OSPF routes. Before accepting the route, you set the route metric to 5. Both match actions are executed in this case.

In this example, if the route was learned via BGP, it's accepted. However, if you assume that the route is rejected because it's not learned via BGP, you'd be wrong.

If a route doesn't match any of the configured terms, a *default action* is taken. The question becomes "What is the default action?"

And as with any complex topic, the answer is "It depends." The default action depends on where the routing policy is applied.

Routing policies must be applied to one or more protocols configured on the router. Each protocol has its own default policy, so the default action depends on which protocol (or protocols) the policy is applied to. The default action is also dependent on whether the policy is applied to routes being imported (brought into the routing table) or exported (advertised from the routing table). Table 14-3 summarizes the default actions tied to some of the more common routing protocols.

Table 14-3 JUNOS Routing Policy Default Actions

Protocol	*Default Action*
RIP	*Import*: Accept all routes received on RIP-enabled interfaces *Export*: Do not export any RIP routes.
OSPF	*Import*: Policies can't be used for imported router. *Export*: Export all routes learned via OSPF and all direct routes associated with the OSPF-enabled interfaces.
BGP	*Import*: Accept all routes learned from BGP neighbors. *Export:* Export all active routes learned via BGP to all BGP neighbors.

Notice that the default action can only be `accept` or `reject`. The default action must be a terminating action to ensure that all routes reach some definitive conclusion. That is, all routes are eventually either accepted or rejected.

Application of policies

The combination of two facts determines how a routing policy is applied:

- Policies are associated with routing protocols.
- Policies control either what gets *imported into* or what gets *exported out* of the routing table.

For example, assume that you want to apply a routing policy to advertise BGP routes via OSPF. Your configuration resembled

```
[edit policy-options]
policy-statement my-sample-policy {
    term my-first-term {
        from protocol bgp;
        then accept;
    }
}

[edit protocols]
ospf {
    export my-sample-policy;
}
```

The policy now begins to take on some meaning. By applying the policy as an export policy for OSPF, you're saying that you'll advertise via OSPF all routes learned through BGP.

What happens if the route is not learned via BGP? Is it automatically rejected? The answer is no. If the route doesn't match the term's conditions, it uses the default action. Because the policy is applied to OSPF, the default export behavior is to accept all routes learned via OSPF. This behavior means that an OSPF route, even though it doesn't match the term, will be accepted because of the default action.

To apply the same policy to explicitly import all BGP routes into your BGP routing table, you simply change how the policy is applied:

```
[edit protocols]
bgp {
    import my-sample-policy;
}
```

By only changing how the policy is applied, the entire meaning of the policy is altered.

Import policies and OSPF

The reason you can't create import policies for OSPF (or IS-IS for that matter) is that OSPF is a *link-state protocol*. Link-state protocols work by ensuring that every node within the network shares the exact same view of the link-state database. If you were to modify or filter inbound routes, you'd create a local copy of the link-state database that wouldn't necessarily match the shared view of the database. If the databases aren't identical, you can't ensure that there are not routing loops in the topology.

If a route doesn't match any of the terms' conditions, the default action will kick in. Because this default action is dependent on the routing protocol and direction (either inbound or outbound routes), it can be less than obvious what will happen to routes not matching your criteria. To avoid confusion, you can explicitly configure a final action that will be executed if a route doesn't match any of your terms:

```
[edit policy-options]
policy-statement my-sample-
   policy {
   term my-first-term {
      from protocol static;
      then accept;
   term my-second-term {
      from neighbor
   10.22.32.1;
      then reject;
   }
   then reject;
}
```

In this example, a final action is configured to reject all routes. If a route doesn't match any of the terms, the final action is evoked, and the route is rejected. This final action is evaluated before the default action for whatever protocol this policy is applied against. So now you can clearly specify what default action to take without worrying about whether the policy is applied to OSPF or BGP traffic, to inbound or to outbound routes.

When you're creating policies, don't get too wrapped up in the words "accept" and "reject." Accept doesn't necessarily mean that your routing table will be accepting the routes. Conversely, reject doesn't imply that your routing table will be rejecting all routes. The behavior depends on whether the routing policy is applied on the inbound side (as an import policy) or on the outbound side (as an export policy).

Evaluation of routing policies

When constructing routing policies, you need to understand how they're evaluated. Multiple policies strung together are called a *policy chain*. The basic flow for policy evaluation in a policy chain is depicted in Figure 14-2.

Just as with policy terms, the order of policy configuration makes a difference. As a route comes in, it's evaluated against the first policy in the chain. The match criteria in the first term in the first policy are checked. If a match occurs, the corresponding match action is taken. If no match exists, the second term is evaluated, and so on. If there is no next term in the policy, then the next policy in the chain is evaluated. If there are no matches in any of that policy's terms, then the evaluation continues until no policies are remaining, at which point the default action is taken.

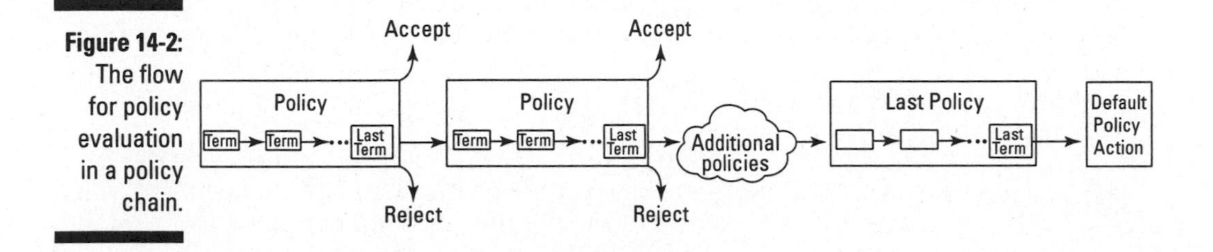

Figure 14-2: The flow for policy evaluation in a policy chain.

Configuring Route Filters

One of the fundamental purposes of routing policies is to gate certain routes from being either accepted into your routing table or advertised to some adjacent router. Sometimes, matching specific routes or a set of routes is useful. To do so, you use a *route filter*.

Route filters match on specific IP addresses or ranges of prefixes. Much like other routing policies, they include some match criteria and then a corresponding match action. The basic configuration resembles the following:

```
[edit policy-options]
policy-statement my-route-filter {
    term router-filter-term {
        from {
            router-filter prefix/prefix-length match-type;
        }
        then {
            actions;
        }
    }
}
```

This basic configuration outline matches a route against the specified filter. If the route matches, the defined action is taken. If it doesn't, the next term or policy is evaluated. As with other policies, if no match occurs, the protocol default action executes.

An important difference between route filters and other policy match conditions is how multiple filters are handled. If you have more than one match condition, the conditions are treated as a logical AND, meaning all of them must be true for it to be considered a match. With route filters, the presence of multiple filters represents a logical OR, meaning it's a match if the route matches any of the configured filters.

Prefixes and prefix lengths

If you want to effectively create route filters, you need to make sure that you understand *route prefixes* and *prefix lengths*. An IP address in dotted decimal notation is really just a shorthand way of representing a 32-bit address. As an example, the address 192.168.32.4 represents the following 32-bit address:

```
11000000 10101000 00100000 00000100
```

So when you add a prefix length to this IP address, you're specifying the number of significant digits in the expanded 32-bit address to include. If you want to match a prefix length of 24 (192.168.32/24, for example), you're really identifying the first three octets in the address.

For more descriptions of how IP addressing works, see Chapter 4.

Match types

The combination of a route prefix and prefix length along with the type of match determines how route filters are evaluated against incoming routes. Table 14-4 shows the half-dozen match types to be aware of.

Table 14-4 JUNOS Route Filter Match Types

Match Type	*Description*
`exact`	Matches if the prefix-length is equal to the route's prefix length.
`orlonger`	Matches if the prefix-length is equal to or greater than the route's prefix length.
`longer`	Matches if the prefix-length is greater than the route' prefix length.
`upto`	Matches if the route shares the most significant bits in the prefix-length and the route's prefix length falls between the prefix-length and the configured upper limit.
`prefix-length-range`	Matches if the route shares the most significant bits in the prefix-length and the route's prefix length falls within the specified range.
`through`	Route falls between the lower prefix/prefix-length and the upper prefix/prefix-length.

In Figure 14-3, each tree represents a set of addresses. For this particular picture, the top node within each tree represents the address 192.168/16. Each set of nodes below the top node represent longer prefix lengths. In other words, as you traverse downward on the tree, the addresses become more specific. (More significant bits are specified.)

Here's what the different match types mean:

- The *exact* match type means that only a route with the same prefix and same prefix length will match. It has to be an exact match, so only the 192.168/16 route is highlighted.
- The *orlonger* match indicates that any route that starts with 192.168 and has a prefix length of 16 or greater will match. In other words, any route that is more specific than 192.168/16 is a match, which is why all the routes are highlighted.
- The *longer* match type is the same as the *orlonger* match type, except that it doesn't include any exact matches. So the only difference is that the top node isn't included.
- If you use the *upto* match type, you must specify the upper limit for the prefix-length. For example, you'd configure `192.168/16 upto /24` to highlight all the addresses between 192.168/16 and 192.168/24.
- The *prefix-length-range* match type allows you to specify the significant bits of an address and then bound addresses with those significant bits between two prefix lengths. In this case, you can ensure that all addresses begin with 192.168, but you want to match only on addresses that have prefix lengths between 20 and 24.
- The final match type is *through*. This match type essentially creates a list of exact matches between the starting node and the ending address. All addresses between the two are considered matches.

Martian addresses

Routes that should never be present in any routing table have taken on an interesting name. These types of routes are called *Martian addresses,* perhaps because they're "out of this world." JUNOS software has a set of Martian addresses that are automatically blocked from appearing in your routing table:

- 0.0.0.0/8
- 127.0.0.0/8
- 128.0.0.0/16
- 191.255.0.0/16
- 192.0.0.0/24
- 223.255.255.0/24
- 240.0.0.0/4

Typically, you want to block bad routes and advertise good routes, which is done using these actions.

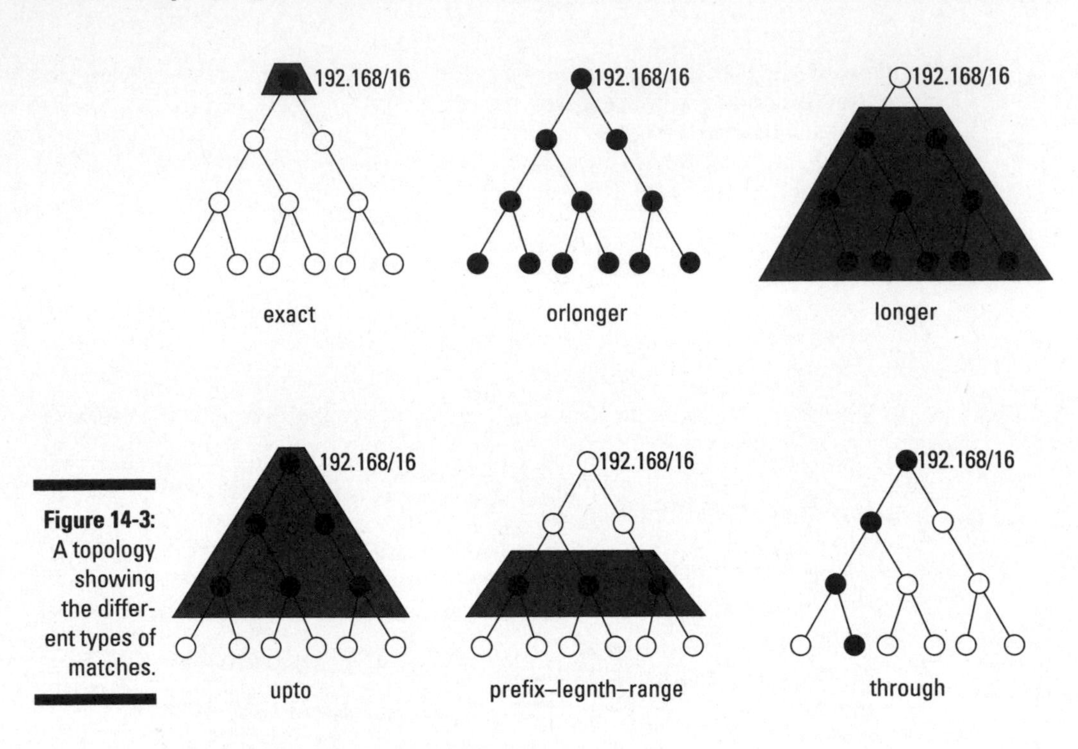

Figure 14-3: A topology showing the different types of matches.

Match actions

The match actions available to route filters are identical to those available for other routing policies. You can accept routes, reject routes, modify attributes that belong to a route, or perform flow control type functions. By far, the most common actions to use with route filters are accept and reject.

Once you know how to construct a route filter, you need to know what routes you want to be filtering. While you may not want a lot for any number of reasons, nobody wants the following routes in their routing tables:

- **0.0.0.0/0:** Nobody wants the default route advertised through their network. Advertising that route can change the default route for all routers that accepted the advertisement.
- **127/8:** Local loopback addresses aren't addresses you'll be routing traffic to.
- **1/8, 2/8, 5/8, 7/8, and 23/8:** The addresses in these ranges haven't been allocated by IANA (the organization that hands out IP addresses to Internet users). Because they shouldn't be in use, you should filter them.

If you want to configure your router so that it doesn't accept these types of routes, you need to create the route filter and then apply it to your protocols. To create the filter:

```
[edit policy-options]
policy-statement filter-unwanted-routes {
    term bad-routes {
        from {
            route-filter 1.0.0.0/8 orlonger;
            route-filter 2.0.0.0/8 orlonger;
            route-filter 5.0.0.0/8 orlonger;
            route-filter 7.0.0.0/8 orlonger;
            route-filter 23.0.0.0/8 orlonger;
        }
        then reject;
    }
}
```

In this example, you specify the routes that you want to make sure never get into your routing table. Notice that the default route and loopback routes aren't included in this list because they're considered Martian routes and are blocked by default. Here, it's worth noting that 0.0.0.0/8 doesn't include the default route (0.0.0.0/0). Additionally, you should know that you can add or delete routes form the Martian table as needed.

Now you must apply this policy to your router. Because you're trying to prevent your router from importing these known bad routes from your neighboring routers, you want an import policy.

Reserved addresses

A number of reserved address ranges are used for internal addressing. RFC 1918 defines these addresses:

- 10/8
- 172.16/12
- 192.168/16

These addresses are reserved, and you should not be receiving route advertisements from other networks containing them. However, they're not automatically filtered because you'll likely want to use these addresses to address your own gear.

It does make sense, though, to ensure that your peering networks aren't advertising these addresses to you, and that you're not sharing these addresses unintentionally with them — so you should configure route filters on the routers that peer with other networks. Configure a single policy to reject these routes and apply that policy as both an import and export policy with your external BGP peers:

```
[edit protocols]
bgp {
    group external-peers {
        import filter-reserved-
    addresses;
        export filter-reserved-
    addresses;
    }
}
```

This policy will now neither accept nor advertise unwanted routes. Being a good citizen and policing your own actions is generally a good thing.

You can't apply import policies to OSPF or IS-IS, which means you want to apply the policy as an import policy for your BGP routes:

```
[edit protocols]
bgp {
   import filter-unwanted-routes;
}
```

Configuring an Aggregate Route

As the number of devices connected to the Internet grows, so, too, does the number of IP addresses assigned to those devices. And the more IP addresses, the more routes your router must maintain. Still worse, as the number of routes increases, so does the time it takes to look up next-hop values. Transit time for traffic is dependent, at least in part, on the number of routes that are in each router's routing table. For example, examine Figure 14-4's topology of interconnected networks.

Look at the Figure 14-4's depiction of three separate networks. Each network has been allocated a 2^{16} prefix. A 2^{16} prefix equates to 216 different addresses. So, if the entire Internet included only these three networks, each device would have to have 3 x 2^{16} routes in its routing table, an amount of data stored that would be prohibitively large, not to mention the time it would take to look up next hops would be prohibitively long.

There has to be a better way? Does a device in AS 15 really need to have a route to every device in AS 7? Isn't it sufficient to provide a route only to the gateway router for AS 7 and then expect that the gateway knows how to route within its own domain?

In fact, if the gateway router for AS 7 advertises only a summary of all the routes that fall within its domain, it could reduce the number of routes it needs to advertise from 2^{16} to 1. As that route gets propagated through the rest of the Internet, each device that wants to send traffic to a device in AS 7 need only know how to get to the gateway.

This type of summary of routes is called *route aggregation*. And if everyone plays nicely, the overall size of routing tables can remain relatively small, even when the total number of devices is quite large.

Aggregate routes must first be configured, and then they must be advertised. Examine the aggregate route shown in Figure 14-5.

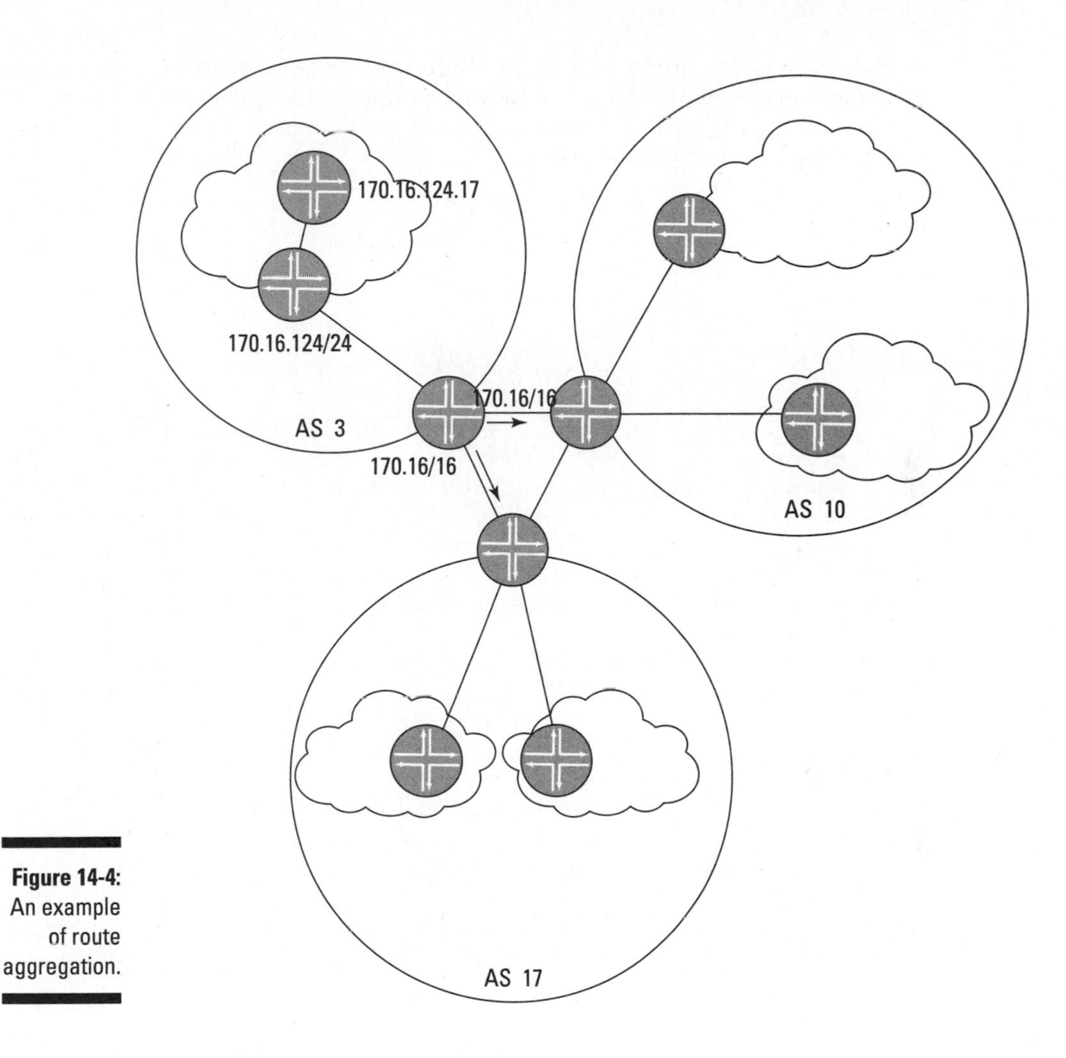

Figure 14-4: An example of route aggregation.

If Figure 14-5 was your network, you'd want to configure an aggregate route on the gateway router and advertise that route to your peering network. In this case, the aggregate route is 192.168.24/24.

To configure the aggregate route, simply identify it as an aggregate within the routing-options hierarchy:

```
[edit routing-options]
aggregate {
   192.168.24.0/24;
}
```

Now all you have to do is advertise this route to your neighbor. Route advertisements are controlled through routing policy. You're peering with your neighbor through a BGP connection, and because it's an outgoing advertisement, you want an export policy:

```
[edit policy-options]
policy-statement advertise-aggregate {
   term find-aggregate {
      from protocol aggregate;
      then accept;
   }
}
```

```
[edit protocols']
bgp {
   export advertise-aggregates;
}
```

This policy matches and accepts all aggregate routes. The policy is applied as an export policy, which means that BGP will send these aggregate routes to all BGP peers.

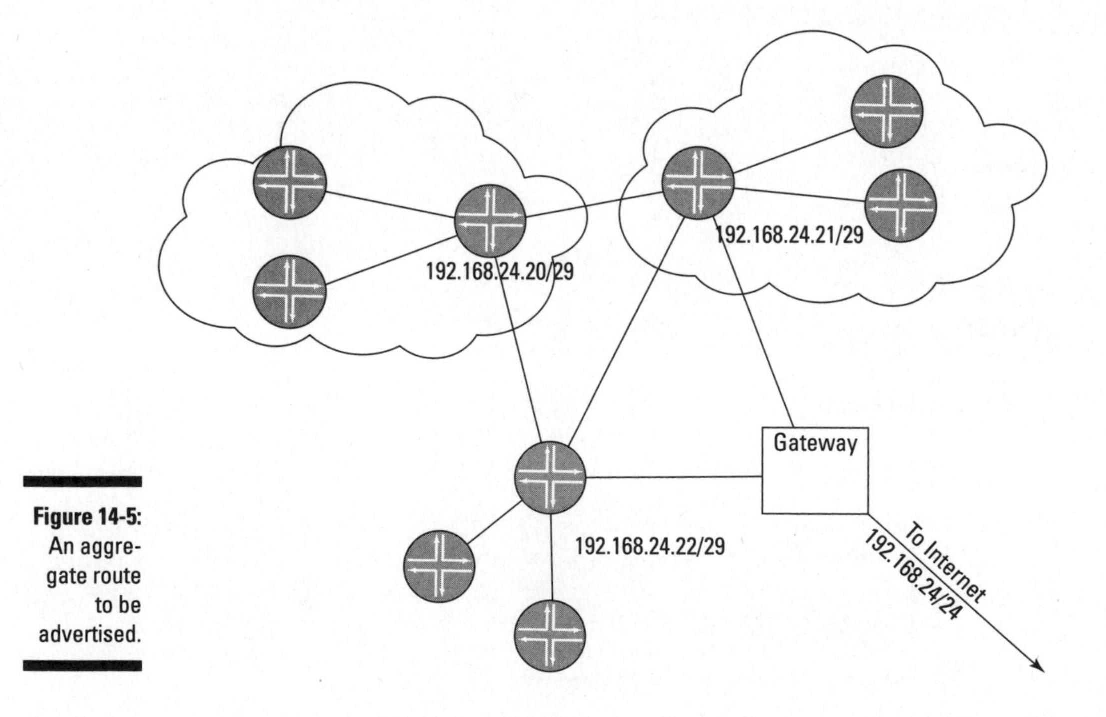

Figure 14-5: An aggregate route to be advertised.

Chapter 15

Enabling Class of Service (COS)

In This Chapter

- Understanding the components of a COS configuration
- Finding out how to classify traffic
- Using multifield classifiers

In a basic network, all traffic is treated the exact same way. Packets come into your routers, and packets go out of your routers, and it really doesn't matter what kind of packets they are or what their transport requirements are.

Class of service allows you finer control over the traffic in your network. By grouping similar types of traffic, you can treat each class of traffic in a specific way, granting preference to traffic that is less tolerant to jitter, delay, and packet loss. Essentially, class of service lets you determine which traffic in your network is a first class passenger and which traffic has to ride economy.

Knowing What Pieces a COS Configuration Requires

The basic idea behind *Class of Service* (COS) is that you examine traffic entering your network to determine what type of traffic it is. Once you know the type of traffic (voice traffic, data traffic, traffic tied to a particular customer, and so on), you can mark that traffic accordingly. As those packets flow through your network, each router can then identify the traffic and make decisions on how to handle it based on its type. In this manner, all of your delay-sensitive traffic can be forwarded faster, or your critical traffic may be less likely to be dropped in times of congestion.

COS is how you control jitter and delay in your network. But what exactly are jitter and delay?

- *Jitter* is the variation in delay over time. The primary contributor to jitter is the variability of queuing/scheduling delay over time.
- *Propagation delay* is the time it takes for signals to traverse a link — basically the speed of light.
- *Switching delay* is the time difference between receiving a packet on an incoming interface and the queuing of the packet in the scheduler of its outbound interface.
- *Serialization delay* is the time taken to clock a packet onto a link.
- *Scheduling/queueing delay* is the time difference between enqueueing the packet of the outbound interface scheduler and the start of clocking the packet onto the outbound link.

Figure 15-1 shows the different components that make up a COS implementation on a router.

A classification stage examines incoming traffic and assigns a forwarding class and loss priority based on one or more fields in the packet header. These forwarding classes are then assigned to input queues.

Input policers ensure that the incoming bandwidth for each traffic flow is within its configured constraints. If a particular traffic flow exceeds its allocated bandwidth, the router can drop the packets within the flow or mark it such that it's eligible to be discarded should congestion occur. If a traffic flow violates the bandwidth set, it's not enough to say that everything that is in violation goes into another queue, because it may lead to out-of-order packets. Instead, you have the option to drop it or tag it so that it can be dropped, if necessary.

On the outbound side of the equation, flows are assigned to output queues. These queues are serviced by the router based on how they're mapped to a scheduler. The scheduler basically dictates which queues get preferential treatment and which queues are forced to wait before they're serviced.

As these queues fill up, they may still overflow. If a queue overflows, packets are dropped as per the configured drop profile.

Finally, when the packet is ready to exit the router and head to the next hop along the way to its destination, the router can rewrite the bits in the header associated with COS so that the next router can examine the header and process the packet based on a new set of COS rules.

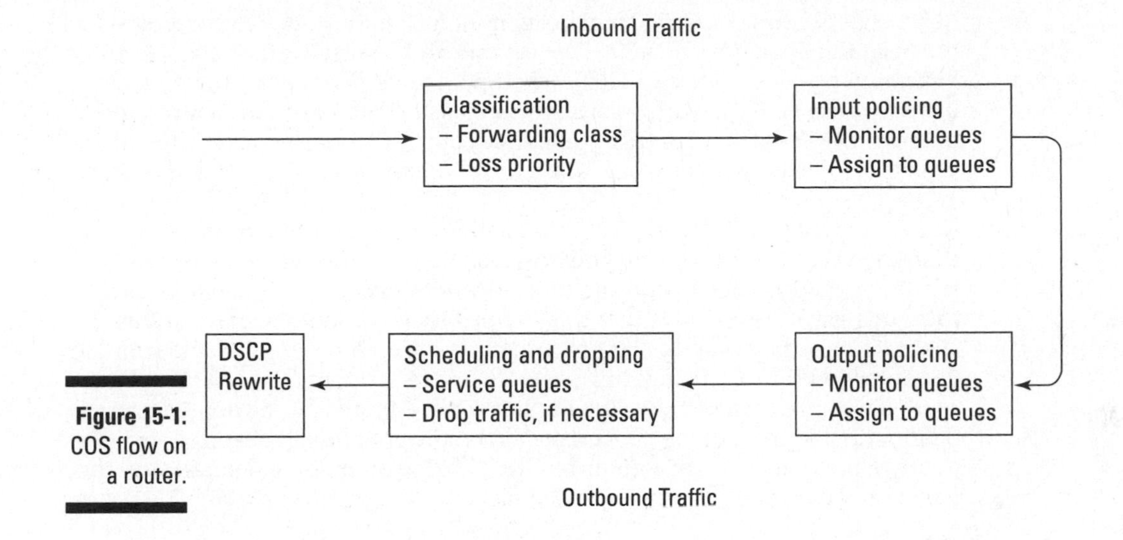

Figure 15-1: COS flow on a router.

This entire description isn't meant to describe how COS works; instead, it's meant to give you an idea of what pieces are required within a COS configuration so that you can better understand each of them as they're described in a bit more detail in the following sections.

Classifying Inbound Traffic

If your router is going to examine packets to figure out whether they're first-class passengers or regular economy-class passengers, you have to know where in the packet this information is stored. There are two fundamental ways to classify traffic, depending on how you have your network set up:

- Assume that all COS settings in a packet are correctly set to conform to your network's COS implementation, in which case you need only look at the COS values in the packet's header.
- Assume that the packet's COS settings aren't set in accordance with your network's COS implementation, in which case you need another way to determine what type of traffic the packet is carrying.

For example, look at Figure 15-2, a typical edge-core network for a couple of different areas of primary concern when it comes to COS.

At your network's core, traffic is being passed from routers you control to other routers you control. In this case, you can be fairly certain that the configuration on those boxes will conform to whatever COS rules you've established within your network. So when you classify traffic, you basically need to look only at COS values that you've set yourself within a packet's headers. This type of classification is known as *behavior aggregate (BA) classification.*

At the edge of your network, traffic is coming to your routers from devices that you don't control. It's anybody's guess how the COS values are set. While it would be nice to imagine a world where everyone classified traffic the same way, the reality is that this uniformity is seldom the case. In this scenario, you may want to classify the traffic based on where it came from, not solely on the COS values in a packet's headers. So, in this case, you need to look at more than just the COS field; you need to look at the source and destination address of the packet, or maybe the source and destination ports. This type of classification requires looking at multiple fields within the packet header, so it has been aptly labeled *multifield (MF) classification.*

Differentiated Services Code Points (DSCP)

The part of the packet header that is examined when classifying traffic for use with a COS implementation is called the *Differentiated Services Code Point* (DSCP). This field has 8 bits, the first 6 of which are important to COS. While you can mark traffic other ways, DSCP is the more popular and powerful choice for COS these days, so we focus on DSCP in this chapter.

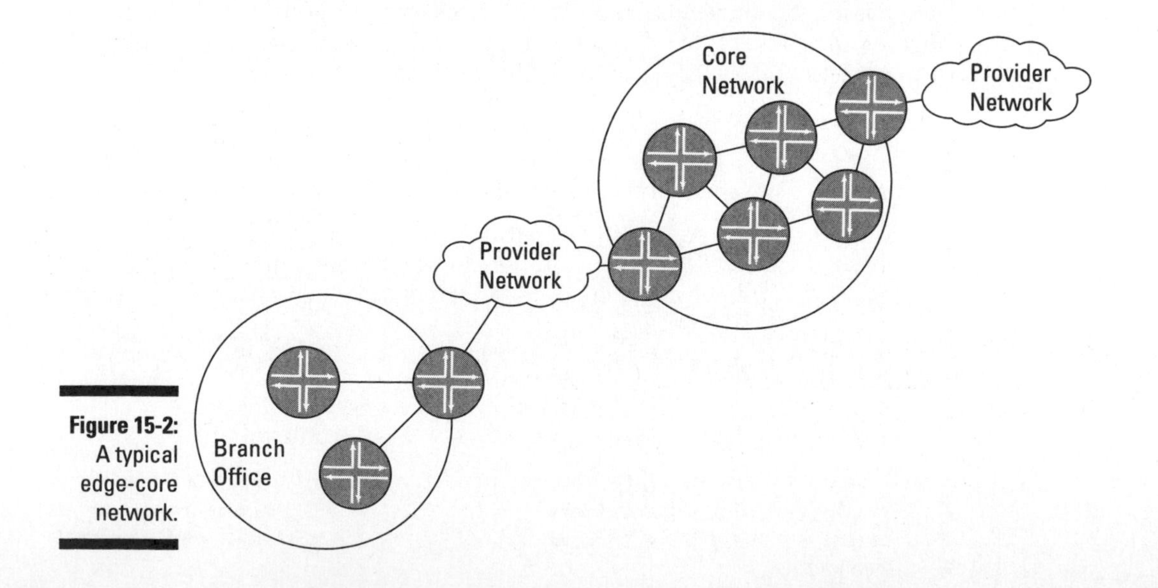

Figure 15-2: A typical edge-core network.

Technical Stuff

Using all the bits in DSCP

DSCPs are 8-bit fields within the packet header (the last 2 bits in the field are used for Explicit Congestion Notification [ECN]). When a router's outbound buffers are full, it sets the ECN bits to let the downstream node know that congestion is on the link. Without going into specifics, the two routers essentially use the information to throttle back traffic on the link.

The DSCP replaces the Type of Service (ToS) field, which used to be the primary field used for COS implementation. The major difference between the two is that the ToS field really uses only the IP Precedence bits (3 bits that identify the type of forwarding to be used for the packet). Conversely, the DSCP uses 6 bits in the field to identify both the type of forwarding as well as the packet loss priority (PLP). As such, it provides more granularity in how a packet is classified and is thus the more common choice in today's networks.

Forwarding classes

The DSCP's 6 bits identify two important pieces of the COS puzzle: the forwarding class and the packet loss priority. The combination of these pieces make up what is called the *per-hop behavior* (PHB), which basically describes what happens to packets for any particular hop in its path. The five classes of traffic are

- **Best effort (be):** Best effort forwarding is the base forwarding for all traffic. Basically, the router does its best to forward the traffic. If congestion develops on the router (its buffers are full, for example), then this traffic is likely to be dropped.
- **Expedited forwarding (ef):** Expedited forwarding is essentially first-class travel for packets in the router. The router provides priority services for this traffic, and it ensures that packets in this forwarding class are the last to be delayed or dropped during times of congestion.

  As packets come in, if the total bandwidth doesn't exceed the allocated bandwidth for this class, the traffic is considered in-profile, and the packet is forwarded normally. If the total bandwidth exceeds the allocation, the traffic is considered out-of-profile. The router will basically do whatever it can to forward the traffic using available bandwidth from the other classes. If there is no available bandwidth, packets can be dropped, though they'll be the last packets subjected to this horrid fate.

  Expedited forwarding is what you use for mission critical traffic that can't be dropped or have excess jitter or delay (think voice traffic).
- **Assured forwarding (af):** Assured forwarding is pretty similar to expedited forwarding. Assured forwarding is kind of like passengers flying business class (that is, they get lots of perks, but not quite the first-class treatment).

As packets come in, they're either in-profile or out-of-profile (just like ef packets). Packets that are in-profile are forwarded normally. The difference is that whereas ef packets are automatically queued up for forwarding if they're out-of-profile, af packets can be subjected to a random early detection (RED) drop profile. Packets in the af class can be assigned a drop precedence (using the PLP bit), and they're randomly dropped to ease congestion.

Assured forwarding is used for applications that need better than best-effort forwarding but aren't quite mission critical (typically applications like PeopleSoft, SAP, or Oracle).

- **Network control (nc):** Network control traffic includes packets like protocol hello messages or keepalives. Packets in this class are forwarded with lower priority, meaning they're more subject to delay. However, these packets are less likely to be discarded. Because the loss of these packets can cause network events (like routing adjacencies flapping), delaying delivery is much better than dropping the packet completely.
- **Class selector (cs):** CS values enable backward compatibility with the older IP-Precedence scheme. The Class Selector codepoints are of the form xxx000. The first three bits are the IP precedence bits. Each IP precedence value can be mapped into a DiffServ class. If a packet is received from a non-DiffServ aware router that used IP precedence markings, the DiffServ router can still understand the encoding as a Class Selector codepoint.

Each of these forwarding classes has at least one PLP associated with it. The combination of forwarding class and PLP is identified by the bit pattern in the DSCP. So when you want to either match on or assign one a particular PLP (that is, you want to specify how a packet is to be handled), you need to specify the specific bit pattern.

Code point aliases

Memorizing bit patterns of forwarding classes can be painful. A better way is *code point aliases.* When determining your COS policy, instead of specifying the bit pattern, you can define the alias name that represents the bit patterns. Such aliases are called code point aliases.

Put simply, use code point aliases, not bit patterns. If you assign English phrases or words to a particular pattern, it's far easier to go back and understand the configuration at a later date. Try looking at 101110; you know immediately that it refers to expedited forwarding. Additionally, if you create a set of rules that you apply to a particular pattern and that pattern changes, changing the definition of the alias is far easier.

To simplify things even more, some well-known bit patterns already have aliases built into the software. Table 15-1 lists the common DSCP aliases along with the corresponding bit patterns, forwarding classes, and PLP values.

Table 15-1 Behavior Aggregate Classification Aliases

Code Point Alias	*Forwarding Class*	*PLP*	*Bit pattern*
ef	expedited-forwarding	low	101110
af11	assured-forwarding	low	001010
af12	assured-forwarding	high	001100
af13	assured-forwarding	high	001110
af21	best-effort	low	010010
af22	best-effort	low	010100
af23	best-effort	low	010110
af31	best-effort	low	011010
af32	best-effort	low	011100
af33	best-effort	low	011110
af41	best-effort	low	100010
af42	best-effort	low	100100
af43	best-effort	low	100110
be	best-effort	low	000000
cs1	best-effort	low	001000
cs2	best-effort	low	010000
cs3	best-effort	low	011000
cs4	best-effort	low	100000
cs5	best-effort	low	101000
nc1/cs6	network-control	low	110000
nc2/cs7	network-control	low	111000
other	best-effort	low	(none)

These combinations aren't exhaustive, but they represent the well-known patterns that you can leverage in your classification of traffic. If you want to add a pattern that isn't already present, you can configure that pattern and name it whatever you want:

```
[edit class-of-service]
code-point aliases {
   dscp {
      my-dscp-alias 110001;
   }
}
```

Using this configuration, you can assign a name to a particular DSCP bit pattern. Every time you want to match on that bit pattern in the rest of the COS configuration, you need to reference only the alias name.

Configuring BA classifiers

Once you match packets to a particular DSCP value, you have to configure the router to match these values. In this context, matching the values constitutes classifying the traffic. That is, once you match the DSCP values, you should know how you want to treat that traffic.

To configure the classification portion of the COS implementation, you want to create logic that says

```
If traffic has a dscp value that matches some pattern,
   Then send that traffic to a particular queue and
   assign a particular loss priority
```

The first part of this logic is straightforward. You need to be able to match the DSCP value of incoming traffic to some values that you want to use to govern how that traffic is forwarded. The second part of the logic is really how you want to treat the traffic after it's been classified.

Forwarding classes

Imagine that a router is like an airline counter. People walk up to the counter expecting to be serviced. But all people aren't equal to the airline. The airline may service its First Class passengers in one line, its Frequent Flyers in yet another line, and finally the remainder of its passengers in still another line. Depending on the type of customer each person represents, people filter themselves into one of the various lines.

The important detail in this example is that two things are going on:

- Passengers are filtering themselves based on the type of ticket they hold.
- The airline is telling them which line corresponds to their particular type.

A router behaves the same way. Traffic that comes in is evaluated to determine what type of traffic it is — is it first class, frequent flyer, or regular — by looking at the DSCP values for the packet. Then the router tells those packets where to go. In the latter case, where to go equates to which outbound queue to use.

When classifying traffic, you must match the traffic and assign that traffic to a queue. The assignment of traffic to a queue is done through forwarding classes. Forwarding classes simply map traffic that is matched to a queue.

Queues

The branch routers (J-series routers) support up to eight different queues, numbered 0 through 7. By default, the first four of these queues are used by the four forwarding classes described earlier:

- **Queue 0 – Best effort.** Any packet without a DSCP value set is forwarded in this queue. This is the default for all non-network-control traffic.
- **Queue 1 – Expedited forwarding.** Note that no predefined schedulers are associated with this queue. If you want to use this queue, you need to explicitly configure the forwarding class and then configure the scheduler to be used.
- **Queue 2 – Assured forwarding.** Note that no predefined schedulers are associated with this queue. If you want to use this queue, you need to explicitly configure the forwarding class and then configure the scheduler to be used.
- **Queue 3 – Network control.** Network control traffic is forwarded using this queue. Remember that this queue is serviced with a low priority, but traffic isn't dropped from this queue. The *low* here means packet loss priority, which is the drop probability bit (with local significance to the device). If the PLP is low, it's less likely to be dropped during congestion than those having a high priority marking.

While the default action is to use these queues for the specified forwarding classes, you can still use these queues for other things. In fact, you may want to define different actions for even these four forwarding classes, assigning traffic to different queues.

So the real question here is "How do you use these in a real network?"

Imagine that network has the different types of traffic shown in Table 15-2 with the corresponding sensitivities to delay and jitter.

Table 15-2 Types of Network Traffic

Traffic Type	*Applications*	*Forwarding Class*	*Queue*	*Forwarding Class Name*
Voice	Real-time voice calls	Expedited forwarding	4	cos_voice
Video	Streaming video	Assured forwarding	5	cos_video
Business critical apps	Sales apps, Oracle, etc.	Assured forwarding	6	cos_buscrit
Noncritical apps	Data sniffers	Best effort	7	cos_noncrit

With these types of applications, you may want to create your own queues and then allocate a certain percentage of available bandwidth to these types of applications. Traffic that doesn't fall into these categories can use the default queues for transit. To use these queues, you have to assign them to forwarding classes, which are then used to forward traffic:

```
[edit class-of-service]
forwarding-classes {
   queue 0 best-effort;
   queue 1 expedited-forwarding;
   queue 2 assured-forwarding;
   queue 3 network-control;
   queue 4 cos-voice;
   queue 5 cos-video;
   queue 6 cos-buscrit;
   queue 7 cos-noncrit;
}
```

This configuration defines eight queues into which packets can be distributed. The assumption is that each of these queues will be allocated some percentage of the total bandwidth. (See the section "Scheduling Configuration," later in this chapter.)

Queues 0 through 3 represent the default queues. You don't need to explicitly configure them. They're configured here for illustrative purposes only. You could even configure your own queues in place of these if you wanted to separate, say, certain other applications or signaling traffic.

Linking forwarding classes to classifiers

The logic you're trying to configure is

```
If traffic has a dscp value that matches some pattern,
   Then send that traffic to a particular queue and
   assign a particular loss priority
```

The DSCP values characterize traffic, and the forwarding classes (and corresponding queues) allow you to classify that traffic so that you can treat it appropriately. To pull these two pieces together, you configure BA classifiers, referencing defined forwarding classes:

```
[edit class-of-service]
classifiers {
   dscp dscp-classifier {
      forwarding-class cos-voice {
         loss-priority low code-points ef;
      }
      forwarding-class cos-video {
         loss-priority high code-points cs1;
         loss-priority low code-points af31;
      }
      forwarding-class cos-buscrit {
         loss-priority low code-points af41
      }
      forwarding-class cos-noncrit {
         loss-priority high code-points cs5;
         loss-priority low  code-points af13;
      }
   }
}
```

This configuration creates your match conditions, and it assigns traffic that meets those conditions to one of the specified forwarding classes, which, in turn, maps to a particular outbound queue.

Specifically, this configuration specifies that any traffic that has a DSCP value of ef (corresponding to a bit pattern of 101110) should be given a loss-priority of low and assigned to the forwarding class called cos-voice. Basically, you're saying that any traffic that is marked as expedited forwarding is voice traffic, and that traffic shouldn't be dropped, so you're giving it a low loss priority. That traffic is then being assigned to the voice forwarding class, which corresponds to queue 5 on the router. Essentially, you're dumping all your voice traffic into a single queue with the expectation that you'll allocate a certain percentage of your total bandwidth to that traffic.

This configuration also classifies video traffic. In the case of video, you want to minimize delay and jitter because it impacts video quality, but the nature of the traffic is such that it's not as critical to your business as the voice traffic on your network. In this case, you want to assign it to an assured forwarding class.

In fact, your network may have multiple sources of video. Imagine that video streaming from one server is being used to send live stock data to a number of different branches in your company. Because decisions are made based on that data, you want to make sure that stream is uninterrupted. Meanwhile, another video stream is sending training or other corporate information that is less critical. While you want that stream to be uninterrupted, if you're forced to choose between that one and the streaming stock quotes, you want to preserve the stock quotes. So this configuration sets a loss priority of high on the training video and a low loss priority on the stock quotes. During times of congestion, the training video is more likely to be impacted, thus preserving the higher priority stock quotes.

For these forwarding classes, no scheduler is defined yet. You must explicitly configure a scheduler before they become useful. See the section "Scheduling Configuration," later in this chapter, for information on configuring schedulers and scheduler maps.

Linking classifiers to traffic

After you create a classifier that matches on types of traffic based on the DSCP value, it then assigns that traffic to a forwarding class that corresponds to some queue on the router. But what flow of traffic is it evaluating?

Classifiers must be linked to one or more flows of traffic before they're useful. The traffic itself flows through interfaces. You must link your newly configured classifiers to the interfaces on the router through which the traffic is flowing.

You have a couple of options here. You can apply your classifiers to all, some, or one of the interfaces on your router. (Applying them to none of the interfaces doesn't make a lot of sense, so we don't include that option.) And even on the interfaces, you can apply your classifiers to all, some, or one of the logical interfaces (units). To make this process a bit easier, JUNOS software supports wildcards.

In this case, you have only a single classifier, so it's easy enough to configure it on all interfaces:

```
[edit class-of-service]
interfaces {
    all {
        unit * {
            classifiers {
                dscp dscp-classifier;
            }
        }
    }
}
```

In this configuration, you're applying the `dscp-classifier` to all interfaces. Notice that you must specify which unit you're applying it to. In this case, you're using the wildcard (asterisk) to indicate that it's to be applied to all units on all interfaces. If you want to apply the `dscp-classifier` to only unit 0 on all interfaces, you can replace the asterisk with a 0.

If you configure several classifiers and want to apply them on different interfaces, you can use the asterisk wildcard with the interface name. For example, if you know that your video traffic travels only on T3 interfaces, and you've configured a classifier to handle only video, you can have a configuration that resembles

```
[edit class-of-service]
interfaces {
    t3-* {
        unit * {
            classifiers {
                dscp dscp-video-classifier;
            }
        }
    }
}
```

In this configuration example, the wildcard indicates that all T3 interfaces should use the specified voice classifier on all units.

Take care when you apply one classifier to many interfaces. In this example, all interfaces share a single classifier, and they're contending for the same classifier. What you want to do is configure *per-unit-classifiers* so that each unit has its own classifier treatment.

Controlling Outbound Traffic

After you've effectively identified the inbound traffic on your router and classified it into one of your forwarding classes, you then want to control the outbound flow of that traffic.

Traffic enters the router, and based on a packet's DSCP value, it's assigned to a forwarding class, which identifies the outbound queue into which it's sent. You may want to control various properties of that queue, including

- Total bandwidth assigned to the queue
- Total buffer memory assigned to the queue for storing outbound packets
- Priority of the queue (the order in which the queue is serviced)

Scheduling configuration

Before you can get into tweaking the various operating parameters of the outbound traffic, you have to understand the underlying mechanism used to configure these parameters.

There are two major components to the scheduling configuration:

- **Schedulers** define the properties of the outbound queues. Once they're tied to individual interfaces and forwarding classes, all traffic matching a particular forwarding class is treated as per the definitions in the scheduler.
- **Scheduler maps** associate a forwarding class with a scheduler. Scheduler maps are then tied to interfaces, thereby configuring the hardware queues, packet schedulers, and RED processes that operate according to the mapping.

In this example, you have four customized forwarding classes, each of which requires a scheduler to be explicitly configured. To create the schedulers, configure the following:

```
[edit class-of-service]
schedulers {
    cos-sched-voice;
    cos-sched-video;
    cos-sched-buscrit;
    cos-sched-noncrit;
}
```

This configuration simply creates the schedulers. No properties are associated with these schedulers yet.

After creating the schedulers, you want to associate each forwarding class with one of the schedulers:

```
[edit class-of-services]
scheduler-maps {
    forwarding-class cos-voice scheduler cos-sched-voice;
    forwarding-class cos-video scheduler cos-sched-video;
    forwarding-class cos-buscrit scheduler cos-sched-
           buscrit;
    forwarding-class cos-noncrit scheduler cos-sched-
           noncrit;
}
```

This configuration maps each of the forwarding classes from the previous examples to its corresponding scheduler.

You're using four of the predefined forwarding classes. While these forwarding classes didn't need to be explicitly configured, only two of them have default schedulers associated with them. By default, only the best-effort traffic associated with queue 0 and the network-control traffic associated with queue 3 have schedulers associated with them. If you want to use either the expedited or the assured forwarding classes, you must explicitly configure a scheduler for those.

Shaping outbound traffic

The most common forwarding characteristic you'll want to control is the bandwidth allocated for a particular application. For example, say that your video traffic is critical to your business, but you don't want it consuming all of your networking resources. You still need bandwidth to handle your voice, business applications, and even network control traffic. Maybe it makes sense to cap the amount of bandwidth available to the video streams, in which case shaping becomes valuable.

Examine the types of traffic on your network and consider these underlying assumptions about bandwidth consumption:

- **Voice traffic:** The most critical traffic for this particular network. Because this business is predicated on communication between employees and customers, voice calls can never be dropped. This traffic needs to be forwarded at all costs.
- **Video traffic:** Because of the dependence on streaming stock quotes, this traffic is critical to the business. However, you don't want this traffic consuming all available bandwidth, so you want to cap it at 40 percent of the available bandwidth.
- **Business critical applications:** These applications are critical to the business and must receive some amount of assured bandwidth. These applications can't exceed 30 percent of the total bandwidth.
- **Noncritical applications:** Noncritical applications don't have a demonstrable impact on business, so they should be treated as best-effort tasks. Because they're not business-impacting, they should not consume more than 10 percent of the available bandwidth.

Given these requirements, you must configure a number of different parameters. The configuration is done within the specified schedulers that are mapped to the forwarding classes to which this traffic is tied.

Preventing queue starvation

With strict priority queuing configured, your voice packets will be serviced as soon as they enter the router. There is actually a problem with this approach, though. If enough voice traffic enters the box, you could effectively starve the other queues because the voice traffic will always be serviced first instead of those queues. To prevent starvation of your other queues, you may want to configure an outbound policer that defines a limit for the amount of traffic the queue can service.

To address this issue, you actually want to configure two separate policers. The first policer identifies the bandwidth limit for the voice traffic. If total voice traffic exceeds 256kpps or the traffic bursts exceed 15kpps, you want to flag the traffic as out-of-profile. As you recall, traffic that is out of profile is sent using available bandwidth from the other queues (if available bandwidth exists). Otherwise, it's dropped.

The second policer sets an upper limit. If the total voice traffic exceeds the upper threshold (set here at 512kpps) or the burst size exceeds 30kpps, you want to discard the packets, regardless of congestion on the interface.

Examine the following firewall policers:

```
[edit]
firewall {
    policer voice-excess-
   policer {
        if-exceeding {
            bandwidth-limit
   256k;
            burst-size-limit
   15k;
        }
        then out-of-profile;
    }
    policer voice-upper-
   limit-policer {
        if-exceeding {
            bandwidth-limit
   512k;
            burst-size-limit
   30k;
        }
        then discard;
    }
}
```

After creating the policers, you have to tie them to the voice forwarding class. Essentially, you want to make sure that all traffic identified as part of the cos-voice forwarding class is policed with the previously configured firewalls.

```
filter voice-filter {
    term upper-limit {
        from {
            forwarding-
 class cos-voice;
        }
        then {
            policer
 voice-upper-limit-policer;
            next term;
        }
    }
    term excess {
        from {
            forwarding-
 class cos-voice;
        }
        then {
            policer
 voice-excess-policer;
        }
    }
    term accept {
        then accept;
    }
}
```

This configuration first evaluates the traffic against the upper limit. If the traffic exceeds the upper limit, you want to discard it, so you should check that condition first. If the traffic isn't discarded, the excess bandwidth policy is evaluated. If the forwarding class exceeds the allocated bandwidth, the traffic is flagged as out of profile and is accepted. It will be forwarded with available bandwidth (if any exists) or dropped.

Configuring strict-high scheduling

Voice traffic is delay-sensitive, so you want to ensure that voice packets in your network are serviced with minimum delay. To do so, you must configure strict priority queuing, which basically means that the voice packets will be processed before anything else is processed.

To configure the strict-priority queuing:

```
[edit class-of-service]
schedulers {
   cos-sched-voice {
      priority strict-high;
   }
}
```

This configuration simply assigns the strict-high priority to the voice traffic. The scheduler map associates this scheduler with a forwarding class so that it can be used to service voice traffic.

Capping a transmission rate

Say, for example, that you want to cap the total bandwidth consumption for video traffic at 40 percent of the available bandwidth on a given interface. To specify the maximum percentage of total bandwidth that a particular forwarding class can use, configure a transmit rate:

```
[edit class-of-service]
schedulers {
   cos-sched-video {
      transmit-rate percent 40;
   }
   cos-sched-buscrit {
      transmit-rate percent 30;
   }
   cos-sched-noncrit {
      transmit-rate percent 10;
   }
}
```

This configuration sets the maximum transmission rate at the specified percentage. If the total throughput on a link is 1.5Mbps, setting a transmit rate of 40 percent means that the forwarding class can, at most, consume 600kbps.

Creating second-rate traffic

You will notice that the examples of schedulers include specific schedulers for various types of traffic that you might see in your network. But where does the generic traffic go? Consider configuring a default forwarding class and associating with it a default scheduler. Any traffic that is best-effort, but at least somewhat notable, can be classified into this forwarding class.

And when it comes to ensuring that this second-class traffic gets serviced, you can configure the scheduler to use up whatever bandwidth is left on a particular interface. Basically, you're saying that you don't want a dedicated piece of the pie; you just want to use whatever is available at the time.

To configure this default scheduler:

```
[edit class-of-service]
schedulers {
   cos-sched-default {
      transmit-rate
   remainder;
   }
}
```

The remainder keyword specifies that this scheduler is to use whatever is left over after the other schedulers have carved out their pieces.

Setting up outbound buffers

The whole point behind constraining the total bandwidth allocated to specific forwarding classes is that you want to prevent a single application or traffic flow from consuming an interface's entire set of resources. Well, if bandwidth is the most important resource to cap, buffer size is a close second.

In this context, buffers refer to the available memory on an interface card available for queuing packets before they're sent downstream. Essentially, after the router performs the next-hop lookup, it sends the packets to the interface where it's stored in memory. The interface then services its queues based on the relative priority of each queue. And while it services those queues, packets being sent by the router for eventual transmission are stored up.

During periods of *congestion* (defined here as times when the total rate of queuing packets exceeds the rate of transmission), these buffers begin to fill. When they're completely full, any new packets being sent to the interface can be dropped because there is no place to store them.

Because some traffic may be less critical than others (or because you can tolerate drops of some types of traffic more than others), you may want to guarantee a slice of the buffer pie. And, similar to capping the transmit rates, you may want to prevent a particular forwarding class or traffic flow from consuming all available buffer space.

The configuration to shape the outbound buffers closely resembles the configuration to shape outbound traffic:

```
[edit class-of-service]
schedulers {
    cos-sched-video {
        transmit-rate percent 40;
        buffer-size percent 40;
    }
    cos-sched-buscrit {
        transmit-rate percent 30;
        buffer-size percent 10;
    }
    cos-sched-noncrit {
        transmit-rate percent 10;
        buffer-size percent 10;
    }
    cos-sched-default {
        transmit-rate remainder;
        buffer-size remainder;
    }
}
```

The deeper the buffer, the more delay that can occur. In a well-functioning network, buffer memory will be low most of the time. Buffers are really intended to absorb bursts of traffic.

Configuring priority scheduling

Each scheduler is assigned a priority. And, by extension, because each queue is linked to a scheduler, each queue has a priority associated with it. When packets are sent to an outbound interface for transmission, they're stored in queues, as defined by their forwarding class. The JUNOS software services these queues based on their priority. If you want to ensure that a particular queue is serviced ahead of others, configure a higher priority for that queue's scheduler.

As an example, the video traffic in your network may be high priority. The business critical traffic in the network may be important but somewhat lesser in priority than the video traffic. And the noncritical traffic may be lesser still. Finally, the default traffic may be the lowest priority. To reflect this prioritization in the configuration:

```
[edit class-of-service]
schedulers {
   cos-sched-voice {
      priority strict-high;
   }
   cos-sched-video {
      transmit-rate percent 40;
      buffer-size percent 40;
      priority high;
   }
   cos-sched-buscrit {
      transmit-rate percent 30;
      buffer-size percent 10;
      priority medium-high;
   }
   cos-sched-noncrit {
      transmit-rate percent 10;
      buffer-size percent 10;
      priority medium-low;
   }
   cos-sched-default {
      transmit-rate remainder;
      buffer-size remainder;
      priority low;
   }
}
```

When you configured the scheduler to handle voice traffic, you configured the priority as strict-high, despite not having yet introduced the notion of priority scheduling — and that was really just an instance of this same concept.

Once you set these priorities, the JUNOS software uses them to determine the order in which queues are serviced. On a particular physical interface, the output queues are serviced as follows:

1. **All high-priority queues currently in profile are serviced.**

   In profile means that the traffic fits within the allocated bandwidth for that particular queue. Multiple high-priority queues are serviced in weighted round-robin fashion. High-priority queues include strict-high priority queues, which are considered to always be in profile.

2. **All medium-high priority queues currently in profile are serviced.**

   Again, multiple queues of the same priority are serviced in weighted round-robin fashion.

3. **All medium-low priority queues in profile are serviced.**

4. **All low-priority queues in profile are serviced.**
5. **All high-priority queues that are currently out of profile and are not rate-limited are serviced.**

   Multiple queues are serviced in weighted round-robin fashion.
6. **All medium-high priority queues currently out of profile are serviced.**
7. **All medium-low priority queues currently out of profile are serviced.**
8. **All low-priority queues currently out of profile are serviced.**

Massaging BA Classifiers for Core Transit

This entire chapter has been predicated on one assumption: the DSCP values have been set correctly before the packets enter your router. If the DSCP values are uniformly applied across an entire network, then it's pretty straightforward. You can trust that the configured forwarding classes match the type of traffic that is inbound, and all your COS configuration just works.

The problem is that at the edge of your network, you're exceedingly unlikely to receive packets that consider your particular COS implementation. As an example, do you typically ask your peering networks what DSCP values they use? Probably not. And similarly, they have no idea what you use. So any traffic that is passed over that boundary needs to be classified independent of the BA classifiers.

The big question is how do you do it? The answer is *multifield classifiers.* MF classifiers work very similarly to BA classifiers in that they examine the packet's header and, based on the contents therein, assign the packet to a forwarding class. The difference is that MF classifiers examine more than just the COS bits in the header.

If you accept the premise that your neighboring networks don't know or don't care what COS bits are set in packets that are sent to your network, then you have to find a different way to match traffic. You can do so in two easy ways:

- Look at where the traffic is from
- Look at where the traffic is heading

Matching traffic based on the source address

In many cases, the source address of a packet tells you the type of packet it is. For example, imagine that you have an application server with the address 192.168.66.77. Any packet that has that source address in its header can be classified the same way. In this case, you basically assign those packets to the forwarding class tied to that application or set of applications.

For this scenario, assume that inbound traffic has a source address of 192.168.66.77, and that traffic from this host is to be classified with the other business critical applications grouped into the cos-buscrit forwarding class. Configure a firewall filter that matches on the source address:

```
[edit firewall]
filter mf-classifier {
   interface-specific;
   term assured-forwarding {
      from {
         source-address 192.168.66.77;
      }
      then {
         forwarding-class cos-buscrit;
         loss-priority low;
      }
   }
}
```

This configuration matches all traffic with a source address matching the specified source. Any traffic that meets those conditions is then assigned to the cos-buscrit forwarding class, and its PLP is set to low.

You must then apply the filter to an interface. Because you're matching on inbound traffic, you want the config to be an input filter.

```
[edit interfaces]
t1-0/0/1 {
   unit 0 {
      family inet {
         filter input mf-classifier;
      }
   }
}
```

All inbound traffic on the specified interface will be matched.

Instead of using the filter input statement, try using the input-list statement:

```
[edit interfaces]
t1-0/0/1 {
   unit 0 {
      family inet {
         filter input-list mf-classifier;
      }
   }
}
```

If you use the `input-list` statement, you can add multiple firewall filters to the same interface if you ever need to. Otherwise, you can configure only one filter per interface at a time.

Matching traffic based on destination port

In addition to being able to match traffic based on where it originates, you can often determine the type of packet (and therefore the proper packet classification) based on the destination port. For example, some applications use well-known ports. SIP is an excellent example. SIP traffic uses the port 5060, so you should be able to match packets based on their destination port. Any packet with a destination port of 5060 can be classified with the other SIP traffic.

In this example, all voice traffic (including signaling) is being handled as part of the cos-voice forwarding class.

```
[edit firewall]
filter voice-mf-classifier {
   interface-specific;
   term expedited-forwarding {
      from {
         destination-port 5060;
      }
      then {
         forwarding-class cos-voice;
         loss-priority low;
      }
   }
}

[edit interfaces]
t1-0/0/0 {
   unit 0 {
      family inet {
         filter input-list voice-mf-classifier;
      }
   }
}
```

This configuration defines another input filter that matches on the destination port. Traffic matching the specified port is classified as voice traffic and uses the voice forwarding class defined previously.

Setting DSCP values for transit

Being able to match on the source and destination addresses certainly solves the problem where you don't know that the DSCP values have been set in accordance with your COS implementation. However, if the values aren't set correctly upon entering your network, you must be able to set them so that the rest of your BA classifiers within your network will function as expected.

A typical COS implementation includes this functionality at the edge routers via the DSCP rewrite capabilities. Essentially, you match on the destination address or port or whatever field you're using to identify traffic. And then based on the type of traffic you know it to be, you configure the router to overwrite the existing DSCP value and use the value that corresponds to the type of traffic you're matching on. When the packet is forwarded to the next hop within your network, that next router can simply look at the DSCP value and treat the packet accordingly.

To configure DSCP rewrites, you simply specify what code points you want associated with a particular forwarding class. This configuration is pretty straightforward; you simply configure what code points you want to match on for a particular forwarding class. Then, you explicitly write those values upon ingress into your network.

Here's where you define the DSCPs to match on:

```
[edit class-of-service]
classifiers {
   dscp dscp-classifier {
      forwarding-class cos-voice {
         loss-priority low code-points ef;
      }
      forwarding-class cos-video {
         loss-priority high code-points cs1;
         loss-priority low code-points af11;
      }
      forwarding-class cos-buscrit {
         loss-priority low code-points af13;
      }
      forwarding-class cos-noncrit {
         loss-priority high code-points cs5;
         loss-priority low  code-points af43;
      }
   }
}
```

To configure rewrites that match the values the rest of your network is keying on:

```
[edit class-of-service]
rewrite-rules {
   dscp rewrite-dscps {
      forwarding-class cos-voice {
         loss-priority low code-points ef;
      }
      forwarding-class cos-video {
         loss-priority high code-points cs1;
         loss-priority low code-points af11;
      }
      forwarding-class cos-buscrit {
         loss-priority low code-points af13;
      }
      forwarding-class cos-noncrit {
         loss-priority high code-points cs5;
         loss-priority low  code-points af43;
      }
   }
}
```

Now you need to apply these rewrite rules to an interface:

```
[edit class-of-service]
interfaces t1-0/0/1 {
   unit 0 {
      rewrite-rules dscp rewrite-dscps;
   }
}
```

All traffic on the specified interface that is assigned to one of the forwarding classes will have its DSCPs rewritten to match the expected DSCP values for the rest of the network. Basically, you use a firewall filter to assign traffic to a forwarding class, and then you use the DSCP rewrite functionality to mark the traffic for subsequent COS processing within your network.

Chapter 16

Using MPLS

In This Chapter

- Understanding how MPLS works and what it can do for you
- Configuring label-switched paths (LSPs)
- Routing LSPs
- Conserving bandwidth on LSPs

Routing protocols are about making your network functional. They allow you to send traffic across the network, and they even allow you to tune your network in some small measure to control how traffic is sent.

Multi-Protocol Label Switching (MPLS) builds on top of that foundation and really grants you a different level of control over how your network transports traffic. By converting your routed network to something closer to a switched network, MPLS offers transport efficiencies that simply aren't available in a traditional IP-routed network. These efficiencies are then augmented with traffic engineering functionality that makes MPLS still more effective. Combined, the switching and traffic engineering capabilities have made something that was once only used in service provider networks one of the emerging technologies in the enterprise.

This chapter attempts to demystify some of these powers, explaining in plain English both how MPLS operates and how you configure it in JUNOS to get more out of your network.

Packet-Switched Networking

Multi-Protocol Label Switching (MPLS) is part new technology, part throwback to older technologies. Its power is really in how it marries both new and old to get the best of both worlds.

To understand how MPLS leverages both new and old, you must have a firm grasp on the following topics:

- Label switching
- Label switched paths
- Label-switching routers
- Labels
- Label operations
- Establishing label-switched paths

Label switching

If you look at how normal IP networks operate, packets are transmitted with headers that contain the address information required to move packets through the network. Packets enter a router, the router examines the header, and then the router sends the packet to the next hop based on the ultimate destination address.

In a label-switched network, the operation is similar but subtly different. Packets aren't forwarded on a hop-by-hop basis. Instead, paths are established for particular source-destination pairs. Look at the network topology in Figure 16-1.

If the topology in Figure 16-1 represents an IP-routed network, traffic from router 1 is forwarded to router 4, which then makes its own forwarding decision, and so on, until the packets arrive at router 9.

In a label-switched network, a path from router 1 to router 9 is created such that all traffic from router 1 to router 9 takes the same deterministic path. Because a preset path exists, individual routing nodes don't need to do a forwarding lookup on the packets as they enter the router. Instead, each node must keep information only on what paths have been established thru it. As packets from that flow enter the router, the router can switch the packets on to a predefined path toward its destination through the network.

Put simply, if router 4 knows that for all traffic from router 1 to router 9, the next stop along the way is router 6, it can just forward the packets to that predetermined hop without ever looking up the route in its routing table, quite similar to the way ATM virtual circuits work.

Label-switched paths

The predetermined paths that make MPLS work are called *label-switched paths* (LSPs). Routers in an MPLS network exchange MPLS information to set up these paths for various source-destination pairs, so in Figure 16-1, information is exchanged through the network to establish the path from router 1 to router 9.

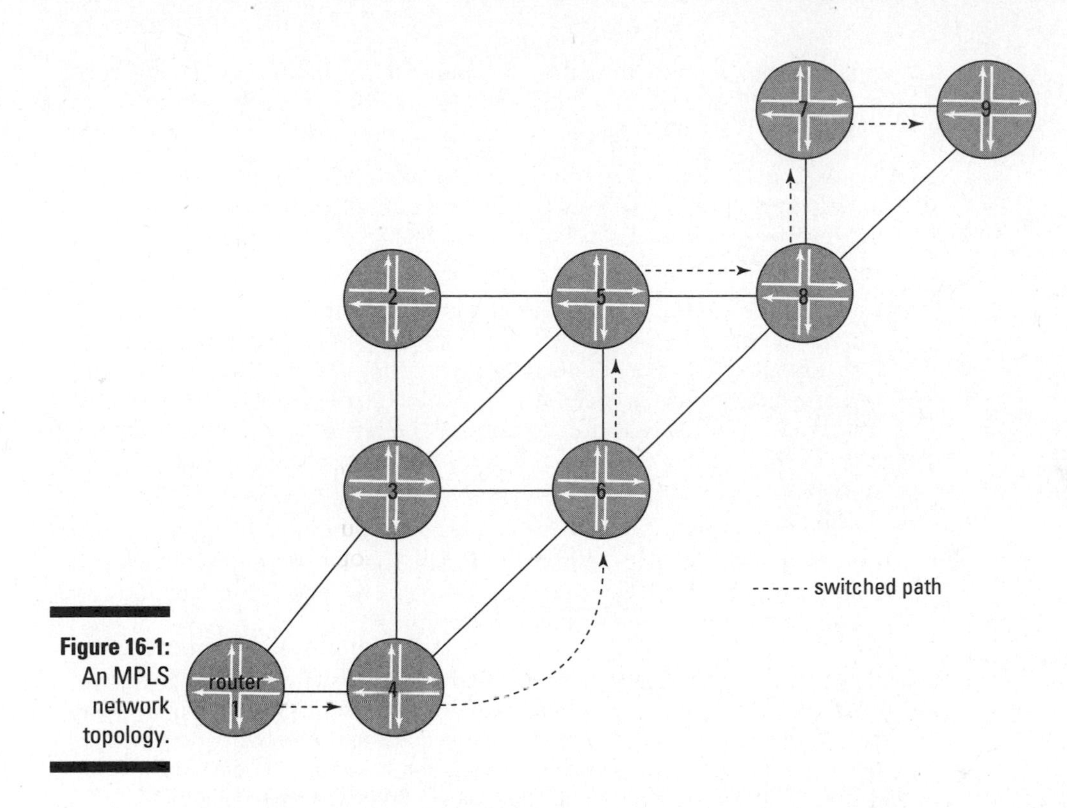

Figure 16-1: An MPLS network topology.

What is important here is that every router in the LSP from router 1 to router 9 must have the same view of the LSP. If a switched path is to have any real efficiencies over typical IP routing, every router in the LSP must be able to switch the packet forward.

MPLS is often called a layer 2.5 technology because it shares both routing (layer 3) and switching (layer 2) characteristics. The fact that paths are preset, much in the same way that Frame Relay or ATM circuits are predetermined, makes MPLS behave quite like a layer 2 protocol. However, MPLS's ability to use signaling protocols which themselves rely on routing knowledge for LSP establishment and traffic engineering and adjust on the fly definitely make it more layer 3ish.

Label-switching routers

The routers that make up an LSP are called *label-switching routers* (LSRs), and they come in a few flavors:

- **Ingress router:** The router at the entry point of an LSP. The ingress router is the only place where normal IP traffic can flow into an MPLS LSP. The inbound router receives IP traffic. When it determines that to reach its destination it must go thru an LSP, the inbound router encapsulates the traffic with an MPLS header and forwards it to the next hop in the LSP.

- **Transit router:** Any router in the middle of an LSP. Transit routers simply switch MPLS packets to the next hop in the LSP, using the incoming interface where the packet came in from as well as the MPLS header to determine where to send the packet.
- **Penultimate router:** The second-to-last router in the LSP. The penultimate router is the router before the last hop in an LSP. Because the last hop in an LSP doesn't need to switch the packet forward to another transit router, it has no need for the MPLS headers. It's the responsibility of the penultimate router to remove the MPLS header before sending it on to the last hop in the LSP. Note that having the penultimate router remove the MPLS label before sending it on to the egress router is optional.
- **Egress router:** The exit point for the LSP. The egress router receives IP traffic from the penultimate router. It does a normal IP lookup, and it forwards the traffic using normal IP routing.

Note that traffic from router 1 to router 9 doesn't have to originate at router 1. Imagine that router 1 is connected to some server. That server is running an application that is being used by someone accessing the network somewhere beyond router 9. Just because the entire traffic flow extends beyond the two endpoints of the LSP doesn't mean that the traffic doesn't use the LSP.

In this case, normal IP routing is used to pass the traffic to router 1. Router 1 does a normal lookup as if the packet were a normal IP packet. The lookup reveals that the destination for this traffic is router 9, and that destination is associated with an LSP. Router 1 then forwards the packet along as per the LSP definition, and each subsequent router treats the packet as an LSP packet. In this case, router 1 represents the starting point for the LSP. As such, router1 is the *ingress router.*

Examining the path again, router 9 is the last router in the LSP. So when the packet arrives at router 9, there is no next hop within an LSP. Therefore, router 9 does a normal IP lookup on the packet, and it forwards the packet as an IP packet. And because router 9 is the last router in the LSP, it's the *egress router.*

All the routers between router 1 and router 8 are *transit routers*. They're responsible for ushering the MPLS traffic along to the next hop in the LSP. The second-to-last router in the LSP (router 8 in this example) is the *penultimate router.* The penultimate router is typically responsible for stripping the MPLS headers off the packets (known as penultimate hop popping, or PHP). (For more information on PHP, see the upcoming section "Label operations.)

Label stacking

You can actually add labels to packets that already have labels (known as *label stacking*). Examine the topology in the figure.

This topology has an LSP defined between router 1 and router 11. But router 4 and router 8 also have an LSP between them. In this scenario, you have an LSP containing an LSP. So as IP traffic enters the first LSP, the ingress router adds an MPLS label. That label is used to switch the packet through to router 4.

Router 4 is an ingress router for a LSP. As the ingress router, it pushes a new label to the packet. That label is used to switch the packet forward to router 8. Router 8, the egress router for the LSP, removes the label and forwards based on the original label, which is exactly what Layer-3 VPNs do.

In the context of a single network, label stacking may not be that interesting, but imagine now that network boundaries appear around the LSPs.

The figure is exactly the same as the previous one except that now carrier networks are identified. You want to switch a packet from the branch office (router 1) to headquarters (router 9). That path traverses your own network as well as a carrier network. You want to switch the packet through your network, so you use an LSP and push your own label to the packet.

Meanwhile, the carrier wants to switch all your traffic through an LSP. So as the packet enters the carrier network, the carrier can add its own label and switch the packet through its transit network. When the packet is handed back to your headquarters, the label has been removed, and you can continue switching the packet to the eventual destination (router 9 in this example).

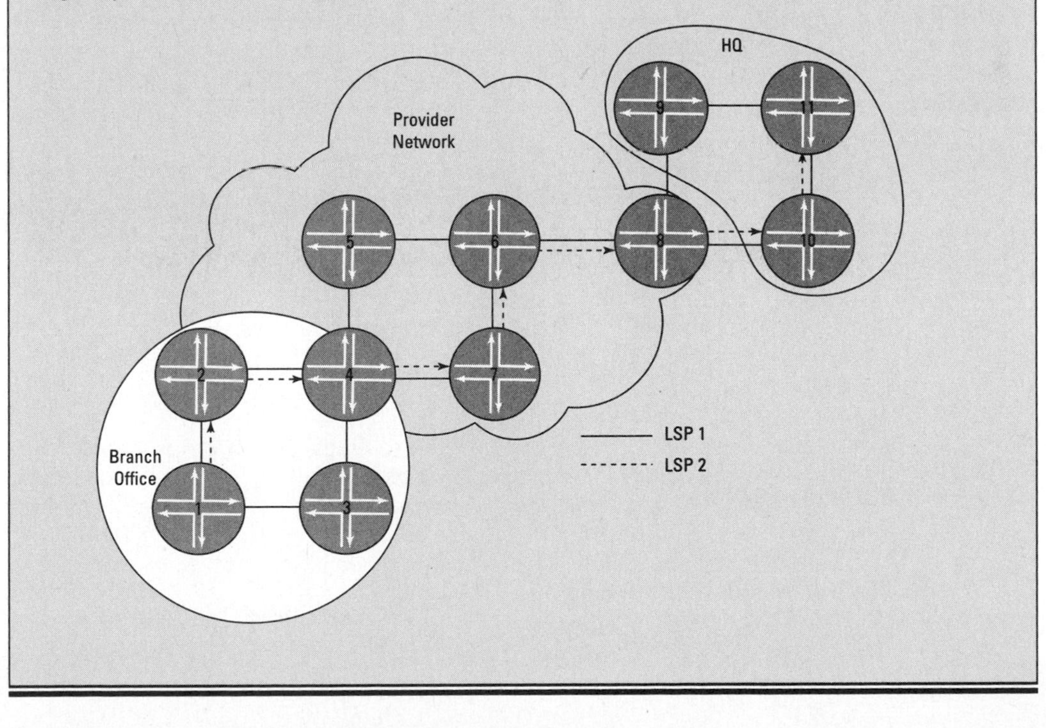

Labels

As packets are forwarded in a label-switching framework, MPLS routers encapsulate the packets with special headers called *labels*. A label basically tells the router which LSP it belongs to. The router can then use the ingress port and the LSP information to determine where the next hop in the LSP is (see Figure 16-2).

In Figure 16-2, the MPLS packet arrives via port 1. The router examines the label and sees that it has a numeric identifier that associates the packet with a particular LSP. Based on the input port and the label value, the router can look up in its MPLS routing table where the next hop in the LSP is. In this case, the lookup reveals that the outbound port is port 4. The packet forwards the traffic out the correct port, and the process repeats at the next LSR.

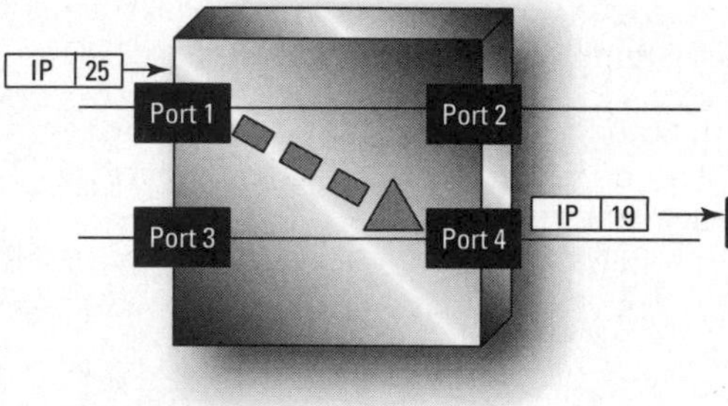

Connection Table

In (port, label)	Out (port, label)	Label Operation
(1,22)	(2,17)	Swap
(1,24)	(3,17)	Swap
(1,25)	(4,19)	Swap
(2,23)	(3,12)	Swap

Figure 16-2: A connection table.

Label operations

How does the label get on the packet in the first place? An LSR's responsibilities extend beyond just looking at the label and forwarding the packet to wherever it needs to go. LSRs are also responsible for managing and assigning the label on the packet.

As an example, when the packet arrives at the ingress router for a particular LSP, that ingress router is responsible for examining the packet so that it can send it through the LSP. However, it must also add the MPLS label so that the next hop in the LSP can process the packet correctly. The act of adding an MPLS label is called *pushing*. The following three label operations form the basis of all MPLS forwarding:

- **Push:** Adds a new MPLS label to a packet. When a normal IP packet enters an LSP, the new label is the first label on the packet.
- **Pop:** Removes the MPLS label from a packet. This is typically done at either the penultimate or the egress router.
- **Swap:** Replaces the label with a new label. When an LSR performs an MPLS lookup, that lookup yields the LSP next hop information as well as the numeric identifier for the next segment in the LSP.

Two other label operations — *multiple push* and *swap and push* — are really just extensions of the first three operations. Because you're unlikely to need these operations, we don't describe them in detail here. Suffice it to say that they perform multiple operations at once.

Establishing Label-Switched Paths

You can create MPLS LSPs in one of two ways:

- **Static configuration:** Static LSPs are a lot like static routes. You basically have to explicitly configure every LSR in an LSP manually. Because no protocols dynamically signal the LSP for you, the load on the LSRs is reduced. However, if you have changes in the topology, the paths can't adapt to the new network. As a result, topology changes can create routing black holes.

  The lack of dynamic update is a significant drawback and one that should not be overlooked. We recommend using dynamic LSPs wherever feasible.

- **Dynamic setup:** Dynamic LSPs use signaling protocols to establish themselves and propagate LSP information to other LSRs in the network. You configure the ingress router with LSP information that is transmitted throughout the network when you enable the signaling protocols across the LSRs. Note that you have to configure the signaling protocols on all of the LSRs. If only a subset of routers are able to exchange information, the LSP isn't established.

  Because the LSRs must exchange and process signaling packets and instructions, dynamic LSPs consume more resources than static LSPs. However, dynamic LSPs can avoid the network black holes of static LSPs by detecting topology changes and outages and dynamically establishing new LSPs to move around the failure.

Signaling Protocols

You need to be aware of two primary types of MPLS signaling protocols, both of which JUNOS supports:

- **Label Distribution Protocol (LDP):** LDP is a fairly simple signaling protocol that behaves much like one of the IGPs (OSPF and IS-IS). LDP runs on top of an IGP configuration, which means you have to get OSPF or IS-IS running first. Moreover, you must configure LDP on the exact same set of interfaces as your IGP.

  Once you've configured both your IGP and LDP on an interface, LDP begins transmitting and receiving LDP messages on that interface. LDP starts off by sending LDP discovery messages to all the LDP-enabled interfaces. When an adjacent router receives the discovery message, it establishes a TCP session with the source router.

  Once the LDP session is established, the routers maintain adjacencies much in the same way that OSPF routers maintain adjacencies. And when the topology changes, those changes generate LDP messages that allow LDP to set up new paths.

  LDP is fantastic in that it's so simple and just works. However, because of its simplicity, it lacks some of the more powerful traffic engineering features that RSVP boasts. For this reason, the major application for LDP-signaled LSPs is in support of Layer 3 VPNs. Suffice it to say that LDP lacks any real traffic engineering capabilities.

- **Resource Reservation Protocol (RSVP):** RSVP is a bit more complex than LDP and offers traffic engineering features that aren't available with LDP-signaled LSPs.

  RSVP works by setting up unidirectional paths between an LSP ingress router and an egress router. In the configuration, you specify what the bandwidth requirements are for an LSP. After you configure these paths and enable RSVP, the ingress router sends a path message to the egress router. The path message contains the configured information about the resources required for the LSP to be established.

  When the egress router receives the path message, it sends a reservation message back to the ingress router in response. This reservation message is passed from router to router along the same path as the original path message (in opposite order, of course). Once the ingress router receives this reservation message, an RSVP path is established that meets the required constraints.

All the LSRs along the path receive the same path and reservation messages, which contain the bandwidth reservation requirements. If they have the available bandwidth (that is, if no other higher-priority RSVP LSP has reserved bandwidth), they're included in the LSP. If a router doesn't have available bandwidth, it generates its own reservation message, and a new route that doesn't include the offending router is found. If no route can be found, the LSP isn't established.

The established LSP stays active as long as the RSVP session stays active. RSVP continues activity through the transmission and response to RSVP path and reservation messages. If the messages stop for three minutes, the RSVP session terminates, and the LSP is lost.

Configuring RSVP-Signaled LSPs

Imagine that you have a network where you're carrying a lot of voice traffic. You want to make sure that voice traffic gets forwarded along a path that has enough bandwidth to support the load without congestion. And because voice packets can't be received out of order, you want the entire voice flow to travel over the same path, as shown in Figure 16-3.

In this topology, you have a source of voice traffic (router 1) that is aggregating all your voice flows from various branch sites. You want to transport this data to headquarters, which requires sending the traffic through router 5 and off through the network and eventually to your headquarters.

You want to ensure that you have reserved bandwidth for all your flows, so you're going to use RSVP as your LSP signaling protocol. To configure the LSP across your network, you must

- Enable MPLS and RSVP on your router.
- Enable MPLS and RSVP on your transit interfaces.
- Configure your IGP to support traffic engineering.
- Set up an LSP from the ingress to the egress router.

Enabling MPLS and RSVP

Assuming that you've already set up your IGP and other routing protocols, the first thing you need to do to establish an RSVP LSP across your network is enable both MPLS and RSVP on your routers.

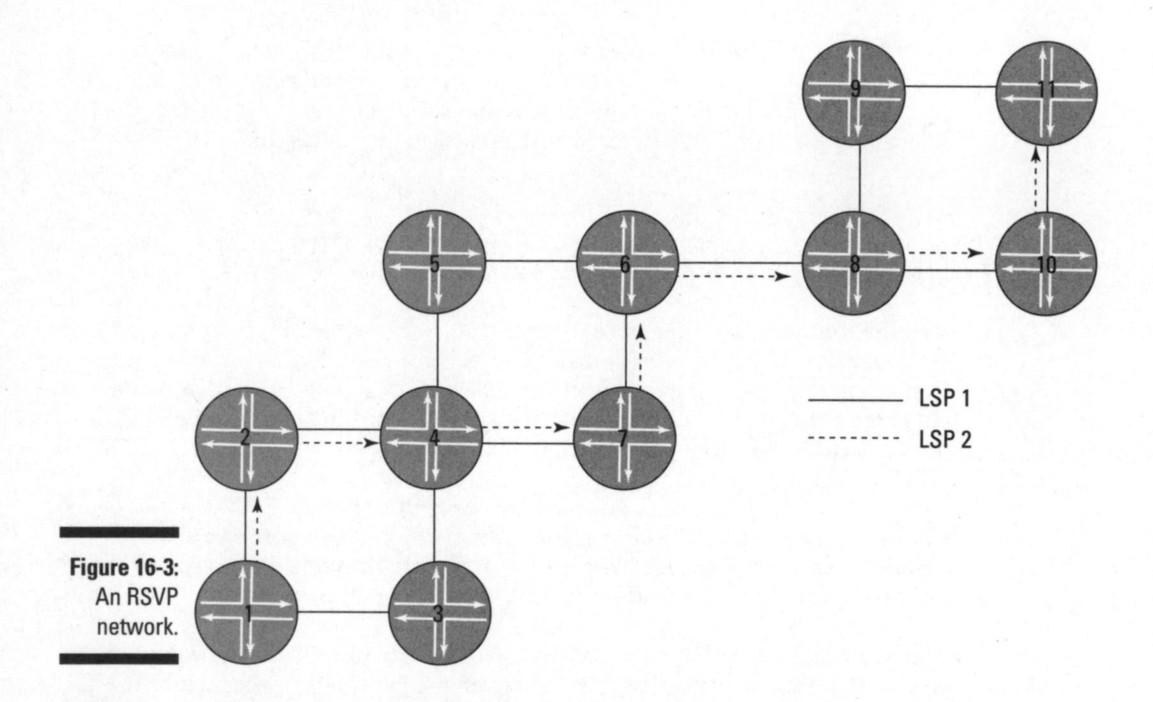

Figure 16-3: An RSVP network.

You have to enable MPLS and RSVP across all the routers in your network, not just the ingress and egress routers. RSVP works by sending path messages and ensuring that all routers within an LSP can meet the bandwidth requirements for that particular path.

To enable these protocols:

```
[edit protocols]
rsvp {
   interface all;
}
mpls {
   interface all;
}
```

This configuration is pretty straightforward. By enabling the protocols on all interfaces, you avoid having to explicitly add each interface, which has the added benefit of making it easy to swap new interfaces in and out.

If you're using management interfaces, you don't want to run the signaling protocols across those LAN interfaces. You can prevent MPLS and RSVP from running on those interfaces by explicitly excluding them using the *disable* statement:

```
[edit protocols]
rsvp {
   interface all;
   interface fe-0/0/0.0 {
      disable;
   }
}
mpls {
   interface all;
   interface fe-0/0/0.0 {
      disable;
   }
}
```

Turning on MPLS on your transit interfaces

After enabling MPLS and RSVP on your router, you must configure your transit interfaces. Refer to the network topology in Figure 16-3, earlier in this chapter.

You must enable MPLS on all the interfaces called out in the topology. To enable the protocols on a transit interface:

```
[edit interfaces]
fe-1/0/1 {
   unit 0 {
      family inet {
         address 10.0.24.1/24;
      }
      family mpls;
   }
}
```

Which router pops the MPLS label matters

The MPLS label on a switched packet is popped by either the egress router or the penultimate router, depending on your configuration. So what makes the determination? And why would you care which router does it?

Picture a network that has a single peering connection with a provider network. Many (if not all) flows from the network to any site outside the network likely will flow through the same gateway. If you've configured LSPs in your network, many of them will have the same egress router.

If you use ultimate hop popping (where the egress router pops the MPLS labels), all those flows and all those packets need to be processed by a single router. If you have a lot of LSPs with a lot of traffic, this step can be resource-intensive.

If you decide to use penultimate hop popping, you essentially terminate the LSP one hop earlier. The MPLS labels, instead of being popped all by the same egress router, are popped by the routers that connect to the egress router. You can effectively divide and conquer when it comes to label popping, which helps avoid running out of resources during heavy loads.

Configure an LSP

After you have MPLS and RSVP turned on and ready to go, the only thing you need to do is configure your LSP from router 1 to router 5. To configure an RSVP LSP, you have to create an LSP on router 1 that points to router 5:

```
[edit protocols]
mpls {
    label-switched-path router1-to-router5 {
        to 10.0.0.5;
    }
}
```

Within the MPLS configuration, creating an LSP is as easy as naming it and identifying the remote loopback address of the router you want to use as your egress router for the LSP.

Creating an LSP that mirrors itself on the egress router is generally a good idea so that you can support bidirectional communication. In this case, you need to also configure on router 5:

```
[edit protocols]
mpls {
    label-switched-path router5-to-router1 {
        to 10.0.0.1;
    }
}
```

Verify the LSPs

After configuring something, you need to make sure that it works as expected. To verify the LSP configuration, use the `show mpls lsp extensive` command. If you issue the command from router 1, expect to see two separate LSPs, as shown in Listing 16-1 (the one to router 5 and the one from router 5).

Listing 16-1: Output from the `show mpls lsp extensive` Command

```
user@router1> show mpls lsp extensive
Ingress LSP: 1 sessions

10.0.0.5
  From: 10.0.0.1, State: Up, ActiveRoute: 1, LSPname: router1-to-router5
  ActivePath:  (primary)
  LoadBalance: Random
  Encoding type: Packet, Switching type: Packet, GPID: IPv4
 *Primary                    State: Up
    Computed ERO (S [L] denotes strict [loose] hops): (CSPF metric: 20)
 10.1.13.2 S 10.1.36.2 S
    Received RRO (ProtectionFlag 1=Available 2=InUse 4=B/W 8=Node
10=SoftPreempt):
          10.1.13.2 10.1.36.2
    6 Dec 13 11:50:15 Selected as active path
    5 Dec 13 11:50:15 Record Route:  10.1.13.2 10.1.36.2
    4 Dec 13 11:50:15 Up
    3 Dec 13 11:50:15 Originate Call
    2 Dec 13 11:50:15 CSPF: computation result accepted
    1 Dec 13 11:49:45 CSPF failed: no route toward 10.0.0.6[6 times]
  Created: Mon Dec 13 11:47:19 2004
Total 1 displayed, Up 1, Down 0

Egress LSP: 1 sessions


10.0.0.1
  From: 10.0.0.5, LSPstate: Up, ActiveRoute: 0
  LSPname: router5-to-router1, LSPpath: Primary
  Suggested label received: -, Suggested label sent: -
  Recovery label received: -, Recovery label sent: -
  Resv style: 1 FF, Label in: 3, Label out: -
  Time left:  127, Since: Mon Dec 13 11:50:10 2004
  Tspec: rate 0bps size 0bps peak Infbps m 20 M 1500
  Port number: sender 1 receiver 39136 protocol 0
  PATH rcvfrom: 10.1.13.2 (so-0/0/2.0) 28709 pkts
  Adspec: received MTU 1500
  PATH sentto: localclient
  RESV rcvfrom: localclient
  Record route: 10.1.36.2 10.1.13.2 <self>
Total 1 displayed, Up 1, Down 0

Transit LSP: 0 sessions
Total 0 displayed, Up 0, Down 0
```

The output does indeed show two separate LSPs to which router 1 is a member. The first LSP is the ingress LSP for which router 1 is the ingress router. The second LSP is the egress LSP from router 5.

Placing Constraints on Packet Forwarding

When RSVP creates the paths for its LSPs, it uses information learned from the underlying IGP configuration. Basically, if OSPF has the shortest route from A to B, RSVP will establish an LSP across that path. At times, however, you may want to dictate your own path. For example, you may know that in terms of hops one path is shorter, but when you talk about actual latency and link speed, a different path is preferable. In these instances, you want to put constraints on the path taken through your network.

Routing LSPs based on these constraints is called *constraint-based routing.* You may want to constrain the path that an LSP takes in a few different ways:

- Reserve bandwidth so that guaranteed bandwidth appears along the path.
- Specify a particular node in the network through which the LSP will pass.
- Identify the exact path for the LSP.

Reserve bandwidth on an LSP

One of the best parts about RSVP is that you can specify a minimum bandwidth that must be supported on each transit router in the LSP. This specification helps ensure that you have enough allocated bandwidth from ingress to egress, particularly for traffic that is particularly sensitive to latency or drop.

As an example, imagine that you're streaming video across your network that you're using to conduct simulations in multiple branch offices. For the simulation to work well, every site has to receive the same feed with the same timing. You may want to ensure that the LSPs you're using to stream the video across your MPLS core all have enough bandwidth to support the rather high requirements for your media. In this case, you can use RSVP to guarantee the bandwidth along the path from source to egress router.

To configure this bandwidth constraint, you can build off your basic MPLS configuration. In the previous MPLS example, you configured an RSVP LSP and verified that it was operating. Taking that LSP, add to it such that the bandwidth requirement is 50MB:

```
[edit protocols]
mpls {
    label-switched-path router1-to-router5 {
        to 10.0.0.5;
        bandwidth 50m;
    }
}
```

The simple inclusion of the bandwidth statement adds that value to the reservation messages that each transit router must respond to. If a router in the network doesn't have the required bandwidth (either because its interfaces don't support that much throughput or because bandwidth has already been allocated to other LSPs), RSVP won't use that router in the LSP. Instead, it sends messages to other routers until it finds a path that meets the bandwidth requirements. Although this path may not be the shortest in terms of hops or overall latency, you'll know that each path segment can support the required bandwidth.

Verifying bandwidth on an LSP

How can you tell that your RSVP-signaled LSP has the appropriate bandwidth allocation? If you want to look at the characteristics, you should use the `show rsvp interface` command:

```
user@router1> show rsvp interface
RSVP interface: 4 active
                    Active Subscr- Static       Available    Reserved    Highwater
Interface    State resv   iption  BW           BW           BW          mark
fe-0/0/0.0   Up         2    100%  155.52Mbps   155.52Mbps   50Mbps      0bps
fe-0/0/1.0   Up         0    100%  155.52Mbps   155.52Mbps   0bps        0bps
fe-1/0/1.0   Up         0    100%  155.52Mbps   155.52Mbps   0bps        0bps
```

In this example, router 1 has three interfaces with RSVP enabled. When you look at the reserved bandwidth on the router, you need to know what bandwidth reservation really means. If you have umpteen flows through a particular interface, what you really want to do is limit some or all of those flows to a specific piece of the overall capacity on the link.

So when you look at RSVP sessions and the bandwidth tied to them, what you're seeing with the `show rsvp interface` command is the total sum of all allocated bandwidth on *all* the LSPs for which this router is an LSR. The totals can be extremely helpful in ensuring that your allocated bandwidth is in line with what you want it to be. If the allocated bandwidth exceeds 100 percent, the LSPs with a reserved bandwidth specified won't use that router as a transit router.

Explicitly configuring an LSP route

When you use RSVP (or even LDP) to signal an LSP, the most basic configuration uses the underlying IGP to calculate the LSP route. That is, the LSP travels whatever route the IGP selects. In some cases, however, you may want traffic to pass through a particular node. (Note that this option is only available if you're using RSVP as your signaling protocol.) Examine the topology in Figure 16-4.

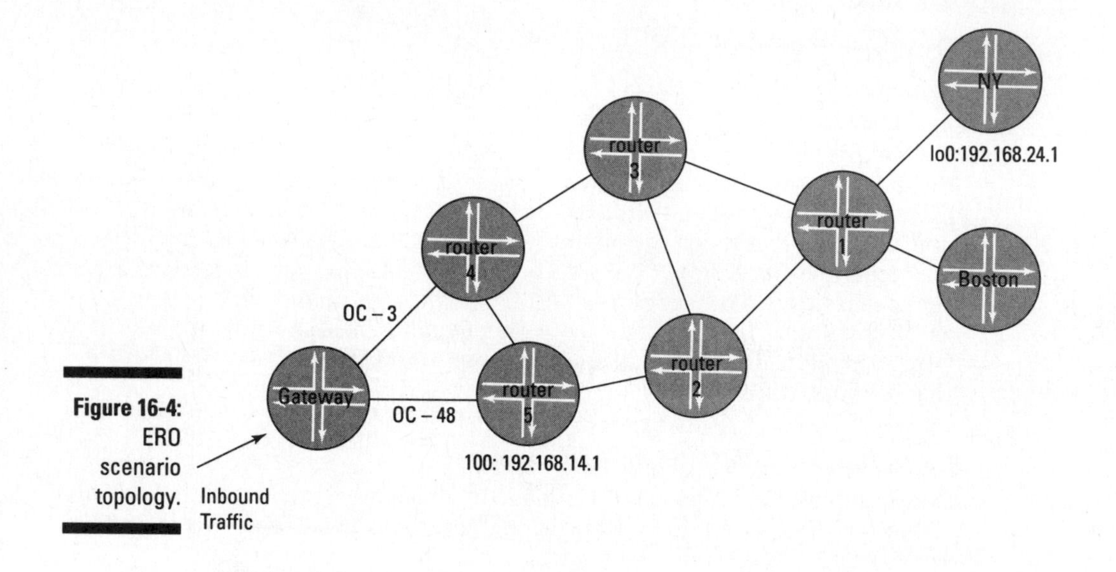

Figure 16-4: ERO scenario topology.

This particular topology has a single ingress point and a single egress point in the MPLS core. Traffic that comes from the corporate headquarters is passed to different branch sites. Maybe the site in New York has more latency-sensitive traffic than the traffic destined for Boston (such as stock trades, for example). You may want to make sure that the New York traffic takes the faster route while the Boston traffic takes the road less traveled.

In the absence of any explicit configuration, if you're using an LSP to route traffic across your MPLS core, the traffic headed to both destinations would take the same path.

Configuring a static route

If you want to make sure that traffic is separated in a particular way, the solution is actually a combination of old and new. First, you want to set up static routes that basically say that if the traffic is destined for New York, then use a particular route.

Static routes are configured under the `routing-options` hierarchy. From the gateway router:

```
[edit routing-options]
static {
   route 192.168.24.1 {
      next-hop 192.168.14.1;
   }
}
```

This configuration is just the standard static route configuration. It defines a static route for all traffic destined for New York, and it sets the next-hop address to route through router2.

Configuring an explicit route

If you want, you can set up an LSP for traffic that includes router 3 so that traffic destined for New York uses the faster path. To do so, you have to explicitly specify that the LSP is to use router 3. This constraint is called an *explicit route object* (ERO).

To configure an ERO that forces the LSP to use router 3, you first have to set up the LSP. On the gateway router:

```
[edit protocols mpls]
label-switched-path ny-traffic {
   to 192.168.20.1;
}
```

You must first enable MPLS and RSVP on the appropriate interfaces. After you've set up the LSP, you have to associate it with a particular path. In this case, we want to specify that the path goes through router 3. To configure the explicit route, use the `path` statement:

```
[edit protocols mpls]
path to-router3 {
   10.0.18.1 loose;
}
label-switched-path ny-traffic {
   to 192.168.20.1;
   primary to-router3;
}
```

This configuration does two things: defines a path and applies that path. The path (called `to-router3`) specifies a particular IP address through which the LSP must traverse towards its destination. Because the path is loosely constrained (configured with the `loose` statement), the only requirement is that the LSP pass through that address. It doesn't matter which interface is used, what path is used to get to that point, or what path is used from that point to the destination.

When RSVP sets up this LSP, it uses the underlying IGP to route from the ingress point to the ERO (router 3 in this case) before continuing to its final destination over the established LSP. RSVP uses the IGP to route from the ERO to the LSP egress point.

In this example, the address used for the path constraint is a specific interface address for router 3. By specifying the interface address, you can pretty much dictate how the traffic will flow through the network. That is to say that traffic will be routed to that interface en route to the final destination. If you use the loopback address of router 3 instead of a particular interface address, you have less control over the path the inbound traffic will take. Traffic is routed to router 3, but it may arrive on any interface. However, your IGP should know the shortest path to reach this loopback interface.

The *primary* statement is what ties the LSP to the path you created. When you apply the path to the LSP, you want to apply it as the primary path so that all traffic on this LSP uses the path. You can configure secondary paths, which would then be used if the primary path is not available (if, for example, an ERO in the primary path was not reachable).

Linking the route to the LSP

After you've configured a static route and created an LSP, the next task is to make sure that all traffic destined for New York travels through the LSP you just created. What you're really doing is specifying that all New York-bound traffic use the LSP as its next hop and allow all forwarding decisions after that to be made based on the LSP.

To link the route to the LSP, use the `lsp-next-hop` statement with the static route configuration:

```
[edit routing-options]
static {
   route 192.168.24.1 {
      lsp-next-hop ny-traffic;
   }
}
```

When traffic comes in with a destination address of 192.168.24.1, the router associates that traffic with the LSP, and it forwards the traffic to the next hop in the LSP.

Verifying traffic using the LSP

Setting up the LSP is all fine and good, but how do you know whether traffic is actually using the LSP? The easiest way to verify the path is by using the `traceroute` command. Examine the topology in Figure 16-5 to see the expected path:

```
user@gateway> traceroute new-york
traceroute to new-york (192.168.24.1), 30 hops max, 40 byte packets
 1  router5 (192.168.14.1)  0.869 ms  0.638 ms  0.536 ms
    MPLS Label-100004 CoS=0 TTL=1 S=1
 2  router4 (192.168.17.1)  0.869 ms  0.638 ms  0.536 ms
    MPLS Label-100004 CoS=0 TTL=1 S=1
 3  router3 (192.168.19.1)  24.968 ms  0.727 ms  0.363 ms
    MPLS Label-100004 CoS=0 TTL=1 S=1
 5  router1 (192.168.20.1)  24.968 ms  0.727 ms  0.363 ms
 6  new-york (192.168.24.1)  24.968 ms  0.727 ms  0.363 ms
```

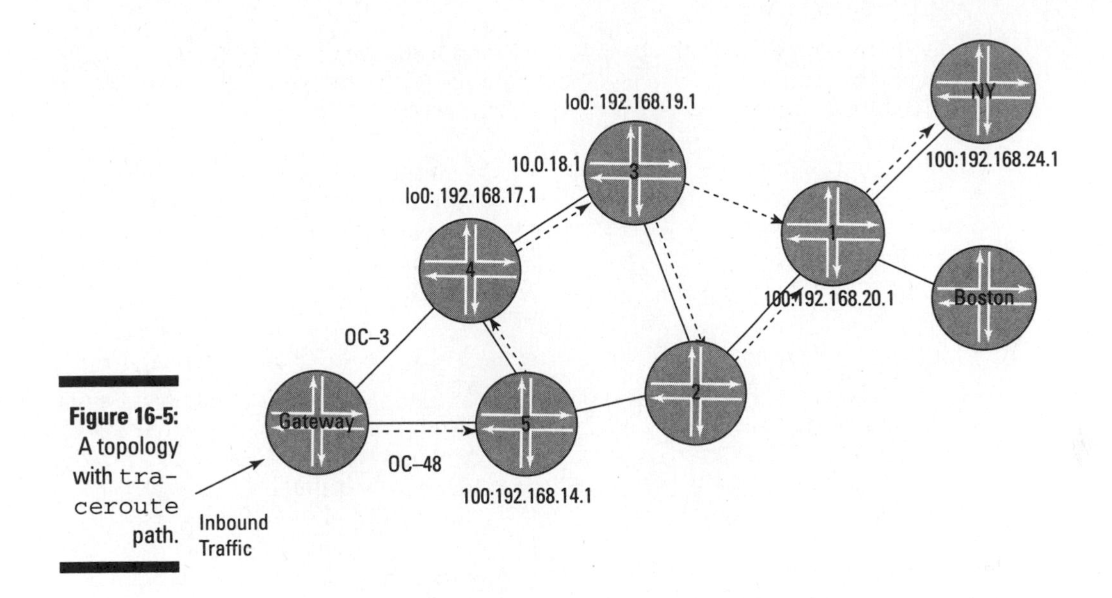

Figure 16-5: A topology with `traceroute` path.

In the output, you want to verify that traffic is passing through the ERO (router 3). You also want to verify that MPLS labels are being used. Typically, it's probably enough for you to verify that an MPLS label is in use. If you want to get more detailed, you can start to check the MPLS labels against the expected label values.

Explicitly configuring an entire LSP path

In some cases, you may want to have a bit more control over the path an LSP takes. For example, you may want to do the following:

- Ensure that the very first hop in an LSP is a specific router.
- Make sure that traffic flows from router 1 to router 2 to router 3, in that order.
- Bound a path at a couple of points, allowing the routers to decide how to get between those points.

Figure 16-6 shows these scenarios.

Imagine that you want traffic in the LSP to travel from the ingress point to router 3 using whatever path is available. From router 3, you want to make sure that the traffic passes through router 2 and then on to router 1, in that exact order. How do you do this?

Configuration for this type of more constrained LSP is handled through the `path` configuration:

```
[edit protocols mpls]
path to-router3 {
    10.0.18.1 loose;
    10.0.22.1 strict;
    10.0.29.1 strict;
}
```

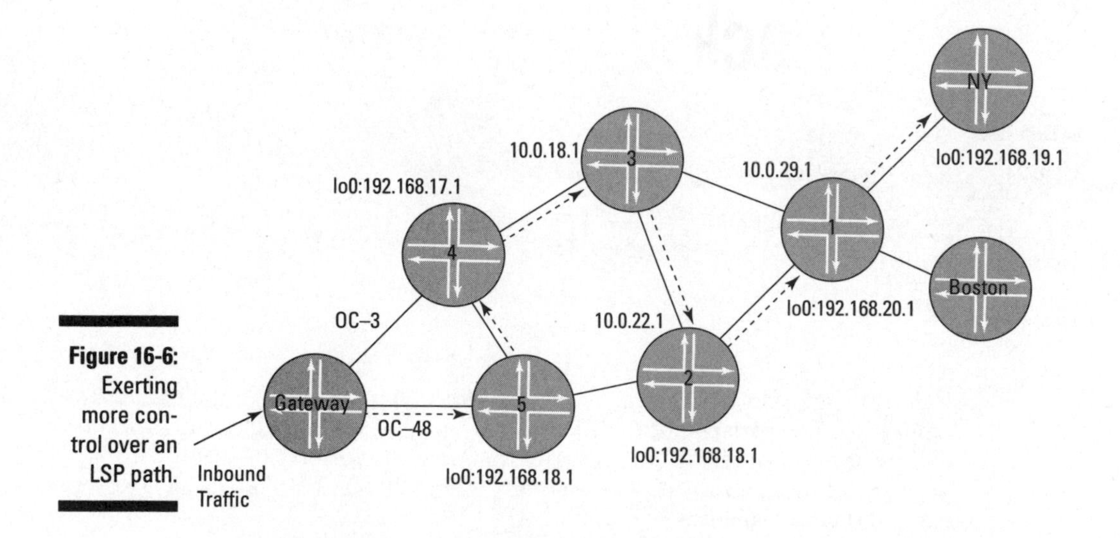

Figure 16-6: Exerting more control over an LSP path.

The strict keyword indicates that traffic has to flow directly to that router. It can't go through any other router in the LSP en route to that router. If you specify two strict addresses in a row, it means that traffic has to flow directly through those two routers without any path deviations in the middle.

Traffic can take any path from the ingress point to the interface on router 3 with the address 10.0.18.1. Then, after traffic flows through 10.0.18.1, it must pass through 10.0.22.1 and then on to 10.0.29.1 before it's eventually forwarded on to the destination.

Again, to verify the path, use the `traceroute` command:

```
user@gateway> traceroute new-york
traceroute to new-york (192.168.24.1), 30 hops max, 40 byte packets
 1  router5 (192.168.14.1)  0.869 ms  0.638 ms  0.536 ms
    MPLS Label-100004 CoS=0 TTL=1 S=1
 2  router4 (192.168.17.1)  0.869 ms  0.638 ms  0.536 ms
    MPLS Label-100004 CoS=0 TTL=1 S=1
 3  10.0.18.1 (10.0.18.1)  24.968 ms  0.727 ms  0.363 ms
    MPLS Label-100004 CoS=0 TTL=1 S=1
 4  10.0.22.1 (10.0.22.1)  0.869 ms  0.638 ms  0.536 ms
    MPLS Label-100004 CoS=0 TTL=1 S=1
 5  10.0.29.1 (10.0.29.1)  24.968 ms  0.727 ms  0.363 ms
 6  new-york (192.168.24.1)  24.968 ms  0.727 ms  0.363 ms
```

Chapter 17

Configuring Tunnels for Secure Packet Exchange

In This Chapter

- Understanding Secure Tunneling and IPSec
- Configuring IPSec VPNs and IKE
- Verifying IPSec and IKE

Most enterprises these days have geographically dispersed workforces. Those workers not located at corporate headquarters, though, still need access to the same tools, applications, and data as the rest of the employees. You need a way to connect up satellite offices to corporate headquarters, using a carrier's network as the transit vehicle.

But just because a site is remote doesn't mean that it can be less secure. The requirements go well beyond simple access; you must provide a secure means by which you can transmit and receive sensitive information. That means is through the use of secure tunnels. By encrypting traffic before sending it through the Internet, you can ensure that your company's data assets aren't compromised.

Getting an Overview of Secure Tunnels

In today's corporate networks, it's becoming increasingly common to have one or more satellite offices connected to a central corporate headquarters. These satellite offices have the exact same needs as the devices and users connected directly to the corporate network (see the sample topology of Figure 17-1). They need fast, reliable, and secure access to data that resides on the same servers and in the same data centers.

The networks depicted in Figure 17-1 are all TCP/IP networks. That is, they're interconnected using IP protocols such as OSPF and BGP. As you now know, IP protocols are tremendously powerful when it comes to exchanging information. They assist in the formulation of routes and the ultimate forwarding of information across diverse networks. However, one of the shortcomings of these IP protocols is that they lack built-in security.

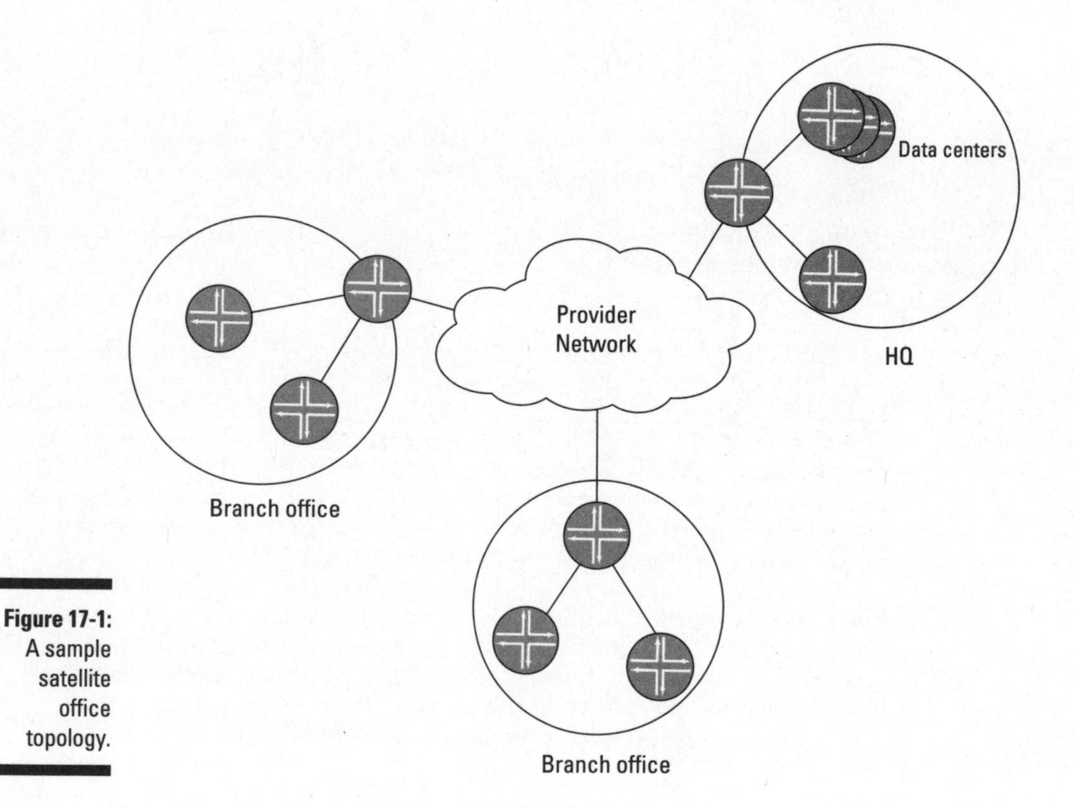

Figure 17-1: A sample satellite office topology.

The IP Security (IPSec) protocol was designed to make up for this shortcoming. Built with security in mind, IPSec provides network-level data integrity, data confidentiality, data origin authentication, and protection from replay. And perhaps more importantly, IPSec can be run on top of any IP protocol on any physical medium.

To fully understand why you need IPSec and what it can do, you must have a firm grasp on these topics:

- Tunneling
- Security protocols
- Security algorithms

- Authentication methods
- Security associations

Tunneling

At the core of IPSec is the notion of tunneling. *Tunnels* in the networking world behave similarly to tunnels in the real world. That is, they provide underground passage from one point to another point.

Say that a satellite office is connected to a corporate core network. If you use the real-world tunnel scenario, you can treat the two networks as cities separated by a big mountain (or a waterway, if you prefer underwater tunnels). You need a way to get from one city to the other city, so you build a tunnel. All traffic from one city travels through the tunnel to the other city, and vice versa.

Conceptually, this idea holds true for IPSec tunnels. The biggest difference here is how that tunnel is created. So under normal conditions, traffic is forwarded from the satellite network's gateway router to the carrier network, and that network forwards the packet through its network en route to the core gateway.

Because you're creating a tunnel, you want your traffic to go underground and emerge on the other side without anyone seeing how it traveled. You encrypt the traffic as it leaves your satellite office, and you decrypt the traffic as it enters your core network. All the transit routers between those two points don't care about (or can't see) the contents of the traffic.

This encryption provides the security inherent in IPSec tunnels.

IPSec protocols

The IPSec security suite includes two different security protocols, each of which serves a different purpose:

- **Authentication Header (AH):** The AH protocol is used to provide data origin authentication, data integrity, and anti-replay protection, it doesn't do any encryption. When you use AH, the IP payload of the packet isn't encrypted, but you can validate the contents of the packet.
- **Encapsulating Security Payload (ESP):** The ESP protocol is used primarily to provide data confidentiality. It encrypts the packet payload, but it doesn't touch the IP header.

Authentication header

The AH protocol encapsulates the packet with a header that includes an authentication value. That authentication value is based on a *symmetric-key hash function.*

Basically, a symmetric-key hash value is called symmetric because the key that is used to encrypt the data is the same key used to decrypt. Your router and the remote route share a secret code (called a *shared key*). You use that key along with a common algorithm to generate a value based on the all the bits in the packet. Your router encapsulates the packet before it sends it outbound with the appropriate header, which includes this calculated value.

When the remote router receives the packet, it uses the bits in the packet along with the preshared key to generate its own value. Because the two routers are using the same key, same algorithm, and same packet, the authentication values should be identical. If they're identical, then you know that the packet sent is the packet that was received, so you can accept the packet and forward it into your network.

If, however, the authentication values don't match, then you know something has changed in the packet between the time that it was sent and the time that it was received. Therefore, you drop the packet.

The AH protocol doesn't actually look at the entire packet. It looks only at the IP payload and the bits in the IP header that never change. It doesn't examine fields like TTL or ToS in the IP header. For example, if you've configured DSCP rewrites on your routers, the DSCP bits change as the packet flows through your network. If you calculate an authentication value based on a changing packet, your authentication value can never be validated.

Note that the AH protocol doesn't encrypt the traffic. Its primary role is to provide data authentication, not data confidentiality. If you want to encrypt your packets for secure transmission, you have to use the ESP protocol.

Encapsulating Security Payload

Certainly, ensuring that traffic received matches the traffic that was sent is valuable, but it really protects you only from malicious attacks; it doesn't prevent other people from taking a peek at your sensitive data. If you want to encrypt your data before you send it so that no one else can see it, you need to use ESP.

When the ESP protocol is used, your router uses a shared key and an encryption algorithm to create *ciphertext* (encrypted text). That ciphertext is the encrypted payload of your IP packet. Your router sends the encrypted text along with an IP header. The IP header allows the transit routers to perform lookups and forward the traffic accordingly.

When the remote router receives the packet, it uses the same shared key and the same encryption algorithm to decrypt the packet. The ESP protocol also creates an authentication header similar to what AH creates, except that it's based solely on the packet payload.

The ESP protocol doesn't do anything with the original IP header. The data authentication doesn't take into account any of the bits in the IP header.

You can actually use both AH and ESP together. AH has the drawback that it doesn't encrypt the packet payload. It does, however, look at the IP header to validate the packet's contents. Meanwhile, ESP has the drawback that it doesn't examine the IP header when doing authentication. It does, though, encrypt the packet payload. Do you see an interesting marriage of ideas here? Using both protocols together is the perfect blend of security.

Security algorithms

Routers need to be able to use a few security algorithms for IPSec to work. Unless you're a total security buff, you really need to know only what they are so that you can answer intelligently when someone asks you how secure your IPSec configuration is.

Encryption protects the packet contents from being viewed on the public network. *Hashing* verifies that the data wasn't altered. But what about validating the source of the data? On the authentication side, JUNOS software uses what is called a *Hashing Message Authentication Code* (HMAC) algorithm. This algorithm is a variant of the more popular Secure Hash Algorithm 1 (SHA-1) and Message Digest 5 (MD5) algorithms.

The *SHA-1 algorithm* takes a data message input of less than 264 bits and produces a 160-bit message digest. It's the most popular of the security algorithms. The *MD5 algorithm* takes a data message input of any arbitrary length and produces a 128-bit message digest. It's more versatile in that it can support longer data messages.

For encryption, JUNOS software supports three different algorithms:

- Data Encryption Standard-cipher Block Chaining (DES-CBC)
- Triple Data Encryption Standard-cipher Block Chaining (3DES-CBC)
- Advanced Encryption Standard (AES)

Again, unless you're a security expert, you don't need to understand the differences between these algorithms.

Authentication methods

Keys can be shared in one of two ways:

- **Preshared keys:** These secret passwords are shared by the two peer devices in an IPSec environment. These keys are configured on each end of an IPSec tunnel, and they must match for any IPSec communication to take place. Preshared keys can be either configured manually or exchanged dynamically using the Internet Key Exchange (IKE) protocol.
- **Digital certificates:** *Certificates* are digital identifiers that validate the authenticity of an individual or a device. A digital certificate implementation uses the public key infrastructure (PKI), which requires you to generate a key pair consisting of a public key and a private key. Certificates are issued by certificate authorities (CAs), which are public or private organizations that manage a PKI.

  The main function of a digital certificate is to associate a device or user with a public-private key pair. Digital certificates also verify the authenticity of data and indicate privileges and roles within secure communication. A digital certificate consists of data that definitively identifies an individual, system, company, or organization. In addition to identification data, the digital certificate contains a serial number, a copy of the certificate holder's public key, the identity and digital signature of the issuing CA, and an expiration date.

Unless you're a security expert, you should probably stick to using preshared keys. Digital certificates and PKI can be quite complex, and you can easily do something that will prevent traffic from flowing across your network.

Security associations

A *security association* (SA) is a set of IPSec specifications negotiated between devices that are establishing an IPSec relationship. These specifications include preferences for the type of authentication and encryption and the IPSec protocol that is used to establish the IPSec connection. A security association is uniquely identified by a security parameter index (SPI), an IPv4 or IPv6 destination address, and a security protocol (AH or ESP).

IPSec security associations are established either manually through configuration statements or dynamically by Internet Key Exchange (IKE) negotiation. In the case of manually configured security associations, the connection is established when both ends of the tunnel are configured, and the connections last until one of the endpoints is taken offline.

In the case of dynamic security associations, you can configure when connections are to be established — either immediately after both ends of the tunnel are configured, or, only when traffic is sent through the tunnel — and dissolve it after a preset amount of time or traffic. You can configure *unidirectional security associations* (separate security associations for incoming and outgoing traffic) or *bidirectional security associations* (one security association for both incoming and outgoing traffic).

Dynamic Security Associations and IKE Protocol

When you deploy and use IPSec on a large scale in the network, manually managing the security associations (SAs) and keys on each device in the network isn't practical. You can configure dynamic SAs in such scenarios so that authentication and key negotiation are automated.

To use dynamic SAs in a router, you must configure the Internet Key Exchange (IKE) protocol and IPSec settings under the IPSec-VPN service configuration. IPSec uses the IKE protocol to dynamically negotiate the security association settings and exchange keys.

The IKE negotiation in a router takes place in two phases:

- Phase 1 establishes a secure channel between the key management processes on the two peers.
- Phase 2 directly negotiates IPSec security associations.

During phase 1, the peers negotiate at minimum an authentication method, an encryption algorithm, a hash algorithm, and a Diffie-Hellman group to create a phase 1 security association. The peers use this information to authenticate each other and compute key material to use for protecting phase 2. Phase 2, also called *quick mode,* results in an IPSec tuple, one security association for incoming traffic and another for outgoing traffic.

Configuring an IPSec Tunnel on an Encryption Interface

Imagine that you have a satellite office that participates in software development for your company. This office may be a remote development office in another country, or it may be just a development office on another coast. The remote office has to access source files that reside within some servers located at corporate headquarters. Because this source code represents your intellectual property, you want to ensure that no one can steal it.

To satisfy your development requirements, you want to configure an IPSec tunnel between your satellite office and your corporate headquarters.

Because we have only a single satellite office in this example, you're going to manually configure your security association.

Configuring an IPSec tunnel requires three basic things:

- Define the security association and the tunnel that will carry the secured traffic.
- Create firewall filters that will place traffic into the tunnel.
- Apply the SA and filters to the appropriate interfaces.

This particular example assumes that you're using an Encryption Services (ES) PIC.

Defining security associations

Security associations basically define your IPSec tunnel. They specify the IPSec protocols to be used, the specific algorithms associated with those protocols, and the shared key required to perform any IPSec actions.

If you have only a few security associations to configure and maintain, you can use manual security associations:

```
[edit security ipsec]
security-association paris-development {
   description "From Paris research center to HQ";
   mode tunnel;
   manual {
      direction bidirectional {
         protocol bundle;
         spi 400;
         auxiliary-spi 400;
         authentication {
            algorithm hmac-sha1-96;
            key ascii-text "$9$...";
         }
         encryption {
            algorithm des-cbc;
            key ascii-text "$9$..."
         }
      }
   }
}
```

The security association configuration does quite a few things:

How IPSec communicates

An IPSec mode describes how the original IP packet is transformed into a protected packet. IPSec supports two modes of secure communication:

- **Transport mode** provides a security association (SA) between two hosts. In transport mode, the protocols provide protection primarily for upper-layer protocols.
- In **tunnel mode**, the endpoints don't need to be configured or be aware of any encryption or IPSEC configuration; they're simply tunneled thru the IPSEC VPN if required to. Tunnel mode helps protect an entire IP packet by treating it as an AH or ESP payload. In tunnel mode, an IP packet is encapsulated with an AH or an ESP header and an additional IP header. The IP addresses of the outer IP header are the local tunnel endpoint and the remote tunnel endpoint. Packets with a destination address matching the private network prefix are encrypted and encapsulated in a tunnel packet that is routable through the outside network. The source address of the tunnel packet is the local gateway, and the destination address is the remote gateway. The IP addresses of the encapsulated IP header are the original source and final destination addresses. Once the encapsulation packet reaches the other side, the remote end determines how to route the packet.

When one side of a security association is a router operating as a security gateway, the security association must use tunnel mode. However, when traffic (for example, SNMP commands or BGP sessions) is destined for the router, the system acts as a host. Transport mode is allowed in this case because the system doesn't act as a security gateway and doesn't send or receive transit traffic.

- **Describe the association.** This is optional text that lets you describe what the security association is.

  Always, always, always enter a description. If you find yourself troubleshooting this router, you'll want to have all the information handy without having to look it up. Much like interface descriptions, there is never a reason not to have a description.

- **Define the mode.** The mode can be either transport or tunnel. For most enterprise applications, the mode should be tunnel, meaning that you're configuring a secure tunnel.
- **Identify the security association as manual.** This configuration differentiates the security association from a dynamic SA. It indicates that the SA parameters are manually configured.
- **Set the direction of the tunnel.** As a general rule, you should be configuring bidirectional tunnels. While you may have reasons you don't need a bidirectional tunnel, you seldom have reasons why you can't have one.

- **Declare which IPSec protocols you are using.** Remember that you can choose from AH and ESP, or you can go with both. If you want to use both (and you should be using both), specify *bundle* for the protocol, which simply indicates that you're using a bundle of both AH and ESP.
- **Define the SPI.** You have to assign a unique numeric identifier to the SA. In this case, the arbitrary number 400 has been assigned. You'll notice that an auxiliary SPI is also configured. You need both the SPI and the auxiliary because the IPSec tunnel is using both protocols. Each protocol needs an SPI to complete the IPSec negotiation. They don't need to be different numbers.
- **Authenticate and encrypt algorithms.** You have to configure which algorithms you want to use. For authentication, use the HMAC algorithm because it provides an additional level of hashing. For encryption, use any of DES-CBC, 3DES-CBC, or AES.
- **Authenticate and encrypt keys.** Use these preshared keys when performing the algorithms. When you configure them, you enter what amounts to a plain-text password. When you look at the configuration, the JUNOS software encrypts the text so that you don't see what you entered.

The security associations are used when the IPSec negotiation is taking place before the tunnel is set up. For the negotiation to work, the security associations on both endpoints of the tunnel must be configured identically.

In this example, you have to configure the gateway router for the Paris development center identically to the gateway router in the corporate headquarters. As you can see from the IPSec description, this example is using the Paris gateway router.

Creating firewall filters

The whole point of an IPSec tunnel is that you want to accept traffic that is transported through the tunnel and reject traffic that isn't secure. After you configure the tunnel on both endpoints, you need to configure firewall filters that will accept traffic only from the remote endpoint.

To filter traffic, you want to match on any traffic that has a source address of the remote endpoint and a destination address of the router:

```
[edit firewall]
filter HQ-to-Paris-traffic {
    term from-HQ {
        from {
            source-address {
                10.0.97.0/24;
            }
            destination-address {
                10.0.12.0/24;
            }
        }
        then accept;
    }
}
```

This firewall filter is pretty simple. It just matches traffic on both the source and destination addresses. If there is a match, the traffic is accepted.

Applying the SA and filters

After you configure the SA and the firewall filters to accept traffic, you have to create the tunnel on the appropriate interface. In this example, the router has an Encryption Services (ES) interface card. To create the tunnel, define the tunnel and then apply the security association and filter to the interface:

```
[edit interfaces]
es-3/0/0 {
    unit 0 {
        tunnel {
            source 10.0.12.33;
            destination 10.0.97.62;
        }
        family inet {
            ipsec-sa paris-development;
            filter {
                input HQ-to-Paris-traffic;
            }
        }
    }
}
```

On the interface, you need to configure the source address for the tunnel. The source address should be the interface address of the outbound interface through which the tunnel is configured. The destination address should be the inbound interface on the remote endpoint through which the tunnel is configured.

Then apply the SA to all the IP traffic on the router. Finally, filter all the inbound traffic on the interface so that you accept only traffic on that interface that originates from the IPSec tunnel.

Checking to see whether the tunnel is functioning

After you configure both endpoints of the IPSec tunnel, you probably want to verify that it's up and running the way it's supposed to. You have to do a couple of things:

- Verify that the SA is active on both routers.
- Verify that the remote endpoint is reachable.

Verify the SA is active

To verify that the SA is active on the router, use the `show ipsec security-association` command:

```
user@host> show ipsec security-associations detail

Security association: paris-development, Interface family: Up

Local gateway: 10.0.12.33, Remote gateway: 10.0.97.62
Local identity: ipv4_subnet(any:0,[0..7]=0.0.0.0/0)
Remote identity: ipv4_subnet(any:0,[0..7]=0.0.0.0/0)
Direction: inbound, SPI: 2908734119, AUX-SPI: 0, State: Installed
Mode: tunnel, Type: dynamic
Protocol: BUNDLE, Authentication: hmac-md5-96, Encryption: None
Soft lifetime: Expired
Hard lifetime: Expires in 120 seconds
Anti-replay service: Disabled

Direction: outbound, SPI: 3494029335, AUX-SPI: 0, State: Installed
Mode: tunnel, Type: dynamic
Protocol: AH, Authentication: hmac-md5-96, Encryption: None
Soft lifetime: Expired
Hard lifetime: Expires in 120 seconds
Anti-replay service: Disabled
```

The first line in this output indicates that the SA is up. You can also verify the configured SA parameters.

Verify the remote endpoint is reachable

As with most configuration tasks, when you're done configuring the IPSec tunnel, you probably want to ping the remote endpoint to make sure that it's reachable:

```
user@router1> ping 10.0.24.2
PING 10.0.24.2: 56 data bytes
64 bytes from 10.0.24.2: icmp_seq=0 ttl=62 time=0.520 ms
64 bytes from 10.0.24.2: icmp_seq=1 ttl=62 time=0.417 ms
64 bytes from 10.0.24.2: icmp_seq=2 ttl=62 time=0.497 ms
64 bytes from 10.0.24.2: icmp_seq=3 ttl=62 time=0.424 ms
64 bytes from 10.0.24.2: icmp_seq=4 ttl=62 time=0.501 ms
^C
--- 10.0.24.2 ping statistics ---
5 packets transmitted, 5 packets received, 0% packet loss
round-trip min/avg/max/stddev = 0.417/0.472/0.520/0.043 ms
```

A successful ping means that you've configured your tunnel correctly.

For configuring dynamic IPSec tunnels on a J-series router or other devices running JUNOS, see its technical documentation for the exact procedure (`www.juniper.net/techpubs`).

Hiding Internal Addresses from the Internet

If you go through all this trouble to make sure that your traffic is secure, you may also want to hide your internal addresses from the rest of the Internet. Hiding them goes beyond just filtering out the internal addresses by using routing policy. You can go so far as to pull them out of all the IP headers that exit your network (not just control packets).

To hide your internal addresses, you configure the local tunnel endpoint to use Network Address Translation (NAT). Whenever traffic comes into your tunnel endpoint router, the router rewrites the source address in the IP header to its own address before sending it through the tunnel. All other routers downstream of the endpoint then see the traffic as having come from the local endpoint.

To configure NAT, you have to do three things:

1. **Define a NAT pool.**

   A *NAT pool* is a list of addresses used to rewrite the packets' source address. In most cases, it's sufficient to have a single address in the NAT pool. That address should be the address of the local tunnel endpoint.

2. **Create a rule to match on all outbound traffic.**

   NAT, like IPSec, is implemented as a service. You need to create a rule for the service that matches on all outbound traffic so that every packet gets translated.

3. **Apply the translation.**

   After matching on packets, you have to apply the translation to the address specified in the NAT pool.

The configuration for these tasks is

```
[edit services]
nat {
    pool ipsec-pool {
        address 10.1.15.1;
    }
    rule nat-rule {
        term {
            then {
                translated {
                    source-pool ipsec-pool;
                    translation-type {
                        source static;
                    }
                }
            }
        }
        match-direction output;
    }
}
```

This configuration creates a NAT pool with a single address in it (the address of the local gateway). The NAT rule has no match criteria, so it matches all outbound traffic. All traffic is translated using the specified pool of one address. Because there is a single address, the translation is static translation. All outbound packets look as though they've come from 10.1.15.1.

To verify that NAT has been configured correctly, use the `show services nat pool` command:

```
user@host> show services nat pool brief

Interface: sp-1/3/0, Service set: blue
NAT pool   Type    Address                              Port       Ports used
Ipsec-pool static  10.0.15.1-10.0.15.1
```

Part IV

Managing JUNOS Software

"This program's really helped me learn a new language. It's so buggy I'm constantly talking with overseas service reps."

In this part . . .

In this part, we cover how to keep your JUNOS network operating and efficient, even when you yourself may be having a bad day. We show you how to run your network with guidance on monitoring, troubleshooting, and automating your network.

Chapter 18

Monitoring Your Network

In This Chapter

- Performing pings and traceroutes
- Monitoring interfaces and routes
- Configuring RPM

Wouldn't it be a lovely world if once you got your network set up and running correctly, you could sit back and relax? Unfortunately, such a world doesn't exist. For your network to remain a lean, mean, routing machine, at least some oversight is required. You need to be able to monitor your network to ensure that things are in order.

This chapter is dedicated to the basic diagnostic tools and instrumentation commands that are essential to the maintenance of a healthy network. It describes how to check connectivity, monitor activity, and ensure that traffic is flowing at breakneck speeds.

Checking Host-to-Host

You'll probably begin monitoring your network immediately after setting up your protocols. The first thing most people do after configuring their router (or other device) is check to see whether they can send traffic across links to other nodes within the network. This test is where the `ping` command comes into play. Examine the network topology shown in Figure 18-1.

If you run OSPF across all the links in the network, you'd expect to be able to reach any host from any other host. But how do you know whether things are working correctly?

From the JUNOS command prompt, you can issue the `ping` command. Log into the router you want to start from and send a ping to an address on the remote host to which you expect a route. For example, in the topology shown in Figure 18-1, you might log into router 1. From there, you want to ensure that you have connectivity to router 7. So you pick any network address on router 7 (any of the interface addresses or even the loopback address will work), and you issue a `ping` command:

```
user@router1> ping 10.0.24.2
PING 10.0.24.2: 56 data bytes
64 bytes from 10.0.24.2: icmp_seq=0 ttl=62 time=0.520 ms
64 bytes from 10.0.24.2: icmp_seq=1 ttl=62 time=0.417 ms
64 bytes from 10.0.24.2: icmp_seq=2 ttl=62 time=0.497 ms
64 bytes from 10.0.24.2: icmp_seq=3 ttl=62 time=0.424 ms
64 bytes from 10.0.24.2: icmp_seq=4 ttl=62 time=0.501 ms
^C
--- 10.0.24.2 ping statistics ---
5 packets transmitted, 5 packets received, 0% packet loss
round-trip min/avg/max/stddev = 0.417/0.472/0.520/0.043 ms
```

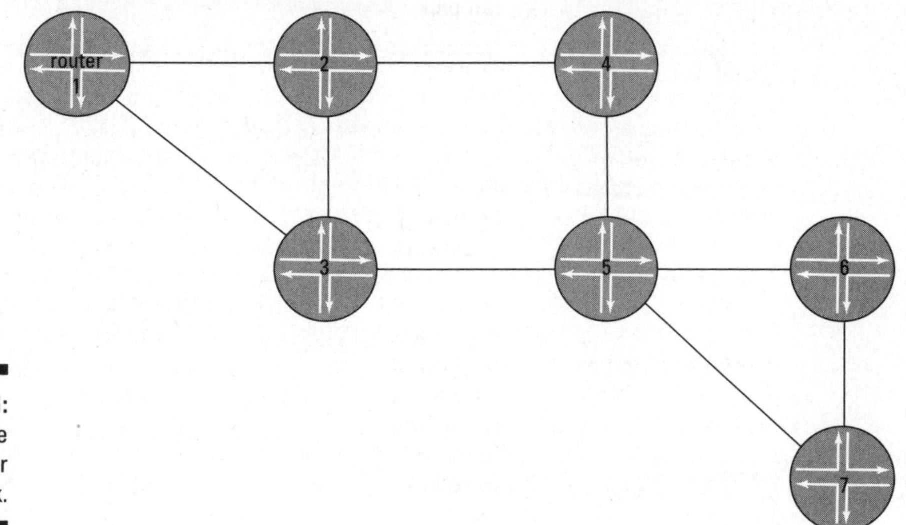

Figure 18-1: A simple 7-router network.

Once you issue the command, your router will send packets to the remote address. When the remote node receives these packets, it generates a response packet and sends that packet back to the original sender. Upon receipt of this response packet, your router records a successful ping and measures the time between sending the original request and receiving the response. This process happens over and over until you stop the command by pressing Ctrl-c.

Associating an address with the host name

If you try to send a ping to the name of the host, you have to make sure that the host names are being resolved on your router. In other words, you have to first configure a DNS server so that an address is associated with the host name.

Typically, when you're using ping to diagnose a new network, you haven't yet added names to the DNS server, so you'd have to use one of the configured addresses.

Now, if you're going with the address approach, which address should you use? You can pick any of the configured interface addresses, or you can pick the loopback address. If you want to ensure that the router itself is up, use the loopback address.

If you pick an interface address, and that interface happens to be down (due to a link error or because it hasn't been configured correctly, for example), your ping will fail. You may think the router is unreachable, but really only the interface is unreachable.

You may notice that in the ping output, each ping has an ICMP sequence number associated with it. Each request and response is flagged with this sequence number so that the devices know which response goes with which request. If you know that you sent request 3 at a certain time, you can check the time that you receive response 3 and record the time it took for the entire round-trip.

The `ping` command gives you a wealth of information. First, you know that the remote address that you chose is up and responsive because the command yielded some output. Second, if you examine the summary data at the bottom of the output, you can see important statistics about the path. For example, notice that there were five packets transmitted and five responses received. This information tells you that all the `ping` requests were received by the remote device. If the network had issues or the packets were lost, you'd see that not all packets transmitted resulted in a received response packet. The packet loss would be an indicator that something is wrong in the network.

Additionally, the summary output shows the minimum, maximum, average, and standard deviations for the response times. In this example, the round-trip transit time for the ping and response is on the order of .500 milliseconds, which is exceptionally fast. If the round-trip time exceeds 150 or 200 milliseconds, you probably want to take a look at the network to determine where the latency is originating.

The origin of ping

The concept of a ping is very similar to the way that SONAR works. Using SONAR, ships send out pulses of sound. The sound waves strike objects in the water and echo back. The transmitter can hear these echoes and use those to map out underwater obstacles. As you've probably seen in movies, these SONAR pulses make a pinging noise, and that noise is the namesake for the `ping` command.

After the concept had been created by Mike Muuss, an acronym was associated with it. David L. Mills called the ping Packet InterNet Groper, but don't let the presence of an acronym fool you as to the origin of the name.

If you look at Figure 18-1, what happens if there is no path to router 7 from router 1? The `ping` command reveals that information as well:

```
user@router1> ping router7
PING router7 (192.168.24.1): 56 data bytes
ping: sendto: No route to host
ping: sendto: No route to host
ping: sendto: No route to host
ping: sendto: No route to host
ping: sendto: No route to host
^C
--- router7 ping statistics ---
5 packets transmitted, 0 packets received, 100% packet loss
```

In this case, router 7 isn't reachable from router 1. The ping fails, and one hundred percent of the packets sent are lost (meaning that there's no response). So does the lack of response mean the router is down? Or does it mean maybe that a problem occurred somewhere between router 1 and router 7? And how do know which is to blame? The way to answer these questions is to issue a `traceroute`.

Tracerouting Your Network

Ping is useful for figuring out if you can reach one host from another host (see preceding section). But what if you care about *how* you reach that host? Or what if you want to know where a particular path is being blocked? Fortunately, `traceroute` helps you with that issue.

In Figure 18-2, the network is running OSPF. OSPF calculates a path from router 1 to router 7 (highlighted in the topology map). If you issue a `ping` command from router1, the ping fails. But how do you know the failure is because router 7 is down? It may conceivably be because an intermediate hop en route to router 7 is down.

To find out the answer, issue a `traceroute` command:

```
user@router1> traceroute router7
traceroute to router7 (192.168.24.1), 30 hops max, 40 byte packets
 1  router2 (192.168.26.1)  0.869 ms  0.638 ms  0.536 ms
 2  router3 (192.168.27.1)  24.968 ms  0.727 ms  0.363 ms
 3  *
 4  *
^C
```

The `traceroute` command works by sending an ICMP packet from the source to the destination node. At each hop, the packet is processed, and the intermediate hop sends a response back to the source letting it know that it was received and has been forwarded to the next hop along the way.

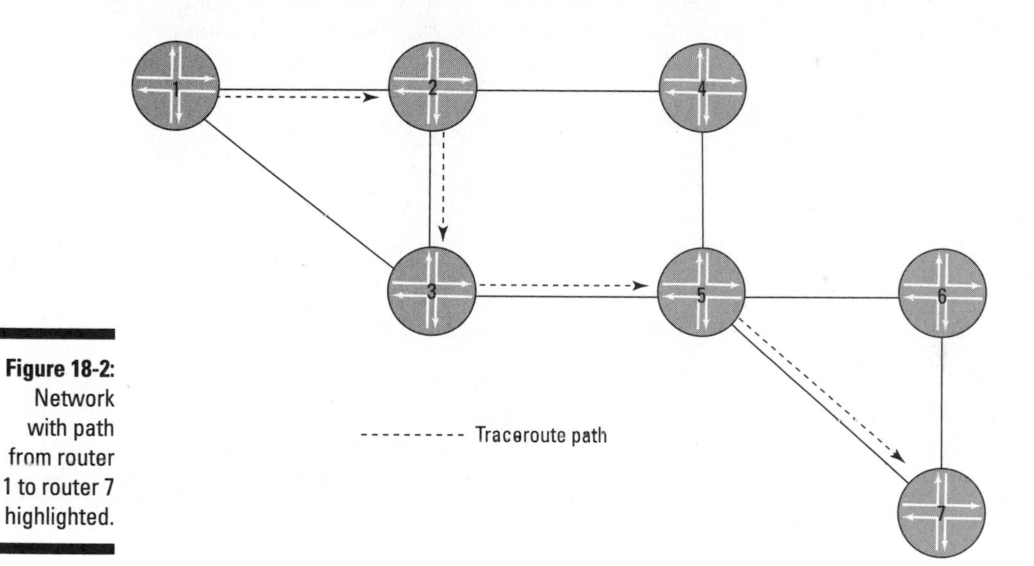

Figure 18-2: Network with path from router 1 to router 7 highlighted.

So as a traceroute makes its way from router 1 to router 7, you start to see responses showing how that packet is traversing the network. In the preceding output, the first hop along the way is router 2. As part of the traceroute, router 1 sends three separate ICMP packets. Router 2 responds to each of these three and then passes the request to the next hop on the way to router 7.

The output shows the round-trip time for each of the three traceroute packets, which gives you an idea not only of which hops are being reached but also how long it's taking to send traffic back and forth between those routers. As with the `ping` command, you want to keep an eye on the round-trip times to identify latency issues within your network.

In this example, the output shows that responses are being received by router 3, but beyond that, nothing is received. Looking at the topology, the next hop in the path is router 5. Because the traceroute isn't receiving a response from router 5, you know that the problem is somewhere between router 3 and router 5. You still don't know what the issue is, but at least now you know where to look.

Working with Common Diagnostic Commands

You'll find yourself using the same commands again and again to monitor, troubleshoot, and diagnose your network. These `show` commands display important information about your interfaces and your routing tables.

Almost every feature within the JUNOS software comes with corresponding *show* commands so that you can see what is happening on the router. The show commands that you'll use the most are

- `show interfaces`
- `show route`
- `show <protocol>`

Monitoring your interfaces

You'll often want to look at how your interfaces are behaving to figure out what is happening to the traffic within your router. As such, you need to become an expert in the `show interfaces` command.

As with all `show` commands, this command has several variations:

- **`show interfaces` (no modifier):** The `show interfaces` command, issued with no modifier, gives you a summary of some of the most important fields and counters tracked for interfaces. This command is an excellent starting point for most interface activities.
- **`show interfaces brief`:** The brief version of the same command pares down the output even more. This command is useful when you're looking for big things like whether an interface is up. If you need detailed statistics or counters, you need to delve a little deeper than the `brief` command.

- **show interfaces detail:** The detailed output for `show interfaces` includes all the information from the previous commands, but it also includes detailed statistics about the interface, including the interface counters for packets and bytes, as well as queuing information, which is useful when you have CoS configured.

Which version of the command you use depends on your goal.

Taking a quick peek

If you just want to see whether an interface is operational, you can start with the `show interfaces brief` command:

```
user@router> show interfaces brief
Physical interface: fe-0/0/0, Enabled, Physical link is Down
  Link-level type: Ethernet, MTU: 1514, Speed: 10m, Loopback: Disabled,
  Source filtering: Disabled, Flow control: Enabled
  Device flags   : Present Running Down
  Interface flags: Hardware-Down SNMP-Traps Internal: 0x4000
  Link flags     : None
```

This command shows all the interfaces on the router, though the preceding snippet shows only a single interface. For each interface, you see the name of the interface, whether it's enabled, and the state of the physical link. For this Fast Ethernet interface, the physical link is down, which means that the interface isn't operational (the link light is down).

The device flags confirm that the interface is *present* (that is, it's on the box and the line card has been detected), *running* (meaning the line card is functioning), and *down* (the link light is down).

The output from the `show interfaces brief` command shows that the interface is Enabled. Remember that you can administratively disable an interface using the disable configuration statement within the interface configuration:

```
fe-0/0/0 {
    disable;
    unit 0 {
        family inet {
            address 10.0.24.2/32;
        }
    }
}
```

Viewing only the output you want to see

A lot of times, you may not want to see every interface on the router. In fact, more often than not, you're checking the status of a particular interface. To see only the output for a specific interface, include that interface's name as an argument in the command:

```
user@router> show interfaces
   brief fe-0/0/0
Physical interface: fe-0/0/0,
   Enabled, Physical link is
   Down
  Link-level type: Ethernet,
   MTU: 1514, Speed: 10m,
   Loopback: Disabled,
  Source filtering: Disabled,
   Flow control: Enabled
  Device flags    : Present
   Running Down
  Interface flags: Hardware-
   Down SNMP-Traps Internal:
   0x4000
  Link flags      : None
```

This command limits the output to only the specific interface included in the command.

Sometimes, you may want to see all interfaces of a certain type. Imagine, for example, that you want to monitor all your Fast Ethernet interfaces. You can use interface wildcards to view all your fe interfaces:

```
user@router> show interfaces
   fe* brief
Physical interface: fe-0/0/0,
   Enabled, Physical link is
   Down
  Link-level type: Ethernet,
   MTU: 1514, Speed: 10m,
   Loopback: Disabled,
  Source filtering: Disabled,
   Flow control: Enabled
  Device flags    : Present
   Running Down
  Interface flags: Hardware-
   Down SNMP-Traps Internal:
   0x4000
  Link flags      : None

(output snipped)
```

If you disable an interface, the output from the show interfaces command will indicate that the interface is administratively down:

```
user@router> show interfaces brief
Physical interface: fe-0/0/0, Administratively down,
          Physical link is Down
  Link-level type: Ethernet, MTU: 1514, Speed: 10m,
          Loopback: Disabled,
  Source filtering: Disabled, Flow control: Enabled
  Device flags   : Present Running Down
  Interface flags: Hardware-Down Down SNMP-Traps Internal:
          0x4000
```

Getting a closer look

If simply knowing whether your interface is up is not quite enough (see preceding section), you can use the base show interfaces command:

```
user@router> show interfaces
Physical interface: fe-0/0/0, Enabled, Physical link is Down
  Interface index: 128, SNMP ifIndex: 23
  Link-level type: Ethernet, MTU: 1514, Speed: 10m, Loopback: Disabled,
  Source filtering: Disabled, Flow control: Enabled
  Device flags   : Present Running Down
  Interface flags: Hardware-Down SNMP-Traps Internal: 0x4000
  Link flags     : None
  CoS queues     : 4 supported, 4 maximum usable queues
  Current address: 00:05:85:02:a4:00, Hardware address: 00:05:85:02:a4:00
  Last flapped   : 2008-03-05 14:30:58 PST (4w3d 23:00 ago)
  Input rate     : 0 bps (0 pps)
  Output rate    : 0 bps (0 pps)
  Active alarms  : LINK
  Active defects : LINK
```

The base `show interfaces` command includes a bit more information than its brief counterpart. In addition to the basic interface information, the `show interfaces` command includes these tasty informational nuggets:

- **CoS queues:** This is the total number of CoS queues configured for the particular interface card. If you've configured eight queues, it shows a value of eight. For this particular interface, only the default four queues are available.
- **Current address and Hardware address:** The current address is the configured MAC address for the interface card. The Hardware address is the actual MAC address tied to the hardware.
- **Last flapped:** The last flapped field indicates the last time the interface went down and came back up. This information can be extremely helpful when you're trying to figure out why traffic is lost on your network. If you look at the last flapped date and time, you can try to correlate that data with changes in your network (maintenance calls, configuration changes, and so on), which can help you track down the source of the flap.
- **Input and output rates:** The input and output rates identify the total input and output in packets per second. In this case, the interface is down, so the values are 0.
- **Active alarms and defects:** The active alarms and defects list the link alarms that are associated with the particular interface. In this case, the link is down, which has generated a link alarm. That alarm is listed as both an alarm and a defect.

Giving a full examination

If you find that the information provided by the `show interfaces` command (see preceding section) isn't enough information, you can try the `detail` version of the same command, as shown in Listing 18-1.

Listing 18-1: Monitoring Output with the `show interfaces detail` Command

```
user@host> show interfaces detail
Physical interface: fe-0/0/0, Enabled, Physical link is Down
  Interface index: 128, SNMP ifIndex: 23, Generation: 303
  Link-level type: Ethernet, MTU: 1514, Speed: 10m, Loopback: Disabled,
  Source filtering: Disabled, Flow control: Enabled
  Device flags   : Present Running Down
  Interface flags: Hardware-Down SNMP-Traps Internal: 0x4000
  Link flags     : None
  CoS queues     : 4 supported, 4 maximum usable queues
  Hold-times     : Up 0 ms, Down 0 ms
  Current address: 00:05:85:02:a4:00, Hardware address: 00:05:85:02:a4:00
  Last flapped   : 2008-03-05 14:30:58 PST (4w3d 23:03 ago)
  Statistics last cleared: Never
  Traffic statistics:
   Input  bytes  :              0               0 bps
   Output bytes  :              0               0 bps
   Input  packets:              0               0 pps
   Output packets:              0               0 pps
   IPv6 transit statistics:
    Input  bytes  :                  0
    Output bytes  :                  0
    Input  packets:                  0
    Output packets:                  0
  Egress queues: 4 supported, 4 in use
  Queue counters:     Queued packets  Transmitted packets   Dropped packets
    0 best-effort                0                    0                 0
    1 expedited-fo               0                    0                 0
    2 assured-forw               0                    0                 0
    3 network-cont               0                    0                 0
  Active alarms  : LINK
  Active defects : LINK
```

When you get to this level of detail, you're usually troubleshooting the interface. This view of the interface gives you even more information, including (but not limited to):

- **Traffic statistics:** The counters displayed here indicate the total number of bytes and packets both received by and transmitted out of the interface. These numbers give you an indication of how much traffic your interface is handling. Note that these statistics are cumulative from the last time the statistics were cleared (cleverly hidden in the field *Statistics last cleared*).

- **Egress queues:** The egress queues correspond to the total number of outbound CoS queues you've configured on the box. In this case, the default CoS queues are all that are configured. Each queue is listed, along with the number of packets in each queue as well as the number of transmitted packets. The dropped packets should be 0 unless you're experiencing congestion. (For more details about CoS and outbound queues, see Chapter 15.)

If you find that you still lack the information you need to troubleshoot your network or even a particular interface, you can use another level of detail: the `show interfaces extensive` command. The output for that command is a superset of the detailed version of the same command. It includes all the same information presented here, along with a detailed listing of input and output errors, and a slew of MAC (layer 2) statistics.

Monitoring your routing information

The foundation command to monitor all the routing information on your router is the `show route` command. This command has a host of various knobs and parameters that you can use to fine-tune your quest for knowledge, and following are the most useful versions of that command:

- **`show route`** (no modifiers): The base `show route` command, issued with no modifiers, gives you a basic listing of the routes in your routing table. This information is helpful when you're trying to figure out whether an expected route is actually present, which is typically a first step toward debugging why devices in your network are unreachable.
- **`show route detail`**: This more detailed view of the routing information includes a significant amount of additional information for each route in the routing table, which is useful when troubleshooting routing issues. This command is typically the second step in diagnosing a routing problem (following the base `show route` command).
- **`show route summary`**: The `summary` command gives you some high-level statistics about the routes that are in your routing table. It tells you how many routes are in the routing table for each protocol.
- **`show route exact`**: The `exact` modifier allows you to see only a specific route or route prefix, which should be used in conjunction with the appropriate detail modifiers (brief, terse, detail, or extensive).

A quick peek at your routes

The most basic task when monitoring the routing information on your router is to look at what routes are in the routing table. See the `show route` command in Listing 18-2.

Listing 18-2: Monitoring Output with the `show route` Command

```
user@router1> show route

inet.0: 10 destinations, 10 routes (9 active, 0 holddown, 1 hidden)
+ = Active Route, - = Last Active, * = Both
0.0.0.0/0           *[Static/5] 1w5d 20:30:29
                       Discard
10.255.245.51/32    *[Direct/0] 2w4d 13:11:14
                     > via lo0.0
172.16.0.0/12       *[Static/5] 2w4d 13:11:14
                     > to 192.168.167.254 via fxp0.0
192.168.0.0/18      *[Static/5] 1w5d 20:30:29
                     > to 192.168.167.254 via fxp0.0
192.168.40.0/22     *[Static/5] 2w4d 13:11:14
                     > to 192.168.167.254 via fxp0.0
192.168.64.0/18     *[Static/5] 2w4d 13:11:14
                     > to 192.168.167.254 via fxp0.0
192.168.164.0/22    *[OSPF/10] 2w4d 13:11:14
                     > via fxp0.0
192.168.164.51/32   *[OSPF/10] 2w4d 13:11:14
                       Local via fxp0.0
207.17.136.192/32   *[BGP/170] 2w4d 13:11:14
                     > to 192.168.167.254 via fxp0.0
```

This command lists the active entries in the routing table, along with some basic information for each route. For each route, you see route, route prefix, and

- **Route origin:** The origin identifies how the route was learned. Listing 18-2 contains *direct routes* (indicating the route is directly accessible through one of the router's interfaces), static routes, OSPF routes, and BGP routes.
- **Route preference:** Listed alongside the route origin is the route preference. Remember that each protocol has a default route preference associated with it, or you can manually override the default. The higher preference values (lower numbers are higher preference) are selected as active routes.
- **Next-hop to the destination:** The address listed after the *to* keyword is the IP address of the next-hop address in the routing table. To get to route 172.16.0.0/12, the router uses the next hop 192.168.167.254.
- **Outbound interface:** The outbound interface tells you the interface that the router is going to use to send traffic to the next-hop address. For the route to 172.16.0.0/12, the router will send traffic out its fxp0 interface.

When you look at the routing table, you should be checking that all expected routes are in the table. If you don't see a route that you expected to see, you know that something wrong with the protocols on the router. You should examine more closely how your device is configured and your routing protocols are operating.

Getting more information about your routes

If a quick glance at your routes doesn't satisfy your hunger for knowledge, you can get a bit more detailed in your examination. To see more routing information, use the `detail` modifier, as shown in Listing 18-3.

Listing 18-3: Monitoring Output with the `show route detail` Command

```
user@router1> show route detail

inet.0: 22 destinations, 23 routes (21 active, 0 holddown, 1 hidden)
10.10.0.0/16 (1 entry, 1 announced)
        *Static Preference: 5
                Next-hop reference count: 29
                Next hop: 192.168.71.254 via fxp0.0, selected
                State: <Active NoReadvrt Int Ext>
                Local AS:    69
                Age: 1:31:43
                Task: RT
                Announcement bits (2): 0-KRT 3-Resolve tree 2
                AS path: I

10.31.1.0/30 (2 entries, 1 announced)
        *Direct Preference: 0
                Next hop type: Interface
                Next-hop reference count: 2
                Next hop: via so-0/3/0.0, selected
                State: <Active Int>
                Local AS:    69
                Age: 1:30:17
                Task: IF
                Announcement bits (1): 3-Resolve tree 2
                AS path: I
         OSPF   Preference: 10
                Next-hop reference count: 1
                Next hop: via so-0/3/0.0, selected
                State: <Int>
                Inactive reason: Route Preference
                Local AS:    69
                Age: 1:30:17    Metric: 1
                Area: 0.0.0.0
                Task: OSPF
                AS path: I
(output snipped)
```

The number after the dot

In the `show` output in Listing 18-2, the router sends traffic destined for next hop 192.168.167.254 out interface fxp0.0. Remember that the number that appears after the dot indicates the logical interface, which is defined as the unit number:

```
[edit interfaces]
fxp0 {
    unit 0 {
        family inet {
            address
10.255.245.51/32;
        }
    }
}
```

The detailed listing for your routes lists a bit more information for each route. Most of that information is a bit esoteric, but some of it can be downright helpful. Here are a couple of output fields that you may enjoy:

- **Age:** The age tells you how long the route has been in the routing table. Imagine that traffic destined for a particular address experiences some problems. You may want to check the age to see whether there was a problem where the route was dropped from your routing table. So you look at the detailed routing information, and if the age is less than anticipated, you know that the route was newly added (or re-added) to the routing table — a certain clue that something is amiss and you need to delve deeper.
- **Inactive reason:** You may have an inactive route that is being supplanted by some other route to the same host. If you've set up LSPs in your network, for example, you may be expecting traffic to flow a certain way. The inactive reason gives you an idea as to why a particular route has been preempted by another route. In Listing 18-3, you can see that you have multiple routes to the destination 10.31.1.0/30. In this case, the OSPF route is inactive because the route preference for an OSPF route is lower than that of a direct route.

Most of the other fields in the `show route detail` output are used very rarely.

Summarizing your routing information

Sometimes you may just want a quick summary of the routing information on your router. As an example, you have just configured OSPF in your network, and you're expecting to see a certain number of OSPF routes in your routing table. You can issue a `show route summary` command to see that all the routes are there (see Listing 18-4).

Listing 18-4: Monitoring Output with the `show route summary` Command

```
user@router1> show route summary

Autonomous system number: 69
Router ID: 10.255.71.52

inet.0: 24 destinations, 25 routes (23 active, 0 holddown, 1 hidden)
Restart Complete
              Direct:      6 routes,      5 active
               Local:      4 routes,      4 active
                OSPF:      5 routes,      4 active
              Static:      7 routes,      7 active
                IGMP:      1 routes,      1 active
                 PIM:      2 routes,      2 active

inet.3: 2 destinations, 2 routes (2 active, 0 holddown, 0 hidden)
Restart Complete
                RSVP:      2 routes,      2 active

iso.0: 1 destinations, 1 routes (1 active, 0 holddown, 0 hidden)
Restart Complete
              Direct:      1 routes,      1 active

mpls.0: 7 destinations, 7 routes (5 active, 0 holddown, 2 hidden)
Restart Complete
                MPLS:      3 routes,      3 active
                VPLS:      4 routes,      2 active

inet6.0: 5 destinations, 5 routes (5 active, 0 holddown, 0 hidden)
Restart Complete
              Direct:      2 routes,      2 active
                 PIM:      2 routes,      2 active
                 MLD:      1 routes,      1 active
```

The route summary includes several key pieces of useful information:

- **Autonomous system number:** The AS number that is configured for your router (if any exists) is displayed here. This number really just validates your configuration.
- **Router ID:** If you've configured a Router ID, it shows up here. If you haven't, the router uses the `lo0` address (the first non-127.0.0.1 address) as the router ID.
- **Routing table name:** Each stanza in the output corresponds to a different routing table within the router. You'll generally be looking in the base table, which is the inet.0 table in this example. If you've configured MPLS, you'll see routes in the inet.3 and mpls.0 tables. The inet.6 table is reserved for IPv6, so you probably won't see too many entries there unless you work with Asian countries or the U.S. Federal government.

- **Routes:** Each routing table has a summary of the total number of routes in the table. In this case, they're categorized as follows:
  - **Active:** Routes that are active (meaning they are being used in the forwarding table).
  - **Holddown:** These routes are in holddown state, which basically means that they're in the process of becoming inactive. This state is rarely seen as it's a transitional state between active and inactive status.
  - **Hidden:** Hidden routes are routes that exist on the router but aren't being used because of some routing policy in use. For example, you may be using a filter of some sort to select one route over another. The route that would have been selected is a hidden route. The route that is selected is an active route.

Getting specific with your output

When you're looking for a particular route or a set of routes, it can be quite painful to have to page through 50 pages of routing information. You don't want your route to be the proverbial needle in a haystack. You need a way to search for a particular route. To find a specific route, use the `exact` modifier:

```
user@router1> show route exact 207.17.136.0/24

inet.0: 24 destinations, 25 routes (23 active, 0 holddown, 1 hidden)
Restart Complete
+ = Active Route, - = Last Active, * = Both
207.17.136.0/24     *[Static/5] 2d 03:30:22
                     > to 192.168.71.254 via fxp0.0
```

This command pretty much limits the output to only the requested route. You can use it with the various detail modifiers (terse, brief, detail, or extensive).

Keeping an Eye on Latency

One of the things you'll want to monitor in your network is latency. *Latency* is a measure of how long it takes for traffic to get from one device to another device. Examine the topology shown in Figure 18-3.

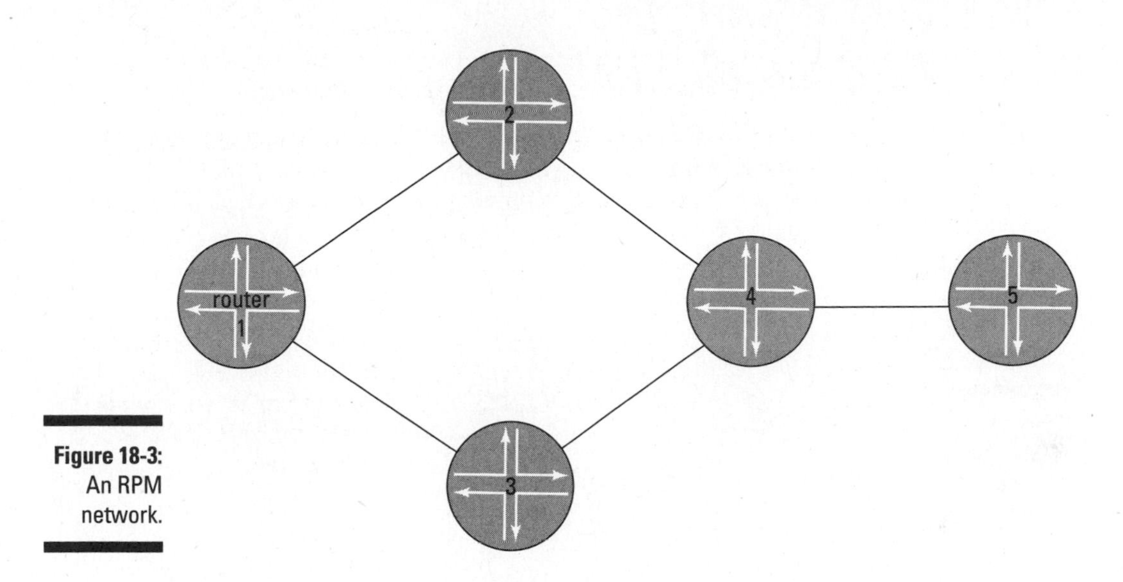

Figure 18-3: An RPM network.

In this simple network, traffic flows from router1 through the network to router5. That path will take some amount of time on a normal day. So if you know what that average time (or *network latency*) is, you can basically monitor your network and evaluate the current performance against the expected performance. So when you see a spike in network latency, it tells you that something has run amok in your network.

Real-time performance monitoring

The JUNOS software supports a tool called *real-time performance monitoring* (RPM). RPM essentially is a set of tests, run periodically, that help you measure the latency between two devices on a network.

RPM only works if the two devices you're measuring between both run JUNOS.

When RPM is enabled, your router generates a bunch of probes that are sent to the target device. These probes are time-stamped when they're sent. When the target device receives the probes, it generates a response and sends that response back to the sender. By measuring the time between sending the probe and receiving the response, your router can tell you what the round-trip time is between the two devices.

This send/receive process is repeated for each probe within a test. By averaging the times over some sample, you can get a better idea of what the average time is across the network. Then these tests are run between fixed intervals to provide you with information about average latency over time.

Configuring RPM

To configure RPM on your network, you need to decide on a few things. First, you have to figure out where you want to do the measurement. If you look at Figure 18-4, you need to select two points in your network that will provide meaningful data.

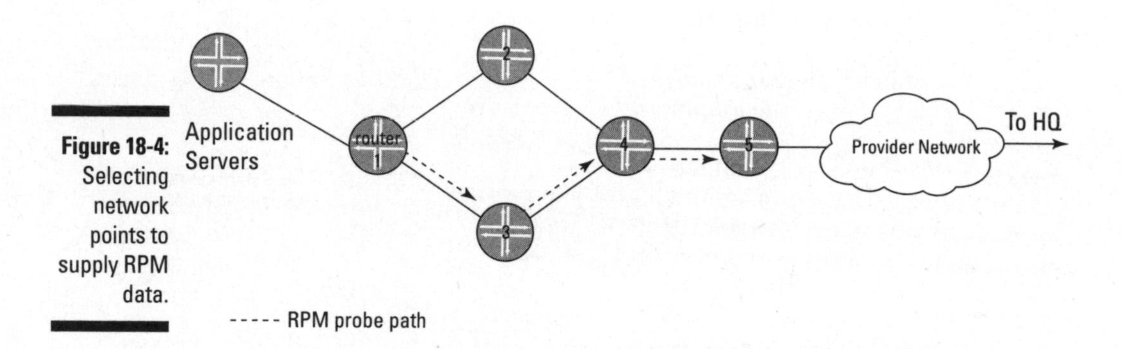

Figure 18-4: Selecting network points to supply RPM data.

In Figure 18-4, application servers are connected to router 1. Ultimately, this traffic is transmitted via VPN through router 5 to your service provider (and eventually back to some headquarters). In this case, you want to measure the latency between router 1 and router 5. Any increase in latency may potentially impact the applications being routed between those nodes.

To configure this test:

```
[edit services]
rpm {
    probe app-server-network {
        test icmp-test {
            probe-type icmp-ping-timestamp;
            target address 192.168.24.1;
            probe-count 15;
            probe-interval 1;
            test-interval 600;
        }
    }
}
```

This configuration defines an RPM test for the app-server-network. The probe owner in this case is really just a name so that you can quickly see what the test is for. Typically, you should name the probe owner after whatever network you're testing (in this case, the application server network).

Most of the RPM configuration is done within an RPM test configuration stanza. Name the test something intuitive (in this case, it's named icmp-test). Then you have to configure the test details.

Use ICMP ping probes because they're easy to configure and generally provide enough information to diagnose latency issues in your network. The savvier user can use TCP or UDP probes, but they require the configuration of the remote end to act as a probe server. If you use ICMP packets, the box already knows how to respond, and the configuration is simpler.

Configure the target address as the loopback address of the remote device (in this case, the loopback address on router 5).

You must also configure the number of probes in each test, the length of time between probes, and the length of time between tests. We recommend configuring between 10 and 20 probes at 1-second intervals. This particular test is going to run every ten minutes.

Monitoring RPM tests

Configuring a test is certainly a great step in the right direction, but you need to somehow see the results of those tests. To view the results of the RPM measurements, use the `show services rpm probe-results` command:

```
user@host> show services rpm probe-results

    Owner: app-server-network, Test: icmp-test
    Probe type: icmp-ping-timestamp
    Minimum Rtt: 312 usec, Maximum Rtt: 385 usec, Average Rtt: 331 usec,
    Jitter Rtt: 73 usec, Stddev Rtt: 27 usec
    Minimum egress time: 0 usec, Maximum egress time: 0 usec,
    Average egress time: 0 usec, Jitter egress time: 0 usec,
    Stddev egress time: 0 usec
    Minimum ingress time: 0 usec, Maximum ingress time: 0 usec,
    Average ingress time: 0 usec, Jitter ingress time: 0 usec,
    Stddev ingress time: 0 usec
    Probes sent: 15, Probes received: 15, Loss percentage: 0
```

The output can be a bit hard to parse, but focus on the following fields:

- **Owner and test:** This field tells you which RPM test is summarized below.
- **Probe type**: Put simply, this field is what you configured as the probe type.

- **RTT**: The RTT fields are the round-trip time measurements. You can see the minimum measurement, the maximum measurement, and the average measurement for the probes over the entire test — in this case, 15 probes.
- **Jitter**: Jitter is the variation in delay over time. The jitter value lets you know how consistent the tests were. If one test took 3 seconds and the second test took 500 usecs, the jitter would be high, an indication that you might want to run the test again because some issues are impacting your network. Ideally, you want a small jitter and a small standard deviation, which means that all traffic more or less takes the same amount of time to traverse your network.
- **Loss percentage**: Although you shouldn't see it as non-zero very often, probes can be lost due to many reasons. If you're seeing probe loss, it indicates that your network is dropping packets somewhere; a firewall filter maybe discarding them; or some device along the path is experiencing congestion. (Pings are generally treated as best effort, and this type of traffic is generally first to get dropped in time of congestions.) Check into the problem accordingly.

In terms of what kinds of times you should be seeing, as a general rule, you probably want to see round-trip-times on the order of 200 to 500 microseconds (usecs). Because these RPM probes are using ICMP ping packets, the times should really be the same as if you issued a bunch of pings to the remote destination.

Chapter 19
Troubleshooting Your Network

In This Chapter

- Knowing what to troubleshoot
- Creating tools to troubleshoot your network
- Using JUNOS commands to analyze network processes

Everyone wants to live in a world without problems, but much to the chagrin of network operators everywhere, such a world doesn't exist. And when things go wrong, you have to be able to diagnose and correct (or at least work around) the issue. This chapter is dedicated to that aspect of networking. While we can't provide troubleshooting information for every conceivable problem, we can establish a framework that you can use to address most problems. As you continue to provision and manage your network, you'll find that having a systematic, repeatable approach to diagnosing and resolving issues is paramount for your success.

Following General Troubleshooting Tips

Whenever you find yourself in a troubleshooting situation, you can take advantage of some general tricks of the trade. None of the following tips are earth-shatteringly profound, but they're in line with the principle of keeping processes simple.

- **Look at your device.** One of the easiest things you can do when diagnosing a problem is to actually look at the device. Take a peek to see whether all the interfaces are cabled correctly. If your problem is that an interface or line card is down, has it been plugged in correctly? If you happen to notice a black smear that is indicative of smoke or fire damage near a component, then you're most likely a bit closer to diagnosing the problem.

  Obviously, if you're managing remote devices, you probably don't want to hop on a plane and fly out to visually inspect your routers, switches, and other devices, but if you are local to your boxes, it's worth a look.

- **Know what is normal.** This trick of the trade may also be fairly obvious, but you have to know what is normal for your device. How can you spot something that is out of the ordinary if you don't know what your baseline is? As an example, how can you know if 30 percent CPU utilization on a system's control board is a sign of a problem or is just business as usual when the first time you look at the CPU is when you're troubleshooting?

  When you get your network up and running, document what is normal for your network. Use the JUNOS monitoring and diagnostic commands to define thresholds for things like

  - CPU utilization on your control board
  - Buffer utilization on your control plane
  - Number of routes in your network
  - Protocol adjacencies for your router
  - Latency between key points in your network

- **Confirm the symptom.** Many problems are transient by nature, and in some cases, testing will cause more disruption than the problem itself. If a transient condition has already cleared, then conducting disruptive tests doesn't provide any benefit. In these cases, you're better off conducting longer term monitoring with testing planned when the problem resurfaces. Basically, if you see a problem, make sure that the problem still exists when you start to look at things.

- **Divide and conquer.** This general approach works well when troubleshooting a problem that is generic enough to have a number of different possible causes. In many cases, you'll be closer to the real cause of the problem when you can effectively eliminate the things that aren't causing the problem. For example, if a joystick card isn't needed to boot a PC and the PC won't boot, start by removing the joystick card. Basically, reduce the system to the minimum number of elements required to reproduce the problem.

- **Test your hypothesis.** The tip here is that if you're going to test a hypothesis, the hypothesis must be testable. It does little good to dream up possible causes for a problem if you can't definitively test whether a hypothesis is valid. Further, when you think up new possible causes, the tests you use to validate these problems should get you closer to the correct diagnosis, even if they fail. That is, each test should eliminate a possible cause of the issue.

- **Keep an open mind.** Many a network operator has failed to correctly diagnose something because of subjectivity that creeps in after years of experience. Many times, operators overlook a potential source for a problem due to their own experiences. You need to be able to leverage your past experiences, but you can't let these experiences prevent you from seeing new possibilities.

Peeling the Onion to See Your Network's Layers

Is there a more ubiquitous cliché in technology than "peeling the onion"? But, as with most clichés, it's popular for a reason. Troubleshooting is perhaps the best example of how you have to peel the onion to see the many different layers within the network.

As an example, imagine that one of the VPNs in your network goes down. The problem may reside in any one of the network layers (see Figure 19-1).

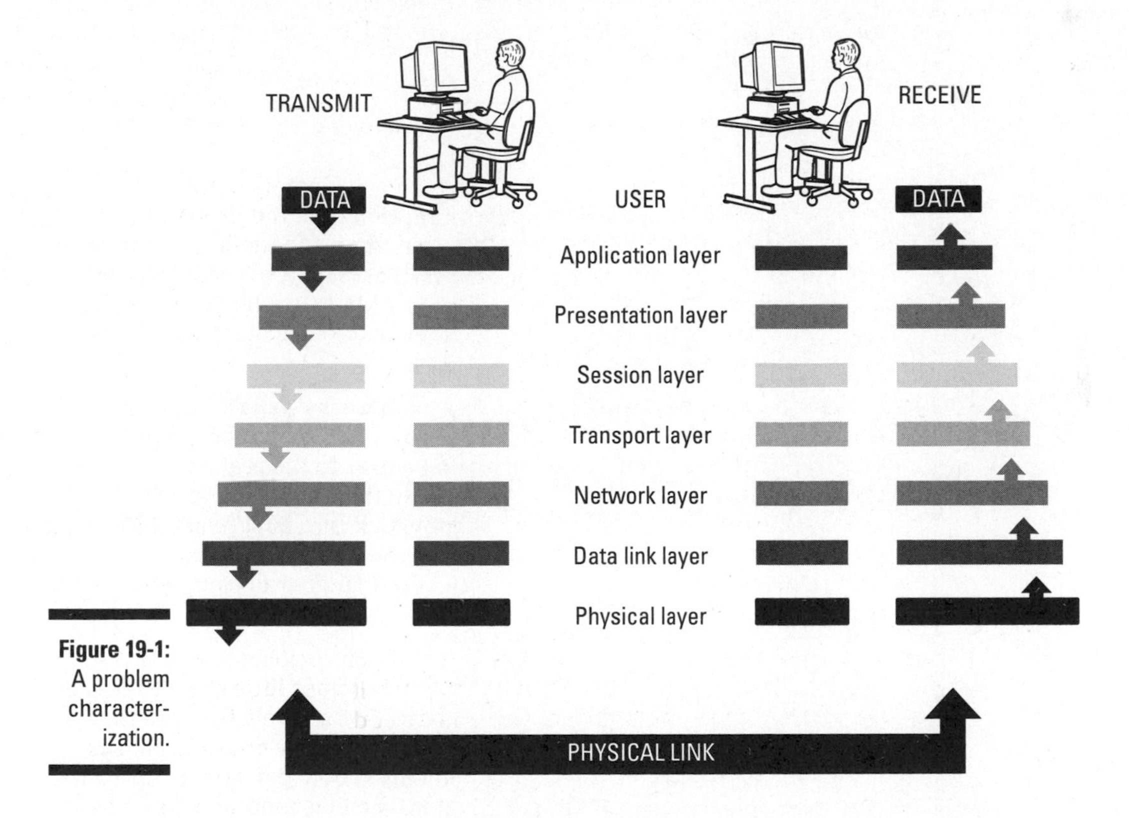

Figure 19-1: A problem characterization.

In this case, you might check the physical layer to make sure the physical links are up. As you peel away that layer, you check the data-link layer to see whether you have a framing mismatch and so on. For you, troubleshooting becomes an exercise in peeling the onion.

As part of peeling the onion, you must also figure out where the problem resides in the network. If you look at your network and the possible sources of issues within, you can characterize problems in several different ways:

- **Local issues** are problems that are local to the device experiencing the problem. Imagine, for example, that something is misconfigured, or the software or hardware has a defect. These types of issues may result in some local effects.
- **Network issues** are problems that impact the way the network functions. The issues may be specific to a particular network segment, an application on the network, or the overall function of the network. This class of issue may be caused by a single device or by something dealing with the implementation of a particular application on the network (CoS, for example). Regardless of the cause, the impact is felt downstream or in other parts of the network.

After you identify the nature and origin of the problem, you're ready to resolve the issue.

This book focuses on the JUNOS software. Sometimes hardware causes problems, however. While we highlight how you can detect hardware issues, we don't provide hardware installation techniques required to swap out bad interfaces or line cards.

Creating a Troubleshooting Toolkit

Don't spend your time worrying about troubleshooting; instead, understand what tools you have at your disposal. Some of the most popular tools you need include

- **JUNOS software CLI:** The JUNOS software CLI is the primary tool for diagnosing the device. The primary functions you'll use are
  - **Monitoring and diagnostic commands:** The various `show` commands (chassis, system, interfaces, and route) form the foundation for most of your base troubleshooting.
  - **Process restart:** In some cases, you may need to restart a particular process on the device.
  - **Network utilities:** Ping and traceroute are troubleshooting staples. You need these tools to diagnose network issues. (For more on these commands, see Chapter 18.)
- **System logs and trace files:** Syslogging and tracing provide information about the operation of the box, highlighting specific events so that you can determine how your box is working. In addition to the normal system log files, individual processes maintain their own log files.

- **Core files:** Core files are basically dumps of information that occur when processes fail. They're not immediately useful when you troubleshoot the device, but they can provide insight so that you can resolve software defects more quickly.

Troubleshooting: A Case Study

The best way to describe how you should approach troubleshooting is to take a look at a network issue and walk you through how to resolve that particular issue. For this case study, reference the topology shown in Figure 19-2.

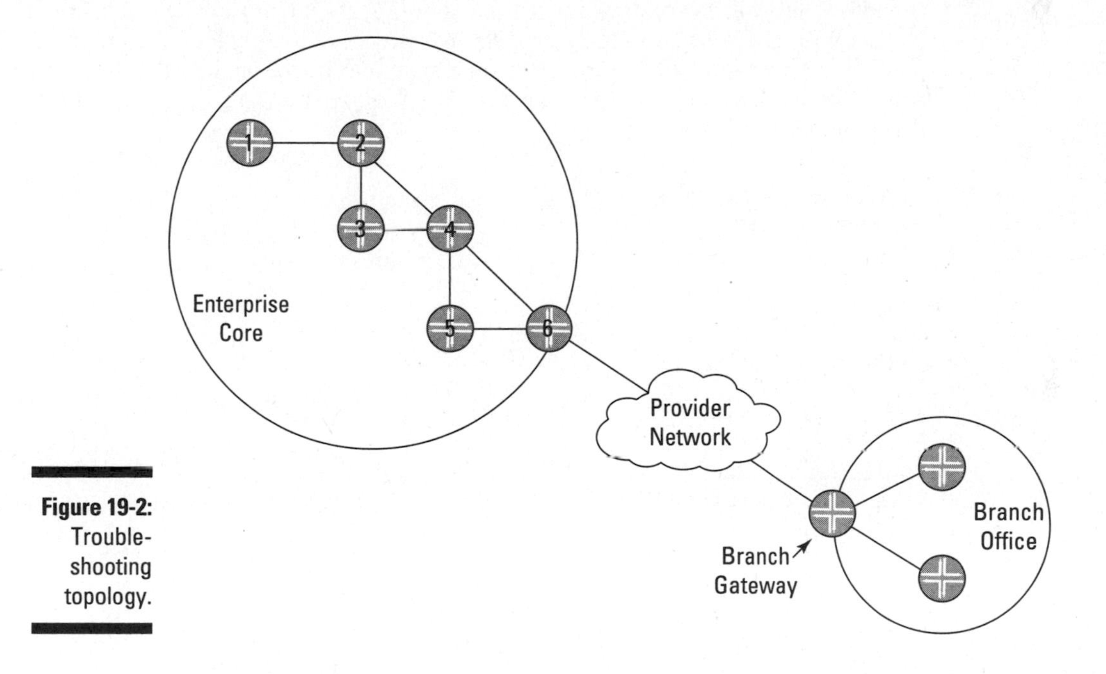

Figure 19-2: Troubleshooting topology.

In this case study, the problem you're looking for is a VPN that has gone down. A VPN can go down for many reasons, so this problem provides a good look at a lot of the different layers involved in troubleshooting.

In this example, you're running both an MPLS core and a branch site. The VPN is set up from the edge of your core to the gateway for your branch network. You're also using an IPSec tunnel over that same link so that your traffic is encrypted for secure delivery.

Within both your core and your branch networks, you're running OSPF as your IGP. Nothing exotic is configured with OSPF in this case. You have BGP sessions between your core and branch networks to a carrier, which is providing an Internet cloud.

You have routing policies set up to both reject unwanted routes and to aggregate routes so that you're not advertising your entire address space. You also have firewall filters set up to prevent unwanted traffic and deny potential attacks on your routers.

Your interface configuration is straightforward. You've specified an MTU value for traffic within your branch network. You have T3 interfaces connecting your branch gateway to the carrier network. On the MPLS core side, you have SONET interfaces.

The VPN is unreachable. What do you do?

The first thing you need to do when troubleshooting anything is establish a workflow. The basic workflow for troubleshooting should always be the same so that you have a programmatic, repeatable way of detecting and diagnosing problems (see Figure 19-3). (For more on a systematic approach to diagnosing problems, see the section "Following General Troubleshooting Tips," earlier in this chapter.)

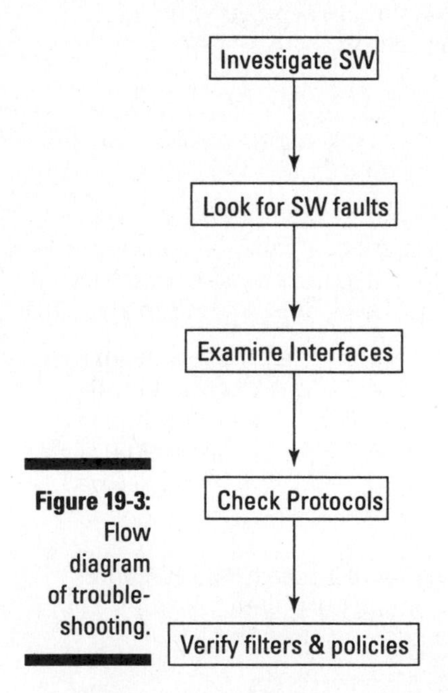

Figure 19-3: Flow diagram of trouble-shooting.

The idea behind this workflow is to identify easy-to-find, big issues first and then to get more granular as you eliminate possible causes. Ultimately, you want the router to work for you, so if the router can tell you something about a particular problem, check there first.

In the case study being used for this chapter, a VPN has gone down. What are the possible sources of that VPN going down? Well, it may be a problem with one of the physical line cards or interfaces. Maybe an interface is down. Or perhaps one of the links on the path has an issue. Maybe you have no route to the VPN endpoint. This workflow is designed to peel the troubleshooting onion, focusing on the lowest layers first and then examining the higher layers.

Being proactive before you experience problems

You should set up your network so troubleshooting a problem can occur even before you experience the problem. For you to be able to access the information you'll need to be proactive, you must configure your router to collect relevant information.

Chapter 11 introduces system logging. At a minimum, though, you should have the following things configured on your router:

- **Remote syslog host:** Having a remote syslog host helps in archiving syslog messages and ensures that these valuable messages are available even in the event of a catastrophic router failure.
- **Archive logs:** You should configure syslog archive settings that will ensure entries are retained for at least two weeks (especially important when remote system logging isn't set up). We recommend configuring 20 copies of the messages file with each copy being at least 1MB in size.
- **Log CLI commands and configuration changes:** You've probably heard the joke about what to do if you break something while no one is watching — just walk away. While this advice is perhaps sound, it's futile when the system has been configured to log interactive CLI commands. When combined with unique user logins, the logging of all commands issued on the box provides an excellent audit trail of who did what and when.

Using these recommendations, your syslog configuration should resemble

```
[edit syslog]
user * {
   any emergency;
}
file messages {
   any notice;
   authorization info;
   archive size 1m files 20;
}
file cli-commands {
   interactive-commands any;
   archive size 1m files 10;
```

```
}
file config-changes {
  change-log info;
  archive-size 1m files 10;
}
```

This syslog configuration does four major things:

1. **Prints syslog messages with *emergency* severity to the terminals of all users.**

   This way, if someone is logged into your router, they'll immediately see critical syslog messages.

2. **Logs all syslog with a severity of notice. Additionally, any authorization messages of info severity are logged.**

   These messages are written to the *messages* file, which is rotated every time it reaches 1MB. Twenty files are kept.

3. **Logs all CLI commands and rotates archive files every time the 1MB limit is reached.**

   Ten files are kept.

4. **Logs all configuration messages and rotates archive files every time the 1MB limit is reached.**

   Ten files are kept.

After you set up your router to provide the level of information you need, you're set to begin troubleshooting as problems arise.

Pinpointing the problem

In the case study in this chapter, a VPN has gone down. The first thing you have to figure out is where you're going to do your troubleshooting. Is the problem in your network or in the carrier's network? If it's in your network, is it in your core or at the branch? Sure, you have a bunch of troubleshooting commands you can run, but on which router do you run them?

You know that traffic has to get from the remote VPN endpoint to the ingress router on the MPLS core. The first thing you want to do is see whether you can reach the remote host:

```
user@core-router> ping branch-gateway
PING router7 (192.168.24.1): 56 data bytes
ping: sendto: No route to host
ping: sendto: No route to host
ping: sendto: No route to host
ping: sendto: No route to host
ping: sendto: No route to host
```

```
^C
--- router7 ping statistics ---
5 packets transmitted, 0 packets received, 100% packet loss
```

The `ping` command shows that the remote host is unreachable. So now you have to determine where the path is broken. Try pinging each of the routers along the path to see where the problem resides. The last router in the path that is reachable is a pretty good place to start.

Hardware troubleshooting

While hardware issues are generally out of scope for this book, you can use your software to detect hardware problems. We focus on those aspects of hardware troubleshooting in this section.

Take a look at the hardware on the last reachable router. In this case study, the last reachable router is the MPLS core's egress router. To check the hardware, you should do three things:

1. **Check alarms.**

   Do any active alarms on the device indicate a problem?

2. **Look at hardware-related log entries.**

   Does anything in the system logs identify a problem with one or more components on the device?

3. **Examine the line cards.**

   Are the line cards operational?

Checking alarms

To see whether the box has any active alarms, use the `show chassis alarms` command:

```
user@router6> show chassis alarms

1 alarm currently active
Alarm time              Class   Description
2008-04-07 10:12:22 UTC Major so-0/0/1: loss-of-light
```

The output from the alarm shows that the SONET interface is experiencing problems. In this case, there is a loss-of-light alarm active, which is why the interface isn't working. Examining the `show interfaces` command output should indicate that the interface is down:

```
user@router6> show interfaces so* terse
Interface               Admin Link Proto Local                 Remote
so-0/0/0                up    up
```

```
so-0/0/0.0                 up    up    inet  10.1.12.1/30
                                       iso
                                       mpls
so-0/0/1                   up    down
so-0/0/1.0                 up    down    inet  10.1.15.1/30
                                       iso
                                       mpls
so-0/0/2                   up    up
so-0/0/2.0                 up    up    inet  10.1.13.1/30
                                       iso
                                       mpls
```

The output of the command verifies that the interface is indeed down. Because you started with the hardware alarms, you already know where to begin resolving the issue (the physical SONET link).

The JUNOS software supports two classes of hardware alarms: environmental alarms that don't need to be configured and alarms that must be explicitly configured. The SONET alarms must be configured explicitly under the `edit chassis` configuration hierarchy:

```
[edit chassis alarms]
sonet {
  lol red;
  los red;
}
```

If the SONET alarms aren't configured, then an alarm won't flag a loss-of-light issue.

Looking at hardware-related log entries

Just because you have no alarms doesn't mean that you don't have hardware-related issues. To verify that the hardware is functioning correctly, look at the log entries.

While it's true that all the logs are written to the general syslog file, you may find it a bit daunting to sift through all that information when looking for specific messages. Some of the key JUNOS software processes write their messages not only to the messages file but also to process-specific files.

Here are a couple of process log files you may be interested in:

- The `chassisd` process is responsible for monitoring and managing the hardware present in the physical router chassis, including ASICs, power supplies, fans, temperature sensors, and hot-swap events.
- The `commits` log file records the commit activities on the router.
- The Class of Service process monitors CoS events in the chassis.

- The Device Control daemon dec communicates with the packet forwarding engine to track the status and condition of the router's interfaces. This interface process configures interfaces as per the router's configuration and the hardware that is present on the box.
- The Error Correction Control daemon eccd deals with memory errors. If you suspect bad or failing memory, check this log.

To view the chassis log file:

```
user@router6> show log chassisd
Jan 16 01:37:06 reading RE i2c
Jan 16 01:37:06 reading host processor dimms
Jan 16 01:37:08 ch_signal_proc: Sent signal 1 to syslogd, pid=4086
Jan 16 01:37:08 SSB0 is now present
Jan 16 01:37:08 hwdb: entry for scb 0 at slot 0 inserted
Jan 16 01:37:08 SSB1 is now present
Jan 16 01:37:08 hwdb: entry for scb 0 at slot 1 inserted
Jan 16 01:37:08 Select SSB0
Jan 16 01:37:08 CHASSISD_SNMP_TRAP10: SNMP trap generated: redundancy
              switchover (jnxRedundancyContentsIndex 6, jnxRedundancyL1Index 1,
              jnxRedundancyL2Index 0, jnxRedundancyL3Index 0, jnxRedundancyDescr
              SSB 0, jnxRedundancyConfig 2, jnxRedundancyState 2,
              jnxRedundancySwitchoverCount 1, jnxRedundancySwitchoverTime 12165,
              jnxRedundancySwitchoverReason 2)
Jan 16 01:37:08 CHASSISD_SNMP_TRAP10: SNMP trap generated: redundancy
              switchover (jnxRedundancyContentsIndex 6, jnxRedundancyL1Index 2,
              jnxRedundancyL2Index 0, jnxRedundancyL3Index 0, jnxRedundancyDescr
              SSB 1, jnxRedundancyConfig 3, jnxRedundancyState 3,
              jnxRedundancySwitchoverCount 1, jnxRedundancySwitchoverTime 12165,
              jnxRedundancySwitchoverReason 2)
Jan 16 01:37:08 Reset SSB0 17
```

The log file shows you any up/down events related to the hardware. If the problem is that one of the system's boards isn't functioning, the log file is where you'll find out.

Examine line cards

One of the possible reasons for an interface to be unavailable is because a line card isn't operational. If you want to make sure that all the line cards are functioning correctly, use the `show chassis fpc pic-status` command:

```
user@router6> show chassis fpc pic-status

Slot 0   Online       FPC Type 1
  PIC 0  Down         4x CC-12, SONET, SMIR
Slot 1   Online       FPC Type 1
  PIC 0  Present      2x OC-3 ATM, MM- Hardware Error
  PIC 1  Online       4x OC-3 SONET, SMIR
Slot 2   Online       E-FPC Type 2
PIC 1  Online       2x G/E SFP, 1000 BASE
  PIC 3  Online       1x Tunnel
```

```
Slot 3    Online       E-FPC Type 1
  PIC 0   Online       1x G/E IQ, 1000 BASE
  PIC 2   Online       1x G/E SFP, 1000 BASE
Slot 4    Online       E-FPC Type 2
  PIC 0   Online       4x G/E SFP, 1000 BASE
  PIC 1   Online       4x G/E SFP, 1000 BASE
  PIC 2   Online       4x G/E SFP, 1000 BASE
  PIC 3   Online       4x G/E SFP, 1000 BASE
Slot 5    Online       FPC Type 2
```

The output shows you how many FPCs are plugged into the router and the status of each one. Additionally, the command gives you the status of each PIC currently plugged into the FPC. In this case, you see that PIC 0 in slot 0 is down, which accounts for the interface being down and the reason the connection between router 6 and the carrier network is down.

Software troubleshooting

If your look into the hardware on your router revealed no faults, you need to check the software. However, before you start looking at individual aspects of the configuration, you want to take a higher level look at the software. To troubleshoot the JUNOS software, look for three things:

- Software-related log entries
- Software processes are running
- Core files on the router

Check software-related log entries

Software-related log entries are pretty similar to hardware-related log entries. Essentially, you want to parse through the main syslog messages file and see whether any significant system events may be causing the VPN to be down.

Check for processes going up and coming down, interfaces flapping, and other events tied to the software on the router. The presence of any of these types of messages indicates a problem, and you should investigate.

Display running processes

If your VPN goes down and the remote endpoint is unreachable, it suggests that you have no route to the host. Without a route to the host, you need to check that all the processes are up and running. To see what processes are up and running, use the `show system processes` command:

```
user@host> show system processes

PID  TT  STAT      TIME COMMAND
    0  ??  DLs    0:00.70  (swapper)
    1  ??  Is     0:00.35 /sbin/init --
    2  ??  DL     0:00.00  (pagedaemon)
    3  ??  DL     0:00.00  (vmdaemon)
    4  ??  DL     0:42.37  (update)
    5  ??  DL     0:00.00  (if_jnx)
   80  ??  Ss     0:14.66 syslogd -s
   96  ??  Is     0:00.01 portmap
  128  ??  Is     0:02.70 cron
  173  ??  Is     0:02.24 /usr/local/sbin/sshd (sshd1)
  189  ??  S      0:03.80 /sbin/watchdog -t180
  190  ??  I      0:00.03 /usr/sbin/tnetd -N
  191  ??  S      2:24.76 /sbin/ifd -N
  192  ??  S<     0:55.44 /usr/sbin/xntpd -N
  195  ??  S      0:53.11 /usr/sbin/snmpd -N
  196  ??  S      1:15.73 /usr/sbin/mib2d -N
  198  ??  I      0:00.75 /usr/sbin/inetd -N
 2677  ??  I      0:00.01 /usr/sbin/mgd -N
 2712  ??  Ss     0:00.24 rlogind
 2735  ??  R      0:00.00 /bin/ps -ax
 1985  p0- S      0:07.41 ./rpd -N
 2713  p0  Is     0:00.24 -tcsh (tcsh)
 2726  p0  S+     0:00.07 cli
```

The output for the command is a list of all the processes running on the router. The actual output can be difficult to parse, so you really just need to know what you're looking for. In the case that a route is missing, you just want to make sure that the routing process (rpd) is running. In the preceding output, rpd is not present, which indicates a problem with that process.

In this particular example, you've determined that router 6 is reachable, because your ping was successful. If you have an issue with a routing process on a router, that problem likely doesn't exist on the last reachable router but rather one of the unreachable nodes. Instead, log into the first unreachable node and check to see whether that router's rpd process is running.

If you determine that the routing process isn't running, you can try restarting it using the `restart` command:

```
user@router6> restart routing
Routing protocol daemon started, pid 5042
```

If you run the `show system processes` command again, you should see rpd in the output.

Find core files on the router

Modern computers and operating systems are complex, which unfortunately leads to equally complex bugs. Diagnosing transient software failures (such as random crashes or boots) is difficult because these types of faults have so many potential causes. In most cases, a crash is the result of a programming error or the failure to anticipate a particular set of events and the software interaction that ensues. However, a crash can also stem from hardware-related causes.

Because transient failures are so difficult to diagnose, well-written code incorporates the ability to `dump` the program's environment in the form of memory pointers, instructions, and register data to a file in the event of a panic or other serious malfunction. A software engineer can analyze the resulting core file by using a debugger and a version of the executable containing debugging symbols. The result of this analysis is generally a very good idea of the sequence of events that lead to the crash. Armed with this information, you can take corrective actions.

These core files aren't generally helpful to the end user who is trying to figure out what went wrong, but they're indicative that something is happening on the router that is beyond your control. As such, they can be helpful in troubleshooting a problem.

To see whether you have any core files on your router, use the `show system core-dumps` command:

```
user@router6> show system core-dumps

/var/crash/*core*: No such file or directory
-rw-rw---- 1 root field 3371008 Jun 18 17:53 /var/tmp/rpd.core.0
/var/crash/kernel.*: No such file or directory
```

This command shows that a core file was generated when RPD crashed. Notice the date and timestamp on the file. Make sure that this data corresponds to the time of the crash so that you're not looking at an old core file unrelated to your current issue. Because you know the process crashed, you should make sure that it restarted correctly (using the `show system processes` command). If it did restart, the core file may not be the source of your issues. Monitor the router to see whether the process crashes again. If it does, you should investigate the process as a possible cause. If the process doesn't crash again, the core file is likely a red herring.

Interface troubleshooting

After you've ascertained that the VPN connection isn't down because of broad hardware or software failures, you can dive into the physical and link layers. Examine the VPN topology in Figure 19-4, this time with more details around the configured interfaces.

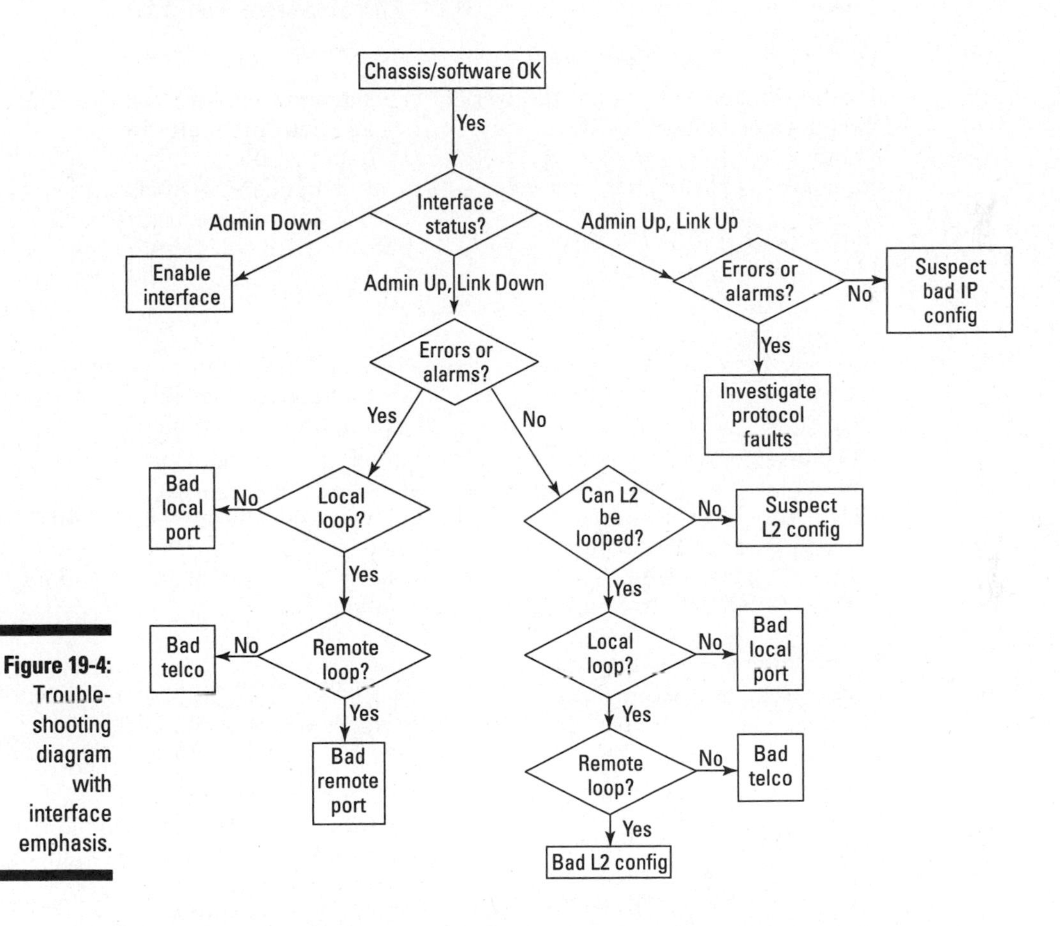

Figure 19-4: Trouble-shooting diagram with interface emphasis.

You want to verify that the interfaces on both sides of the particular network segment in question are operational. In this case, though, you control only router 6; your carrier owns and operates the immediately adjacent router. To troubleshoot this particular problem, you need to be able to identify where the problem resides and then determine what the likely cause of that problem is.

As with any of the troubleshooting tasks, you need a plan of attack so that you know what you're looking for and how to find it. Figure 19-4 shows the basic flow for troubleshooting interfaces.

In essence, you want to first find out whether the interface is up. If the interface is down, you need to figure out why. If it's up, you need to figure out why traffic isn't flowing along that particular segment.

Checking the interface status

The first thing to check on the interface is whether it's up or down. To check the interface status, use the `show interfaces terse` command:

```
user@router6> show interfaces terse

Interface               Admin Link Proto    Local                 Remote
s0-0/0/1                up    up
s0-0/0/1.0              up    down inet     10.0.26.2/30
t1-0/1/0                up    up
t1-0/1/0.0              up    up   inet     10.0.25.1/30
t1-0/1/1                down  up
t1-0/1/1.0              up    down inet     10.0.30.1/30
```

When an interface is administratively disabled, the physical interface has an Admin status of down and a Link status of up, meaning that you had turned off the interface, but the physical link is still working (there are no alarms). A logical interface configured on the disabled interface would have an Admin status of up and a Link status of down, meaning the physical link is working, but the data link layer can't be established end to end.

When an interface isn't administratively disabled and the data link layer between the local router and the remote router isn't functioning, the physical interface has an Admin status of up and a Link status of up. The logical interface, meanwhile, has an Admin status of up and a Link status of down.

If the physical interface is down, both the physical and logical interfaces will have a Link status of down.

In this example, the interface through which the VPN runs is administratively up, but the link layer has failed. This failure indicates a problem with the interface.

Had the interface been up, you would need to ping the remote end of the link to see whether the problem was a data-link layer issue or a routing issue. A successful ping indicates a likely routing issue, which means that the interface isn't to blame. If your ping fails, the likely culprits are an IP address misconfiguration on either end of the link (they're not configured on the same subnet, for example) or a firewall filter blocking the ping.

If the interface is administratively down, you need to enable the interface. Remove the `disable` command from the interface configuration.

Detecting bad ports

If your interface shows as administratively up but the data-link layer isn't established, you need to figure out where the problem lies. The first thing to do in this case is to check the port through which the connection is wired up.

To check the local port of the network segment, ping the interface address you've configured on that port:

```
user@router1> ping 10.0.24.2
PING 10.0.24.2: 56 data bytes
64 bytes from 10.0.24.2: icmp_seq=0 ttl=62 time=0.520 ms
64 bytes from 10.0.24.2: icmp_seq=1 ttl=62 time=0.417 ms
64 bytes from 10.0.24.2: icmp_seq=2 ttl=62 time=0.497 ms
64 bytes from 10.0.24.2: icmp_seq=3 ttl=62 time=0.424 ms
64 bytes from 10.0.24.2: icmp_seq=4 ttl=62 time=0.501 ms
^C
--- 10.0.24.2 ping statistics ---
5 packets transmitted, 5 packets received, 0% packet loss
round-trip min/avg/max/stddev = 0.417/0.472/0.520/0.043 ms
```

In this case, the interface is functional, which implies that the reason behind the data-link failures lies with either the remote end or the physical lines connecting the routers. At this point, you should begin exploring loopback tests to identify the problem.

A failed ping on your local address likely indicates a bad port.

The physical path of a leased line usually has a number of segments or spans interconnected by repeaters. When the line has a break or signal noise, you can test the line on a segment-by-segment basis.

Essentially, what you do is loop traffic that is received back out the transmit line, allowing the router to establish a data-link layer session with itself. If you perform the loopback test one segment at a time, you can verify which network segment isn't functioning. If a loop is set back toward a router and it's not detected, then you can assume that the problem lies somewhere between the router and where the loop was set.

This loopback testing is typically handled by your telecom provider, which means that you may need to contact your carrier in the event that you suspect line problems.

Ensuring compatible settings

If you find that both the local and remote ports are functional, you should check that the physical properties on both sides of the link are configured identically.

Check the following settings on your interfaces:

- **Frame checksums:** By default, E3 and T3 interfaces use a 16-bit frame checksum. You can configure a 32-bit checksum, which provides more reliable packet verification. However, some older equipment may not support 32-bit checksums. If you're using T3/E3 interfaces and you're experiencing problems, make sure that you haven't changed the default value.
- **Payload scrambling:** Payload scrambling is disabled by default. If you have it enabled, it must be enabled on both ends of the link. Ensure that both ends are configured identically.

Physical links may be down for a slew of other reasons. These reasons are more tied to the physical interfaces than they are to the JUNOS software. If you have other issues with your interfaces, consult the Juniper Networks documentation for your particular interface.

Routing troubleshooting

If you have no hardware, software, or interface issues, the next place to look is your routing protocols, routing policies, and firewall filters. Your goal is to see whether the route to the remote host exists, and if it does, what else might be stopping traffic.

Checking for a route

In the VPN case study, it isn't that interesting to see whether a route to the last reachable node exists. Indeed, there must be one if you can successfully ping that router. Instead, you want to make sure that you have a route to the final destination.

In this particular topology, the next hop is a router in your carrier's network. This route should be learned via BGP. You should be able to look at the forwarding table and see a BGP route to the destination. To check whether you have a route to router 12, use the `show route forwarding-table` command:

```
user@router1> show route forwarding-table destination 192.168.5.220

Routing table: inet
Internet:
Destination        Type RtRef Next hop         Type   Index  NhRef  Netif:
192.168.5.220/32   dest     0 0:0:c0:e8:69:db  ucst      21      2  so-0/0/1.0
```

This command shows that you do indeed have a route to the host. If you didn't have a route, the command would have returned nothing.

The presence of a route indicates that your filters or VPN configuration likely have a problem. Had the route been missing, it would indicate a problem with your routing protocols (either your IGP or BGP).

The forwarding table is the lookup table that contains all the best routes to the destinations in your routing table. Your routing table is the collection of all the routing information your router has, but that table doesn't determine directly how traffic is passed. If you want to make sure that you're troubleshooting the information actually being used by the forwarding plane, use the forwarding-table version of the `show route` command.

Checking your protocols

If the route doesn't appear in your forwarding table, you'd begin by checking your routing protocols to see that the route is present on the adjacent router. Consider a couple of scenarios here:

- Your router and the problem router are both within the same network, connected via an IGP (like OSPF).
- Your router and the problem router are in different autonomous systems, connected via BGP.

Verifying OSPF adjacencies

If your router is in the same AS as the problem router and you don't have a route to the box, check your protocol adjacencies using the `show ospf neighbor` command.

In Figure 19-5, you expect router 7 to have OSPF adjacencies with router 6 and router 4. To verify that route 6 has established an adjacency with router 7, use the `show ospf neighbor` command:

```
user@host> show ospf neighbor brief

  Address          Intf                State      ID               Pri  Dead
10.1.2.1          t1-1/0/0.0          Full      10.250.240.9      128   32
10.1.2.81         e3-2/0/0.0          Full      10.250.240.10     128   33
```

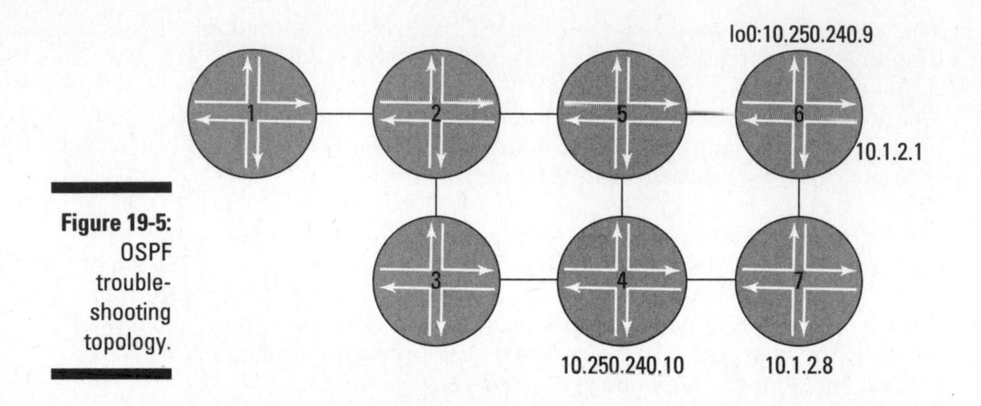

Figure 19-5: OSPF trouble-shooting topology.

In this case, the adjacency isn't there. You should check the configuration on each device to make sure that

- Both routers have OSPF enabled on the correct interfaces.
- Both routers are configured within the same OSPF area.

Correcting the configuration mistakes and re-running the command verifies that the adjacency is now up:

```
user@router6> show ospf neighbor brief

  Address         Intf                State     ID              Pri  Dead
10.0.24.1       so-0/0/1.0          Full      10.250.240.32   128   36
10.1.2.1        t1-1/0/0.0          Full      10.250.240.9    128   32
10.1.2.81       e3-2/0/0.0          Full      10.250.240.10   128   33
```

Verifying BGP peering relationships

Regardless of whether your router is in the same AS or a different AS as the problem router, you need to make sure that you have a BGP session configured.

If the two adjacent routers are in peering ASs, you obviously need a BGP peering relationship between the two routers. However, even if the routers are in the same AS, remember that you need to configure the routers as IBGP peers. So regardless of where the routers are located in the network, you need to make sure that you have the expected BGP peering sessions established on both devices.

In the following output, you can see several BGP peering sessions:

```
user@router6> show bgp summary

Groups: 2 Peers: 4 Down peers: 1
Table          Tot Paths  Act Paths Suppressed    History Damp State    Pending
inet.0                 6          4          0          0          0          0
Peer               AS      InPkt     OutPkt    OutQ   Flaps Last Up/Dwn
State|#Active/Received/Damped...
10.0.0.3        65002         86         90       0       2       42:54 0/0/0
0/0/0
10.0.0.4        65002         90         91       0       1       42:54 0/2/0
0/0/0
10.0.24.1        65002        87         90       0       3           3 Active
10.1.12.1       65001         89         89       0       1       42:54 4/4/0
0/0/0
```

Peering sessions that show a state of 0/0/0 are established sessions, indicating that the BGP session is up and running correctly. If you still don't have a route, you need to look at your routing policies.

If the BGP peering state shows Active (as with 10.0.24.1), it means that the BGP session isn't yet established and that the session is actively being set up (that is, the two routers are exchanging TCP messages). If you see this state for a peering session, you should check the BGP configuration on both sides to ensure that they're both pointing to the right addresses.

Checking policies and filters

If your routing adjacencies are established, then the next thing to check is your routing policies and filters. You may have configured a routing policy that prevents the route from being injected into your forwarding table. To validate your routing policies, you need to examine the route filters and check that no large aggregate routes are being discarded or rejected.

Similarly, if you have the routes in your forwarding table but traffic is still not reaching the destination, you should check your firewall filters to make sure that you're not blocking traffic on a particular port, destined to a particular address, or of a particular type.

MTU troubleshooting

If you've checked your hardware, software, interfaces, and routing properties, another possible root cause of the failure is *maximum transmission unit* (MTU). The MTU specifies the largest packet size that a particular router or interface can handle. If a packet exceeds the MTU, it's broken up into smaller pieces (fragmented) and sent along. The remote end must put the packet back together before it performs any additional forwarding.

If the MTU values aren't consistent across a network (that is, they're not set to the smallest common value), you can experience packet loss. In the VPN example, invalid MTUs may be leading to the loss of the VPN connection.

To diagnose this condition, you have to ping each hop in the path using variable packet sizes. When you use the `ping` command, you can optionally specify the size of the ICMP packet to send. By changing this size, you can see if the packets fail to reach their destination at a certain point.

Where you're likely to run into issues is around the 1500-byte mark. Some devices will choke on packets that exceed that 1500-byte size. To see whether you're experiencing this problem, you want to issue a ping with packets smaller than 1500 bytes and then issue a subsequent ping with packets greater than 1500 bytes. Additionally, you want to make sure that the device doesn't fragment the ICMP packets sent as part of the ping request.

To ping the remote endpoint with 1500-byte packets:

```
user@router1> ping 192.168.20.1 size 1500 do-not-fragment
PING 192.168.20.1 (192.168.20.1): 1500 data bytes
ping: sendto: Message too long
ping: sendto: Message too long
ping: sendto: Message too long
ping: sendto: Message too long
^C
--- 192.168.20.1 ping statistics ---
4 packets transmitted, 0 packets received, 100% packet loss
```

Notice that the ping output shows that fragmentation is required even though you specified only 1500 bytes. The ping packet carries an additional 20 bytes of IP overhead as well as 8 bytes of ICMP header. The payload of the packet, then, is the 1500 bytes you configured plus the additional 28 bytes, which puts it over the 1500-byte limit.

If you try the same exercise but specify only 1400 bytes, you should see a different result:

```
user@router1> ping 192.168.20.1 size 1400 do-not-fragment
PING 192.168.20.1 (192.168.20.1): 1400 data bytes
1408 bytes from 192.168.20.1: icmp_seq=0 ttl=64 time=4.826 ms
1408 bytes from 192.168.20.1: icmp_seq=1 ttl=64 time=2.378 ms
1408 bytes from 192.168.20.1: icmp_seq=2 ttl=64 time=2.299 ms
1408 bytes from 192.168.20.1: icmp_seq=3 ttl=64 time=2.417 ms
^C
--- 192.168.20.1 ping statistics ---
4 packets transmitted, 4 packets received, 0% packet loss
round-trip min/avg/max/stddev = 2.299/2.980/4.826/1.067 ms
```

Chapter 20

JUNOScripting

In This Chapter

- Battling the effects of network downtime
- Understanding the power of automation scripts
- Writing automation scripts with JUNOScript
- Examining sample scripts that do amazing things

If you're like most of the people managing networks for a living, you probably have enough work to fill the calendars of three or four other people besides yourself. The reality is that most networks are growing, both in terms of number of devices and the number of users relying on the network. While that growth continues at astronomical rates, the number of people managing those devices and servicing those users is increasing much more slowly — and sometimes even decreasing (due to cost cutting, for example). This growth leaves the unfortunate network architect and operations team desperate for some way to simplify or automate tasks in an effort to improve efficiency and protect the valuable uptime of the network.

This chapter introduces some fairly slick ways of both automating tasks and reducing total downtime in the network through automation scripting. It's beyond the scope of this book to cover it in superb detail, but we guarantee once you're introduced to it, you'll want to write your own scripts.

Minimizing Network Downtime

The most basic requirement for your network is that it be up and running. Period. If your network is down, nothing else really matters. So it's in your best interest to do whatever it takes to ensure that your network doesn't suffer from excessive downtime. You need to constantly evaluate the reasons for downtime within your network and evaluate what you or your vendors can do to address those issues.

The major causes of downtime within networks can generally be lumped into three broad categories:

- **Human factors:** Loss of service tied primarily to misconfiguration or other user mistakes.
- **Unplanned events:** Outages or degradation of service that are caused by either software or hardware issues in the device.
- **Planned events:** Downtime associated with software or hardware maintenance and upgrades.

But how does each category impact the network? If you look at the sources of downtime in networks (see Figure 20-1), most networking folks attribute the lion's share of service interruption to human factors. In fact, at more than 50 percent of total downtime, human factors dwarf both unplanned events and planned events. Unplanned events ring in at No. 2, and planned maintenance events take up the rear at around 15 percent of total downtime.

These results should catch your interest because the largest contributor to overall downtime within the network is you.

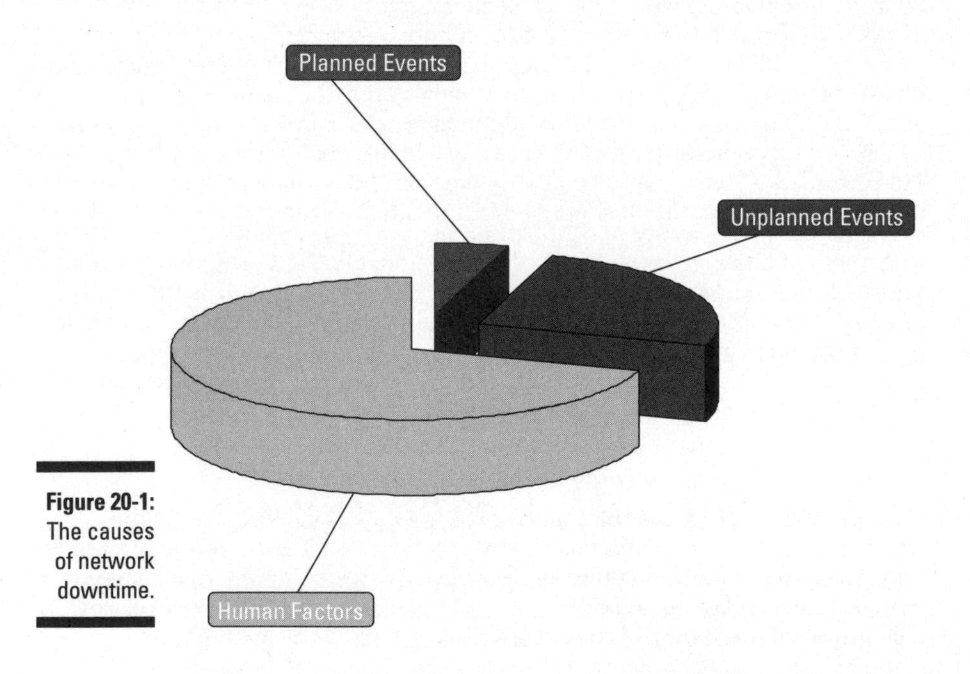

Figure 20-1: The causes of network downtime.

Why is it always my fault?

It may come as a surprise that human error is, statistically, the largest contributor to downtime. (Then again, depending on your own experiences, it may not.) Basically, it all comes down to the single biggest reason for issues to arise: Change. Whenever you change something within your network, you risk causing an outage or degradation of some service.

And what's the one thing that changes the most? It's not the networking gear or the software running on that gear. Typically, it's the configuration of the devices on your network. It shouldn't be terribly surprising that those changes are directly related to downtime in most networks.

The following sections reveal what you can do to make sure that changes in configuration don't have an adverse effect on your network.

Committing with logical rules

You can create a router configuration that is syntactically correct but doesn't do what you want it to do. For example, you can create a stateful firewall quite easily, but what if you cut yourself off from the router? Or you can create a routing policy that checks out, but did you really mean to flood all your BGP routes into your IGP routing table?

The point is quite simple: You need more than mere syntax checking to make sure that changes you introduce into your network via configuration don't bring down the network. You need a means with which you can check that a configuration complies with a set of logical rules that suit your particular network.

The JUNOS commit model offers the opportunity to enforce such a set of logical rules.

The commit model gets you a lot of nifty capabilities, including the ability to make sets of changes active all at once or roll back configuration to the last known good one. Most appreciated by many an administrator is the ability to check the configuration one last time before it's made active. You can parse it to make sure that what is being checked in meets higher level requirements, and you can enforce your set of business rules to make sure that the configuration does what you want it do.

Archiving and passing rules across the organization

Creating a set of business rules and having those be enforced across the devices within your network takes a little effort on your part. You may already be in the situation where you're struggling to find enough time to manage your network without having to add in more work in your copious free time. How can you archive a bunch of rules and roll them out when needed?

Remember the mistakes you made when you first started working with networks? Now that your network is growing, you may want to bring new people in to help. As good as these people may be, they will undoubtedly make the same mistakes you made.

The problem is that those mistakes will actually cost you more money today than they did, say, five years ago. Your network is larger than it was five years ago. Maybe you have more devices on it. Perhaps you have more people using it. You probably have more traffic on the network today. So that very same mistake today actually has a higher impact than it did five years ago and, by extension, is more costly today. How much more expensive will that same mistake be in another five years?

If you can create a rule that prevents a mistake from happening a second time, you can start to weed mistakes out of your network — not only today, but tomorrow, too (and that's the power of rules). Over time, your rules will become more robust because you will add to them from the collective experiences of your entire operations and architect teams. Every time a configuration mistake is made, that mistake becomes a prime candidate for inclusion into your business rules to ensure that it doesn't happen again.

Results from this line of thinking can be amazing. Imagine that you want to get seven to ten years of service out of your routers. If in that time you can avoid even one outage that you otherwise would have run into, you can effectively drive the costs associated with your network down. How much does downtime cost in your network? Can you afford to spend the time to create these business rules? Can you afford not to?

The average cost of an impaired network is around $3 million per day. An outage that lasts only 2 hours still adds up to a large number:

```
2 hrs x $3,000,000/24 hrs = $250,000
```

All you have to do is calculate what the average length of an outage is within your network. Avoiding even one of these types of outages can result in significant operational savings.

Minimizing the effects of software issues

If human factors are the largest contributor to overall downtime in most networks (see preceding section), then system issues triggering unplanned events are the second contributor. You may be wondering what you can do on the box to mitigate this problem.

When looking at the outages and performance impacts caused by system issues, it is worth noting where you can minimize the effects of the issues. For example:

> A large company indicated that it had recently experienced an outage that lasted some four hours. For this particular company, its network was the major portal for new business, so this outage was particularly costly. When asked about the cause of the outage, the company reported that the source of the problem was a bad Ethernet port on one of the routers. Now, changing the cabling from a bad port to a good port should be a fairly straightforward task. So why was the outage so long? In the company's words, "It was the last thing we thought to check for."

This story highlights the problem with system issues and gives some insight into what you can do to minimize the downtime associated with them. In this example, the operations team was certainly impacted by the hardware failure, but its inability to quickly diagnose the problem was the reason the outage was so long.

In fact, if you have ten people working on your operations team and all ten of them joined the company on the exact same day, each one would have diagnosed the problem slightly differently. Based on each person's experience, or based on some piece of information each had, or even based on the hairs of the back of their neck, each of these ten people would go through different steps to diagnose the problem. The total downtime associated with this particular issue is dependent, in some measure, on who of those ten happens to get the page at 2 a.m. indicating that something is wrong.

The perfect scenario is that each of your ten people would diagnose the problem in exactly the same way. Or, better yet, maybe the router can diagnose itself. Basically, you want a systemic, programmatic way of monitoring and diagnosing your network. You want to be able to leverage the collective knowledge of your most senior and skilled networking team members so that your newest employee is armed with a set of tools with which he can do battle.

In the previous example, if the company had an automated way of performing the troubleshooting tasks, the outage may have been reduced from four hours to 30 minutes, reducing the cost of this outage from $250,000 to $62,500.

Reducing Network Downtime with JUNOScript

JUNOS provides a way to address both the human error and the response time associated with system issues. The use of a scripting framework called JUNOScript allows you to enforce business rules on the configuration end while automating the monitoring and diagnostic tasks required to maintain a network. JUNOScipting has five key benefits for your network battles with downtime that you should be aware.

No. 1: Constrain the configuration

The most basic requirement for policing configuration is to be able to create a set of network-specific business rules and the block configurations that violate those rules.

As an example, you may want to use a specific MTU size in your network. You can make it mandatory that all configurations use that particular MTU size. If a configuration has a different MTU size set, you can fail the commit so that the configuration file is never active on the device. The failure would generate an error message, and the network operator would get a custom description of the problem and how to correct it.

You may want to ensure that all routers in the network have the correct route filters or security policies in place. You can check the configuration at the time it's committed and fail any configurations that don't have their security mechanisms in place.

Have you ever tried to troubleshoot an issue with an interface, but you don't know where the interface is connected, because the interface description isn't configured? You can force configurations to comply with your own internal configuration standards, which can save oodles of time down the road as you monitor these devices.

No. 2: Change the configuration

Validating the configuration is certainly cool and can definitely save you the potential headaches of what may have otherwise been an outage of some sort. But if the router knows that it's supposed to have a filter for the default route, why not just correct the problem rather than automatically fail the commit?

A second benefit of JUNOScripts is that you can automatically change the configuration. In this case, if the configuration doesn't have a filter for the default route, at commit time, the router can add that filter to the configuration.

In the preceding section where the MTU size was checked, instead of failing the commit, you can correct the problem. The script can essentially be used not only to detect but to configure aspects of the device.

Or imagine that you're using a SONET interface that has Automatic Protection Switching (APS) enabled. APS basically allows you to configure two interfaces in exactly the same way so that, in the event of a fiber cut on the first link, the router automatically switches over to the second link. The requirement here is that both interfaces be configured identically, which can be difficult to police over time. And now you have a network operator who wants to quickly make a change to an interface. He doesn't even know that APS is enabled, so he makes the change only to the primary interface. The commit succeeds because it's syntactically correct. In fact, the only time you know you have a problem is when the fiber is actually cut. In this situation, the reason you've configured APS is to avoid downtime associated with a fiber cut. But because the configuration isn't correct, you experience the very downtime you're trying to avoid.

In this case, a JUNOScript that automatically configures the backup interface identically to the primary would have spared you the difficulty of troubleshooting a configuration error amidst the chaos that ensues when a physical line is cut.

No. 3: Simplify the configuration

Configurations can be complex and a bit unwieldy at times, but for the most part, configuration across multiple boxes in your network seems kind of the same. Sure, each router has different interfaces and IP addresses, but the base set of configuration parameters is largely the same. So why do you have to configure all these things when the only real differences between each box are relatively small?

JUNOScript's ability to simplify configuration is part of its automation capabilities. You can reduce configuration to only the set of router-specific parameters that you want to use to guide the router's configuration.

No. 4: Create custom logic for operational commands

The other benefits of JUNOScript were associated entirely with the configuration of the box. You can also gain efficiencies by providing powers around monitoring and diagnosing the health of your devices. JUNOScripts allow you to create your own diagnostic logic.

Huh? Imagine that you issue a `show interfaces extensive` command. You get pages and pages of output that you then have to parse through. It's unlikely that you care about everything in the output. In fact, in this case, you may just be looking for the interface counters that show a nonzero packet loss. And your intent is to take a closer look at those specific interfaces.

Or, perhaps, you want to look at your BGP neighbors so that you can more closely inspect the BGP sessions that are down. You don't need to monitor the sessions that are working properly. Instead, you just want to take a peek at the problem areas.

JUNOScripts allow you to execute a command and parse its output. Based on what you find, you can execute a different command and parse that output. Then, based on what you find, maybe you want to issue yet another command. Essentially, what you're doing is creating a decision tree: Based on the output of one command, automatically issue a second command.

This process enables you to script out your most common debugging procedures. If you perform the same set of tasks every time a link goes down, you can script them and change the output of the commands to only give you what you want to see.

No. 5: React to live events

JUNOScripts can simplify a lot of the debugging and troubleshooting tasks, but wouldn't it be great if the router could just debug itself — well, guess what? JUNOScripts have the ability to trigger their commands based on some event happening on the device.

Whenever a link goes down, it's normally one of half a dozen things. So when the link goes down and generates a syslog event, one of your JUNOScripts is invoked. That script runs through the 15 most common commands that you would use to diagnose the router. Now, when you get the page in the middle of the night saying that you have an issue, the message includes a pile of diagnostic information so that you know what the issue is (or, at the very least, what the issue is *not*). To make things even easier, that information can be automatically pared down so that you get only the meat (that is, you only need to look through the most important information).

Invoking JUNOScripts

The powers of JUNOScripts can absolutely be network-changing. But to take advantage of them, you have to first understand what a script is, how a script is created, and how to invoke the script on the device.

JUNOScripts are scripts that reside on the box that leverage the device's underlying XML framework (see Figure 20-2).

Whenever you interact with the device, whether it's configuring things or just monitoring the health of the router, you're using the management process (MGD) as the conduit between you and the router. And whether you know it or not, all your communications are actually taking place using XML. Everything that goes into or comes out of the box is in XML.

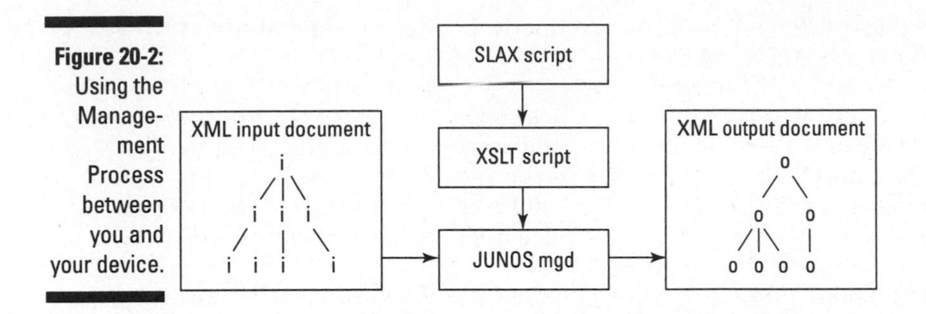

Figure 20-2: Using the Management Process between you and your device.

Here is the `show interfaces` command, this time with pipe (|) and modifier `display xml` added in:

```
user@host> show interfaces terse | display xml
<rpc-reply xmlns:junos=http://xml.juniper.net/junos/7.6R1/junos>
    <interface-information xmlns="http://xml.juniper.net/junos/7.6I0/junos-
              interface" junos:style="terse">
        <physical-interface>
            <name>dsc</name>
            <admin-status>up</admin-status>
            <oper-status>up</oper-status>
        </physical-interface>
        <physical-interface>
            <name>fxp0</name>
            <admin-status>up</admin-status>
            <oper-status>up</oper-status>
            <logical-interface>
                <name>fxp0.0</name>
                <admin-status>up</admin-status>
                <oper-status>up</oper-status>
          ...
```

The output is rather difficult to read, but it explains why MGD strips off the XML tags before sending the output to your screen. But what these tags show is the underlying XML structure that forms the framework for the JUNOScripting capabilities. If you know what the structure is, then you can look for specific values or fields and take action based on the content found there.

JUNOScripts are essentially scripts that anticipate information and take action based on whether that information is present.

Writing scripts

JUNOScripts are written in one of two scripting languages: Extensible Stylesheet Language Transformation (XSLT) or a more Perl-like Stylesheet Language Alternative Syntax (SLAX). Because XSLT is a bit onerous to use, SLAX is the programming language of choice.

SLAX doesn't affect the expressiveness of XSLT; it only makes XSLT easier to use. The underlying SLAX constructs are completely native to XSLT. SLAX adds nothing to the XSLT engine. The SLAX parser parses an input document and builds an XML tree identical to the one produced when the XML parser reads an XSLT document.

SLAX functions as a preprocessor for XSLT. The JUNOS software automatically converts SLAX programming instructions (such as `if`, `then`, and `else` statements) into the equivalent XSLT instructions (such as `<xsl:choose>` and `<xsl:if>` elements). After this conversion, the XSLT transformation engine — which, for the JUNOS software, is the JUNOS management process (MGD) — is invoked. The flow of this process resembles the one shown in Figure 20-3.

Of course, a full how-to for writing scripts in SLAX is beyond the scope of this book, although it's pretty cool and fun to see working. For a detailed reference guide, see the Juniper Networks JUNOS documentation manual Configuration and Diagnostic Automation Guide at `www.juniper.net/techpubs`.

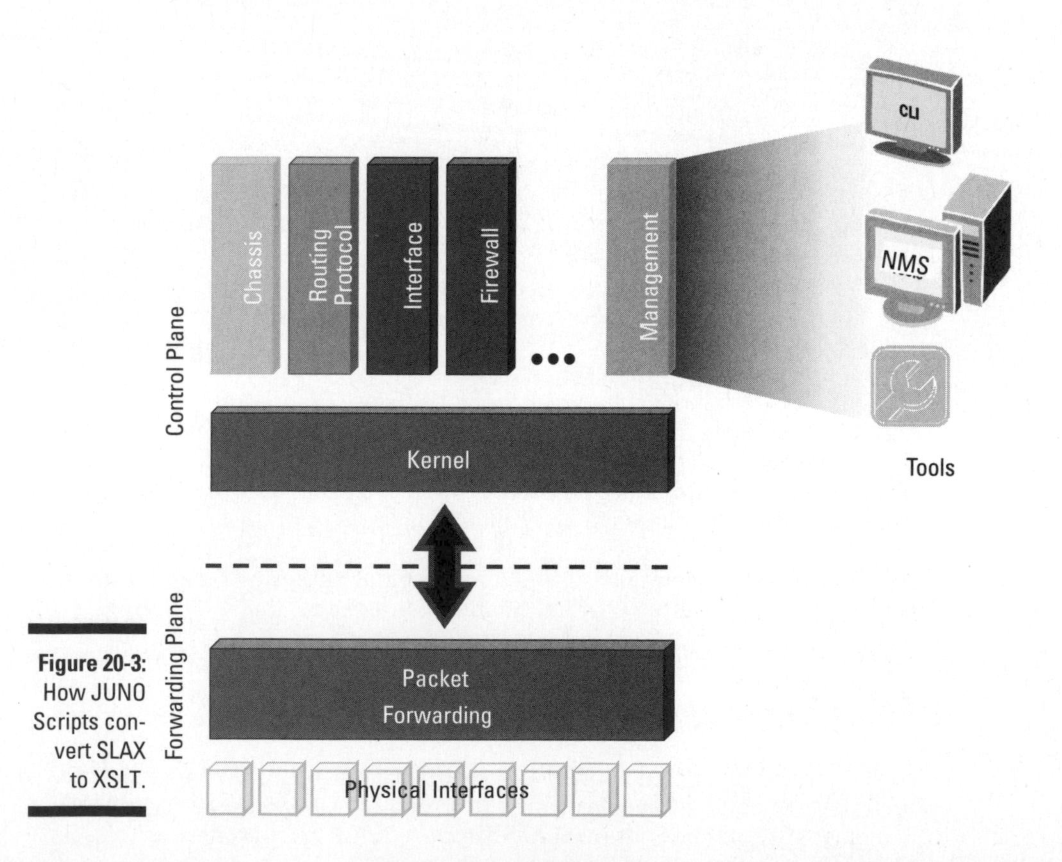

Figure 20-3: How JUNO Scripts convert SLAX to XSLT.

Invoking scripts

Scripts are saved on the device and executed on each individual box. As such, scripts must reside somewhere the device can access them. Scripts are stored in one of these directories:

```
/var/db/scripts/commit/
/var/db/scripts/op/
```

Only users in the superuser JUNOS login class (or with other login classes that have been explicitly assigned superuser privileges) can access and edit files in this directory (see Chapters 7 and 9). This safety precaution ensures that well-intentioned scripts aren't replaced by malicious scripts designed to take your network down.

For `commit` scripts, you must enable the script by including a file statement in the configuration:

```
[edit system]
scripts {
   commit {
      file script-name.slax;
   }
}
```

Files listed in this configuration execute every time a commit is issued. Multiple files are executed in the order in which they're listed, allowing you to specify multiple `commit` scripts, each of which addresses a different issue within your network.

For operation scripts, you must enable the script by including the file statement in the configuration:

```
[edit system]
scripts {
   op {
      file script-name.slax;
   }
}
```

To execute the script, you must issue the `op` command followed by the name of the script. For example, if you want to invoke your `bgp-dead-peers` script:

```
op bgp-dead-peers.slax
```

If your script takes name-value pairs as an input, those are included in the command line after the name of the script.

Putting JUNOScripts in Motion

Even though a reference on how to write and create scripts is beyond the scope of this book, it's really useful for you to look at a few scripts that showcase some of the power waiting there for you.

Example 1: Constraining configuration

In the earlier section "Reducing Network Downtime with JUNOScripts," we discussed the ability to constrain configuration, and the notion of MTU size was used as an example. So what would a script look like that requires the MTU to be set a certain way?

```
param $min-mtu = 2048;
match configuration {
    for-each (interfaces/interface[starts-with(name, "so-") && mtu && mtu <
       $min-mtu]) {
        <xnm:error> {
[. . .]
            <message> {
                expr "SONET interfaces must have a minimum mtu of ";
                expr $min-mtu;
            }
        }
    }
}
```

This example specifies that the minimum MTU value to be allowed in this configuration is 2048. The match configuration stanza then evaluates every interface whose name starts with the string `so-`, which limits the search to only SONET interfaces on the device. If the interface has a matching name and that interface's MTU is less than 2048, it generates an error, which fails the commit. The message that is displayed when the error is generated is `SONET interfaces must have a minimum mtu of 2048.`

Example 2: Changing configuration

A good example of the cosmic power of JUNOScripts is the automatic configuration of LDP on your OSPF and ISIS interfaces. For example, you may want to ensure that all your OSPF and ISIS-enabled interfaces also have LDP enabled on them. This example tests for interfaces that are configured with OSPF or ISIS. If no LDP is configured, it configures it. The scripts also check that all LDP-enabled interfaces have corresponding IGPs configured. If not, the script generates a warning.

```
match configuration {
    var $ldp = protocols/ldp;
    var $isis = protocols/isis;
    var $ospf = protocols/ospf;

    if ($ldp) {

        for-each ($isis/interface/name | $ospf/area/interface/name) {
            var $ifname = .;

            if (not(../apply-macro[name == "no-ldp"]) && not($ldp/interface[name
               == $ifname])) {
                <xnm:warning> {
                    call jcs:edit-path();
                    call jcs:statement();
                    <message> "ldp not enabled for this interface";
                }
            }
        }

        for-each (protocols/ldp/interface/name) {
            var $ifname = .;

            if (not(apply-macro[name == "no-igp"]) && not($isis/interface[name
               == $ifname]) && not($ospf/area/interface[name == $
ifname])) {
                <xnm:warning> {
                    call jcs:edit-path();
                    call jcs:statement();
                    <message> {
                        expr "ldp-enabled interface does not have ";
                        expr "an IGP configured";
                    }
                }
            }
        }
    }
}
```

Example 3: Simplifying configuration

One of the most tedious configuration tasks (and therefore one of the most prone to human error) is the configuration of many similar things, each of which is only slightly different. It may be the configuration of multiple interfaces, or, in this example, the configuration of many similar LSPs, each of which has a different destination address but is otherwise the same.

The configuration you'd like to use is simple:

```
protocols {
    mpls {
        apply-macro blue-type-lsp {
            10.1.1.1;
            10.2.2.2;
            10.3.3.3;
            10.4.4.4;
            color blue;
        }
    }
}
```

This configuration is ideal because it's straightforward and easy to read. The actual underlying configuration resembles:

```
protocols {
    mpls {
        apply-macro blue-type-lsp { … }
        label-switched-path blue-lsp-10.1.1.1 {
            to 10.1.1.1;
            admin-group include-any blue;
        }
        label-switched-path blue-lsp-10.2.2.2 {
            to 10.2.2.2;
            admin-group include-any blue;
        }
        label-switched-path blue-lsp-10.3.3.3 {
            to 10.3.3.3;
            admin-group include-any blue;
        }
        label-switched-path blue-lsp-10.4.4.4 {
            to 10.4.4.4;
            admin-group include-any blue;
    }
}
```

Your scripts need to translate the input provided from the actual configuration, so the script might resemble:

```
match configuration {
    var $mpls = protocols/mpls;

    for-each ($mpls/apply-macro[data/name = 'color']) {
        var $color = data[name = 'color']/value;
        <transient-change> {
            <protocols> {
                <mpls> {
```

```
                for-each (data[not(value)]/name) {
                    <label-switched-path> {
                    <name> $color _  '-lsp-' _ .;
                    <to> .;
                    <admin-group> {
                        <include> $color;
                    }
                }
            }
        } …
```

Example 4: Creating custom logic for operational commands

One of the potential uses for creating custom logic is the ability to issue a single command and get the required information about all your dead BGP peers. You want to be able to execute a single command and have the output be limited to only what is relevant in diagnosing the dead peers.

In this case, you define a dead peer as any BGP peer whose last state wasn't Active. Anything that had an Active state is functioning correctly (see Chapter 13). You want to check the `show bgp neighbor` command and then return any of the peers that aren't active.

Such a script may look like

```
param $peer;

match / {
    <op-script-results> {
        if ($peer) {
            call dead-peer($peer);
        } else {
            var $summary =
                jcs:invoke('get-bgp-summary-information');

            for-each ($summary/bgp-peer
                                [peer-state == 'Connect']) {
                call dead-peer($peer = peer-address);
            }
        }
    }
}
template dead-peer ($peer) {
    var $query = <get-bgp-neighbor-information> {
        <neighbor-address> $peer;
    }
    var $answer = jcs:invoke($query);
```

```
    <output> "Peer: "   $peer;

    var $info = $answer/bgp-peer;
    if ($info/last-error) {
        <output> "Last error was: " _ $info/last-error;
    }
    if ($info/last-state != 'Active') {
        <output> "Last state was: " _ $info/last-state;
    }
    /* ... */
}
```

This script first defines a parameter to be passed to it. If the variable is included in the invocation of the script, the script queries only that particular peer. If no peer is specified, the command invokes the `show bgp summary` command. It then parses the output and matches on any peer whose state is Connect.

This process identifies which peers are of interest to you. You now want to get information about each of those peers and return it as the command output. The script invokes the `show bgp neighbor` command, using each of the dead peers determined previously.

The output your looking for may be

```
user@router1> op dead-peers peer 10.5.14.2
Peer: 10.5.14.2
Last error was: Cease
Last state was: OpenConfirm
Next-hop: 10.11.3.4
Interface: ge-1/2/3.0
Interface is up (14212 errors)
Next-hop is reachable via ping (5/5)
No authentication found in local configuration
No authentication errors found in syslog
...
```

Part V
The Part of Tens

"It's okay. One of the routers must have gone down, and we had a brief broadcast storm."

In this part . . .

No *For Dummies* book is complete without the irreverent, lighthearted Part of Tens. In this part, we cover two info-rich areas that can help you be a JUNOS star: the top-ten JUNOS command categories you'll use every day and the ten best places you can go to find help and assistance.

Chapter 21

The Ten Most Used Categories of JUNOS Commands

In This Chapter

- Breaking down common commands by category
- Showing a few commands that you'll use over and over

You'll likely use a few commands in JUNOS repeatedly while administering your network. In this chapter, we list the top ten categories of usage and some of the more useful commands within each type of administration.

Show Me the JUNOS Software Running in the Device

`show version`: Lists which version of JUNOS software is running on your device. It also shows the hostname of the device and the Juniper model number. *Use:* Checks which version of JUNOS software is running on the device. Check that all components of JUNOS software are at same version level.

`show version detail`: Also shows the version of all JUNOS processes running on the device. *Use:* Checks that all JUNOS software process are at same version level.

Show Me Something about the Device

`show chassis hardware`: Displays hardware inventory of device and components installed in the device. Shows version, Juniper part number, serial number, and description of each component. *Use:* Perform hardware inventory to track components in your possession and to provide information to support if a component fails.

show chassis hardware detail: Also shows version, part number, and serial number for all memory installed on device components. *Use:* Inventory memory components.

Show Me and Confirm My Configuration

configure: Enters configuration mode. *Use:* Modify the configuration running on the router, switch, or other device.

show configuration: Displays the configuration currently running (active) on the device. *Use:* Verify that the configuration is what you expect.

commit confirmed: Activates configuration changes, but returns to previous configuration automatically if you don't actively accept the new configuration. *Use:* When you're committing a configuration that you think may lock you out of the device or otherwise disrupt access to the device, use this command to guarantee that you'll be able to log in to the device.

Commit: Activates changes made to the router configuration. *Use:* Have changes you made to the configuration take effect. You need to `commit` (or `commit check`) following the use of `commit confirmed` so that the device knows to continue using the most recent configuration.

Back Up and Rollback My Configurations

request system snapshot: Backs up the device's file systems, including configurations. *Use:* Archives all the directories and files on the device so that you can restore them if necessary.

rollback: Returns to the previously active device configuration. *Use:* If a newly committed configuration doesn't work as expected, use this command to return to the previous configuration.

file list detail /config and file list detail /var/db/config: Lists the backup configuration files on the router, switch, or other device. *Use:* Shows when the previous configuration files were saved (committed).

Show Me the Interfaces in the Device

`show interfaces terse`: Lists all interfaces (network cards) present in the box, shows whether they're operational (up or down), and lists IP addresses of each interface. This command shows one interface per line, so it's easily scannable. *Use:* One of the first steps in tracking down a network problem is to make sure that all installed and configured interfaces are up and running and to check that IP addresses are properly configured.

Give Me More Detail about the Interfaces

`show interfaces`: Multiline output per interface lists properties of the physical (hardware) interface, including MAC address and hardware MTU, and of the logical (unit or subinterface) interface, including protocol MTU configured protocol addresses. *Use:* Adds more detail when tracking down network problems.

`show interfaces` *`interface-name`*: Multiline output for a single physical interface. Shows both physical and logical interface information. *Use:* Narrows down output to a single interface of interest.

`show interfaces detail`, `show interfaces detail` *`interface-name`*, `show interfaces extensive`, and `show interfaces extensive` *`interface-name`*: Increasingly more detailed information about all interfaces or about a specific interface. The `detail` version adds interface statistics, and the `extensive` version adds error counters. Output is long, so you generally specify an interface name. *Use:* Adds more detail when tracking down network problems.

Show Me Something about Routing

`show route`: Lists the entries in all the device's routing tables. *Use:* Check which routes the device knows about, and see which ones the device has calculated to be the best ones (the active routes). Check that the device has a route to a specific destination. Variants include

- `show route inet.0` lists all IPv4 routes
- `show route inet.6` lists all IPv6 routes
- `show route detail` adds route preference, next hop, and other information
- `show route` *`protocol`* lists all routes learned by the specified routing protocol

`show route forwarding-table`: Lists the entries in all the device's forwarding tables. *Use:* Checks which active routes are actually being used to forward traffic from the device towards network destinations.

Give Me More Detail about Routing

`show rip neighbor`: Lists the RIP devices (neighbors) in the network. *Use:* Shows the device interfaces on which RIP neighbors can be reached, along with the neighbor's IP address and distance (metric, or hop count) to the neighbor.

`show isis interface`: Lists the device interfaces running IS-IS. *Use:* Verifies that IS-IS is configured on the desired interfaces.

`show isis adjacency`: Lists the OSPF devices (adjacencies) in the network. *Use:* Shows the device interface on which IS-IS routers can be reached.

`show ospf interface`: Lists the device interfaces running OSPF. *Use:* Verifies that OSPF is configured on the desired interfaces.

`show ospf neighbor`: Lists the OSPF devices (neighbors) in the network. *Use:* Shows the device interface on which OSPF neighbors can be reached.

`show bgp neighbor`: Lists the BGP routers to which this router is connected. *Use:* Shows which neighbors the router has established peering sessions with.

`show bgp summary`: Lists BGP group, peer, and session state information. *Use:* Helps determine whether a BGP session has been established.

`show route protocol bgp`: Lists the routes learned from BGP. *Use:* Confirms that the router is learning routes only from desired neighbors.

Show Me Something about Switching

`show Ethernet-switching interfaces`: Lists information about the switched Ethernet interfaces. *Use:* Find out the name, state, VLAN membership and other details about each configured Ethernet interface.

`show vlans`: Lists the configured VLANs. *Use:* Check configuration of the default and other VLANs.

`show virtual-chassis status`: Lists the role and member ID assignments in of a virtual-chassis configuration. *Use:* Verifies and provides status, interfaces and other data about the interconnection of platforms in a virtual chassis configuration.

`show spanning-tree bridge`: Lists configured or calculated Spanning Tree Protocol parameters. *Use:* Shows bridge domain configuration and status.

`show spanning-tree interface`: Lists configured or calculated interface-level Spanning Tree Protocol parameters. *Use:* Verifies that spanning-tree is configured on the desired interfaces

Show Me Details for Maintenance

`show log messages`: Lists the system log messages in the default syslog file messages. *Use:* The syslog family monitors all systemwide operations on the device and records them to syslog files. This command displays time-stamped entries so that you can see what has occurred on the device and when it occurred. Useful for tracking down device, network, and traffic flow problems.

`show system uptime`: Lists how long the device has been up and running. *Use:* Check the last time that the device powered on or restarted, or was rebooted.

Chapter 22

The Ten Best Places to Get Help

In This Chapter

- Finding help online
- Getting help from a live person

If you still have a few more questions about JUNOS software, you can turn to many places for assistance. In this chapter, we provide out our top-ten list of go-to sources to find more about software operations, training, and support — all the extra details that you may need to help you configure and operate JUNOS software in your own network deployments.

Command Line Interface

Are you looking for more background on how a particular feature works? You don't need to turn any further than the various Help commands, which you can use while logged in to the router through the CLI:

- ? — Lists all the valid entries at any point of the command line.
- `Help topic` *`command_name`* — Displays configuration guidelines for any command entered as the `command_name`.
- `Help syslog` *`syslog_message`* — Displays the meaning of specific `syslog_messages`.

Technical Publications

All Juniper-developed product documentation is freely accessible at this site. Find what you need about JUNOS software under each product line.

```
www.juniper.net/techpubs
```

Forums

The Juniper-sponsored J-Net Communities forum is dedicated to sharing information, best practices, and questions about Juniper products, technologies, and solutions. Register to participate at this free forum.

```
http://forums.juniper.net/jnet
```

Literature/Media

Find brochures, white papers, flash files, videos, and other media presenting relevant topics of JUNOS software.

```
www.juniper.net/products_and_services/junos
```

Books

Juniper Networks actively supports a book program that works with in-house engineers and subject matter experts to publish books like *JUNOS for Dummies* and other pertinent titles.

```
www.juniper.net/books
```

Training

Juniper Networks Education Services offerings include a curriculum of introductory and advanced courses on Juniper networking and security products.

```
www.juniper.net/training
```

Certification

Take certification courses online, on location, or at one of the partner training centers around the world. The Network Technical Certification Program (JNTCP) allows you to earn certifications by demonstrating competence in configuration and troubleshooting Juniper products. If you want the fast track to earning your certifications in enterprise routing, switching and/or enhanced services using online courses, student guides, and lab guides, navigate to

```
www.juniper.net/training/fasttrack
```

Support

Do you have a question or an issue that requires assistance from technical support? Perhaps, you want to upgrade your software. For quick and easy problem resolution, Juniper Networks offers an online self-service portal: the Customer Support Center (CSC) at `www.juniper.net/support`.

Customer Care

For nontechnical customer assistance issues:

- Phone (toll free, United States and Canada): 1-800-638-8296 and select Option 2 for Customer Care
- Phone (outside the United States): 1-408-745-9500 and select Option 2 for Customer Care
- Web: Open a Customer Care Case via the CSC Case Manager: `www.juniper.net/cm/case_create_customer_care.jsp`

JTAC

For technical assistance issues:

- Phone (toll free, United States, Canada, and Mexico): 1-888-314-JTAC (1-888-314-5822)
- Phone (outside the United States): 1-408-745-9500
- Web: Case Manager `www.juniper.net/cm` (requires login)

Juniper doesn't permit opening JTAC cases via e-mail. For a listing of local telephone numbers, visit `www.juniper.net/support/support_contacts.html`.

Index

• B •

• C •

• E •

• F •

• G •

• H •

• J •

• K •

• L •

• M •

• N •

• Q •

• R •

• S •

• T •

• U •

• V •

• W •

• X •